REMIXING EUROPEAN JAZZ CULTURE

I0593022

Remixing European Jazz Culture examines a jazz culture that emerged in the 1990s in cosmopolitan cities like Amsterdam, Rotterdam, Berlin, London, and Oslo – energised by the introduction of studio technologies into the live performance space, which has since developed into internationally recognised, eclectic, hybrid jazz styles. This book explores these oft-overlooked musicians and their forms that have nonetheless expanded the plane of jazz's continued prosperity, popularity, and revitalisation in the twenty-first century – one where remix is no longer the sole domain of studio producers.

Seeking to update the orthodoxies of the field of jazz studies, *Remixing European Jazz Culture*:

- incorporates electronic and digital performance, recording, and distribution practices that have transformed the culture since the 1980s;
- provides a more diverse and multifaceted cultural representation of European jazz and the contributions of a variety of performers; and
- offers an encompassing picture of the depth of jazz practice that has erupted through Northern Europe since 1989.

With an expansion of international networks and a disintegration of artistic boundaries, the collaborative, performative, and real-time improvisational process of remixing has stimulated a merging of the music's past and present within European jazz culture.

Kristin McGee is Associate Professor in Popular Music in the Arts, Culture, and Media Department at the University of Groningen in the Netherlands.

Transnational Studies in Jazz
Series Editors
Tony Whyton,
Birmingham City University, UK, and
Nicholas Gebhardt,
Birmingham City University, UK

Transnational Studies in Jazz presents cross-disciplinary and global perspectives on the development and history of jazz and explores its many social, political, and cultural meanings.

The Cultural Politics of Jazz Collectives
This is Our Music
Edited by Nicholas Gebhardt and Tony Whyton

Jazz Sells
Music, Marketing, and Meaning
Mark Laver

Austral Jazz
The Localisation of a Global Music Form in Sydney
Andrew Robson

Jazz Diaspora
New Approaches to Music and Globalisation
Bruce Johnson

Voices Found
Free Jazz and Singing
Chris Tonelli

Remixing European Jazz Culture
Kristin McGee

For more information, please visit: www.routledge.com/music/series/TSJ

REMIXING EUROPEAN JAZZ CULTURE

Kristin McGee

Routledge
Taylor & Francis Group

NEW YORK AND LONDON

First published 2020
by Routledge
52 Vanderbilt Avenue, New York, NY 10017

and by Routledge
2 Park Square, Milton Park, Abingdon, Oxon, OX14 4RN

Routledge is an imprint of the Taylor & Francis Group, an informa business

Library of Congress Cataloging-in-Publication Data
Names: McGee, Kristin A., author.
Title: Remixing European jazz culture / Kristin McGee.
Description: New York : Routledge, 2020. | Series: Transnational studies in
jazz | Includes bibliographical references and index.
Identifiers: LCCN 2019038522 (print) | LCCN 2019038523 (ebook) |
ISBN 9781138585485 (hardback) | ISBN 9781138585492 (paperback) |
ISBN 9780429505232 (ebook)
Subjects: LCSH: Jazz–Europe–History and criticism. | Jazz–Social
aspects–Europe.
Classification: LCC ML3509.E9 M35 2020 (print) | LCC ML3509.E9
(ebook) | DDC 781.65094–dc23
LC record available at https://lccn.loc.gov/2019038522
LC ebook record available at https://lccn.loc.gov/2019038523

ISBN: 978-1-138-58548-5 (hbk)
ISBN: 978-1-138-58549-2 (pbk)
ISBN: 978-0-429-50523-2 (ebk)

Typeset in Bembo
by Wearset Ltd, Boldon, Tyne and Wear

For Wiebe

CONTENTS

FIGURES

SERIES FOREWORD

Since the 1990s the study of jazz has changed dramatically, as the field continues to open up to a variety of disciplinary perspectives and critical models. Today, as the music's meaning undergoes profound changes, there is a pressing need to situate jazz within an international research context and to develop theories and methods of investigation which open up new ways of understanding its cultural significance and its place within different historical and social settings.

The Transnational Studies in Jazz Series presents the best research from this important and exciting area of scholarship, and features interdisciplinary and international perspectives on the relationships between jazz, society, politics, and culture. The series provides authors with a platform for rethinking the methodologies and concepts used to analyse jazz, and will seek to work across disciplinary boundaries, finding different ways of examining the practices, values, and meanings of the music. The series explores the complex cultural and musical exchanges that have shaped the global development and reception of jazz. Contributors will focus on studies of the music which find different ways of telling the story of jazz with or without reference to the United States, and will investigate jazz as a medium for negotiating global identities.

Tony Whyton
Nicholas Gebhardt
Series Editors

ACKNOWLEDGEMENTS

My sincere gratitude is first and foremost expressed to the many musicians, dancers, festival organisers, event planners, DJs, and various other artists and actors who have shared their time and stories with me. In a cultural moment in which so much of musicians' lives is spent not only performing, recording, and rehearsing, but also attempting to make their mark in an expanding digital landscape through a complex field of promotion and discourse, I was especially grateful that many of these were willing to talk with me face to face. Special thanks then go to all of the dancers, DJs, and founders of the Herräng Dance Camp (in no particular order), including Bärbl Kaufer, Bianca Locatelli, Felix Berghäll, Fredrik Dahlberg, Hasse Mattsson, Jessica Oldin, Judy Prichette, Lennart Westerlund, Marcus Koch, Marie Nahnfeldt Mattsson, Mats Oldin, Mimmi Gunnarsson, Nils Anders, Rikard Ekstrand, and fellow dancers and friends Sven Dupuits and Kersten Gavander.

In Amsterdam, I am especially grateful for the conversations and many performances of various members of the Wicked Jazz Sounds collective, including platform founder Manne van der Zee, vocalist Berenice van Leer, DJ Phil Horneman, and saxophonist Susanne Alt. I also appreciate my conversation with trumpeter Rob Van de Wouw, who shared insights about his work with the Blue Note Trip Series in Amsterdam as well as his own solo group. Also from Amsterdam, I was very grateful for the revealing conversations with producer and composer David Scheurs and with musician Caroline Esmeralda van der Leeuw of the project Caro Emerald. Both shared fascinating insights about musical performance and composition in the era of digital media and performance and distribution networks.

In Oslo, I was very happy to speak with several musicians from the Jazzland label and most importantly its founder Bugge Wesseltoft, as well as artists Beady Belle and Ellen Andrea Wang. In connection with the impressive Nasjonal Jazzscene

Club, Jan Ole Otnæs graciously offered to talk to me about his club, in connection with other jazz networks and initiatives in Norway. Before and after the Punkt Festival, I was thankful for the chance to speak with percussionist Erland Dahlen and performer and remixer Jan Bang, one of the long-time curators and organisers of this festival.

During two trips to Berlin, I was able to meet with several of the key collective members of Jazzanova, including manager Daniel Best, producer and performer Stefan Leisering, and bassist Paul Kleber. Before an outdoor festival in Germany and in France, I was honoured to see performances and later interview members of Electric Swing Circus, including guitarist Tom Hyland, sound artist and guitarist Rashad Gregory, and vocalist Fe Salomon. In Hamar, Norway, after a captivating concert by GURLS, vocalist Rohey Taalah shared some insights regarding strategies for performing and touring as well as her musical influences.

In Saumur, France, I met with festival organiser Isabelle Montanier, Lindy Hop promoter and dancer Mikael Bretagne, and I was especially grateful for the extra contacts and expert translation assistance of Eléonore Guillot. If you are looking for an excellent young colleague in your arts organisation, hire this young woman!

Sections from two of this book's chapters are reworked and republished with the generous permission of the original editors and publisher. I therefore want to acknowledge and thank Fabian Holt, Carstin Wergin, and Elizabeth Levine for allowing me to reprint parts of the chapter "Collectivities, Cosmopolitanisms and Mixed-Mediations in Amsterdam's Crossover Jazz Scene" from C. Wergin and F. Holt (eds) multi-authored Routledge collection *Musical Performance and the Changing City: Postindustrial Contexts in Europe and the United States* (2013).

I'd also like to thank the wonderful colleagues who were willing to read drafts of particular chapters throughout the process. I'm indebted to the conversations and comments of the series editors Nick Gebhardt and Tony Whyton as well as Routledge's editors Constance Ditzel and Peter Sheehy, copy editor Amanda Picken, and production manager Matt Deacon. I'd also like to thank the anonymous reviewers of the manuscript. I'm especially grateful for the comments of various chapters of Fabian Holt, Chris Tonelli, Christina Baade, Tom Perchard, Ioannis Tsioulakis, and I thank Lynn Hooker for her literature suggestions on Balkan Beats. I'm very lucky to have had come into contact with Aubrey Williams, who provided excellent editorial work on all of the chapters and magically reduced them down from monster trucks to mere SUVs. (There is always more work to do!)

Finally, I'd like to thank my husband and confidant, who has motivated me to leave the comfortable home environment to attend these diverse and exciting musical events throughout Europe. He has also pushed me to finish this project and allowed me to vent when I experienced some of the barriers which made research difficult. Sometimes these related to the normal experiences of researchers within neoliberal institutions (including little time for actual research), but other times, I felt an unconscious bias influenced if and how club owners, record owners, managers, and musicians responded to my questions (such as not responding at all).

I remain grateful for the support of friends and family, including my loving parents Kathy and Charles and my two affectionate cats (I hope this is the first jazz book which acknowledges the important work of felines), and I am excited that even in this moment of great ecological and geopolitical crisis, that we all find a way to make, listen to, talk about, and dance to music. These persistent acts contribute meaningfully to music and arts worlds, which themselves sometimes offer the best spaces to make sense of what seems overwhelming and unintelligible.

INTRODUCTION

Remixing European Jazz Culture – Historical Precedents, Methodological Approaches, and Theoretical Interventions

Setting the Stage – Punkt 2018 – Kristiansand, Norway

At summer's close, southern Norway's coastal city of Kristianstad hosts the annual Punkt Festival, promoting the artistic concept and practice of remix in music. Curated by Jan Bang and Erik Honoré, two music producers and electronic musicians committed to both improvised and experimental electronic music since the 1980s, Punkt maintains its reputation for bridging the experimental improvised community with the technologically mediated sound production world of the recording studio.

This festival provided the finale of this book's ten-year research endeavour, posing a fitting end to the subject, *Remixing European Jazz Culture*. In August 2018, I flew to Kristiansand for two immersive days of concerts and talks with musicians and attendees. The first concert I attended on Saturday, September 1, featured a Norwegian pairing of the duo guitarist/composer Geir Sundstøl and drummer Erland Dahlen, with a live remix by German sound artist Peter Schwalm. Dahlen's playing appears on hundreds of recordings, including those of Norwegian artists Xploding Plastix, Ellen Andrea Wang Trio, Nils Petter Molvær, Eivind Aarset, Hanne Hukkelberg, and Anja Garbarek, with guest appearances from John-Paul Jones and Mike Patton. For many years, Dahlen was also the drummer with the popular Americana band Madrugada. Equally renowned guitarist Geir Sundstøl has also performed with a wide variety of musicians, including electronic jazz trumpeter Nils Petter Molvær, and featured as a session player and sideman on hundreds of albums. Punkt founder Bang depicted his solo debut *Furulund* as "David Bowie meets Brian Eno while improvising with John Coltrane".[1] Such fondness for inter-generic, intercultural, and transnational mixing proved an apt description for the entire festival.

This first set delivered a markedly melodic and metric approach towards improvised music. After guitarist Sundstøl appeared on stage at the modern and well-equipped Kick Scene nightclub, he sat down behind his kit, his face obscured in darkness while his hands and instrument were projected onto a screen above. His modest musical exposition entailed slow moving passages, filtered through timbral distortions and decays. After some minutes, he sampled himself playing a simple four-note passage; languid whole-tones descended in step-wise motion which too were sampled and looped. This dirge-like phrase became the *cantus firmus* for textual enhancement and manipulation, with glitches, low vibrations, and wirery pre-programmed patches. Sundstøl's set evolved gradually, before Dahlen approached his percussion assemblage. He carefully entered, gently animating various instruments, enhancing the minimalistic yet eclectic loops of Sundstøl. His playing immediately synced with Sundstøl's sampled groove, adeptly enhancing the soundscape with a mild wash of colour. Later, Sundstøl too captured one part of Dahlen's phrase, and faded out the original loop of the steel guitar.

Interviewed the following morning, Dahlen revealed that he'd prepared particular programmes for this set, but also freely improvised others through self-sampling with his Korg Vocal Beats Sampler (Erland Dahlen, Interview with the author, September 2, 2018). This began his solo set, which evolved from live improvised acoustic drumming to sonic manipulation, sampling, and sequencing of his own passages. His performance was visually and sonically embellished with three tuned Indian bells (purchased at a vintage furniture store in Montreal) positioned high above his head. Eventually foregrounding his bass drum, he amplified a low frequency drone and, although not easily heard, it vibrated through our chairs and into our bodies. This moment guaranteed the music's hyper-present and corporeally immersive experience. Finally, Sundstøl re-entered the stage, and the two expanded various textures, loops, and dynamics, while intermittently drawing from earlier musical ideas. Their performance flowed back to the original minimalistic texture of Sundstøl's first four-note loop until each sonic event eventually faded to nothing.

Immediately after, the *live remix concert* began, remixed by accomplished German producer and composer Peter Schwalm. Schwalm established his career in several musical worlds, from electronic music to ambient pop, and from radio and film to theatre and ballet. Like many of the artists at Punkt, Schwalm's artistic credentials reflect international affiliations and aesthetics; and famously via his well-known collaboration with Brian Eno in the late 1990s.[2]

Schwalm's 'live remix' technique employed primarily analogue and digital outboard effects. During this concert, his remix approach cohered with the softer and spacious ambiance of the duo's preceding set. First, he cautiously re-incorporated the original loop of Sundstøl, adding occasional sonic booms, each one understated, and nearly unperceivable. These progressed in texture, creating a trance-like, or perhaps, low deep-sea exploration soundscape, until the duo's original loop was completely transformed. He then excavated textures from Dahlen's drumming sequences, drawing out timbres of the various instruments, from the bamboo sticks to the bells and low bass drum drone. His spacious style prioritised low-tone resonances which aesthetically complemented Sundstøl and Dahlen's improvisations.

During Punkt, Schwalm's reconfiguration and mixing of sonic material within the context of improvised music demonstrates how remix culture has permeated European jazz culture in the twenty-first century. Distinguishing itself from other genre-oriented jazz festivals, Punkt promotes its ethos of 'experimentation for experimentation's sake', but it also points to the ways that remix increasingly resists characterisation as a musical skill connected to discreet musical genres such as hip hop or electronic dance music (EDM). In short, remix can no longer be placed exclusively within pre-production spaces such as the studio.

Bang's objective for the first Punkt Festival in 2005 was "to bring the studio onstage in concert situations, improvising with electronics". He stated they wanted to create an environment "where [remixers] had access to entire concerts – like a spider's web of musical material to sample from". Such concerts would become "the basic sound source for the next performance", what they called "the *live remix* of the previous concert". The aesthetic goal of such concerts further betrayed their desire to distance themselves from dance-oriented remixes. Bang emphasised this point stating: "By inviting friends more from the improv scene, it was – and still very much is – our goal to create new music" (Jan Bang, email correspondence, November 17, 2017).

This large-scale, multi-instrumentalist principle entailed the likelihood of artistic 'failure', due to the mechanics and spontaneity of remixing entire concerts. Reiterating this aesthetic goal, Bang visualised this festival's parameters:

> By bringing the studio onstage, with empty hard disks and only three quarters of an hour to gather samples and prepare for the performance – it is an exercise in finding solutions or possible musical language with a sense of danger involved, in that it has a real possibility of failing.
>
> *(Jan Bang, November 17, 2017)*

Within its fourteen years, the festival has collaborated with musicians involved in the aforementioned scenes who expressly enjoy the 'danger' involved at the borders of improvising and remixing.

Expanding jazz praxis outside of orthodox geographical, performance, and reception contexts, the Punkt remix festival embraces the possibilities afforded by interaction, where technologies first introduced in the studio have now migrated to the live performance space. The riskiness entailed by such techniques evidences the contemporary broad-based application of remix. Remix is no longer the sole domain of solitary producers in the studio, but now asserts itself as a collaborative, performative, real-time improvisational process linking a wide pantheon of practices from mainstream dance music cultures to experimental improvised musical communities worldwide.

This experience encompasses many of the interactions and themes which motivated this book some ten years ago. At this juncture, while remix extended into a variety of musical spheres, an overview of European jazz studies revealed a particular insider culture and a consistency replicated within a canon of musicians and their recordings – even as the subjects and materials differed by period and nation. Around 2000, currents appeared to be changing and jazz practice, experience, and creativity itself was turning away from existing Eurocentric definitions of what jazz had been and could be in the 'New Europe'. Despite these currents, the field seemed to be dominated by mostly mature male academics, who had inherited the traditions of the early jazz critics and their well-cited polemics. For a new generation of jazz scholars, it was up to us to either accept their insider's view of what European jazz was and continued to be, or to reject it.

Indeed, a reliance upon a limited canon of players and their recordings seemed incongruous to the multifaceted history of jazz-making. Fortunately, in recent years, a number of treatises have begun to complicate these narratives, including compelling works by Wipplinger (2017), Braggs (2016), Atkins (2003), and others. Furthermore, it seemed clear that a certain set of practices and interactions were overlooked in existing histories. Engagements with new media in particular remained under-recognised within academic literature. Finally, the long-held 'masculinity' of jazz practice, visibility, and research appeared sedentary, and this remains problematic considering the important role that women and more complex gender processes have held for prior and existing European jazz cultures.

Responding to this, as a younger jazz researcher, I had early cultivated a desire to transform the orthodoxies of the field from a larger recording-based, male canon of players, involved with orthodox modes of jazz performativity, to prioritise an alternative type of study. Indeed, I have intentionally conceived of this book as an intervention – not of the radical sort, but something more modest. First, it relates to a desire to incorporate some of the dominant (digital) media performance, production, and reception practices occupying jazz and art culture more broadly since the 1980s. Second, this project is an attempt to provide a more diverse and multifaceted cultural representation of European jazz. Third, the project seeks to reveal the contributions of a variety of performers from various musical backgrounds and identities than is typical for most academic writings on jazz, which remain focussed on white male performers within modernist music-making communities. Finally, by incorporating new theoretical frameworks (for jazz criticism) such as media studies, gender, and feminist theory, as well as the important role of the body within cultural studies, I hope to offer a more encompassing picture of the depth of jazz practice erupting through (especially) Northern Europe since 1989, a moment when the 'New Europe' was itself occupied with accommodating new cultural and artistic forms as a vehicle to define and situate its new set of geographical, cultural, artistic, and political affiliations.

Within this introduction, I will first synthesise some of the important theoretical concepts (and especially the role of remix) as a compelling framework with which to better understand and situate jazz culture within Europe. In the following section, I offer a review of the critical debates surrounding the importance and influence of remix upon contemporary culture, and in relation to development within jazz culture. Then in Part I, I review relevant literature regarding European jazz and its histories more broadly. Later in Chapter 1, I sketch a brief history of post-war development of various streams of remixed, popular, transnational, and remediated jazz within Europe, especially from the 1980s on, or within the New Europe and throughout the digital era more broadly, primarily since such a history does not yet exist comprehensively. This overview provides important context for subsequent chapters. After this brief synthesis of debates regarding European jazz histories, in Part II, I offer a summary of the objectives and themes of the book's chapters.

Theorising Remix within Music Cultures

Upon the widespread experimentation and adoption of studio editing and manipulation techniques, first implemented within the Jamaican studios of groundbreaking reggae producers – famously King Tubby and his Waterhouse remixed dub plates during the 1970s (Hebdige 1987) – remix later came to characterise not only the altered takes of reggae but, increasingly, hip hop. By 2000, sampling was built into the remix approach, and would significantly dominate the adaptations of popular musics, which reworked existing material from archives into new songs. Remix too was increasingly connected to the reworking and mediation of current jazz-oriented recorded material, and often referenced a body of creative production-led practices shared between and across *polygeneric* jazz collectives. Here jazz producers remixed material of interconnected producers from other cities, conveying a process of cultural influence and transnational interactivity.

From the 1990s onward, remix increasingly encapsulated an entire ethos, symbolising the philosophically disruptive and fast-paced turnover of contemporary culture. In this century, remix has been positioned by many popular music and media scholars as the defining artistic and cultural concept of our time (Gunkel 2015; Miller 2008; Lessig 2008; Navas 2012). Since the accelerated artistic practices engendered by digitalisation, recent generations have acquired concepts from prevailing movements which also crystallised the overarching milieu of particular decades, from the Jazz Age to the Velvet Revolution. Remix also consolidated many of the defining cultural debates about the transition from the twentieth to the twenty-first century, where human subjects increasingly interacted with expanding technologies of machines and computers, and with the historical artefacts accessible from an exponentially expanding archive. Such interactions led to broad-based artistic and ideological questionings of conventional notions of artistry, authorship, cultural heritage, memory, and creativity, as well as challenging and destabilising the surrounding judicial and governing bodies which continued, in some form, to promote nineteenth-century conceptions of ownership and creativity (Lessig 2008, *RiP! A Remix Manifesto* 2008).

While remix encompasses broader beliefs subsumed within several facets of contemporary life, from new forms of amateur arts participation on social media to the intertextual citation practices of film-makers and DJs, remix can also be understood as a philosophical imposition upon the Platonic ideals of the classical and modernist era, from the constraining concepts of originality, innovation, and individuality to universal notions of truth and beauty. An interrogation of these values is central to remix arts movements. The repurposing of old media, technologies, and especially the role of music recordings (once the 'official' texts of jazz culture), challenges the notion of the author and of individual music consumers. Remix can be said to foreground *practices* and *processes* which by their very nature are interactive and performative. Remix obscures the concept of an origin, and promotes instead artistic forms which destabilise and recalibrate concepts such as source, truth, and musical authorship. Remix arises within the broader frame of postmodernism in its ahistorical approach towards cultural configuration; remix expands the geographical, technological, and economical field, providing technological tools for both cultural exploitation (and expropriation) and for disruptive artists outside of the Global North.

Within audiovisual media studies, a number of authors have contextualised and theorised remix in all of its artistic, philosophical, and ideological complexity. Notably, remix scholar David Gunkel adapts Jameson's seminal late-capitalist formulation to position remix as the cultural logic of "networked global capitalism" (Gunkel 2015, 18). As Gunkel argues, remix challenges the notion of a singular author's authenticity, and instead demonstrates how "the concept of authorship has itself always been equivocal and something of an artifice" (xxx). In his book, *Sound Unbound* (2008), Paul Miller (DJ Spooky) similarly perceives remix as the defining arts impulse of digital culture; remix and sampling practices represent collective forms of ownership. Miller understands remix as driven by computer-ordered mnemonics, and as systems of memory created within a "database-driven logic" where reconfigured sounds act as "thawed architecture", and where architecture represents the "frozen sound" of older musical practices (Miller 2008, 17). Mashup scholar Aram Sinnreich identifies remix as dialectically engaging the entire modernist tradition, where such values as labour, craft, individualism, innovation – as staples of "modern aesthetic theory" – inform remix culture's contemporary critique (Sinnreich 2010). Others have positioned new genres within remix culture as vehicles to transform corporate pop music into new and innovative art forms. For example, remix artist Girl Talk (Brett Gaylor) regards sample-based performances and practices as the "folk art of the future" (*RiP! A Remix Manifesto* 2008). Each of these theorists, many working within electronic music, provide useful concepts for how jazz artists too have explored new performative and aesthetic practices since the 1990s.

As Gunkel and others remark, remix stimulated debates about notions of authorship, artistic quality, and innovation, and these were broadly ignored by jazz scholars. Even within popular music, not all arts practitioners and cultural pundits reacted favourably to these new forms of cultural mediation. In their synthesis of current debates, once progressive (and now reactionary) artists David Byrne and Henry Rollins, denigrated the sample- or phonographic-driven art of remix artists in their characterisations of DJs (and by extension remix artists) as "record player players" (Gunkel 2015, 33). These tensions, connected to the artistic and often unorthodox use of technology, overlap with earlier artistic debates within jazz, such as those exchanged between the so-called 'moldy figs' and modernists of the post-war era as bebop emerged as the new modernist art form, *avant la lettre*, which displaced swing while internalising the modernist rhetoric connected to the perceived higher authenticity of New Orleans small-scale jazz (Gendron 1995). Such debates within the earlier jazz wars and in contemporary popular music critical discourse betray continual tensions surrounding the transformation of artistic practices and the role of a wide-reaching modernist arts philosophy. Ultimately, both belie their reference point within the aesthetic and moral principles of modernism.

Mark Katz conceptualises the variety of practices developing especially from recorded music technologies as "phonographic effects". These include techniques derived from both performative turntable-driven art and new techniques attached to the analogue sampler. Here, the phonograph features as the single most important medium in the development of new artistic practices, some influenced by earlier signifying practices from African American culture, such as the citation aesthetic of much instrumental jazz and its adaptation of riffs (Katz 2004). Particularly within jazz culture, the careful study of recordings remains paramount in the musician's development of improvisational and performative vocabularies (Berliner 1994; Monson 1996). New practices connected to remix within the recording studio then feature as another phonographic effect, enabled by the (once) unorthodox yet artistic use of hardware and later sampling software for aesthetic aims (Morey and McIntyre 2014).

Lawrence Lessig, one of the first scholars to receive significant attention for his views on digital culture, was inspired to radically transform the entire notion of authorship and its legal and economic implications within the cultural field. He argued that the artistic impulses inherent in the remix forged the defining cultural attitude of the 2000s (Lessig 2008). He claimed that the older modernist pursuits of reading and writing had been replaced by remixing, a participatory art that recycles existing culture for the creative and interactive aims of contemporary culture. In such processes, the notion of collective culture is prioritised over individual innovations. It is here too that a call for copyright revision was staged, as such increasingly complex and fragmented phonographic practices led to activities further away from the ideals founding the production of music recordings (as records of individuals' artistic works) before the era of both live interactive practices and studio-led innovations such as versioning, turntablism, sampling, beat construction, and remix more broadly.

Despite its far-reaching commentary within cultural studies, law, sociology, popular music, and media studies, remix theory and culture has received an uneasy welcome within the jazz culture pivoting between our two centuries (Gibson 2005). Jazz scholars of pre-digital cultures understand the combined role of musical mentorship and the study of iconic recordings as instrumental in forming kinships and developing artistic skills, and remix could be simply configured as an extension of such ideals. If the phonograph is a form of music writing within jazz history, the study of such writings proves critical for engagement with such records, especially those circulated within a canon of perceived exceptional and authentic artistry. Within developments of jazz education from the 1980s, this attitude certainly prevailed, yet rarely in institutional contexts did such phonographic values extend to include new artistic skills within digitally mediated forms of jazz.

Within digital record studios and work stations, remix artists approach the study and adaptation of jazz recordings differently. Rather than favouring the most iconic, canonised recordings, they have adopted genres less studied within dominant jazz histories. In particular, remix or sample artists of the 1990s turned to recordings of the 1960s and 1970s, including tracks from soul, jazz fusion, or jazz funk (Perchard 2011). This process of incorporating samples from these less prestigious (jazz) recordings stimulated an alternative phonographic effect – that of revitalising interest in so-called forgotten or marginalised (jazz influenced) recordings of the post-1960s or 'jazz is dead' decades. As Perchard (2011) and Williams (2014) have argued, excavating 'lost' jazz recordings served both aesthetic and affective aims for new music communities. Gunkel too understood remixing as something deeply committed and connected to human history:

> As with writing, the inherent redundancy of remix can be validated as a kind of archival effort to preserve the memory of something that could be lost to the dust-bins of history by reanimating one's appreciation for the original and even creating new markets for source material and the artists who created it.
>
> *(Gunkel 2015, 50)*

The sometimes-uneasy relationship between DJs, producers, remixers, jazz musicians, and jazz scholars during the 1990s and early 2000s then spoke to the negotiation of the role that jazz records should play in contemporary jazz and more broadly in contemporary dance culture.

After an era of successful and widely distributed jazz sampling-based projects in the 1990s, the potential of DJs, producers, and remix artists to stimulate interest in forgotten recordings or lesser-known jazz styles of recent decades was evident. Unsurprisingly, therefore, certain twenty-first century jazz labels such as Blue Note happily contributed prior recordings to DJs and remixers for new releases. Thus, remix constituted another node in the trajectory of ascribing value to particular recordings as a form of cultural distinction, what one of the Berlin-based DJ/promoters depicted as the process of 'meaning making' surrounding the reconfiguration of recorded jazz into new musical contexts (Daniel Best, Interview with the author, November 27, 2017). Naturally, jazz culture remains steeped within a discourse of authenticity related to a body of 'star' players featured within a corpus of canonised recordings. However, other equally compelling values such as originality and the necessary liveness of non-American jazz cultures challenges and complicates our understanding of jazz media, even as the current recordings-based history and its canonisation has been influenced by perceived cultural hierarchies and power dimensions of the transnational music industry, such as access to important media channels and institutions and prominent record labels financing expensive recording studios. During the 1990s, such tensions were then re-staged, yet remained at the centre of jazz artistry debates within the neo-classical movement.

As Bernardo Attias (2013) reminds us, this apprehensive embrace between new musical practices such as sampling and remixing in relation to a body of authentic and now canonised – yet arguably highly mediated – jazz records led to a mixed reception of the interactions between jazz recordings and European remix artists during the last three decades. In this period, new performance techniques such as real-time sampling of the 'live remix concert' emerged alongside new forms of jazz media, which transformed the spaces of music creativity and participation, from 'live' music performance contexts to the dance-oriented spaces dominated by turntable practices, and to the producer-led hybrid recording studios, where the artful repurposing and configuration of recordings took prominence. All of these practices, performance contexts, and musical transformations thus speak to larger transformations within European music cultures since the 1990s, when remix began a continuous thread within each stage of musical flows of people, artefacts, and music technologies, which feature in the following chapters and case studies of this book.

Remix and European Jazz Culture

In this section, the concept of the remix is explored both metaphorically and musically as an ideal and action epitomising our current culture. Remix is too understood as infiltrating most facets of contemporary European jazz culture. As a principle and practice, remix occupies not only the spaces of professional music making, such as studios and live events, but informal sites such as amateur bedroom studios and the related online interactive sites of digital creativity, reception, and promotion. As an ideology, discourse about remix too features within the online critical reception of jazz, such as artist-driven zines (magazines) connected to live music scenes. The process-oriented values of remix also factor within the distribution networks of musicians and the transnational collaborations of producer-led projects. Finally, as an aesthetic, remix relates to the re-combinatory reconfigurations of writers and performers working at the borders of electronic, pop music, and jazz, whose creativity is encountered in established and emerging contexts ranging from music videos to festivals, and all the myriad platforms constituting Europe's performance networks. Interrogating remix from a variety of perspectives allows an exploration of contemporary European jazz culture in connection to overarching phenomena, especially digitalisation and transnationalism. Additionally, it embraces the full spectrum of interactive jazz musical cultures – from instrumental, vocal, improvised, live, and digital iterations, to the most heavily produced and technologically mediated. Ultimately, such a concept forces a reconsideration of jazz culture beyond existing narratives as either essentially African American, or as imitative of Black canonical figures. Here, remix and European jazz culture remain beholden to forms of intercultural contact as well as responsive to larger transformations within contemporary European society, such as the restructuring of national borders or the growing movement of people and ideas across nations. In recent decades, European jazz culture has been transformed too by overarching economic, environmental, and political pressures; thus, the processes and debates surrounding remix have responded to such larger phenomena.

Connected to remix as ideology, disposition, and praxis, within this book, *technology* and *mediation* upon jazz practice emerge as core themes. By embracing this facet of jazz culture, this book seeks to accentuate other media and performative engagements which remain peripheral within academic scholarship on jazz. These include the role of popular music aesthetics, the prominence of crossover vocalists within jazz spaces, the increasingly pivotal role of music videos for jazz promotion, corporeal engagements with jazz such as through social dance communities, and finally, the polygeneric record labels which established connections to instrumental jazz voices but also embraced connections to pop, rock, and electronic dance music in recent decades. Such an approach seeks to reflect a multifaceted and inclusive European musical culture, where a broader variety of participants and contexts are illuminated and where new media expressions are given greater attention through online mediation.

Part I

European Jazz Star Circuits, Transnational Routes, and Institutional Networks

In their *Jazz Worlds/World Jazz* anthology, Goffredo Plastino and Philip Bohlman qualify the study of jazz in Europe as one previously prioritising narratives of intercultural encounter between Black American jazz "heroes" and Europeans who "discover" jazz at the "edge of empire" in the early twentieth century (Bohlman and Plastino 2016, 38). Within such approaches, histories have primarily focused upon the exposure of Europeans to touring American jazz musicians and the concomitant spread of their recordings during the 1920s with the recording industry's internationalisation (Panassié 1934; Delaunay 1948; Hodeir 1945; Stendahl 1987; Zwerin 2000; Poiger 2000; Shack 2001; Jackson 2003; Regnier 2009; Fry 2014; Lotz 2012; Tackley Parsonage 2012; Hasse 2012; James 2015; Jost 2012; Arndt 2016; Bohlman 2016; Jankowsky 2016; Wipplinger 2017). This is unsurprising considering the obvious role that African American as well as other international jazz musicians and their performances and recordings held for emerging European jazz cultures. Indeed, jazz entered and further sprang from the forces of modernity in part via its complex movement through the Caribbean, Latin America, North America, and across the Atlantic within Europe in the decades leading up to and during the radical and transformative Jazz Age (Atkins 2003; Gilroy 1993; Gebhardt 2012).

Atkins (2003) and others have rightly critiqued overly reductive narratives which continue to proffer origin myths proclaiming jazz as the syncretic offspring of the European and African populations (and related musical phenoms) within New Orleans in the late-nineteenth century, which later spread to Europe in the early twentieth century. This myth promotes jazz's genesis within the United States exclusively; as a quintessential product of this culture, before it would stimulate confrontations and later imitations abroad. Conversely, Gebhardt and others imagine jazz's eruption as something equally 'foreign' in the more recent territories of the New World, emerging from the deeply complex and multicultural interactions within South America, the Caribbean, North America, and beyond. Within the new jazz studies, scholars have increasingly sought a more transnational or global perspective which highlights jazz's complex negotiation of such matters, alongside expanded forms of travel and intercultural contact as modern societies were forged during the transition from "proto-industrial plantation societies" to modern nation states (Gebhardt 2012). Accordingly, jazz can better be understood as a cultural, aesthetic, and artistic force simultaneously inheriting, mitigating, encompassing, and coalescing a variety of artistic and aesthetic genes into its modern design. Ultimately, jazz's eternal (re)constitution has always involved the incorporation of disparate musical and cultural sources, making it essentially *polygeneric*, a concept which guides the theoretical analyses of this entire project.

During a formative period of transnational encounters, especially during the two world wars, the touring routes of American and other international jazz musicians alongside the cultivation of specialised jazz scenes, and series in countries including Britain, Germany, and France, ultimately encouraged and later stimulated now (overly) romanticised and often narrowly canonised recorded collaborations between European and American jazz musicians (Jackson 2003; Lotz 1985, 2012; Brown *et al.* 2014).[3] Naturally, other jazz musicians from Africa, Latin America, and to a lesser extent Asia, were also present in various emergent jazz locales within Europe before and after the Cold War.

In Europe, music's technical reproduction first occurred during the late-nineteenth century, as entrepreneurs raced to invent and implement new entertainment mediums. In France, the now firmly entrenched media transnational Pathé, as the European counterpart to Columbia records and later MCA and others, connected the nascent European film and phonograph industries in the early twentieth century (Jackson 2003).[4] From the First World War to the present, European record companies emerged in various local and national contexts, but most were influenced by the burgeoning metropolitan music scenes. Charles Delaunay and Hugues Pannasié's Paris-based *Disques Swing* (Swing Records) immortalised European jazz artists Stéphane Grapelli and Django Reinhardt alongside touring African American musicians such as Louis Armstrong and Sidney Bechet. Other transnational examples include the German and British label Parlophone (purchased by EMI in the 1930s), an important label for recording and disseminating (European) jazz recordings during the 1920s (Wippingler 2017, 38). Another was the prominent competitor, the Swedish-based transnational Metronome Records, which also recorded many jazz artists within Europe. The UK's Decca records had recorded many well-travelled European jazz musicians, namely Jack Hylton, the European 'King of Jazz', and his orchestra in the interwar period (Fry 2014, 85–95). Next to staged collaborations between European and African American jazz musicians, American jazz soloists including Valaida Snow, James Reese Europe, Paul Whiteman, Sam Wooding, Ben Selvin, The Ingenues, Benny Carter, Louis Armstrong, Sidney Bechet, Duke Ellington, Billie Holiday, and Hazel Scott were offered important recording and performing opportunities. The travels of these artists greatly impacted the course of national and international jazz styles developing during the interwar and post-war period (Gilroy 1993; Brown 2006; Lotz 2012: 144; Tackley Parsonage 2012; Bakriges 2007; McGee 2016). In addition to encountering jazz through phonographs, within this transformative century, European musicians critiqued jazz, attended performances in theatrical contexts, watched films, collected and studied recordings, joined aficionado jazz clubs (Hot Clubs), and established their own performing groups (Delaunay 1948; Panassié 1942; Tournès 1999; Fornäs 2003, 2012; Jordan 2010; James 2015; Tackley Parsonage 2012, 2017).

In the post-war period, new independent recording companies and performance networks dedicated to jazz emerged. Notably examples included East Germany's Amiga Records (Poiger 2000, 155) and Delaunay's Disque Vogue in 1948 (Delaunay 1948). From the 1950s on, especially Black American musicians aspiring to extend the boundaries of jazz and improvised music settled in Europe, and collaborated with European musicians. As Christopher Bakriges points out, after the 1960s, African American expatriates such as Archie Shepp, Cecil Taylor, and Anthony Braxton, especially those seeking to sidestep the proscriptive expectations of jazz (and the industry's established racialised essentialisms), found more progressive musical climates in Europe where their "creative music" was recorded for European labels, famously Enja (Germany), ECM (Germany), Fontana (the Netherlands), and H'Art (Switzerland) among others (Bakriges 2007, 258–261).

Initially, critics of European jazz culture fervently debated the validity of the cross-fertilisations resulting from such performing jazz musicians, and of their national and transnational mobility (Tackley Parsonage 2005/2017, Jordan 2010, Wipplingler 2017), while eventually identifying 'authentic' European jazz sources and inspirations, as is so often attributed to Django Reinhardt's Quintette du Hot Club de France during the 1930s and 1940s (Delaunay 1961/1982, Dregni 2004). Equally prominent for the reception of a cosmopolitan European jazz culture were the jazz-influenced theatrical groups and Black revues such as the *Chocolate Kiddies* and *La Revue Nègre* featuring eclectic star performers, notably Josephine Baker, whose musical, physical, and theatrical performances appealed to colonial, modernist-driven attitudes during the pre-war years (Dvinge 2013; Jackson 2003; Brown 2008; James 2015). These celebrated while often exoticised performances profited from new architectural spaces of cabarets, music halls, and international musical theatres erupting in late-nineteenth and twentieth-century Europe metropoles. Paris's famous cabarets and theatres the Olympia and the Moulin Rouge featured Black American stars Baker, Adelaide Hall, and others who dominated the headlines; these provided the model for newly erected jazz-oriented music halls throughout Europe in the early twentieth century.

Fortunately, some of these cosmopolitan albeit culturally essentialising performances were recorded in films, such as Baker's celebrated Charleston dance in *Siren of the Tropics* (1927). Such media reinforced the kinetic and corporeal connection to jazz culture in the post-war period – a feature often ignored in current European jazz histories, and one which was revitalised in the last two decades of the twentieth century in dance-centred jazz scenes such as the UK's jazz-dance explosion in the 1980s and 1990s (Cotgrove 2009) and the more recent swing revivals in Sweden and Germany (Sékiné 2017). Such scenes emerged organically and outside of more orthodox jazz spaces, developing local styles and promoting local DJs for initiated series such as "Jazz Junction" and related competitive dance collectives including the innovative I Dance Jazz (I.D.J.) crew, which performed with both DJs and live jazz groups and competed throughout the UK in the 1980s (Cotgrove 2009, 49–50). The UK's jazz dance scene was just one of many which encouraged collaborations between jazz instrumentalists and DJs in various dance clubs and post-industrial spaces throughout Europe since the 1980s, scenes and performances which are examined within this book.

The symbiosis evolving between live jazz, popular culture, and reproduction technologies (including film, radio, and the phonograph) is a thread running throughout the course of social and cultural jazz histories, but one infrequently and inconsistently examined in scholarship on European jazz culture (Baade 2011; Fry 2014; Gabbard 1996; Heile, Elsdon and Doctor 2016; McGee 2009, 2018). However, these relations between modern media technologies, popular (dance) culture, and jazz performance and recording facilitated the modern star system, a system which precipitated the internationalisation of the twentieth-century music industry. This system dominated until the 1990s, when digitalisation and new distribution networks such as Napster significantly disrupted this model (although not entirely). In jazz circles, these media had provided the means for promoting international stars throughout the industrialised world; through the spread of both jazz media and the proliferation of jazz performance spaces, and from the recorded LP, soon a transnational European touring "jazz star network" evolved (McGee 2011). The early stars of jazz culture, Josephine Baker, Louis Mitchell, Jack Hylton, Duke Ellington, and Count Basie, soon became veritable royalty in cosmopolitan European cities (Hasse 2012). Currently, performing jazz artists cultivate careers profoundly informed by such legacies, cognisant of how such narratives and musical aesthetics colour the reception of Europe's own international touring routes and forms of stardom. The role that these early mobile jazz performers played in the mythology of Europe's nascent jazz culture heavily depended upon this collision of technology, mobilisation, and later the digitalisation of popular culture, especially after the reunification of Eastern and Western Europe (Fornäs 2003, 2004; McGee 2011; Arndt 2012; Whyton 2012; Salvatore 2012; Hellhund 2012; Dvinge 2013; Toynbee, Tackley and Doffman 2014).

While early twentieth-century jazz circuits encountered jazz in musical theatres, cabarets, and night clubs, contemporary jazz artists enjoy a variety of performance spaces from online interactive media platforms to revanchist warehouse party spaces, and from outdoor raves to large-scale popular music festivals. In addition to the proliferation of new kinds of popular spaces, the global jazz network relies upon a shared recognition by Europeans of an institutionalised jazz canon, largely formed through a set corpus of recordings, with a codified jazz lexicon within European institutions, including conservatories and academic programmes (Whyton 2012; Ake 2010). Next to historicised recordings, Europe's jazz spaces and networks emerged to promote both local jazz affiliations connected to this canon, which was partly articulated by leading European critics, collectors, and writers such as André Hodeir, Hugues Panassié, Joachim-Ernst Berendt, and others who promoted a range of ideological tropes from the 'jazz as freedom' metaphor or notions of racial purity and authenticity to eroticist and primitive-inspired fantasies and eventually to narratives of 'heroic' African American jazz artists. This canon and the related jazz-oriented myths became instrumental in later decades in guiding jazz education programmes in European conservatories (McGee 2011; Whyton 2012). It also provided the impetus for early European music scenes, where local musicians created their own jazz performances often inspired by American jazz stars and their recordings. Historians of European jazz (Delaunay 1948; Zwerin 2000; Jackson 2003; Fornäs 2003, 2004; Baade 2008; Cerchiari *et al.* 2012; Nicholson 2005; Knauer 1994; Jost 1987; Bohlman and Plastino 2016; Stendahl 1987; Martinelli 2018; Wasserberger, Matzner and Motyčka 2018; Tackley Parsonage 2005) would reveal how these earlier enthusiasts' communities would later evolve into more entrenched European jazz cultures driven by local cultural impulses and transnational encounters.

One of the first compilers of a modern European jazz history, Wolfram Knauer, admitted the complexities of endeavouring a comprehensive European jazz treatise, especially regarding the vast differences in the structural, political, linguistic, and cultural particularities of individual national or city-based jazz scenes (Knauer 2009). Finally, in 2018, an important European jazz anthology was released which attempted the ambitious task of presenting the totality of various European jazz histories. Francesco Martinelli's monumental *The History of European Jazz: The Music, Musicians and Audience in Context* provided individual jazz histories and related phenomena in over thirty-four countries (Martinelli 2018). Earlier anthologies had also provided important multinational contexts for European jazz, especially Cerchiari, Cugny, and Kerschbaumer's *Eurojazzland: Jazz and European Sources* (2012), which offered wide-ranging studies on largely transnational European jazz phenomena such as postmodernism, the role of avant-garde movements, the spread of cool jazz throughout the continent, and the development of new technological means within performance practice and recording. These important studies provide foundational historical evidence of a thriving European jazz culture.

This book acknowledges the relevance of these studies, yet it begins where such histories concluded, interrogating contemporary European jazz culture from an entirely new era of transnational jazz practice, partially motivated by the phenomena of globalisation, digitalisation, the popularisation of jazz, and the large-scale transformation of the music industry beginning in the 1990s. It departs from the entrance of digitalisation within European jazz cultures as they evolved, either self-consciously or organically, from these earlier enthusiast, sometimes subcultural, other times imitative, collaborative, and often canonical pursuits. Considering its breadth and diversity, European jazz culture is explored in a variety of genres, locations, and recording contexts, but its cases are primarily drawn from Northern Europe within Scandinavia, Germany, France, the United Kingdom, and the Netherlands. However, within each of these cases, the transnational character of 'post-industrial' jazz output is highlighted. Especially prominent themes are the processes related to transnationalism and the restructuring and expansion of European cities in the formulation of a so-called 'New Europe' after the fall of the Berlin Wall, and the expansion of the European Union. Since 1989, European jazz culture has been radically impacted by the unique cosmopolitan character of the European metropolis after the reunifications of Eastern Europe and of Germany. This year remains critical for understanding the particular quality of current European jazz scenes, such as those in Amsterdam, Paris, Berlin, Oslo, Birmingham, and London, as their populations expanded and diversified because of such transformations. Especially in the transitional decades leading to the new millennium, new technologies played a prominent role in European jazz innovation. Therefore, the relationship between new recording and performance technologies related to digital manifestations such as sampling, editing, and sequencing within remix culture are given prominence.

Simultaneously during these last three decades, a counter-movement materialised rejecting the technological neophilia within some production and performance sites. Such preservationist or 'retro' movements included the many jazz revivals which self-consciously resisted the incorporation of new technologies and cross-over genres, such as those promoted within electronic dance cultures. Jazz revivals revisited the recordings of the early jazz culture as conceived within particular European centres during the two world wars. The tensions arising between a move towards jazz's re-popularisation through, for example, the incorporation of jazz aesthetics within popular music recordings, and conversely, the ideologies underpinning the more conservationist revivals betray the oppositional and dialogical nature of contemporary popular jazz developments. This book attempts to uncover and interrogate these tensions, while also specifically illuminating those other, less conservative streams, which embraced new distribution networks, performance practices, technologies, and interactions within pop music and dance culture.

The chapters contained observe select European jazz cultures at the cusp of the millennium as they expanded into exponential transnational networks, and responded to changes within the music industry. These transformations are now often attributed to the processes of fragmentation, wealth accumulation, and consolidation under neoliberalism. In some sense, jazz cultures of this period have been remixed, revived, and reconfigured to facilitate their connections to contemporary popular musics, but also to reincorporate European youth cultures, as the growing cosmopolitanism and cultural diversity of European cities reflected changes in world culture, in digital distribution networks, and in the increasing incorporation of jazz into such networks. Indeed, more contemporary youth cultures and their transnational interactions with the jazz phonographic object destabilised some of jazz's high art connotations from earlier decades (Katz 2004; Perchard 2011; McGee 2011; Williams 2014). Ultimately, in many youth-oriented remix or post-sampling cultures (Behr *et al.* 2017), jazz has simply become normalised as one of many possible music practices and genres with which to express creativity through the various outlets of sampling, recording, performance, production, and participation through both live music cultures and through online sound creation, mediation, and discussion platforms (Dubber 2015).

During the last decades of the twentieth century, European jazz educational systems and government subsidies also provided infrastructure and transnational networks for the expansion of European jazz in the twenty-first century, resulting in the emergence of transnational bodies such as the European Jazz Federation (1969) and European Jazz Network (1987) (Martinelli 2018, 3). Connected to such transnational alliances, jazz culture incorporated some of the values and training inherited from these institutions, as well as integrated the routes of the international jazz star circuit and of the everlasting New York global trajectory, which dominates both touring routes, educational pilgrimages, and historical imaginations of many of today's most versatile, virtuous, and prestigious performing and touring jazz artists (Nicholson 2005; Mäkelä 2010; McGee 2011).

Part II

Remixing European Jazz Culture in Seven Chapters

The following chapters explore European jazz culture in a number of cities, spaces, contexts and periods, from the 1990s to the present.

Chapter 1 provides a brief history of European jazz developments and predominant phenomena since the Second World War. This chapter does not claim to be comprehensive, but rather seeks to uncover and illustrate developments and themes especially relevant for the book's case studies in the context of remix culture and trans-cultural developments within European jazz. It traces the role of European and transnational record companies, of jazz collectives during the counterculture and of the role of festivalisation and popular music networks from the 1980s on. It also reviews the important and growing connection between electronic music techniques to new forms of jazz creativity. Prominent phenomena within this chapter are digitalisation, popularisation, and transnationalism within jazz and popular music networks in the New Europe.

Chapter 2 explores two facets of twentieth-century jazz scenes within Amsterdam: mixed-mediated *crossover jazz* platforms and jazz dance *club series*. It especially highlights the role of the jazz performance and media platform Wicked Jazz Sounds, a group of DJs, instrumentalists, media artists, and party planners promoting jazz dance events in Amsterdam, and integrating improvisation into jazz and crossover music networks. The chapter looks at improvisational practices within the club setting through two established series, the Blue Note Trip and the Wicked Jazz Sounds club nights. It explores the role of electronic jazz within medium-sized popular music clubs in Amsterdam, one of the most visited tourist destinations of Europe, where processes of migration and tourism influence the development of such dance-oriented jazz series. It further examines the role of jazz conservatories and of established jazz labels within these transnational music and interactive spaces, arguing that values relating to liveness, to embodied corporeality, and to cosmopolitan hybridity foreground the enjoyment of such series, making jazz popular again for transnational youths of mobile, multicultural, and various gender backgrounds.

Chapter 3 examines the PLO (producer-led outfit) Jazzanova within post-reunification Berlin, a collective of music producers, DJs, and instrumentalists active since the mid-1990s. The role of the *hybrid studio* takes prominence, as it relates to producers labouring and excelling in crafting new jazz-oriented recorded material. The role of the jazz archive and of Black music and recorded jazz is pivotal for this chapter's understanding of sampling and of jazz vinyl for contemporary remixes exhibiting jazz-oriented sensibilities. This chapter argues that conventional priorities in relation to the jazz praxis are transmitted within particular studio-oriented practices, including: intimate knowledge of jazz records, collective organisation and forms of sociality surrounding such collections, and the studio-driven practice of creating hybrid jazz-inflected grooves through sampling and live beat construction. This chapter traces the growth of a jazz and Black music record-collecting community to highly specialised hybrid-studio producers and DJs during the last three decades within Berlin, now a European musical capital.

Chapter 4 highlights the role of an electronic jazz *record label* based in Oslo, Jazzland Recordings, which gained a coveted reputation since the early 2000s within Northern Europe. The chapter examines particularly to what extent this record label offered a 'New Conception of Jazz' by embracing and recording those artists willing to engage with and update the widely celebrated 'Nordic tone' conception, while also exploring especially broader global cosmopolitan movements, including electronic dance and world music. Furthermore, it explores to what extent Norway, as a well-financed, social welfare state, has nurtured the careers of contemporary jazz artists, breaking the conservative mould dominant across the Atlantic in the 1990s. Consequently, it looks at the spaces and organisation of neighbourhoods within Oslo during an intense period of urbanisation and regeneration followed by the competitive incursion of capital within jazz spaces through the industrial and economic processes of neoliberalism. Here two artists, Bugge Wesseltoft and Beady Belle, and their Jazzland recordings, produced over two decades, are examined to delineate the transformation from more locally based but transnationally driven jazz scenes to transnational networks of performance and promotion.

Chapter 5 offers an alternative look at contemporary jazz culture through the role of 'social' jazz dance and the influence of European *jazz dance revivals*, providing a close reading of the centre of such revivals, through an ethnographic and practice-based investigation of the Herräng Dance Camp in Sweden. Divided into three sub-chapters, this chapter focuses upon two aspects of contemporary jazz dance culture. The introduction and first part explore the 'Black Atlantic' connection between the camp's organisation and promotion of this revival/continuum, and the Black American jazz dancers who cultivated long-term relationships with European dancers from the late 1980s. By proposing a *swing dance continuum* within Sweden, this chapter aims to refocus the role of corporeal jazz cultures within contemporary European jazz cultures. These two sections also provide a context for the 'vintage' jazz-oriented media which informs current dance styles within Europe. The third part of this chapter especially highlights the current musical aesthetics and practices of this camp, with a focus upon the complex intermediated values expressed through a relation to mostly Black American swing music recordings and the current European Lindy Hop professionals, who combine their roles as teachers at this prestigious camp with other (virtual and live) performance contexts throughout Europe. This focus upon the dancers aims to elevate the role of jazz dancers within European culture, while also drawing attention to the critical relation to recorded and audiovisual media paid by this professional, trans-local community.

Music festivals and *music videos* assume prominence in Chapter 6, especially in relation to polygeneric and trans-cultural jazz genres such as electro swing, which often appear within vintage remix or popular music festival contexts. Electro swing (and vintage remix more broadly) became popular in the late 2000s and often featured in both mixed-arts and large-scale popular music festivals. This chapter highlights the role of *vintage festivals* and transnational consortiums for the promotion of crossover jazz styles since 2000, especially those featured in small-scale spaces such as the Anjou Vélo Vintage festival in Anjou, France. The outdoor festival is connected to the online promotional ecosystem of YouTube, where especially music videos of electro swing artists have replaced recordings as promotional 'calling cards' for such jazz-inflected genres. Here, vintage remix artists acquire transnational festival performances and other forms of remuneration with their multi-generational performances, especially attuned to the revival of pre-bebop oriented jazz culture. Here such groups engage with the European 'jazz past' to offer a compelling albeit festive 'survival technology' to the current global crisis. This chapter focuses upon the recordings and performances of three contemporary crossover groups, Electric Swing Circus (UK), Caravan Palace (France), and Caro Emerald (The Netherlands). All three groups have embraced the role of sampling 'vintage' jazz as a core facet of their music and performative aesthetic. Finally, such a connection to a vintage jazz past is explored through the promotional videos of these groups.

Finally, in the Epilogue, I review the major critical themes and values within European jazz culture which have persevered into this millennium as well as those transformed because of the paradigmatic aesthetic phenomena of popularisation, digitalisation, and remix aesthetics, and of broader geopolitical phenomena such as globalisation and the restructuring of Europe since 1989. These three decades have witnessed a dramatic shift in how music is consumed, organised, performed, and made profitable for those aspiring jazz artists. By querying how remix has altered jazz culture in this century, I hope to motivate further studies which too consider the role of the remix, of popular music, of contemporary media such as the music video and of dance for contemporary jazz culture.

Notes

1 See "Artists" on the Punkt Festival website, November 11, 2018: www.punkt festival.no/artists.php?posts&entry_id=1531842932&title=geir-sundst%C3%B8l (accessed August 1, 2018).
2 Schwalm's appearances and courses are listed on his record company's website, Rare Noise Records, www.rarenoiserecords.com/j-peter-schwalm, accessed September 10, 2018.
3 Examples include Louis Mitchell and the Jazz Kings with Sidney Bechet in Paris (Jordan 2010, 70); Benny Carter in Britain in the 1930s (Tackley Parsonage 2012);

Coleman Hawkins with Django Reindhardt in Paris in 1935 (Nettlebeck 2004, 51); Han Bennink and Misha Mengelberg with Eric Dolphy in the Netherlands in the 1960s (Heffley 2005); vocalist Monica Zetterland singing American jazz tunes in Swedish accompanied by, among others, Bill Evans in the 1960s (Brown *et al.* 2014); Stan Getz with Bengt Hallberg in Sweden in the 1950s (Kan 2016); Don Cherry with Swedish drummer Bengt Berger in Sweden during the late 1960s (Kan 2016); and Jan Garbarek with Keith Jarrett and others in Norway in the 1970s (Nicholson 2005). Later examples also include interactions between other types of jazz labourers, including jazz dancers such as Frankie Manning and Norma Miller with the Swedish Swing Society in the 1990s and 2000s in Sweden (Sékiné 2017).

4 Later the record company Metronome established bases in cities throughout Northern Europe including Stockholm, Helsinki, Hamburg, Berlin, and New York (Brown *et al.* 2014, 67).

1

JAZZ IN POST-WAR EUROPE

From Free Collectives to Electronic Jazz

This chapter prefaces the subsequent chapters, offering an overview of critical elements of European jazz culture following the Second World War, especially those developing following the free, collective networks of the 1960s and 1970s. Phenomena addressed include the expansion of transnational record labels, popular music's role for stimulating crossover jazz movements, the influence of new technologies and media practices such as DJing within electronic jazz, online jazz zines, and the role of compilation albums for emerging artists. Additionally, interactive dance culture and new audiovisual contexts, from niche festivals to videos for expanding networks, will be treated, along with new modes of visibility within remixed European jazz cultures.

Relatively few jazz scholars have seriously examined contemporary European jazz. While 'polygeneric' (those inheriting multiple socio-cultural and musical genes) jazz projects have proliferated throughout Europe since the 1990s, most coverage has occurred within the field of music journalism. One example is music critic and historian Stuart Nicholson, in his book *Is Jazz Dead?: Or Has It Moved to a New Address* (2005), arguing that America's previously dominant cultural position and contemporary cultural significance demanded reconsideration. In his now well-cited thesis, Nicholson claimed that during the last quarter of the twentieth century, the most innovative jazz was produced not in the US, but in Europe, particularly in Scandinavia. Within particular cities and scenes, he posited the emergence of a 'glocalised jazz dialect', noting especially electronic and folk music collaborations within European jazz contexts, most notably artists and labels such as the Munich-based ECM label, which first supported Jan Garbarek's 1960s and 1970s 'ethnic-jazz' recordings.

From the productive intermingling of European folk, popular, and jazz styles, Nicholson witnessed a meaningful and engaged jazz culture stimulated by the national funding of jazz, and engendered by an open approach towards education and experimentation. Notably in Scandinavia, the combination of jazz funding and infrastructure, alongside the desire to develop a local jazz culture, cultivated what ECM's Manfred Eicher referred to as the 'Nordic Tone', a phrase quickly adopted by the jazz press to distinguish Northern European jazz from other regional styles. Here, jazz artists eagerly embraced new technologies such as sampling and sound manipulation within both live performance spaces and digital recording studios. Some more advanced technologically mediated European electronic jazz projects positioned themselves as bold criticisms and reactions to the growing conservatism of American jazz during the 1980s (Nicholson 2005, 208). Furthermore, by 2000 such genre-fusing recordings were influencing jazz artists in the US, reversing the perceived one-directional process of influence. Herbie Hancock, for example, studied the tracks of Norwegian electronic jazz trumpeter Nils Petter Molvær for his crossover, hip hop-influenced jazz and funk recordings of the early 2000s (Hancock's *Future2Future* from 2001). This process of influence and interaction, Nicholson argued, proved essential for new forms of mobility and creativity, when he claimed in 2005: "Where once the dynamic for this change and evolution in jazz came from within America, it is now shifting to these glocal communities around the world" (Nicholson 2005, 222). Nicholson thus, like Gebhardt and others, demanded a global or transnational recognition of jazz and its transformation within the New Europe.

Europe's Free and Collectivising Jazz of the 1970s and 1980s

Parallel to Nicholson's European exceptionalism, in his book *Northern Sun Southern Moon: Europe's Reinvention of Jazz* (2005), Mike Heffley focused especially on avant-garde and political jazz activities within Europe during the 1970s and 1980s. In this period, a general shift from the American star system to the European collective marked much of Europe's free-jazz movement, whilst most non-conformist jazz activities remained tied to state-sponsored finance. Contrary to Nicholson's positive review of Scandinavian jazz support, European jazz often failed to acquire the generous subsidies given to European art music organisations, including national orchestras and opera companies. As Heffley remarks: "A grassroots network of activist fans and musicians has been the main international and local support of the music since the beginning" (Heffley 2005, 91). Unlike earlier movements in America, where jazz's concertisation transpired in part due to influential jazz promoters such as Norman Granz, or through the support of civic organisations like the NAACP, new jazz movements in Europe relied upon a combination of subsidised individual artist collectives, and independent entrepreneurs, festival organisers, and transnationally oriented record labels willing to support individual jazz artists and new aesthetic movements (Bakriges 2007).

In addition to independent jazz labels like Munich's ECM and Enja (which stood for European New Jazz), music festivals increasingly played a pivotal role in sustaining jazz musicians' careers (McGee 2016; Webster and McKay 2016). These ranged from large-scale pop music festivals such as Sziget to the prestigious European jazz festivals such as the Netherlands North Sea Jazz Festival. They extended to the recently expanding smaller vintage jazz festivals, jazz clubs, and series such as the Vintage Reboot events in Paris. Such festivals provided import-ant sites for the middle-layer of polygeneric jazz performers and their promotion of electronic jazz recordings or reconfigured projects in the neoliberal era.

In the Netherlands, certain expressionistic jazz networks and collectives emerged alongside artistic and semi-political movements such as the Provo or Fluxus movements (Whyton and Gebhardt 2015). The Instant Composers Pool was perhaps the first broadly organised Dutch jazz collective to actively engage, record, and program the works of contemporary improvisers and performers (Rusch 2015; Schuiling 2019), founded in 1967 by avant-garde saxophonist Willem Breuker, pianist Misha Mengelberg, and drummer Han Bennink. Both Bennick and Mengelberg had played and recorded with Eric Dolphy in Hilversum in 1964 for his final recording, *Last Date*, before his death in Berlin (Rusch 2015, 45). This organisation evolved into one of the Netherlands' most influential umbrella organisations for a variety of jazz events including combinations of clas-sical, free, and theatrical works regarding improvised jazz (Heffley 2005; Rusch 2015; Schuiling 2019).

In 1973, the organisation split twofold; the Kollectief led by Breuker, and the ICP independently led by Mengelberg (Rusch 2015). The Kollectief gained a rep-utation for ironic, humorous, and experimental improvised works, later connected to similar free jazz experiments throughout Europe during the late 1960s and 1970s (Heffley 2005, 63–116). Both Bennink's projects and Breuker's Kollektief were responsible for international collaborations with European jazz and art music composers, and additionally American free jazz players including Cecil Taylor, Sun Ra, and Eric Dolphy. They were also inspired by musical explorations in tonality, including compositional and performance structures from surrealism, drawing from the philosophical and sociological explorations of John Cage and the Fluxus move-ment (Whitehead 1998). Furthermore, these organisations profoundly increased awareness of Dutch and European jazz more broadly, helping invite government support through Dutch institutions such as the BIM (The Union of Improvising Musicians, 1971), SJIN (*Stichting Jazz en Geimproviseerde Muziek Nederland*, Associ-ation of Jazz and Improvised Music in the Netherlands) and STEIM (Studio for Electro-Instrumental Music) (Heffley 2005, 78). The Dutch free jazz movement has since been stereotyped and even belittled for its ironic and theatrical detachment from serious or spiritual explorations (Whitehead 1998). However, such European movements emerged as self-conscious alternatives to the star system and the pop-ular music driven by the Anglo-American music industry in the 1960s and 1970s. For Heffley and others, these groups "shared with other Dutch initiatives and voices an ethic of offering an alternative popular music to counter that of commercial mass culture" (Heffley 2005, 79). His term "emanzipation" recalls social protest, media expansion, and student activism characterising the late 1960s and 1970s. Such musical explorations, free jazz, and outdoor music festivals provided the most palatable forum for expressing a modern resistance and reluctance to eager adoption of the American music industry's commercialism and capitalism.

Whyton and Gebhardt's recent publication *The Cultural Politics of Jazz Collectives: This is Our Music* (2015) provides further evidence of the role performed by processes of music collectivism, leading up to and within New Europe. Illustratively, Arvidsson and Adolfsson's chapter on the Swedish music collective Ett Minne för Livet (A Lifetime Memory) explores the role of the musical performance style during countercultural political dissent, as well as resistance to mainstream American musical styles. Their examination of a 1975 broadcast concert revealed how this collective's integration of folk, jazz, and rock styles relevant for Swedish culture in the mid-1970s facilitated a means of departing from Anglo-American popular music and the modernist art tradition, while critiquing the decolonisation processes of the 1950s and 1960s. They argue that this initiative led to more autonomous musical spaces and practices after the 1970s (Arvidsson and Adolfsson 2015).

Also in this edition, Christa Bruckner-Haring and Michael Kahr (2015) examined varieties of contemporary Austrian jazz forged from the *Jazz Werkstatt* collectives in Vienna and Graz, which, in recent decades, led to the formation of an increasingly trans-cultural identity within their local jazz scenes. Similarly, Scott Currie examined the *Freie Initiative Improvisation Berlin* (FIIB) collective as something beyond a collective, rather a registered association of artists and impresarios. For Currie, this "collective organization and its festive manifestation played a central role in establishing and maintaining a presence for improvised music in Berlin". Further, FIIB brought together musicians from the newly unified east and west of Berlin, offering "a common meeting ground that ... held together ... the fractious constituents of scenes otherwise divided by stylistic markers of generation and geography" (Currie 2015, 65). These recent free collectives directly mediated the transitional periods of unification or reorganisation characterising post-reunification cities in the 1990s and 2000s.

Similarly, Tim Wall and Simon Barber examined the Cowcob Collective's role in Birmingham as a progressive transnational music endeavour. They revealed the complicated layers of jazz making within a range of spaces, genres, and institutions from the official cultural space of Symphony Hall to local festivals (Mostly Jazz, Funk & Soul Festival), through local jazz Arts Council funded platforms such as Jazzlines, and within local pubs promoting weekly jazz nights. These activities were uncovered as multifaceted approaches towards contemporary jazz practice (Wall and Barber 2015). Finally, Andrew Dubber explores the modern "associative vernacular mediation" practices of the Kitchen Orchestra's Pulse Online multimedia project which took place in Stavanger, Norway in 2012, exploring not the place-specific character of contemporary jazz collectivism, but rather the affordances of specific media objects for particular modes of interaction and participation. Dubber reveals how, through online mediation, jazz audiences collaborated "rather than simply witnessed" performances within the Tou Scene (Dubber 2015, 223).

As evidenced from these studies, by the 1980s, some political reactions and insular aesthetic dogmatism of the earlier free collectives had given way to a new generation of musicians, exposed to a greater variety of transnational popular musics and performance networks. These were not merely the mass-mediated music industry's top 40 hits, but world music, transnational jazz collectives, and field music recordings of smaller, but now digitally distributed record labels. With increased access to world musics, younger and often conservatory-trained European musicians sought other forums for improvising and engaging with jazz. This generation was less interested in rejecting Anglo-American mass-mediated musical styles, and some critics argued it lacked a collective political voice in relation to performance. Trends in popular music, and especially electronic dance music, prompted new engagements with youth culture which re-incorporated some of jazz music's interactive, pre-war, and war-time proclivities such as dance and studio experimentation with soundscapes and textures, which reintroduced the aesthetics of groove into jazz-influenced spaces and recordings.

European Jazz in the Digital Era

Before digitalisation, the recording crisis necessitated new ways of financing music. During the 1970s and 1980s, less established and often younger jazz musicians developed techniques to engage with contemporary culture while simultaneously promoting their work. Musicians naturally sought to modernise jazz practice by connecting jazz performance aesthetics with contemporary popular music genres (Fellezs 2011). The commercial success of fusion, smooth, or crossover jazz artists led to an increase in jazz performers within major labels like Verve and Blue Note (McGee 2013). Parallel to this, during the 1980s and 1990s, other technologically experimental while less industrial forms of jazz began to feature in local clubs and electronic music festivals, reflecting both the ad hoc and 'improvised' interactivity of new music scenes. Especially prominent were those most impacted by popular styles driven by DJing networks; from these, new sonic techniques emerged, adopting sampling techniques and sound manipulation capabilities of electronic hardware. Within recording projects, the technical standards of earlier studio fusion and contemporary jazz projects gave way to projects highlighting the danceability and interactive aspects of live jazz. The outcome of such cross-fertilisations quickly gained currency via promoters and fans of these cosmopolitan club circuits as 'acid jazz'. The appellation was attributed to early UK jazz dance and world music promoter and DJ Gilles Peterson, who had produced his own jazz dance series in London during the late 1980s and 1990s. He later promoted a variety of electronic and mixed-mediated jazz discs on his weekly BBC music programme, *Worldwide*. In the 1990s, Fiona Talkington too became an important early promoter of genre-fusing electronic jazz projects on her numerous radio programmes for BBC's Radio 3.

Early acid jazz projects successfully negotiated the prior boundaries between popular music and jazz, and between dance, electronic, hip hop, and digital production technologies, new configurable genres which had radically altered the musical landscape. Since the 1990s, with the acid jazz boom in major urban centres throughout Europe, new styles of jazz continued to attract dancers and younger audiences exposed to a greater variety of audiovisual artists, including live jazz instrumentalists, but also turntablists, sample-based sound producers, dancers, VJs, and DJs.

According to *Billboard*, acid jazz scenes first emerged in the UK in the 1990s. The UK's acid jazz scene spawned mainstream artists such as The Brand New Heavies and Jamiroquai. Yet acid jazz was only the latest of a longer trajectory of DJed jazz-dance events throughout the UK since the late 1970s where jazz records, competitive dance crews, and the eruption of new fashions and lifestyles culminated around 'rare jazz' records, independent record shops, and post-industrial or sometimes disused holiday locations for immersive jazz dance activities. These ranged from jazz dance club nights, to 'day-timers' and 'weekenders', to designated radio programmes featuring jazz, soul, funk, and Latin music (Cotgrove 2009).

The proliferation of electronic jazz networks was not simply a European phenomenon but, by its very nature, attuned and connected to musical developments within cities throughout the world such as Jakarta (Maliq & D'Essentials), Rome (Jestofunk), and Kyoto (Kyoto Jazz Massive). Music industry journalist Martin Johnson linked the club scene of the 1990s to the mammoth success of mainstream crossover jazz influenced groups prior to 2000, including Beck, Us3, and the Fugees. He further credits mainstream crossover groups for negotiating a more prominent place for jazz in pop culture. Arguably, the role of jazz-influenced dance music and its growing popularity further stimulated multiple sub-genres, including styles such as trip hop, drum 'n' bass, and ambient groove in prominent jazz dance cities such as Manchester and London (Hesmondhalgh 2000). These sub-styles of electronic music provided important pathways for younger audiences to experience new currents in jazz. By the mid-1990s, the more local or regionally distributed acid jazz recordings of specialised jazz record stores moved online as these businesses failed to survive in the new digital environment. This was precipitated by the rise of digital distribution networks such as Napster, alongside the incorporation of mass-mediated crossover jazz styles by the majors who increasingly marketed compilations through larger distribution outlets or online (Johnson 1997, 18).

Interestingly, this decade marked the era of the *compilation album* for smaller record labels, a strategy taken as regional networks of independent record stores faltered. Independent jazz labels produced compilation records that highlighted complementary artists from local acid and crossover jazz scenes. Major and independent record companies reacted swiftly by releasing compilations of both crossover and acid jazz artists on more generic series such as Instinct's *This is Acid Jazz*. Drawing on the long-tail distribution and reception model (Anderson 2004), these mixes curated current and past artists within compatible playlists of jazz, Black music, hip hop, and urban dance music intended to appeal to club goers, instrumental jazz fans, and urban music fans. Instinct, a British jazz label, released their own series featuring mixes of jazz and electronic projects from the UK's many DJed jazz-dance clubs, within scenes which stimulated and depended upon the collaboration and promotion of local zines, event promoters, dance crews, independent record stores, and local band managers such as London's DJ Patrick Forge and event planner and record label owner Eddie Piller (Cotgrove 2009, 237). Along with Gilles Peterson, Piller was instrumental in successfully distributing Acid Jazz Records, one of Britain's first independent acid jazz labels (Cotgrove 2009, 239–240). Island's 4th and B'way series *Rebirth of the Cool* highlighted more underground trip hop, jazz, and drum 'n' bass combinations in the 1990s. Other polygeneric jazz labels emerged outside of the UK including the German label Compost and their *Future Sound of Jazz* series, similarly promoting jazz and electronic beats projects. In the US, Blue Note's *The New Groove* released an original collection of hip hop and classic jazz, apparently inspired by Us3's success. Moreover, their *Rare Groove* series spawned a number of re-releases of older jazz artists including John Patton and Donald Byrd. Fantasy Records also licensed some of its catalogue to the San Francisco Bay Area label Luv N' Haight, eventually initiating its own *Legends of Acid Jazz* series (Johnson 1997, 21).

By 2000, the internet facilitated numerous forums for dispersing new sounds and cementing new sub-genres related to dance musics, electronic soundscapes, and jazz instrumentals. Such online, digitally driven output sometimes led to cross-generational and mixed-mediated interactions in live music settings. Notably, British DJs and electronic producers such as Roni Size incorporated older jazz recordings in their sets and toured with instrumental soloists from these re-released records. The British electronic duo Lamb similarly collaborated with soloists such as trumpet player Kevin Davy and revived a post-war jazz aesthetic by adding small groups to live performances such as the London-based string trio Chi 2 Strings and the jazz rhythm section comprising bassist Jon Thorne, Icelandic guitarist Oddur Mar Runnarsson, and Danish drummer Nikolaj Bjerre.

The Black music networks of jungle and drum 'n' bass in the UK too came about partly through the configurable synergy between these projects' producers and their corresponding online and physical participants. However, the sampling of old recorded jazz beats, manipulated through accelerated tempos, dynamic sequences of break beats, and the incorporation of live jazz instrumentalists further connected this music to its Black diasporic (Caribbean) musical origins (Hesmondhalgh 2000). Associations to an older and progressive Black jazz culture continued to drive its inspiration and aided in reviving live jazz in cosmopolitan, electronic lounges, and dance clubs throughout the world.

Outside of the UK, Vienna's electronic music scene had absorbed the 'rare groove' compilations, electronic break beats, and sampled jazz recordings into its many electronic jazz events, yet the style of this scene's most famous duo, Kruder & Dorfmeister, transmitted a relaxed, downtempo aesthetic (Mazierska 2018). Electronic music magazine, *Resident Advisor*, depicted the early sound of these two creatives as purveyors of a "musical *beutekunst* that owes … to rare funk tunes, electric jazz arrangements, the feeling of deep soul, hiphop, dub, reggae, ambient, fusion, brazil, chansons, dope beats and drum + bass …" ("Biography: Kruder & Dorfmesiter"). The mellower soundtrack quality of their early mixes appealed to Gilles Peterson, who in 1993 played "High None" from their EP *G-Stone* (G-Stone Recordings 1993) on his programme *Worldwide*. Upon its international reception, Kruder & Dorfmeister quickly garnered an international following, creating their own downtempo, acid jazz label which continued to attract fans of polygeneric electronic music. This label connected fans of similarly eclectic labels such as Jazzland in Oslo, Ninja Tune in London, and Compost Records in Munich ("Biography: Kruder & Dorfmesiter"). Stefan Niederwieser described the slower grooves and highly eclectic sounds of K & D as indicative of the "newly won Western appetite" for international musical combinations, remade for the "post-reunification generation", creating "a very international sound" within an era where the "western way of life had won over the old Eastern Bloc" (Niederwieser n.d.). In 1996, K & D released their *DJ Kicks* 'mix-tape', selling over a million copies and inspiring a new genre, the *remix compilation album* (Niederwieser n.d.). The remix album soon evolved as a staple for electronic jazz producers to promote their skills and versatility, a topic addressed especially in Chapter 4.

Elsewhere in Northern Europe, the trend for incorporating live jazz artists into established disco and dance circuits emerged during the 1990s in transnationally connected dance cities, especially Amsterdam, London, Paris, Vienna, and Berlin, scenes supporting lively dance cultures and a constant flux of musicians, tourists, and local music and dance enthusiasts (Rapp 2009). Amsterdam gained an international reputation during the late 1980s for interactive discos such as the RoXXY, which provided professional opportunities for up-and-coming DJs such as KC the Funkaholic and Eddy de Clercq (*All That Jazz* 2009, 367). In 1995, tenor saxophonist Hans Dulfer appeared in the Dam Square with DJ Dmitri, a performance initiating a new dance-oriented public to live crossover jazz performances (Dulfer and Determeyer 1998). By the early twenty-first century, Amsterdam's electronic jazz events centred around multimedia venues like the Melkweg and the Sugar Factory, some sponsored by major jazz companies such as Blue Note, with dance and electronic jazz themes and sets suitable for dancing *and* listening.

Within these networks, DJs continued to forge new territory by interweaving more densely manipulated soundscapes with recorded jazz improvisations in the studio. As producers and DJs built basement studios and digital workstations, they eventually branched out to nightclubs, where a younger generation of dancers and electronic music lovers enthusiastically embraced these 'sample-driven jazz' experiments. From the early 1990s, mid-sized nightclubs, influenced by the informal culture of raves, increasingly adopted the performance aesthetics of acid and electronic jazz as they featured sample artists, DJs, turntablists, and MCs with equal prominence to bands, pop stars, and instrumentalists. As rave culture declined in the early twenty-first century, commercial discos and nightclubs consolidated the musical and participatory networks between acid jazz and the electronic dance and rave culture of the prior decade. Current electronic jazz projects still favour the live moment and the aesthetics of participatory discrepancies (Keil and Feld 1994), yet also rely upon audiences' knowledge of sample-based dance music and interactive DJ mixes.

Since the 1990s, digital distribution networks have importantly dispersed remixes outside the purview of the majors or commercial radio networks. Digital music platforms stimulated new pathways to disseminate music with unprecedented speed and efficiency from community music sites to local dance clubs, from local radio to internet streaming services, and from peer-to-peer (P2P) networks to mobile devices. As transnational networks promoted increasingly sophisticated remixes and mashups, electronic jazz artists honed their techniques with sometimes free, open-source software such as Acid Pro and Ableton Live, and eventually developed more specialised genres, including sample-based or cinematic jazz. Single-producer electronic jazz projects frequently began in home studios but quickly branched out to spawn electronic jazz collectivities (McGee 2015). As producers and DJs forged new musical communities, the internet enabled new networking channels such as recruiting visual artists for performances. These sometimes resulted in original promotional videos appearing on dance floors but also through digital fora such as SoundCloud and YouTube.

Contemporary electronic-based jazz collectivities engage in various promotional, performance, and recording projects from soliciting user participation during performances or on artist websites (e.g. Kitchen Orchestra's 'Pulse' video phone interactions) to multimedia festivals and all-night dance parties. These collectives often register their own labels to produce and promote the work of collaborating and related groups, such as the case with Jazzanova's Sonar Kollektiv label, which in 2017 celebrated its twentieth anniversary. In 2007, the collective had already formed the Sonar Kollektiv Orchester, a fifteen-musician ensemble which collaborated with and recorded acoustic 'remixes' of the producer-led project Jazzanova.

Independent Electronic Crossover Jazz Labels

Since 2000, European labels such as Sonar Kollektiv and Jazzland Recordings have importantly supported new polygeneric European electronic jazz groups. To illustrate, the highly respected British label Ninja Tune promoted numerous transnationally active, polygeneric cosmopolitan groups including Skalpel, Jazzanova, Funki Porcini, and the Cinematic Orchestra. These independent record companies arose partially to fill the gap left by the majors and their disinterest in such collectivities. Furthermore, independent record companies functioned more as mobile networks than geographically fixed entities, no longer solely comprising traditional recording, distribution, promotion, and A&R branches.

In the 2000s, the breadth of activities subsumed within such platforms, both musical and non-musical, as well as the trans-locality of independent collaborations, hinged upon transnational connections for distribution in other regions as well as for transnational performance routes. However, electronic jazz or mixed-genre labels also depended upon artistically motivated, well-connected individuals contributing to thriving local music scenes of cities such as London, where jazz dance and electronic music networks complemented each other. Within such scenes, these electronic labels' artists were typically discovered less through traditional routes, often through more informal and international networks of DJs, producers, sound artists, and instrumentalists working interactively through DIT (do-it-together) alliances.

Countering the transnationalism or even seeming 'placelessness' of such networks, trans-local jazz collectives often integrated geographically rooted, historically significant artefacts (i.e. vintage local jazz club recordings), which in turn they re-circulated through mobile, virtual, transnational routes. Ninja Tune recorded a number of 'nu' jazz electronic collectives who forged aesthetic links to national forms of cultural heritage, most notably Skalpel from Poland, led by Marcin Cichy and Igor Pudło, both DJs/producers from Wroclaw. Skalpel's unique sound resulted from fervent excavations and remixing of Polish jazz samples hulled from the smoky, dusky environs of 1960s and 1970s Polish jazz clubs. A 2009 BBC interview with Skalpel's DJ/producers Cichy and Pudło explored their interest in scavenging old Polish records:

> You have an idea of sounds in your mind, and then you must find them for it to be a real record.... So sometimes we are looking for a sample for a very long time. It took us over three years to make this LP.... It's a mixture of breaks and ambient sounds, and a hip-hop way of producing it.... We were thinking about doing something original and we decided that the Polish jazz is something we could give to the rest of the world.
>
> *(Walton 2004)*

This desire to mediate national or regional historical jazz to "the rest of the world" reflects the international "aesthetic cosmopolitanism" (Regev 2013) of electronic jazz in an era of increased mobility and interaction for artists throughout Europe. European jazz artists also appeared keenly aware of the persistent visibility of canonical jazz stars. In response, these locally rooted yet progressive artists sought to position their own jazz histories against the dominance of jazz narratives, which perpetually foregrounded Americans from the early twentieth century (Whyton 2013).

Outside of the US, such trans-locally inclined groups actively connected with other electronic jazz collaborations in different scenes – indeed, German electronic jazz collective De-Phazz claimed that such sample-driven jazz groups appeared on similar radars with producer-led outfits (PLOs) like Amon Tobin and the Cinematic Orchestra. However, such alliances did not preclude producers and label owners of electronic jazz to establish contracts with the majors for increased distribution. For example, De-Phazz, led by producer Pit Baumgartner, released material on major label subsidiary Universal Jazz Germany, although these producer/artists often first developed their careers performing with local DJs and within independent labels and record shops. While DJ/producer-driven jazz collectives established trans-local recording companies, their particular "logics of circulation" (Straw 1991) dramatically differed from traditional majors versus independent models of pre-internet decades.

DJ as Gatekeeper/Taste-Maker/Curator

Eventually, jazz record companies and jazz subsidiaries of the majors acknowledged the relevance of underground currents in electronic jazz and their networks of musicians, producers, labels, and event organisers. They realised that dancers and clubbers were discovering new music through live DJ events and through various mediums, such as YouTube mixes. In the Netherlands during the 2000s, for example, Blue Note embraced the opportunity to solicit the popularity and reputation of nu jazz and electronic dance music DJs to release multi-genre compilations of back catalogue material along with new urban, hip hop, soul, and dance tracks. This practice had worked exceptionally well with British electronic jazz dance group Us3, whose breakthrough success owed significantly to their digital sampling of previous Blue Note jazz recordings (e.g. Herbie Hancock's "Cantaloupe Island") with new beats and dance sequences. During the 2000s, Blue Note Netherlands began releasing mixed-genre compilations under local electronic jazz DJs such as Dutch artist DJ Maestro. While not 'authentic' reproductions of electronic jazz club mixes, these compilations attracted listeners due to such connections. In this context, producers of electronic jazz projects adopted the radio disc jockey's role of cultural curators or 'taste-makers', displacing the A&R divisions as they were valued for their unique knowledge of recorded jazz history and newer currents in electronic or mixed-mediated jazz culture.

Electric Jazz Zines – *Straight No Chaser*

During the 1990s, the promotion of electronic jazz occurred mostly in progressive online magazines like *The Wire* or in the transnationally distributed British zine *Straight No Chaser: The Magazine of World Jazz Live*, a quarterly zine launched in the late 1980s. Paul Bradshaw, its author, initiated the magazine to create attention for the cross-currents between contemporary Black (diasporic) music, jazz, and electronic music, especially within London's electronic clubs. The slogan of the zine, "Interplanetary Sounds: Ancient to Future", betrayed an expansionist (Afro-futuristic) jazz at the centre of the magazine's focus in connection with other progressive Black musics from around the world – especially soul-oriented electronic music. This slogan obviously referenced two prior forward-looking jazz currents: Sun Ra's musical explorations and Funkadelic's funky jams and psychedelic recordings of the 1970s and 1980s. The title also expanded the Black Atlantic connections of recent international Black music currents in the European crossover or electronic jazz scenes.

The magazine also reflected a wider gambit of jazz sources, from internationally successful artists to lesser-known underground scenes not connected to the conventional music industries of cities such as London or Paris. Its transnational readership related to the world music exploration during the 1980s and 1990s, which brought new international currents into live and DJed jazz programmes within both informal dance music gatherings and into the expanding club scenes of the 1990s. Making such connections to an earlier non-essentialist and fundamentally international Black music diaspora was especially important for the acid jazz and later nu and electronic jazz communities within Europe, as it provided a counter discourse and musical milieu against the discourse of conservatory-oriented jazz within the United States.

Within Bradshaw's twenty-year run, artists featured on the zine's cover included Roni Size, Fema Kuti, Bjork, 4Hero, Guru, Cinematic Orchestra, Meshell Ndegeocello, Anita Baker, A Tribe Called Quest, and Gilles Peterson. From this broad international mix, the role of the nu jazz vocalist, the jazz instrumentalist, world jazz artist, world music promoter, and electronic jazz DJ all featured as prominent actors within this international landscape, all styles complexly interrelated. Based upon statements of electronic jazz practitioners examined in this book, who religiously consulted this publication, *Straight No Chaser*'s treatment of various styles positioned it as the international voice for new currents in jazz, electronic dance music, and new digital sampling techniques in studio and on stage. Considering that many of its reviewed artists sampled progressive jazz artists from the 1960s to the 1980s, one may argue that particular recordings provided inspiration and a progressive model for electronic jazz collectives during those last three decades. Amongst others are frequent references to both the recordings and overall musical aesthetic and philosophy of especially Miles Davis, Herbie Hancock, Sun Ra, and Roy Ayers – all musicians frequently referenced or listed as important influences for the musicians and artists interviewed for this study.

Jazz Festivals, Revivals, and the Participatory Bodies of European Jazz Culture

Next to the promotional, journalistic, and critical representation of new streams of jazz, the performance world has dramatically transformed due to a growing and now saturation of jazz, popular music, and mixed-arts festivals (Delanty *et al.* 2011; McGee 2016; Webster and McKay 2016). Dedicated jazz clubs still exist, but many jazz consumers encounter this music more frequently within festivals or other mixed-arts settings. The European jazz festival network, first established in the post-war period, also professionalised and expanded during the 1990s. In addition to more conventional jazz genres, such festivals currently offer a broader range of Black music-oriented popular genres from jazz, soul, and R&B to crossover pop and electronic jazz. For example, the North Sea Jazz Festival competes with other large European festivals such as Jazz à Vienne in France or Italy's Umbria Jazz Festival to attract travelling jazz artists to perform alongside global Black music stars (Delanty *et al.* 2011; Santoro and Solaroli 2013; McGee 2016). These large festivals remain important for travelling jazz musicians who depend upon them for their income.

Related to the expansion of jazz music festivals, other kinds of inter-arts festivals erupted since 1990. The mid-1990s swing and exotica revival in North America fuelled similar fascination in Europe. It manifested in both mainstream commercial projects and exhibitions and within developing structures in the European entertainment industry. Simon Reynolds famously theorised such revivalist movements as indications of popular culture's obsessive consumption of prior popular music aesthetic forms, a notion he referred to as 'retromania' (Reynolds 2011). The electro swing revival in cities like Paris exemplified this asynchronous retro obsession, yet filtered through a technologically driven and remix aesthetic, as both earlier swing dances and swing dance records were re-integrated in European dance culture of the 2010s. In this climate, artists promoted themselves through individual social media with their own music videos, but they also adopted mass-mediated promotional opportunities such as the interactive reality television format. For example, the transnational Dutch-based PLO Caro Emerald incorporated vintage-oriented production aesthetics, whose retro soundscapes made them attractive candidates for use within reality TV dancing contests (this is discussed in Chapter 5).

Rather than in jazz clubs, remixed or sample-based polygeneric genres (and especially those which incorporate electronic dance music aesthetics) are more likely programmed in either large-scale pop festivals or smaller arts-themed and niche festivals such as vintage or mixed-arts events. Since 2000, the vintage festival movement has manifest in smaller cities throughout Europe as a forum to highlight local jazz artists who travel these outdoor live music circuits, but not necessarily as the headliners for the major European jazz festivals.

While large-scale festivals provide critical performance opportunities during the summer and autumn months, European swing revival musicians and dancers such as Herräng's professional Lindy Hop performers too depend upon small-scale festivals. Through the growth of jazz dance instruction camps and summer "festivals" (as they are called by dancers), a cottage industry of competitive performance, educational, and showcase festivals has emerged to provide viable professional opportunities for various creative artists. These workshops depend upon professional dancers who dedicate their weekends to spreading jazz dance to European enthusiasts. Such a transnational network has achieved a truly trans-local community, which starkly differs from the professional music industry networks of the major, large-scale jazz festivals of pre-internet decades.

Another elusive facet of contemporary jazz culture are the online promotional outlets occupied by jazz artists, producers, filmmakers, and dancers. The role of music video has profoundly altered the ways new artists network and promote their performances. Indeed, most of the new jazz artists working across genres such as electro swing or electronic jazz (and even more so for the swing dance community) depend upon audiovisual media, especially music videos for their current visibility and viability in the European jazz world. While many music videos have replaced albums as the preferred musical media for younger audiences (Vernallis 2013), other media has assumed a greater role within the entire network of artistic activity. This media, for example, has profoundly impacted and hastened the growth of a transnational competitive swing dance community, where a body of digitally circulated dance films are studied and evaluated within a transnational arena and then such media influence the experiences, aesthetics, and expectations of 'live' jazz dance events.

Finally, the various revivals and reconfigurations of prior jazz media through contemporary platforms including YouTube have enabled dialogical explorations and adaptations of pre-digital jazz media. Through the remix, historical analysis, or interactive performative jazz remake, prior jazz cultures and their media have featured as the prominent markers of contemporary remix cultures. One example are the films made by the jazz dance troupe, the Harlem Hot Shots from Stockholm, who rigorously studied older jazz films from the 1930s and 1940s, and recreated particular routines for short films which then circulate to the international Lindy Hop dance community through YouTube. The particular expansion of media genres through YouTube has profoundly impacted how contemporary jazz artists navigate their profession.

Cumulatively these developments stimulated a multifaceted, inter-connected and multi-dimensional jazz culture in various scenes and cities since the period of reunification. In the following chapter, Amsterdam's dance tourist jazz club nights are examined to uncover how new symbiotic alliances emerged in the context of musical migrations, jazz education, and new relationships between the jazz majors, local institutions, and recording networks as evidenced within two long-time series (Wicked Jazz Sounds and Blue Note Trips) taking place at two established multimedia dance clubs, Melkweg and the Sugar Factory.

2

WICKED JAZZ SOUNDS AND BLUE NOTE TRIPS

Dance Tourists and Musical Migrants in Amsterdam's Crossover Jazz Scene

> The new jazz constituency got here in part by following their own agenda through pop music and have no intention of discarding their fondness for it.
>
> *(Johnson 1997, 17)*

> You have many crossover bands where there is a sort of movement creating attention for a larger music stream and from where the local scene only becomes bigger and stronger. Ultimately because of that you receive more exposure and more creative possibilities.
>
> *(Trumpeter Rob Van de Wouw, July 5, 2009)*

In August 2008, the Melkweg's *Blue Note Trip* event featured DJ Maestro and trumpet soloist Rob van de Wouw, two of the series' most visible artists.[1] I arrived at 11:00 p.m., guested-in with an older, bearded Dutch man wearing loose-fitting overalls. We then entered a medium-sized hall featuring an elevated stage, state-of-the-art sound system, well-equipped lighting booth in the balcony, and a small bar. A massive poster prominently displayed behind the stage promoted *Blue Note Trip*, with a photograph of a young, fashionably dressed man in panama hat carrying a tattered suitcase – the quintessence of the cosmopolitan, travelling urbanite. DJ Maestro entered minutes later carrying two crates of vinyl, ordered a drink, and waited quietly for the last DJ to finish his set. Those occupying the hall numbered not more than twenty – a mix of tourists and Dutch music fans, most in their twenties. Approaching midnight, he began his set with Latin-tinged lounge music as the small crowd directed themselves towards the stage – but few ventured onto the dance floor, for by Dutch standards, the hour was far too early for dancing. Gradually warming up the room, Maestro incorporated the sounds of Brazilian rock, salsa, hip hop, house, and big beat into his non-stop four-hour set as the hall steadily filled up.

As the first dancers approached, a range of overlapping musical genres blended seamlessly to accommodate the cosmopolitan crowd. Populating the room were equal numbers of women and men – most eager to dance to the DJ's eclectic grooves.[2] Eventually, the music evolved into a percussive funk break, and a young, casually dressed Van de Wouw came to the microphone with his trumpet. He began sparsely with a few blues licks, increased the intensity with funk-based rhythm and blues, and at the height of his solo, delivered the more ornamental hard bop phrases in the style of Roy Hargrove. A lesser DJ may have buried his solo, yet Maestro aptly programmed the appropriate space during his most chromatic passage. His playing – highly polished and rhythmic – drew an immediate slew of whoops, hollers, and hand-throwing from the crowd – who continued to dance while facing the stage. Women showed off their versatility with salsa steps and belly dancing, while men swayed back and forth, or bopped their heads to and fro as if listening to some down-tempo hip hop. Occasionally, one or two displayed more contemporary urban moves, but a more reserved physicality prevailed. It was clear that dancing, flirting, and talking were central to the experiences and social interactions favoured by both locals and tourists.

I eventually conversed with a few people hanging around the bar or seated in chairs lining the back of the walls, including a group of younger, Scottish tourists who had been dancing throughout the night. They told me that they were enjoying the opportunity to dance unabashedly, drink beer, and had indulged in marijuana before their arrival. Their enthusiasm was both catching and pleasantly derided by less adventurous members sitting on the side-lines who giggled and pointed. Indeed, even the light technician began to tease them – following the most uninhibited of dancers with a small spotlight, on which the young man began to pounce as if admonishing his persistent shadow.

Later, I approached three Indian men who spoke neither Dutch nor English, but nevertheless entered the modest dance floor and stood close to Van de Wouw as he began his riveting solo. Surprisingly, the lone elder gentleman seated discretely at a table also came to dance, jabbing his hands in the air and stomping anachronistically in a 1960s beatnik style. Two tall, young Dutchmen standing by the bar came for the jazz, they told me, alerting me to a well-known radio station, Arrow Jazz, playing a similarly eclectic mix of urban contemporary music, such as Nora Jones, Stevie Wonder, and the New Jazz Collective, a Dutch instrumental jazz funk group. Until 2012, DJ Maestro's weekly Arrow Jazz radio programme, *Dig This*, promoted the Blue Note Trip recordings and weekly events in Amsterdam and Utrecht. According to Blue Note's Dutch site, *Blue Note Trip* is a jazz series that combines the Blue Note's back catalogue with hip dance recordings. In Amsterdam, the Blue Note Trip series cultivated symbiotic relations between collective members and fans. However, they equally depended upon commercial

FIGURE 2.1   DJ Maestro record cover, *Birds Beats*, Blue Note Trip Series (2008)[3]

stations and transnational music corporations to promote events, release recordings, and present their music on national radio programmes.

Through such ethnographic encounters within Amsterdam crossover jazz club nights, I realised that international tourists, often students from other European universities, comprised an important segment of these collectives' late-night audiences. Many travelled to Amsterdam to visit clubs, coffee shops, and stroll through the city's elegant neighbourhoods. In this respect, much of Amsterdam's mobile party tourists share affinities with what D'Andrea terms "expressive expatriates", representing a cultural-artistic elite interacting with musical media and appropriating "alternative formations in commodity form" (D'Andrea 2007, 3–4).

Introduction

Amsterdam's increasingly multi-mediated, technologically driven crossover jazz scene accommodates contemporary transnational youth cultures within local dance venues promoting a variety of electronic music styles. In particular, this city's contemporary electronic jazz collectivities embody cosmopolitanism through mixed-genre predilections supported by local music lovers and international tourists, who expressly visit clubs to experience Amsterdam's unique blend of social and sexual inclusivity, vibrant nightlife, and musical mutuality. Crossover jazz series occupy the physical spaces of Amsterdam's historic neighbourhoods, while also transforming digital social landscapes. Since the late 1990s, the proliferation of socially organised networks has provided new forums for musical sociality and creative musical interaction. These digital engagements inspired cross-fertilisations of jazz instrumental styles with earlier European urban music trends, themselves originating in African American derived genres such as soul and funk, and precipitated cosmopolitan European and American dance genres from techno to house (Mutsaers 1998).

Within this scene, new generations of jazz soloists from local conservatories seek forums for expressing their affinity for jazz and popular music, as well as integrating new media. During the 2000s, collaborating with local DJs and producers, collectives provided new foundations for distinctively European, multi-mediated, mixed-genre events. Amsterdam's DJ Maestro, for example, spun an eclectic mix of Euro-American electronic dance music beats, Latin rhythms, and urban African dance genres, while supporting live instrumentalists. Maestro began his musical life in Groningen as a classical violist and later began spinning jazz with other popular music styles during the 1990s. Since then, he has released eleven albums with Blue Note, remixing Blue Note recording artists including Horace Silver, the Buddy Rich Big Band, Janet Lawson, Joe Williams, Les McCann, and collaborated with such European jazz soloists as saxophonist Candy Dulfer and trumpeter Rob van de Wouw. Maestro continues to perform across Europe for jazz festivals with international jazz instrumentalists.

Maestro's aforementioned work, his weekly radio programmes, and frequent appearances in such established mixed-media clubs speak to the complicated yet necessary interactions between corporate transnational entities and local bodies as they structure mutually beneficial relationships. These intermediated productions inspire new forms of musical sociability. Indeed, fans of Maestro can visit his website, purchase his Blue Note compilations, log playlists on streaming platforms, tag musical genres – as well as meet virtual friends and comment about current electronic jazz events.

Another Amsterdam venture, Wicked Jazz Sounds – a loosely connected network of artists, DJs, VJs, and party planners – brings together young jazz instrumentalists and vocalists with a variety of other cultural participants, eschewing the traditional boundaries to organise events which appeal to a younger, highly mobile, and dance-oriented public. During boat trips, club evenings, and summer beach parties, fans interact, dance, and socialise in mutually interactive settings more akin to the all-night rave than the small club jam session. While scholars of traditional jazz often prioritise improvising jazz instrumentalists over technologically mediated, crossover jazz genres, these multimedia collectives initiated trends for a dance-oriented European jazz culture, which increasingly combined the mediated mutuality of technologically driven forms of sociality and the interactivity of older jazz styles.

In this chapter, I examine Amsterdam's contemporary crossover jazz scene through both ethnographic and historical channels. Based on interviews with participants of two collectives and jazz/dance series, Wicked Jazz Sounds and the Blue Note Trip series, I address the performative, social, and hyper-mediated format through which individuals interact, invigorating more traditional forms of sociality. Increasingly, cosmopolitan collectivities disentangle traditional binaries within the industry (major versus independent, men versus women, acoustic versus electronic) and disrupt distinctions between professional and amateur worlds. Within popular music, these collectives also drew upon an expanded body of arts and music participants than those historically represented by historicised groups, previously epitomised by all-star jazz groups, led by esteemed soloists represented by jazz impresarios and critiqued by the jazz press.

I enlist the term *trans-local collectivity* to depict the fluid activity and sociality of participants and fans, a distinction which becomes increasingly opaque from 2000 onwards. I further highlight several core qualities of Amsterdam's trans-local collectivities, which both accommodate and deviate from previous models of performativity, sociability, and promotion within the popular music field. In Northern Europe, Amsterdam has effectively integrated human capital and creative labour into the city's historic cultural sphere, making it one of the area's most successful tourist destinations. Crossover jazz scenes provide a forum for facilitating new forms of sociability between international tourists and local music participants. In this context, a variety of relations evolve between tourists and local fans, and between professionals and amateurs, which challenges historical notions of scenes while blurring codified European musical signifiers. In Richard Florida's terms, Amsterdam's reputation for social and sexual inclusivity stimulated creative capital for music participants and arts entrepreneurs who first envisioned, then enlivened, the form and contours of musical events and interactivity (Florida 2005).

In this manner, several foundational processes have come to characterise Amsterdam's trans-local collectivities. These processes incorporate traditional jazz performance values, yet remix and renew them to accommodate younger and more technologically inclined music participants. First of all, these series both solidified digital networks of reception and promotion through processes of *hypermediation*. Since the early 2000s, these networks have inspired and incorporated a broader field of participants including instrumentalists, DJs, producers, photographers, video artists, graphic artists, event planners, concept developers, and volunteers – all of whom contributed because of the flexible penetration of social media. Additionally, these collectivities reflected a growing and necessary *symbiosis* between the industry and participants within the neoliberal industrial environment. In this manner, representations of collectivities were inherently imaged as a reflection of their audiences – i.e. larger groups of creatives reflected in and participating with final products (in contrast to intentional distance promoted between audiences and rock star bands). Next, Amsterdam's audiences – a mix of young dance tourists with local jazz fans – stimulated the activities within the collectivity as well as the ways they chose to represent themselves as they encourage participation from audiences, while affiliated with local clubs and entrepreneurial arts workers, blurring boundaries between the professional, consumer, entrepreneur, and amateur.[4] Furthermore, these series both stimulated and mediated a sense of *liveness*. The scene exhibited (and continues to exhibit) a return towards notions of "liveness" in the social musical space, partly as a reaction to the non-human quality of digital media, the overwhelming choice presented by internet sources, and music television's promotion of a limited number of transnational pop music. Liveness is symbolically connected to earlier jazz and Black music cultures, including the cabaret and dance hall jazz of the interwar periods. Additionally, participants expressly valued physical participation through *dance* and other forms of expressive movement. Within these nightclubs, a mixed-gendered physical interactivity prevailed, overriding exclusively consumption-based social behaviours or traditional norms presented in rock concerts or jazz-oriented jam sessions. Finally, this trans-local scene reflected an "*aesthetic cosmopolitanism*" (Regev 2013) typifying polygeneric jazz within the New Europe in late modernity through an appreciation of diverse musical styles, whilst privileging African American influenced genres. Cosmopolitanism continues to characterise interactions between international tourists and local music participants/fans.

These characteristics are neither exclusive nor exhaustive, but constitute novel combinations of new and more traditional forms of urban musical sociality. In this chapter, I argue that the confluence of technologically driven social networks, as well as Amsterdam's interest in both urban dance musics and live instrumental jazz, provide a late-capitalist forum for such crossover collectivities, as they connect with other European cosmopolitan jazz developments. However, they have remained passionately connected to forms of locality. In the following sections, I survey recent theorising about popular music scenes and public culture networks to project current scenes beyond modernist and postmodernist paradigms. By contextualising thought about scenes in popular music studies, I advance groundwork for new conceptions of musical collectivism which actively promote notions of trans-local identifications. I then situate Amsterdam's electronic jazz collectivities within European developments in crossover jazz from the 1990s. Finally, I highlight the various flows and matrices of Amsterdam's trans-local collectivism to examine this chapter's case studies, Wicked Jazz Sounds and the Blue Note Trip series.

Scenes, Networks, and Circulations

Since the 1970s, theorising about the subcultural value of music scenes in urban spaces, a focus of the Birmingham school, has dominated theoretical methodologies in popular music studies. Hebdige's iconographic work on British punk and ska provided new models for envisioning the resistive potential of popular music scenes as they position themselves against conservative social and cultural hegemonies (1979). Will Straw's 1991 reformulation of scenes rejected earlier correlations between disenfranchised socio-cultural groups and the politics of style, and instead laid claim to recent ruptures in the historically mapped rock canon. Borrowing from Bourdieu's systems of logic, Straw investigated two international music scenes, alternative rock and dance music, to illuminate "local systems of articulation" ("localism" as a musical value) and "universal systems of articulation", and further queried the intensified impact of economic and cultural globalisation (1991, 369). In 1994, Lipsitz expanded scene theory to encompass notions of "musical mobilities", claiming that as popular musics travelled and engaged local practices, they also responded to mass-mediated commodities, engendering transformations as well as reified notions of place. Popular music theorist Sarah Thornton further underscored the emerging subcultural value of recordings as they began to acquire aura, superseding live performances through their use in new musical and social spaces such as the discotheque and recording studio (1996, 51).[5]

Peterson and Bennett (2004) also revised prior theoretical conceptions, which regularly dichotomised scenes as either subcultural or a set of alliances amongst participating locals. In their survey of scene theorising, they replaced outdated frameworks with a tripartite model encompassing local, trans-local (and national), and virtual contexts. Carrington and Wilson had previously noted how trans-local scenes depend increasingly upon global flows of people such as DJs and "dance tourists" (2002). Lee and Peterson posited the idea of the virtual scene as a setting bounded by words and discourse about musical styles in contrast to the face-to-face interaction of physical scenes (2004). In contrast to scholars segmenting scenes according to their physical or virtual manifestation, Bennett and Peterson argued for examining the technological, social, *and* personal elements underpinning virtual musical social networks.

This study of Amsterdam's crossover jazz scenes proposes an "ethnography of circulation" (Parameshwar Gaonkar and Povinelli 2003) while also positioning the physical spaces of this cosmopolitan city by mapping the value of mass and social media into its most prominent sonic social spaces. I prioritise the movement and engagement of collectives and their creative vitality as guided by flows and circulations over fixed geographies, static players, and historically recognised musical styles. This circulatory logic of trans-local, multi-genre performative scenes encompasses both virtual and physical mobilities as they co-exist, intersect, and ultimately facilitate the interactive practices of creatives and consumers. The notion of scene remains apropos, even in its virtual and trans-local dimension, as musicians and music travellers envision themselves as part of the scene, one which organically circulates through different worlds, seeking new spaces to accommodate twenty-first-century technologies of production, creativity, and social engagement. Indeed, it is in these physical spaces that the virtual discourse and interactivity of social media is cemented and most pleasurably experienced through the interaction with real musicians and their remixing and regeneration of various musical styles.

Contemporary Amsterdam's music collectivities are largely guided by young promoters with exceptional social network acumen, designing, promoting, and extending these networks' interactive capabilities with fans, distributors, and other creatives. These young entrepreneurs differ from more traditional, industry-funded promoters through their creative engagement with social media as well as their role in incorporating a broader range of arts participants into their networks. Manne van der Zee, the digitally skilled promoter and manager for WJS (Wicked Jazz Sounds), maintains an essential role in the collectivity through a variety of flexible positions, from engaging relations between musicians, visual artists, photographers and technical staff, to securing venues and recordings. He remains committed to developing a digital landscape, establishing profiles on a number of network sites including Facebook and YouTube. Videos of events, excerpts from recordings, and photos of dancers at weekly club events constitute but a few of the circulating texts populating WJS's digital landscape. On WJS's homepage, participants ask questions about upcoming events or comment upon past events. On YouTube, WJS posts a number of crossover jazz mixes created by leading DJs Phil Horneman and Leroy Rey to accompany video collages and animated films made by local artists. Promotional pieces for these soundtracks also include collages of the scene's physical participants, including, for example, silhouettes of hip hop dancers interspersed with photographs of past events. Florida's (2005) simple formula connecting economically successful cities to large creative classes corresponds with the creative patterns of Wicked Jazz Sounds promoters, who negotiate variable and mobile environments while harnessing the unique yet flexible talents of artists, fans, and musicians from an ever expanding and adapting field of creativity.

Steve Jones' (2002) mapping of audiences and localities onto digital networks proves relevant when we consider how Amsterdam's electronic crossover jazz scene is partly mediated by social network users referencing local groups and performances on network radio sites like *3Voor12* as well as established local spaces, deeply connected to Amsterdam. Conversely, while Amsterdam's crossover jazz collectives thrived within the context of the city's attractive neighbourhoods and squares, the members of these jazz aggregates further challenged spatial genre associations as they themselves promoted the transnational, cosmopolitan quality of their music, or registered their performances in a variety of cities and for international music festivals. To illustrate, Wicked Jazz Sounds resists an exclusively Dutch national characterisation on their website by choosing to write in Dutch and English, and by networking on digital radio stations, where names of internationally famous clubs such as the Melkweg accrue cosmopolitan currency through casual recommendations of migrating dance tourists, as well as through discourse circulating in travel books like the Lonely Planet guides. However, these clubs simultaneously maintained symbolic internal associations for Amsterdam's local cultural and political participants by maintaining weekly club evenings and by establishing local and physical relationships with jazz fans, dancers, and volunteers from the city's artistic neighbourhoods, who commandeer clip boards and lamp posts of local cafés, record stores, and supermarkets to promote the collectivity. In this sense, the unique physical and geographical quality of Amsterdam as a cosmopolitan Dutch city mattered for the success and conviviality of crossover jazz events. Indeed, it is the combination of *gezellig* (cosy) neighbourhoods esteemed for their tolerance and the desire for new forms of musical participation that enhanced and sustained the flexible and fluid movement between musicians, international tourists, artists, and promoters.

In the following ethnography, I envision the circulation of mobile musical networks through the local (Amsterdam's neighbourhoods), the trans-local (the interaction between international musicians and tourists, and between established record companies and local multimedia music clubs), and the virtual (the promotion of the collective through various digital platforms on the internet). I first briefly connect the rise of Amsterdam's crossover jazz scene to the popularity of electronic jazz beginning during the 1990s.

Amsterdam's 'Cosmopolitan' Jazz Scene

In the Netherlands, the trend for incorporating jazz artists into the more established disco and dance circuit emerged during the 1990s, especially in cities like Amsterdam and Utrecht, supporting lively dance cultures and a constant flux of musicians, tourists, and local enthusiasts. Amsterdam gained an international reputation during the late 1980s for ebullient, eclectic, sexually inclusive, and multicultural discos such as the Paradiso and the RoXXY – clubs providing professional opportunities for dance, funk, and techno DJs, most notably KC the Funkaholic and Eddy de Clercq (*All That Jazz* 2009, 367). By 1990, Amsterdam's dance circuit attracted instrumental musicians eager to contribute to this vital scene. In 1995, jazz tenor saxophonist Hans Dulfer appeared in Dam Square with DJ Dmitri, a performance causing ripples in the jazz press and cultivating a whole new dance-oriented public to live crossover performances. By 2000, Amsterdam's electronic jazz events crystallised within multimedia venues like the Melkweg and the Sugar Factory, some sponsored by major jazz companies (Blue Note), with dance and nu jazz themes. Current electronic jazz projects still favour the live moment and the aesthetics of "participatory discrepancies" (Keil and Feld 1994), yet also rely upon audiences' knowledge of and desire for electronic-based dance music and DJ mixes. In Amsterdam, thus, the DJ enjoys an unprecedented status.

During this period, distinguishing themselves from their American counterparts, European DJs mixed genres in ways catering to European dance sensibilities. The mashup and genre-clashing phenomena of the early 2000s often entailed juxtaposing contrasting musical tracks from distinct fields such as mainstream pop hits circulated through music television and commercial radio and the underground indie or electronic dance musics of European clubs and discos. In 2002, 2manydjs' popular mashup radio programme, *Radio Soulwax*, symbolised this particular aesthetic. Airing on local Belgian radio, the Dewaele brothers (as 2manydjs) mixed popular hits with underground garage rock and electronic dance beats. This programme spurred a Northern European dance floor sensation wherein mashups of such pop anthems as Nirvana's "Smells like Teen Spirit", Destiny's Child's "Bootylicious", and Michael Jackson's "Billy Jean", when mixed with European electronic acts such as Dakar & Grinser (Germany) and Vitalic (France), became common disco fare.[6] As locals became increasingly exposed to Anglo-American musical hits promoted by commercial radio and music television and intensified by the swift and profound consolidation of the music industry, local producers adopted techniques to 're-territorialise' the hits, talking back so to speak to the ubiquity of the (then) Big Four.[7] European dance music fans enjoyed the music of Destiny's Child and others, but sought opportunities to remix and re-contextualise mass-mediated music through their own unique experiences, injecting these overplayed tunes with local dance dispositions. For European DJs, transnational pop hits provided malleable sonic material for radio sets, club events, and digital productions.

As DJs increasingly dispersed mashups and remixes outside of commercial radio or the purview of the Big Four, they initiated new pathways to disseminate sounds with unprecedented speed, from local radio to online streaming platforms, and from social networks to local dance clubs. As internet-driven mashups became more sophisticated, electronic jazz artists honed their techniques through software, and developed more specialised genres. Contemporary electronic-based jazz collectivities engage in a variety of interactive projects from soliciting user participation on artists' websites and remixing transnational hits, to multimedia festivals and all-night dance parties.[8] During the last decade, record labels including Wicked Jazz Sounds' United Recordings or the Dewaele's Deewee Records increasingly released their own genre-clashing material in a similar vein with other European record labels such as Ninja Tune and Jazzland Recordings.[9]

Independent record companies such as Deewee (2manydjs' record company) also frequently fulfilled multiple roles such as record labels and publishing houses. Deewee depicted these roles as both multifaceted as well as locally bound: "Deewee is a building, a studio, a label, a record collection and a publishing house. Every DEEWEE release is written, recorded or mixed in the building by David and Stephan Dewaele".[10] Increasingly, independent record companies functioned as mobile performance and recording networks. Wicked Jazz Sounds' United Recordings, begun in 1998, quickly established connections with other independent labels/platforms within Europe. Label owners Theor Verplancke and Rob Bouhuis characterised this network as one built upon experiences with other independents such as the "highly acclaimed Outland Records in Amsterdam". United Recordings survived in this decade's difficult industrial climate by forging alliances with other 'sub-labels' including "After Midnight, Alien Recordings, Disque Deluxe, Flammable, Forbidden Planet Records, Fundamental Recordings, Groove Alert Records, Hi9, Long Life Recordings, Nightfever, Quest For Trance, Music For Cocktails, Therapy Recordings, Touché and Music For Cocktails".[11] These independent crossover record companies arose partially to fill the gap left by the majors and their disinterest in more subcultural electronic sample-driven jazz collectivities. Producer-driven jazz collectives promoted trans-local recording companies while also exploiting the distributing potential of jazz majors, and in so doing, they introduced novel trans-local circulations, dramatically mutating traditional majors versus independent models of pre-Internet decades.

Since the late-1990s, European jazz record companies began to realise that dancers and clubbers were discovering new music through live DJ events and local social media. In the Netherlands, Blue Note embraced this opportunity to solicit the popularity of electronic jazz DJs to release multi-genre compilations of back catalogue material along with new urban, hip hop, soul, and dance tracks. In the United States, this practice had worked exceptionally well with British electronic jazz dance group Us3, whose breakthrough success owed significantly to their artful digital sampling of prior Blue Note jazz recordings (e.g. Herbie Hancock's "Cantaloupe Island") with new beats and dance sequences. In 2009, Blue Note Netherlands released mixed-genre compilations under DJ Maestro's name, a confusing practice as fans of Maestro might expect to hear original 'mix-tapes' of beats and soundscapes with local jazz artists. Nevertheless, these compilations continue to attract listeners for various personal and social purposes.

Since 2005, Wicked Jazz Sounds also released seven multi-artist compilations through United Recordings. When asked about the impetus for the WJS compilations, DJ Horneman stated emphatically that the music on WJS compilations was intended to represent the total sound of Wicked Jazz Sounds, and not meant to re-enact the live events. According to Horneman, "the live thing you have to experience live, you can never put that on CD" (Phil Horneman, Interview with the author, July 5, 2009). To illustrate, their fourth series featured many British and American artists, old and new as well as tracks by Serbian, Brazilian, Ukrainian, Japanese, and Finnish groups. Genres range from nu jazz to hip hop and broken beat, to soul, avant-garde and lounge music. Some of the better-known artists include Omar, Q-Tip, Chick Corea, and Jamie Lidell. In a Bourdieusian sense, esteemed DJs acquired distinction through their role as cultural tour guides (replacing 'gatekeepers' and its connotation of industry elitism), entrusted to exhibit the necessary taste and network affiliations to curate old and new sounds. Thus, independent DJs gradually displace traditional radio DJs as purveyors of popular taste. Participants of Amsterdam's crossover collectives articulate their preference for compilations produced by local DJs, who actively work in the scene over commercial national radio programmes sponsored by media transnationals like Live Nation or Rupert Murdoch's European radio syndicates.

The Netherlands' music conservatories are the origin for many of the city's crossover jazz instrumentalists. Most of those I interviewed were once music students at nearby Dutch conservatories.[12] The University of Amsterdam's Conservatory jazz programme provides training in a variety of styles, including Afro-Cuban, crossover, big band, R&B, and funk. The programme also features artists in residence, incorporating yearly guest teachers and performers from the international jazz community. These soloists make up an increasingly tightly knit group of 'stars', many from New York, who travel the conservatory circuit to offer semester-long workshops, perform with big bands as guest soloists, and to gig in local clubs in these cosmopolitan cities. The movement of these 'jazz stars' from North America to Europe and all over the world – first initiated during the 1980s as jazz education expanded in universities and provided a viable career path for young musicians – mirrors some of the trajectories of students who combine established educational backgrounds with local weekly jazz sessions while networking with other international students to form contemporary crossover jazz groups (McGee 2011).

Musicians participating in Amsterdam's crossover jazz scene acknowledge the place of African American culture in nurturing American jazz stars, yet their relationship to this music constitutes another of the many inroads into musical performance. As will be seen later, Dutch jazz musicians experience and internalise canonical American jazz recordings alongside other musical influences from famous European jazz stars to local Dutch jazz artists and more distant musical influences from Euro dance to Anglo-American popular music. Contemporary musicians and participants alike maintain multiple musical identities and unproblematically value transnational, national, and local musical styles.

Amsterdam's Jazz Club Night Series: Wicked Jazz Sounds and Blue Note Trips

In the following, I highlight two of Amsterdam's most popular and active crossover jazz series that since 2000 have drawn talent and activity from each other, and also epitomised the interactivity favoured in Amsterdam's musical collectives, through their fluidity of participation, their presentation of expert jazz instrumentalists, and prioritisation of mixed-musical genres. I highlight two events, the *Blue Note Trip* series at the Melkweg and the *Wicked Jazz Sounds* dance evenings at the Sugar Factory, due to the manner in which musical and cultural identifications were performed, ultimately guiding Amsterdam's "remix" (Lessig 2008) jazz collectivity culture – a confluence of active participation and digital discourse that heralds transformations in the kinds of behaviour characterising urban sociability in the European post-industrial city.

Most 'nu' and electronic crossover jazz in Amsterdam occurred near one of the city's most famous squares, the *Leidseplein*,[13] one of the main hubs for Amsterdam's famous tourist industry, attracting thousands of locals, nationals,

FIGURE 2.2   Wicked Jazz Sounds at the Sugar Factory, 2018[14]
Source: Photograph by Jordi Wallenburg.

and internationals especially. The square itself accommodates diverse street performers and musicians. All provide night-goers both local and exotic symbols of Amsterdam's reputation as the 'carnival of the North'. For locals, the square contains some of the city's most historically rooted small-scale, multimedia event clubs, and because of their historic prestige, they remain subsidised by inter-arts organisations. In the height of the summer months and in the early morning hours, the square becomes a beacon for both locals and tourists embracing the Netherlands' relaxed marijuana policy, and seeking revelry, dance music, affordable beer, and the friendly interaction between Dutch party-goers and international travellers.

Historic buildings on the square include the elegant *Stadsschouwburg*, which recently converted its lobby into a cocktail bar and café, and the Café American in the American Hotel, a luxurious building of a faded early-twentieth-century art deco design, popular with business tourists and globe-trotting trust-funders. Irish-, American-, and Dutch-style pubs surround the '*plein*' with tables sprawling into the square. The area supports a casino (Holland Casino), the Amsterdam Hard Rock Café, and a plethora of *eetcafés*, fast food chains, and a host of international restaurants. This square, more than any other in Amsterdam, betrays the influence of post-colonialism, global capital, and transnationalism with its mixture of early-twentieth-century Dutch architecture, arts theatres, pubs and cafés, and modern transnational food and clothing chains.

FIGURE 2.3 The Melkweg, Amsterdam, the Netherlands, photograph courtesy of the Melkweg

Source: Photograph by Dan van Eijndhoven (DigiDaan, https://www.digidaan.net/album/info.php).

Adjacent to the Leidseplein are the two most important multimedia music clubs, the Melkweg and the Sugar Factory. These two clubs face each other and attract even younger music lovers than those frequenting Amsterdam's more traditional jazz club, the Bimhuis. Music programmes complement each other and often program similar events on similar evenings, with Thursdays and Sundays favoured evenings for dance events. Indeed, one can often see clubbers wandering from the Factory to the Melkweg to compare DJs and crowds.

The Melkweg

During the 1970s, historians portrayed the Melkweg as the centre of musical and artistic life, coining Amsterdam the 'San Francisco of Europa'. The organisation was awarded subsidies by the minister of culture and from Amsterdam's civic government. By the 1980s, the venue reputedly became the meeting point for travellers wanting to experience "rock music, light shows, hash, and love and peace" ("Historie" n.d.), and hosted multi-discipline performances including video, poetry, and music. In the same period, the venue chose to revive its image, renouncing its hippy vestiges and foregoing hash consumption, tapestries, and tearooms. Many of the rooms, recently revamped, facilitate more professional presentations of culture, film, and music. In the early 1980s, the Melkweg became one of the first Dutch venues to program non-European musical groups, including bands from Africa and South America, and initiating the first world music festival in 1983. Amsterdam further extended its reputation as a socially progressive and culturally innovative city with its initiation of 'world music' series in some of its most respected clubs such as the Paradiso.

Blue Note Trip Club Nights at The Melkweg

During the 2000s, the Melkweg hosted a variety of dance club evenings, including the *Blue Note Trip* events, featuring musical mixes of jazz, fusion, dance, hip hop, and electronic music. These corporate-sponsored events featured instrumental soloists collaborating with celebrated DJs including Amsterdam's well-known DJ Maestro. From around 2002 to 2012, Blue Note organised dance and club events throughout the Netherlands with various DJs and jazz instrumentalists, although the Melkweg remained its musical outpost. Its incorporation of the weekly *Blue Note Trip* events supported mixed-genre experimentation, sanctioned through the established channels of a jazz record company icon. The collaboration between transnational music companies (Blue Note), nationally subsidised professional multi-arts cultural spaces (the Melkweg), and 'underground' Amsterdam artists and musicians (DJ Maestro and other local jazz instrumentalists) indicated new kinds of infrastructures characterising European cities, suggesting a gradual departure from distinct cultural spaces intentionally separating high art and popular culture and discouraging the kinds of fluid interactions now transpiring between commercial, entrepreneurial, and local artistic underground communities. Moreover, multimedia spaces embraced the characteristics of liveness associated with popular music of earlier decades by reincorporating the jazz instrumentalist and vocalist into the DJed dance context. In contrast to counterculture aesthetics, hypermediation animated the promotion and participant–artist interaction culminating in multimedia spaces. Additionally, the collective–audience symbiosis was also evident as transnational record companies worked with local clubs and local arts entrepreneurs to maintain locally situated yet cosmopolitan identities.

The *Blue Note Trip*'s featured star was DJ Maestro (Martijn Barkhuis) and one of Maestro's frequent soloists was jazz trumpeter Rob van de Wouw, who also works with DJs in Amsterdam and in his hometown, Rotterdam. Van de Wouw leads his own jazz group, for which he writes and records for local Dutch jazz label Embrace Records. Van de Wouw also currently records for the Oslo-based Jazzland Recordings. He first established networks through his conservatory training in Rotterdam during the 1990s but after 2000 also worked with DJs in Amsterdam and for club events such as the *Blue Note Trip* series at the Melkweg. Now Van de Wouw enjoys an international reputation as a cosmopolitan jazz soloist. His movement from conservatory to mixed-media club and on to the transnational European jazz festival circuit speaks to the kinds of trans-local trajectories taken by young European jazz musicians.

Like other contemporary jazz instrumentalists working in crossover jazz collectives, Van de Wouw articulated some of the challenges presented by mixtures of digital technologies and electronic beats in live music settings. He regards the biggest challenge working with DJs as creating spontaneous musical dialogue, paralleling the improvisational calibre of the best acoustic jazz musicians. He depicted these kinds of combinations (DJs and musicians) as often too facile, explaining:

> Actually you want to find an interesting vibe where you think, hey I can say something here. That is what you are waiting for. You hope that the record provides something that you can use. Sometimes I find it very difficult to play with a DJ. To me, if you want to do it well, then you actually have to do more than what is typically done. It is usually pretty simple for everyone. To me, you can get a lot heavier with it.
>
> *(Rob van de Wouw, July 5, 2009)*

Similarly, saxophonist Susanne Alt – who also performs with DJ Maestro – depicted the challenges performing with DJs, claiming that timing, tuning, and stylistic challenges differ from the more traditional jazz combo setting. For Alt, finding the right kind of groove, establishing a rewarding and proficient interaction between the DJ and instrumentalist, and having the space to develop a coherent idea presented the most distinct challenges.

FIGURE 2.4 Jazz saxophonist Susanne Alt
Source: Photograph by Michel Zoeter.

For jazz vocalist Berenice van Leer, working with *Wicked Jazz Sounds*, traditional challenges of jazz no longer exist. She reports that performing with a DJ allows one to move beyond the proscriptive jazz changes such as the standard 8, 12, or 32-bar progressions, to choose something more open. Furthermore, concepts of time become increasingly fluid as the layering conception of electronic beats and repetitive melodic phrases trumps traditional harmonic and rhythmic forms. Van Leer's attitude about performing with the group mirrors other participants of *Wicked Jazz Sounds* in her desire to break from more traditional moulds. It was through *Wicked Jazz Sounds* that Van Leer began to experiment with improvisation and mixed-genre jazz styles. She regards the series as bridging the gap between an active dance public and jazz fans who seek innovation, appreciating live spontaneity and challenges of jamming over difficult rhythms, harmonies, and electronic beats. Here all three musicians recognise 'liveness' as an essential component of the experience. This return to liveness was in many ways inspired by the overly static laptop and CD DJ performances during the onset of digitalisation during the early 1990s. However, liveness in acoustic jazz sessions remained an important value, even as acid jazz and earlier dance projects dis-incorporated live instrumentalists in the early 1990s.

Like many young multi-genre Dutch jazz musicians, Van de Wouw's first influences came from American jazz artists including Charles Mingus, Horace Silver, and Roy Eldridge. He also considers the popular music of his youth, including European dance music and rock, as essential aspects of his performative musical template. Many Dutch jazz soloists report similar stories concerning their relationship to American jazz, nourished by the careful study of canonical (African) American jazz recordings and eventually developed through more formal channels of education. They eventually establish performing relationships with German, Belgian, or other Western European musicians, many revering the same American jazz stars of the hard bop era. Thus, contribution to the scene is predicated upon the network of local and international musicians who circulate through Europe's cities and profit from Europe's highly connected jazz festival circuit.

Van de Wouw depicted Amsterdam's crossover jazz scene as collegial, identifying a symbiotic relationship amongst bands:

> You have many crossover bands wherein you can say that because of that, there is a sort of movement which creates attention for a larger music stream and from where the local scene only becomes bigger and stronger. Ultimately you receive more exposure and more creative possibilities.
>
> *(Rob Van de Wouw, July 5, 2009)*

This characterisation of the scene suggests the influence of trans-local networks and the successful integration of popular music styles with live jazz interactivity. Indeed, during the Melkweg series, clubbers consistently exhibited their fascination with live jazz soloists while valuing the interactive potential for dancing and engaging with performing musicians, activities frequently discouraged in purist jazz venues and concert halls featuring established jazz stars.

Musicians, DJs, and participants from both collectives cited the spontaneous inter-action with the public as their greatest reward. Such events required a heightened awareness of the crowd, and as a performer, an intense but more sporadic physi-cal performativity. During sets, performers must not only impress with improvised solos, but also inspire dancing and interactivity. Van de Wouw considered his generation's experience with jazz and popular music as less 'purist', claiming that younger audiences are more interested in a wider variety of musical genres and much more enthusiastic about recent crossover jazz projects. For him, this gener-ation's exposure to popular music, Black music, and traditional jazz have led them to consider jazz as one part of music's broader history.

Saxophonist Alt and vocalist Van Leer, both performing in the WJS series, sim-ilarly identified Black music and dance music as essential for attracting younger, diverse audiences who, during the 1990s, came to miss the physical interactivity characterising the grassroots cultures of soul, funk, and hip hop. Ingrid Monson writes of the cultural capital acquired by 'white' musicians and fans who incor-porate Black musical tastes, slang, and manners of dress into their performances, a practice predating the expansion of hip hop to white audiences in the 1980s (Radano 1995; Monson 1995; Wald 2000). While Amsterdam's electronic jazz scene draws from American popular music, much of this has been mediated through mainstream outlets including music television and radio since the 1970s. Musicians and fans are inspired by Black cultural sources often through recorded media rather than through a deeper face-to-face engagement with Black Amer-ican culture. However, discourse surrounding racial encounters in European contexts differs from the racialised discourse attached to American culture, espe-cially considering Europe's reifying of the 'folk' in modernist colonial contexts (Raphael-Hernandez 2003). For Amsterdam's musicians and electronic jazz fans, notions of ethnicity, race, and class remain prominent and problematic tropes for negotiating cultural identification, which have historically established precedents in European history and its diverse musical cultures (Bohlman 2000). Contempo-rary references to musical cultures borrow both from historical European mythoi, yet also betray the influence of American popular culture and the media's perpet-uation of perceived Black musical essences.

The Sugar Factory

The crossover jazz series *Wicked Jazz Sounds Club Nights* found its home in the adjacent Leidseplein club, The Sugar Factory, which opened in 2003 with the goal of pioneering late-night theatre for multi-mediated, musical experiences. In one report (Bellen *et al.* 2003), the biggest complaints issued by Amsterdam's creative class (artists, upstart party organisers, DJs, bands, and visitors) was the lack of exhibit spaces for multi-discipline activities, such as small parties, experimental meetings, fashion shows, and multimedia performances. The report, dismayed by far "too few buildings promoting the larger line between DJ-cafés and the commercial halls and clubs", emphasised the need for new non-commercial spaces housing between 100 and 500 persons (Bellen *et al.* 2003, 58). The Sugar Factory's proximity to the Melkweg proved a strategic move for such a multimedia, late-night exhibition space.

WJS's weekly club events at the Sugar Factory generally attracted a very stylish and relatively sober crowd, a mix of dancers and music revellers in their mid-twenties, with some thirty- and forty-year-olds peppering the crowd. During the second week of July 2009,[15] most arrived between 24:00 and 1:00, and by 1:30 queues of dancers formed near the entrance. Clubbers chatted while queuing, sending messages and photos to friends, updating them on their whereabouts and their experience – a confluence of twenty-first-century social media practices enhancing the live music club experience. Most were very well dressed and included 'hipsters', bohemians, and university students. The smallish dance floor was demarcated by a narrow, illuminated bar and two large video screens, directly opposite the stage, levitated high above the dance floor. The low podium in front of the dance floor provided a small performance space where musicians stood directly in front of the DJ and within feet of the dancing fans.

By 11:00 p.m., the band and DJs finished their sound check, which seamlessly transitioned into the first down-tempo set. The instrumentalists left the stage, still wearing their day clothes, and packed up their gear in order to retreat to the green room. I was led to the newly built smoking room by German alto saxophonist Susanne Alt for a brief interview before beginning her set with the other DJs and musicians. Intermittently, couples came in to smoke, but we remained largely unbothered save for two Australian university students. One girl, with crimped, bleached blonde hair, and glistening tanned skin, stumbled in, clearly feeling the effects of marijuana. She rushed over to us and emphatically proclaimed, "I can't find my friend". She continued incoherently, stating again her concerns, then proclaiming in a panicked voice, "You don't understand she only speaks English". For emphasis, she yelled: "She's not Dutch, she doesn't speak Deutsch". Susanne paused, rolled her eyes, and continued contrasting her experiences performing with her own quartet and Wicked Jazz Sounds. While this incident appeared random and inconsequential to the evening's musical development, it reflected the number of tourists who visit Wicked Jazz Sounds dance events, many hoping that their unique desires are fulfilled in evenings out. Tourists visit dance events not only to dance and meet other international tourists, but also to experience Amsterdam's marijuana coffee houses. Dance tourists often begin their evenings in smaller coffee houses before attending some of the charming brown bars and eventually ending their nights at mid-size dance venues such as the Melkweg. These young women clearly intended to socialise with other tourists, dance and experiment with alternative mental states, choosing electronic jazz as the backdrop for such explorations. Some would even meet at local hostels, hearing of the event from other travelling dance tourists (Rapp 2009; D'Andrea 2007).

Regarding crossover jazz, Dutch jazz instrumentalists engage different performative values for various contexts. For example, Alt claimed that with her jazz quartet, she develops longer, more complex solos, highlights her own material, extends communication with other instrumentalists, and performs for a "musicians-dedicated" audience. However, during WJS's events, she sees her music reaching new audiences through the mixing of dance music with improvisation. This combination enabled new forms of sociability by participants, who became excited by the visceral spontaneity and physical stamina of live improvised solos, yet demanded the bass-centred aesthetics of electronic sequences mixed with recognisable dance hits to inspire physical modes of interactivity. It is this combination of transnational dance hits, groove-oriented Black musics, and the live performativity of jazz instrumentalists that is so valued by crossover jazz audiences in Amsterdam. Fans and musicians alike persistently cite Black music sources for their musical fusions, while also revelling in this cosmopolitanism.

WJS's lead vocalist Berenice van Leer's experience with the band broadly corresponds with Alt's. Both had extensive training in Amsterdam's Music Conservatory and have parents who are musicians. As a child, Van Leer gained essential musical experience travelling with her father's band, attending gigs, and listening to his soul, funk, fusion, and jazz-inspired record collection including such greats as Earth, Wind and Fire, Herbie Hancock, and Miles Davis. She also gained inspiration from 1980s pop icons such as Janet Jackson and Michael Jackson. Van Leer similarly highlights the critical role that Black music held for the appeal and interactivity of the group, claiming:

> People want to experience a new tradition by reinvigorating the old soul – currently reflected by popular groups and singers like Duffy … that is actually very traditional and this combination with live DJs, electronica, mixed with old elements – that is something very surprising.
>
> *(Berenice Van Leer, Interview with the author,*
> *September 29, 2009)*

Leer's comments reflected the values posited within this remix culture. Again, the cosmopolitanism presented by the group's live mixing of diverse musical genres is couched within the grooves and performative values of Black music. Van Leer, like Alt and Van de Wouw, similarly prioritised the live element of crossover jazz performances as central to their success for young, mobile audiences.

Wicked Jazz Sounds' cosmopolitanism is further reflected in their use of both English and Dutch for promotional material and during live shows. Van Leer confirmed the use of both English and Dutch for club evenings and with the Wicked Jazz Sounds band. The need to communicate with tourists and with local Dutch residents is taken very seriously by the collective. The singers also draw upon the most popular MCing traditions, again from Black diasporic music sources, in order to create the right atmosphere and to connect with dancers. However, Van Leer also stressed the need to throw in local conversational phrases in Dutch, as the band identifies themselves as a Dutch group playing for Dutch audiences.

While verbal communication remains important, the greatest pleasure that Van Leer receives is through the intensity with which the group reaches people musically: "Although it may sound cliché", says Van Leer, "Dancing with a smile" as the Wicked Jazz Sounds' website declares, is really the essence of their popularity and their relationship with fans. What you see in the crowd, admitted Leer, "is a really mixed group, men and women, and that you are reaching people, as they dance, then go completely crazy and really express themselves" (Berenice van Leer, September 29, 2009). Both Van Leer and others correlated the success of the collective with the interactivity of their fans, and in this sense, the collective imagines its own values vis-à-vis interaction and participation reflected back to them before, during, and after live shows, as fans post links to video performances and photographs, and rate shows on social sites. For example, photographer Marc van Oers posted photos taken of WJS's events on their Facebook site.[16] Van Oers' willingness to share his photographs reflect Lessig's sharing economy as well as the persistent interactivity that characterises electronic jazz dance events. Eventually, these photos appear on other Facebook accounts as well as in slide shows before, during, and after WJS events, which in turn promote not only the musicians in the collective but the fans that breathe creativity into this digitally mediated community.

The 1990s witnessed more women gaining positions within the music industry. Female artists such as Liz Phair and Alanis Morissette broke into the transnational rock market as singer songwriters or solo rock artists. By the end of the decade, *Rolling Stone* proclaimed 1999 the "Year of the Woman" (Garofalo 2005, 393). Yet today, rock music's traditionally male-gendered performance dynamics continue to dominate, encouraging more traditional types of sociality during live shows. In general, concerts at smaller European rock and jazz clubs attract mostly young men, while dance-oriented electronic jazz surmounted the gender culture presented in other types of venues, attracting much larger groups of young women to live shows, who came to dance and interact. Not only do electronic jazz events attract equal numbers of men and women, but they also feature greater numbers of female talent in Amsterdam including expert vocalist Van Leer and award-winning saxophonist Alt.[17]

Additionally, the collective attracted entrepreneurial contributions by local female photographers and artists who regularly attended shows and provided their work to promote the group. One of the group's most prolific photographers (and sometimes DJ) is Ester K. (Esther Duijn), who regularly contributes her professional work for CD covers and for networked media sites. Eventually, other women are attracted to the collective because of its reputation for enhancing and valuing the artistic creativity of Amsterdam's many young female artists.

DJ Phil Horneman is the creative originator of *Wicked Jazz Sounds* and is largely responsible for the organisation's musical and artistic sound. He claims that he and co-collaborator Manne van de Zee wanted to bring jazz and nu jazz to a younger public, but that they were not the first to coordinate DJs with live musicians. Instead, stated Phil, "We were simply in the right place at the right time". Horneman introduced the concept of Wicked Jazz Sounds in the early 2000s by imagining a youth radio programme that might extend beyond traditional jazz programmes. He promoted this concept for a local radio programme in Amstelveen, claiming:

> I wanted to make a radio show which was mostly for younger people, presented in a way that the music was going from traditional jazz to contemporary to hip hop to house, drum and bass, nu jazz whatever. That is why I came up with Wicked Jazz Sounds … I mean I can go really far. And sometimes you think is this jazz and sometimes it isn't but it has a jazz feel. Soul, black music is in it and that's the most important thing.
>
> *(Phil Horneman, July 5, 2009)*

Consistently, the producers and musicians within Amsterdam's crossover jazz scene trace their current musical inspiration to more historical Black music sources. Some might argue that this scene suffers from a kind of provincial cosmopolitanism. Nevertheless, Black music remains central for the reception of these collectives as hip, danceable, and interactive – long-time tropes presented and appropriated in the history of European dance music.

Together with partner Manne van de Zee, the two decided to extend the radio format for live events, which could more freely integrate the newest dance and electronic grooves with currents in hip hop, soul, R&B, and even house and techno. Eventually the events became so successful that the organisation had accrued a group of like-minded creatives and club owners to extend its reach. As suggested by their promo, Horneman and Van de Zee stressed the openness and flexibility of the group's mission, and emphasise the diversity and plurality of participants:

> They aim to bring quality music in an open and accessible way to a wide group of people. The platform features DJs, live musicians, producers, VJs and most of all: a lively community of diverse people, all dancing with a smile.

While participants reflect both the collective's core members as well as the participation of its fans, the scene's cosmopolitanism owes largely to the combination and interaction between international dance tourists and local Dutch jazz and dance music lovers.

After conversations with Alt and DJ Horneman, I wandered back down towards the stage, surprised to see how quickly the venue had filled. Dutch club culture begins exceptionally late, with dancers arriving no earlier than midnight and attendance peaking at around 2:00 a.m. Young and fashionable fans sat on the risers and lined the bar and dance floor, chatting, drinking, and observing the general 'talent'. Most were enjoying listening to the down tempo grooves of DJ Leroy Rey, who later wowed the crowd and musicians with his spontaneous electronic drum improvisations. Two 'nerdy' white guys, one with stringy dread locks whom I recognised from the green room, were dancing on the sparsely populated dance floor. Both moved out of tempo and in self-mocking ways with quirky angular moves, attempting to engender an informal atmosphere free from the judgement and physical expectations of 'slick' professional events. They seemed to suggest to other, shyer dancers that "it's ok, even guys like us can dance and have fun". Arguably, the reverse tactic of featuring 'nerdy' guys worked well in this venue, in contrast to larger urban European discotheques where sensuously dressed, glamorous female dancers attract crowds to the floor. These amateur Wicked Jazz Sounds go-go dancers clearly betrayed the organisation's participatory aesthetic that this was music for anyone to enjoy and to dance to. The dancing mascots convincingly continued their antics as others gradually but steadily filled the floor. While the collective's platform of Black music provides the impetus for dancing and other forms of interactivity, most of the scene is populated by young middle-class whites. Amsterdam's Moroccan, Turkish, and Black population generally support hip hop clubs and smaller venues specialising in reggae, hip hop, and reggaetone.

During their set, saxophonist Alt and vocalist Van Leer began quietly negotiating with both DJs, working out their entrances and submitting their musical groove requests. Alt stood before the DJ, brandishing some Maceo-inspired funk to Horneman's harmonic, down-tempo loop. Her timing was impeccable and the crowd instantly acknowledged her with claps and whoops. After a brief solo, MC/vocalist Van Leer took the mike from the side of the stage and assertively addressed the crowd, announcing the goal of the evening's proceedings: "Yeah Wicked Jazz Sounds. Are you ready dance floor to give it up for Susanne Alt on the saxophone? …" Leer continued hyping the crowd with verve and pep before entering the stage directly in front of the DJ. She began her vocal incantations with slow, drone-like melodies, as if feeling her way into the crowd and into the hypnotic, repetitive loop and riffing on repeated texts, including "I can see you there, I know you, so far away, so far away …". Skilfully improvising her melodic lines, she extended her range from high to low, revealing her ease with modal jazz techniques. Alt and DJ Horneman provided the pulsating riffs and grooves for Van Leer's build-up until Alt reclaimed the spotlight, extending her two-note funk riff to more complicated blues, funk, and eventually chromatic bebop motifs. Horneman enriched Alt's cutting sound by layering more complicated beats over the four-bar, repeated chord sample towards the end of Alt's solo. This was well-coordinated electronic improvisation at its best. Suddenly, the clock ticked 2:00 a.m. and my ride awaited. As I hastily departed, I took one last look around the crowded dance floor and realised, this party had just begun.

Conclusion

In Amsterdam, the variety of electronic jazz collectives remain popular because of their connections to electronic dance movements, their regeneration of popular and Black music sources, their use of digital production techniques and networks, and their collaboration with local talent. As Wicked Jazz Sounds' saxophonist Susanne Alt stated, younger crowds, seeking new forms of sociability, persistently expressed their desire to dance to the newest electronic music, but also witness the live element that is often missing in single DJ sets. Similarly, DJ Phil Horneman of WJS emphasised the necessity of engaging audiences by moving, dancing, and reacting to the music as a form of live performativity. His disdain for the so-called "static DJ" clearly points to live performative values, which persist in European post-industrial crossover jazz scenes.

Audiences of these mobile collectivities substantiate their own mobility through transnational pleasure pilgrimages to historically mediated tourist zones, featuring digital media exhibition spaces such as the Melkweg in the Leidseplein. Audiences migrate from virtual worlds to live dance events, and jazz musicians themselves migrate from home towns to Europe's prestigious jazz conservatories to be trained by highly esteemed 'in residence' American and European soloists.

Both *Wicked Jazz Sounds* dance evenings and the celebrated *Blue Note Trip* series exhibit and reflect the changing dynamics between scenes, fans, amateurs, and arts entrepreneurs – further blurring boundaries between professionals and consumers of musical cultures. Amsterdam's regenerated post-industrial sites, such as the Melkweg's old factory, encapsulate their lineage to older counterculture ideals and initiatives, thus reinforcing these institutions' European progeny. Moreover, the use of arts initiatives and multimedia event spaces by Amsterdam's city government reflect the growing *symbiosis* between previously segmented urban sectors and underground or local arts entrepreneurs. Furthermore, the scene clearly reflects urban arts participants changing values as traditional modes of musical sociability (*interactivity, dance*) are reinvigorated through *hypermediated* processes including the use of digital media to remix live events and recordings by fans to the casual discourse and evaluation of events distributed through social network sites. Amsterdam's crossover jazz scene betrays its connection to prior European jazz scenes and especially those promoted within the cabaret and dance hall culture of the interwar decades which appropriated music as a vehicle for *dancing, live* music interactivity, and musical *cosmopolitanism*. In Amsterdam's thriving electronic jazz spaces, tourists and locals together revel in the urban festivity and live performativity provided by cosmopolitan electronic jazz collectivities.

These fluid expressions of musicality, sociality, and interactivity in turn evidence trans-local, post-industrial flows, selectively circulated through digital, geographic, temporal, and musical zones.

Notes

1   This chapter expands research from a 2013 publication in an anthology entitled *Musical Performance and the Changing City: Post-Industrial Contexts in Europe and the United States* (London: Routledge, 2013). Part of this chapter is also inspired by sections of the chapter "New York Comes to Groningen: Jazz Star Circuits in the Netherlands" in *Migrating Musics: Media, Politics and Style*, Byron Dueck and Jason Toynbee (eds) (London: Routledge, 2011). I would like to thank Fabian Holt, Carsten Wergin, Celia Cain, Byron Dueck, Iván Orosa Paleo, SJ Moenendaar, and the peer reviewers for their helpful commentary and criticism of this chapter.

2   This is in contrast to most indie and acoustic jazz concerts, which are typically attended predominantly by men.

3   This is cited from the page "Maestro" on Blue Note's website, cited 22 October 2009, www.google.com/imgres?imgurl=www.bluenote.nl/media/db_images/original/2225. jpg&imgrefurl=www.bluenote.nl/page/series/62&h=350&w=350&sz=49&tbnid= BzJnR7lxuVBhVM:&tbnh=120&tbnw=120&prev=/images%3Fq%3Dblue%2Bnote% 2Btrip%2Bmaestro&hl=en&usg=__Ea1cJJCo4BMHtzi3f2YmJAIeDco=&ei=uy_gSt-sEsSx4QaWwpUO&sa=X&oi=image_result&resnum=3&ct=image&ved=0CA8Q 9QEwAg

4   In George Lipsitz's terms, artists in post-industrial collectivities illustrate a new kind of politics which "take commodity culture for granted" but which produce "an immanent critique of contemporary social relations" having the power to illuminate "affinities, resemblances and potentials for alliances among a world population that now must be as dynamic and as mobile as the forces of capital" (Lipsitz, quoted in Born and Hesmondhalgh 2000, 27).

5   As the Internet transformed distribution processes in the late-1990s, music scholars began to investigate new social practices embedded in digital networks. Music industry scholar Steve Jones examined the particular technologies directing new distribution modes to stress people's continued role in driving popular music circulations in particular localities. With respect to music distribution channels, Jones envisioned the internet as an important site of disintermediation and re-intermediation, processes most recognisable within music and social network communities (2002, 224).

6   See 2manydjs' *Disc Jockey's Delight Vol. 2* (2002) featuring tracks with Kaw-Liga [Prarie Mix], Frank Delour, The Residents, and Michael Jackson's "Billy Jean". In 2009, DJ Morgoth added to this legacy by mashing Rick Astley's "Never Gonna Give You Up" up with Nirvana's "Smells like Teen Spirit", widely circulated in dance clubs and on internet social networks and blogs.

7   Referring to these four-multinational music/media corporations: EMI, Sony Music Entertainment, Universal Music Group, and Warner Music Group.

8   These collectives often promote networks by registering their own labels to produce and promote the work of collaborating and related groups, such as the case with Jazzanova's Sonar Kollektiv label, which in 2007 formed the Sonar Kollektiv Orchester, a fifteen-musician ensemble. The orchestra, led by Volker Meitz, has worked with other European jazz collectives including Jazzanova and De-Phazz.

9   See Ninja Tune's website for a list of artists and current new jazz projects, accessed January 10, 2011, http://ninjatune.net/.

10   This description is published on the Bandcamp website under "Deewee", accessed December 22, 2018, https://deewee1.bandcamp.com/.

11   United Records history is published on Discogs under "United Records", accessed December 22, 2018, www.discogs.com/label/2966-United-Recordings.

12   First in 1976, the Amsterdam Conservatory, the Haarlem Conservatory, and the Association for the Music Lyceum, fused into the overarching Sweelinck Conservatory. In 1994, the Sweelinck Conservatory and the Hilversum Conservatory fused into the now existing Amsterdam Conservatory. In 2008, the conservatory relocated to a newly designed building at the Oosterdokskade, near Central Station, boosting three main concert halls. The Amsterdam Blue Note hall features jazz and pop concerts ("The Building"). These kinds of fusions, precipitated by national cultural initiatives, speak to the new values promoted within the European Union, as governments invested more money in arts education and asserted its cultural value for cities and their musical offerings as well as articulated the role of arts in 'branding' the unique character of European cities.

13   The square's history dates back to the seventeenth century, when it first provided a gateway for traders and farmers (*Green Guide: Netherlands* 2001, 118). During the late nineteenth century, as European cities expanded to accommodate its growing populations and European industrialisation, the square erected a number of theatres, cafés, and hotels for a variety of pleasure-seekers and businessmen in industries including textiles and electronics. During the 1970s, at the height of the VPRO (Progressive Protestant Radio Broadcasting Company) period, some of the square's surrounding historic sites, including the abandoned dairy factory, became artist sites or anti-squatting residences. A period of post-Fordist restructuring accompanied ideological and philosophical shifts with regards to capitalism and corporate culture. Driven by these shifts, Dutch cities underwent dramatic changes with regards to the social use of public spaces, spaces often democratised and redirected for popular music and culture. In Amsterdam, students demanded democratic transformations in the educational system and changes in the design and use of industrial buildings. In districts like the Leidseplein, the counterculture further positioned themselves in surrounding historic warehouses and factories reclaiming them from their industrial sources into sites for artistic regeneration, cultural expression as well as cheap DIY housing, a phenomenon eventually accepted by policy leaders and regulated as 'anti-kracht' housing. By the end of the twentieth century, city planners and arts organisations had transformed many of its earlier squatter buildings into multi-mediated artistic spaces, and in this respect, these buildings have maintained much of the multi-disciplinary predilections introduced by arts activists of the 1970s.

14   This is taken from the user 'agitproper' on *Flickr*, accessed October 22, 2009, www.flickr.com/photos/agitprop/2382419711/in/set-72157604359495385/

15   This performance took place on July 5, 2009.

16   Posted on December 5, 2010, on WJS's Facebook page, www.facebook.com/#!/pages/Wicked-Jazz-Sounds-Band/40813875311.

17   Alt was nominated for the Edison Jazzism Publieksprijs for her 2016 album *Saxify* (Venus Tunes 2016).

3

DJS AND PLOS IN BERLIN'S ELECTRONIC JAZZ SCENE

The Hybrid Production Aesthetics of Jazzanova

Jazzanova's sustained success has been their vision for using the traditions of the roots of jazz to make the music more accessible; sharp musicianship and sophisticated production flair that pleases the mature listener whilst all the while maintaining contemporary aspects for both stalwarts and new fans alike. And by refusing to adhere to any one musical style, Jazzanova has become one of the most durable artists in their field.

(Smith 2003)

It is difficult to disentangle sampling from song writing, impossible to draw firm lines between a cover version and an original song. Songs are texturally dense palimpsests, accreted rather than authored.

(Fisher 2013, 53)

Technology, Sampling, and Authenticity

In "Subjectivity in the Groove", Bernardo Attias uncovers two reoccurring anxieties expressed as new technologies transform musical cultures: that they "degrade the fidelity of musical recordings" and "threaten to undermine the development of musical technique" (Attias 2013, 20–21). These anxieties were first expressed when experimental recording technologies were introduced in the early twentieth century, yet they return within debates in the digital era. The prevalence of these judgements speaks to the endurance of values such as technical virtuosity, knowledge, and authenticity within the cultures of jazz and dance music.

As electronic dance music cultures proliferated in the 1980s and 1990s, the role of the DJ and producer became more prominent, stimulating intense discussion about the hierarchies of musical prestige, performance practice, and recording techniques. By the 2000s, sampling as a practice had become so deeply embedded into popular music conventions that Behr, Negus, and Street would proclaim our current popular music era as a "post-sampling" one dominated by a "sampling continuum", and "informed by" and emerging from "the affordances of near ubiquitous digitalisation – a kind of 'post sampling' musical environment wherein sampling and other musical practices intermingle" (Behr *et al.* 2017, 224).

Jazz culture too was transformed by such developments relating to emerging sampling practices, notably in the collaboration between DJs and producers who created sample-based works from older recordings or circulated remixes of prior jazz recordings within dance music contexts. Such collaborations stimulated old anxieties, naturally, but also prompted new ones. These anxieties were interestingly shared by mixed-genre producers and instrumentalists collaborating in 'record-collecting' collectives, which treated the phonographic object as the foundation of aesthetic and artistic experimentation.[1]

Indeed, the artistic evaluations of producer-led outfits (PLOs) within new jazz-related genres led to discussions about newer practices such as remixes or real-time sampling (Harkins 2010). Some, including the producers of the Berlin-based collective Jazzanova, discussed the old in relation to new technologies. For example, Berlin Producer Stefan Leisering argued that older techniques, such as beat construction and first-generation sampling equipment, offered more interesting possibilities than those developed for digital workstations (Stefen Leisering, Interview with the author, November 25, 2017). However, behind these debates loomed the role assumed by the vinyl recording as the core ideological and aesthetic object of new music. Those involved in remixing, sampling, or creating dance music inspired by jazz appeared driven by "phonograph effects" (Katz 2004, 146), and a broader phonographic logic which viewed the archive as the basis for new musical output. Because producers within production networks maintained a preference for discs prior to the widespread accessibility of digital formats, their discourse and practices reflected a deep-seated fascination with vinyl collections thought to consolidate entire affective life-worlds, and especially those prior to 1980. These included the network of relations from a particular record label, to a spatially located music scene, or community of players from the pre-globalisation era.

Within a growing body of scholarship on both analogue DJ culture and digital sampling practices, scholars positioned sound recordings as the dominant artistic artefact of remix culture (Schloss 2004; Butler 2006; Gunkel 2015). The prominent role of recordings for DJs and producers foregrounds significant discourse within the critical and technical sphere, and also in the studio and performance space. Members of the trans-local electronic jazz collective Jazzanova not only favour vinyl collections, but their study of recordings have endowed them with extensive knowledge of both jazz and other genres of recorded popular music, a process profoundly influencing their art. It is therefore from the vantage point of music recordings that this chapter seeks to connect the history of jazz and Black music recordings to the producer-led practice of remixing and modern song composition practices within the jazz-based PLO. In particular, this chapter interrogates the role of the Black music recording archive to the sample-based remixes of the Berlin-based collective Jazzanova, an electronic jazz outfit locally and internationally active within both Berlin's live music scenes and transnationally oriented recorded music projects during the last two decades.

Listening with Jazzanova – Good Remix, Bad Remix

In 2017, Jazzanova producer, beat maker, and instrumentalist Stefan Leisering explored common motivations for making remixes. One aim, he asserts, is to expand one's network to gain exposure, while affiliating with a respected artist (Stefen Leisering, November 25, 2017). Furthermore, producers seek to develop the established practice of 'versioning', a process with roots in reggae culture; for electronic jazz producers, versioning allows creating alternative textures, forms, and danceable styles connected to an artist's most popular hit. Remixes often circulate in a number of platforms in the digital environment, yet the remixes of Jazzanova were originally intended for dance clubs.

Despite the engagement with this practice by Jazzanova's producers, there is often ambivalence about remixing, especially since this process has become more expedient. In this environment, some less experienced DJs even boast their ability to produce remixes in mere hours, which often evidences the (lack of) quality and artfulness of these mixes (Stefen Leisering, Interview with the author, Berlin, November 25, 2017).

Nina Simone – The Remix 'Stomp Treatment'

Within the neoliberal environment of the current music industry, most requests for remixes offer little financial remuneration, so producers aim for increased exposure for their other recordings, or seek invitations to produce a record, or DJ at a prestigious club. Leisering depicted the typical facile remix as one where a popular song is remixed with a predictable house beat – the so-called 'stomp treatment'. It begins by programming in a high-hat loop, eventually dropping in the bass drum, and finally the bass. He recalled hearing one such underwhelming example while touring with Jazzanova:

> We were just having some food and drinking but they had loud music and every song they played was kind of danceable and then they played Nina Simone to a beat and I said, wait, the bass drum will be coming in and it really did. I thought, okay, [he laughs] do we really need that? Maybe had they played that Nina Simone tune in that kind of club that I don't go to – it needs that remix but artistically it's a mess.... And if you listen for instance to St Germain, they did it in a nice way, so when you want to make people dance to jazzy house grooves, then play that and

why Nina Simone? … I suppose that it's related to "I know that song, wow and it has a beat that I can dance too". That's all it's about.

(Stefan Leisering, November 25, 2017)

Implicit in this are the aesthetics surrounding sampling practices in relation to particular genre cultures, and in this case jazz, especially its iconic artists. Here, the repurposing of such recordings for the more functional goals of remixes is then weighed against alternative engagements with Black music recording artists.

In this new context, however, knowledge of Simone's own career likely colours Leisering's discomfort in hearing her music quantised in such a manner. Her background is de-emphasised in favour of the reconcilability of the 'grain' of Simone's voice, or for the collective recognition of a familiar melody. Hearing a jazz phrase through the practice of *citation recognition* remains a common value within jazz culture, where musicians engage in borrowing as a way of building upon prior works, sharing an insider's discourse about its citable canon (Berliner 1994, Monson 1996). Recognition, however, also implies socio-political knowledge of the challenges Simone encountered when striving to gain recognition first as a pianist and later as a jazz musician within a traditionalist and masculinist jazz world (*What Happened Miss Simone?* 2015). Hearing these recordings also sparks memory of her politically oriented musical output, including, *Forever Young, Gifted and Black: Songs of Freedom and Spirit* (1967), which contained her famous civil rights song 'Mississippi Goddam'.[2]

In this listening climate, adapting Simone's voice for a danceable mix precipitates the kind of "context collapse" argued by ethnomusicologist Kyra Gaunt (2015). It also recalls Steven Feld's theorising of "schizophonia" prompted by sampling practices within popular music recordings (2000). The remix is then a logical extension of such practices which relied upon the rendering of familiar material to a more generalised rhythmic pattern, wherein recorded material elicits vague recognition, but only in so far as its new context enables distracted listening within the aesthetics of sampling and layering guiding electronic dance music.

'Stimela' – Engaged Remixes

Remixes, however, can offer a form of aesthetic and cultural encounter, emulation, and study that jazz artists have long negotiated in their performative citation of recorded music. Interestingly, Jazzanova chooses to remix material to which they feel both musically and culturally connected. For instance, Leisering offered to share and discuss his remix of Hugh Masekela's 'Stimela', a track composed over a two-week period in 2016. For this project, he studied its cultural narrative, which foregrounds socio-economic inequality subsumed within the system of apartheid. Masekela's song evokes the experiences and sounds of the trains carrying young, marginalised men from neighbouring countries and from the townships of Lesotho and Botswana to the coal mines near Johannesburg. These labourers suffered harrowing conditions during apartheid and Masekela's song bears witness to this system.

Furthermore, Stefan studiously analysed the *mbaqanga* strains of this recording, as well as Masekela's unique approach to jazz. Like Leisering, Masekela had earlier absorbed diverse musical traditions from his cultural milieu, including local music genres such as the soul-tinged African pop of Miriam Makeba and international musical influences from the fusion of Herb Albert to the Latin jazz of Antônio Carlos Jobim. By remixing Masekela's original recording and adding elements of funk and ambient textures, Leisering extends the eclectic tradition of African pop rendered in this earlier recording.

Such study of the cultural and musical context also inspired a performative approach within the recording studio, greatly impacting the form and contour of the Jazzanova remix. Stefan described part of the process:

> We are really placing mikes on the piano; we are experimenting with diving into the sounds; we are not just making a beat with the sounds that we use every day … I press the pedal there on all the sides and we were hammering. I don't know how many people do that for a remix … I like to be a little bit off.… So, most sounds you hear are from the piano or from the plucked sounds. I recreated the melody. That is the upright bass, re-recorded … it is really interesting how we got away from just sampling and into *recreating* the sound.… And here for instance I have programmed all of the drums and they sound like a live drummer. I just wanted to have a little contrast from the original. It sounds like a slo-mo house track and then it turns into an Afro-funk song, [after the drums are fully present in the mix he exclaims] "yeah like that".
>
> *(Stefan Leisering, November 25, 2017)*

Our shared listening evolved into a discussion of the ethics of remixing. How did a techno reworking of a Nina Simone song differ from Leisering's remix of Hugh Masekela's 'Stimela'? While each remix alters the melodic and rhythmic material for a new transnational audience, Leisering's remix recognises the aesthetic and ethical impulses of the original song. Furthermore, this remix gradually evolves before incorporating the human textures of the choir, highlighting the antiphonal nature of this vocal genre (*mbaqanga*). This slow build-up is antithetical to the dictates of a dance-oriented remix, where tracks quickly adopt the four-to-the-floor pattern for club music dancing.

This remix foregrounds the core themes of this chapter in relation to the changing practices of record production, especially those which still adapt to the prior aesthetics of citation and influence within the earlier era of jazz recording before the widespread expansion of digital studios (Behr *et al.* 2017). It also speaks to changes within sampling-based musical cultures upon the availability of digital sample-based productions, namely within the cultures of hip hop and

EDM where the practice of the remix has fragmented into a myriad of contexts, stimulated by a variety of aims.

Moreover, the chapter examines how transnational or diasporic Black music movements from the twentieth century inform ideas about cultural memory, ultimately within the PLO production process wherein jazz recordings by Black artists become the locus for new sampling practices within the recording studios of Europe. I highlight the role of Jazzanova's Berlin-based producers, whose relation to a Black jazz past differs from that, for example, of the Black jazz rap collectives (such as the Native Tongues) of the 1990s, whose members maintained connections to the hip hop communities in cities like Detroit and Philadelphia (Perchard 2011). However, dismissing the value of the Black jazz past would negate the personal and collective to collective connections of contemporary European artists working trans-locally with and for Jazzanova in a process resembling yet altering the transnationalism of earlier decades (Gilroy 1993).

Additionally, this chapter explores the practice and prevalence of remix within electronic jazz culture, an important development since the onset of digitalisation and hyper-globalisation of the 1980s. While this decade is typically depicted as an era of growing conservatism within jazz media, I argue that an alternative arena of particularly progressive jazz practice within Europe led to its resurgence in these same decades. Its vitality resulted from the confluence of technological experimentations within jazz networks of performance and recording, alongside the integration of performative values within youth-oriented electronic dance cultures. I investigate how new techniques developed within what I refer to as the modern *hybrid recording studio*, affording the expansion of jazz timbres and compositional methods especially as adapted within other production-oriented techniques such as sampling, looping, and beat construction. Critical to developing an aesthetics of electronic jazz was the fundamental role of the vinyl record archive, as both primary source material for new works and as a critical arena to circulate a jazz discourse and establish credibility within a network of jazz curators and meaning-makers.

I focus particularly on how remixing has featured as a core musical activity and outcome of collaborations between the producers and DJs of the durable PLO (producer-led outfit) Jazzanova, an influential electronic jazz collective from Berlin, which developed from the informal DJing, record collecting, and dance café culture of the mid-1990s. This PLO has since graduated from an informal coterie of record collectors, amateur DJs, and music promoters to a highly professional, internationally esteemed outfit, running a record company, booking international tours, and releasing professional quality recordings of both remixed and new material in collaboration with other professional artists. Since 2000, Jazzanova has released a variety of recorded formats for fans of both electronic jazz and modern sample-based groove tracks from compilation albums to EPs, and from remixed recordings of mainstream pop artists to newly composed works.

Through analysis of Berlin's contemporary electronic jazz culture, I argue that Jazzanova, like other similarly motivated PLOs, reinforce three logics underpinning this culture's committed relationship to the study of recordings. These logics prove instrumental in defining the jazz-influenced sound art of Jazzanova and of electronic jazz more generally since the late-1990s. The first is the dedicated, comprehensive study of performance practice as captured within a now canonical body of recordings. The second is an interest in extending the artistic and aesthetic possibilities of prior sampling activities through techniques such as time-shifting, chopping, or the recreation of recorded sounds through a semi-performative digital sound construction craft. The third is an expanded interest in reanimating older recording practices, such as recording acoustic instrumental parts and combining them with the newly created digital sequences, effects, and beats in something akin to a *'sampled-not-sampled'* compositional practice. It is this last stage which signals a new era of recording practice, where the studio re-emerges as compositional medium and where the live aesthetics of instrumental jazz are re-staged within the sample plus live recording object. Such hybrid combinations are a staple of all popular music recordings since the 2000s (Behr *et al.* 2017), but the ways in which a particular set of jazz values are adapted into this hybrid studio setting profoundly reflects upon how these two worlds have encountered and responded to each other since jazz samples prevailed within recorded hip hop and sub-genres of electronic music prior to 2000.

Building a Jazz Archive, Cultivating 'Jazz Ears' for Electronic Jazz Producers

In November 2017, I visited Berlin to meet members of Jazzanova and to attend two DJ events of its members. After interviewing producer Stefan Leisering, I was invited to view Jazzanova's Prenzlauerberg Recording Studio. This is a hybrid studio, containing a drum room, vocal room, piano room, computer editing room, and a large control room. The main rooms are filled with both acoustic instruments and synthesisers of various eras, an eclectic collection partly defining the asynchronous sound of Jazzanova. It also houses Stefan's studio, containing a digital workstation adjacent to numerous computers and sampling equipment, keyboards, and a plethora of records. Here Stefan composes, samples, and sequences his drum parts and beats. The room houses his Atari computer, an E-mu sampler, a full mixing consul, and a small midi-synthesiser for his sample patches. He creates his own samples rather than using pre-existing sound libraries or pre-made patches from various editing programs (such as Ableton or Logic). For sampling, he uses an older version of the program Creator. Ergo, Stefan retains the same general sampling and editing format he first acquired in the 1990s.

During our meeting, Stefan demonstrated his method. First, he calls up the drum samples, many of which he played himself, while others are taken from vinyl

FIGURE 3.1   Jazzanova in their studio, Prenzlauerberg, Berlin
Source: Photograph by Georg Roske.

recordings such as a Chucho Valdés instrumental record. He then created various versions of each of these hits, resulting in over twenty dynamic ranges from which to choose. This was a considerable difference from drum sequencing programs which typically disable such dynamic differentiation. Finally, in an expedient and impressive demonstration – using Creator – he first recorded two measures of various snare hits from his numerous versions of the same snare instrument. Using his mouse, he created a rhythm pattern which would become the basis for a funk beat. He then called up his sample banks and applied the same process for the bass drum and high hat. Once satisfied, he then tweaked the pattern for more dynamic range and rhythmic irregularity, such as adding a few ghost notes on the high hat or increasing the dynamic on the bass drum before beat three of the funk pattern. When he replayed his final groove, it sounded so much like an acoustically performed drum kit that I asked him if he could differentiate between sample-produced beats and acoustically recorded drums on other similar recordings. He said he usually could tell because computer or sampled drums often lack the ambience of the room or they sound dynamically static. An example given was of an Amy Winehouse track from her *Back to Black* album.

While this compositional/recording set-up demanded greater time commitment, it informed and distinguished Jazzanova's musical aesthetic. Stefan depicted the Jazzanova percussion sound as "weird, live but also programmed". After finishing editing his beat, the original was no longer recognisable. The core of these recordings as well as knowledge about the performance styles of artists inspired his work. Justin Williams depicted this process as a form of 'allosonic' quotation, "achieved via re-recording or quoting" rather than 'autosonic' quotation, "achieved by using the recording itself" (Williams 2014, 208). However, these beats exhibited an affiliation with the iconic drummers of jazz, soul, and funk rather than a simple reconstruction. Indeed, it extended the citation practice of the 'jazz tradition' by borrowing and more importantly adapting existing jazz vocabularies to reconfigure within a new voice. In his 'hauntology' framework, Reynolds argued that these new sample-based creations contained an uncanny and haunting residue of the originals (Reynolds 2011, 326–361). This residue, however, manifests through an active studio performance.

Leisering also stressed that because he used only single hits from various recordings or his own sampled drum hits, arranged in an idiosyncratic manner, it was highly unlikely that one would confuse his beats with those of the drummers sampled. Stefan's lengthy process is considered tedious to many beat makers, who prefer sampling an entire funk beat from an existing recording or from the thousands of banks offered through programs like Logic. Notably for Jazzanova, this earlier citational practice lacks the creative transformation necessary for the development of a compelling new sound.

During this demonstration, Leisering also reflected upon how certain performers established iconic sounds. For example, when wanting to produce a pattern inspired by Jack DeJohnette, Leisering would add a ghost note right before the four, typifying DeJohnette's style. Other drummers studied in terms of their unique style included Bernard Purdie, who during the 1960s played with Aretha Franklin, and later with Idris Muhammad and dozens of musicians from Nat Adderley to Ahmad Jamal. Ultimately, Leisering's incorporation of various drum samples reflected his intimate knowledge of the recorded history of Black drummers active from the 1950s to the 1970s. These drummers had all grappled with the unique possibilities of recording technologies in studios connected to various genre cultures.

Because of the methodical study of recordings, Leisering was not only an avid jazz performance and recording expert, but he was able to artistically recreate different drummers' signature styles in his own beat constructions. This mirrors the pedagogical process of live jazz drummers who study and borrow other drummers' stylistic elements to 'say something' new (Monson 1995). However, Leisering's instrument was unorthodox, as he used his Atari computer and E-Mu sampler to deconstruct, record, and then reconstruct beats according to his own aesthetic.

Through this complex practice and engagement with players and their recordings within Jazzanova's electronic jazz style, the ambience of particular recording studios' influence remains foundational. During our conversation, Stefan argued that particular recordings exude their own milieu, a concept not easily reducible to a particular rhythm or melody. For Leisering and others, recordings' particular ambient *soundscapes* materialise from the combination of various factors such as from particular miking techniques or from contrived effects such as echo and reverb (Doyle 2005), or from the unique combinations of instruments favoured by producers within particular contexts and locales. Certain studios, such as King Tubby's Waterhouse in Kingston, also transformed conventional recording equipment with techniques and acoustics which situated dub plates in a particular time and place, and especially in relation to an active and mobile dance public. Despite a common understanding of recordings as abstract objects or cultural commodities, the patina of the subjective intervention and invention of technologies is always recognisable in particular recordings. Indeed, Stefan played the introduction of Ramsey Lewis's 'If Loving You is Wrong, I Don't Wanna be Right', and asked me to identify it as sampled in a major contemporary hit. I suggested De La Soul, but it was the Fugees 'Oh La La'. When listening again, he said: "I can see why they chose that sample – the whole combination of the sound of the recording and the sound of the Wurlitzer is special" (Stefan Leisering, November 25, 2017). By recognising the sample's overall milieu, Jazzanova's producers recognise how sample-based works act as "thawed frozen architecture", a concept conceived by DJ Spooky (Miller 2008). By deconstructing the histories and performance practices mediated through recordings within a particular soundstage, the locations, values, and sets of relations are brought to life. In combining them within new hybrid recording processes, these recombined musics illuminate the foundation of past expressive cultures, making them meaningful for newly emerging ones.

Jazzanova's Trajectory from Record-collecting Cafés to Producer-led Studios

Jazzanova was one of the earliest European DJ and producer-led collectives to establish a reputation outside of local studios and dance clubs. Today, they still feature performances and projects of many of the original members. For example, DJ, booking agent, and manager Daniel Best has been working for and with Jazzanova for over twenty years. He recalls the development of this consortium from the 1990s in relation to electronic music, hip hop, and jazz within the improvised spaces of Berlin's artistic communities. For him, the 1990s was a rather informal period wherein 'digging in the crates' was still the primary manner of finding new and interesting music. He reports a number of crate-diggers who regularly congregated within an ad hoc place called Delicious Doughnuts in Berlin's Mitte district. Here they played and shared records in a fashion closely resembling the jazz record-collecting and discursive activities of jazz enthusiasts' clubs (Jazz Hot) from the 1930s and 1940s, centred around Berlin's internationally celebrated multi-arts café culture (Zwerin 2000; Wipplinger 2017).

There, spaces retained their social function, sharing knowledge and collectively listening to jazz and Black music recordings when particular recordings where still difficult to locate in the reunification period. Best recalls that in the mid-1990s, a certain synergy grew around this café. Jazzanova and Sonar Kollektiv bassist Paul

Kleber also remembers Berlin as an exciting place to discover new music. He recalls other important spaces for this crew including WMF (later renamed Café Moskau) and Kaleidoskop, stating "many of the clubs were in old factory buildings" and that they "invited DJs from all over the world". According to Kleber, the collective listening of these spaces motivated this affective community at the cusp of the internet's more pervasive influence on dance music cultures. He recalls, "It was at that time that it was really cool to go there and listen to some new music. There was also internet but you didn't listen so much to music on the internet". For him, these weekly recordings-based evenings also provided a connection to developing local communities:

> It was exciting because all the districts which weren't yet gentrified now started, like really hip underground parts of Berlin and districts where people lived and it is still like that. The interesting thing is that the creative people go to places which are like down and cheap and they are doing their stuff there and in the new clubs and the galleries and then it becomes interesting for the investors and then it gentrifies.
>
> *(Paul Kleber, Interview with the author, November 26, 2017)*

Because of his affiliation with electronic jazz, Kleber remembers the nature of on-stage interactions between electronic sound artists and live jazz instrumentalists. For him, the creative quality of such interactions depended upon the vision and skills of both the instrumentalists and the DJs or sampling/sound artists. He described the challenges related to live interactions with these new technologies:

> When I started with Micaton with this band, when we played live it was the new thing for us to mix it with machines or to mix it with a sampler. There was this one guy who did sounds from the samples and we mixed it. You are really tied to this line and you cannot break out of this and you have to play with the machine and the machine never plays really with you. So, it is different, it is more like you have to play your part in the song and it starts here and there is not much space for development or to be spontaneous. So, I think many guys I know, now they prefer more to play without machines to get the freedom to do something on stage. To improvise on stage again. On the other hand, it depends a little bit on the music. If you have the music in a pop style and you have to really nail it on stage for example on a big festival stage. You don't have so much space to be really into small stuff and you don't have so much time to develop so you have to like nail it and rock the crowd and then it helps to make it more powerful and to add instruments or sounds that you can't produce with your acoustic instrument.
>
> *(Paul Kleber, November 26, 2017)*

Evident are the obvious challenges of upholding the aesthetics and values of jazz improvisation, such as the freedom to extend and alter rhythmic feels, harmonic changes, and dynamics with the fixed musical components of sampled and sequenced recordings. However, in certain settings, real-time sampling of digital soundscapes can boost the energy of a performance, making it more spectacular for large audiences.

Eventually, Jazzanova began to promote events for larger parties. Initially, they adopted a DIY approach. In this pre-internet moment, Leisering recalls the attractive and informal atmosphere of their first meeting place (Delicious Donuts), with one café-like room in the front and a slightly larger room in the back for listening and dancing. Most of its DJs appeared regularly, two to three times a week, and it became a central meeting place for sharing new records and planning music events. This was also one of the first informal spots to hear and dance to hip hop records, especially those sub-genres (jungle and drum 'n' bass) from the UK. In this ad hoc curatorial and sociable space, a connection with like-minded international collectives was established including the Rogue Beats Crew, 4Hero, and the Broken Beat scene in London. Later parallels could be made to the Kyoto Massive collective in Japan. In this sense, the 1990s witnessed a truly international expansion of DJed jazz, which later led to a hybrid Black recorded music production aesthetic.

Leisering recalled meeting DJs at Delicious Donuts in the Mitte district in the mid-1990s. Allegedly, when some DJs were approached by an agent about making a compilation for use in clubs, they sought out particular producers to assist in the recording. As a result, three DJs (Alex Barck, Juergen von Knoblauch, Claas Brieler) and three producers (Axel Reinemer, Stefan Leisering, Roskow Kretschman) began to collaborate under the name Jazzanova. Initially, recordings ranged from new releases within the jungle and trip house genre to older jazz and soul records passed down from the nearby American army bases during the 1970s and 1980s. Again, the parallels to interwar jazz culture are clear. Within the occupied zones and cultural spaces of Berlin, such contact occurred on various levels – a set of connections and interactions conceptualised as the 'Jazz Republic' by Wipplinger (2017).

Decades later, cultural encounters were driven by a new set of relations within the once occupied zones of Berlin. Because of a growing demand, Leisering was asked to host a radio programme on jazz and hip-hop-influenced dance music in the mid-1990s. This became another outlet for sharing musical tastes and promoting neighbourhood parties. During the 1990s, each DJ of the collective contributed to some of Berlin's many informal series and club nights. For example, Best established and promoted a reggae night called Escobar every Monday at an illegal club, Pfefferbank, in Berlin-Mitte. This was before the fully established techno clubs attracted large groups of tourists and before significant capital was invested by international music corporations in Berlin's expanding transnational techno tourism industry (Rapp 2009).

One of the collective's early series was the Kaleidoscope events hosted by the WMF club and later the Moskau Club. Here they performed their own sets, but they also invited international DJs such as Theo Parish (Detroit) and Quest Love (from the Roots) as well as live bands, many from Brazil including the electrified 'samba doido' of Azymuth and Delata. The Brazilian funk sound of these instrumental groups influenced the overall sound of Jazzanova's studio projects, leading to a long-term interactive transnational musical aesthetic. However, according to Best, this earlier period was less international than the current DJ-driven jazz and electronic scene in Berlin, partly because the affordable tourism industry had not yet peaked. Most of the DJs of the scene were not only German but also men; Best referred to them as record 'nerdies'. Apparently, there was one woman who occasionally DJed, Emanuele De Luca, a Tunisian who now lives in Paris and still spins records (Daniel Best, Interview with the author, November 27, 2017).

Jazzanova swiftly developed their own record label (Jazzanova Compost Records) to distribute mix-tapes, newly produced material, and compilation albums. After the release of their first 12-inch in 1997, the collective began working with jazz instrumentalists in various settings. Best depicted this new way of working as the basis for the early artistic success of Jazzanova. In fact, the DJs would often share new records with the producers, lending their opinions about what was valuable or 'cool', and then the producers would use these recordings as the basis for new compositions. Through this process, a particular ecosystem and creative flow materialised; DJs would dig crates and spin new records in the revanchist spaces of Berlin, then the producers would use these recordings for both remixes and sample-based records. Arjun Appadurai (1996) would describe these processes as cultural flows driven by particular media and technoscapes within late capitalism, but such interactions reflected the social and informal interactions of music scenes depicted by Sara Cohen in her study of the rock music scenes in Liverpool (Cohen 1991). Here, the discourse and ideologies of music scenes was driven by the histories connected to particular spaces and recording objects within the larger history of German popular music and its long-time connection to Black music and jazz (Lotz 2012; Wipplinger 2017; Zwerin 2000).

Best views the development of Jazzanova as connected to several movements throughout the world, especially in Europe but also in Japan. One significant development in the context of digital music circulation was the expanding and increasingly prominent role of the DJ as record curator and taste-maker. Since the late 1990s, a number of record curators gained international reputations for scouting and promoting noteworthy records. Promotion could occur during live events or through weekly radio shows, and finally by releasing record compilations created by such taste-makers. Within electronic jazz, the most revered DJ/ music curator from this period within Europe was Gilles Peterson, a 'taste-maker' who has DJed and promoted new music in London and abroad since the 1990s.[3]

Peterson's promotional efforts aided the success of Jazzanova's first EP, which featured the track 'Fedime's Flight' released by JCR, a merged label between Jazzanova and Compost Records (also German) in the early 2000s. Jazzanova created several LPs from remix compilations to LPs featuring new compositions which combined samples, live instrumentations, and vocals. The first full-length album featuring this new hybrid method was their 2001 LP *In Between*, released in Europe under JCR. The recording was shortly thereafter licensed by Ropeadope in the US for use by various US-based ad agencies and media companies (Stein 2002). In this period, Ropeadope was a subsidiary of Atlantic Records with whom they held a production and distribution contract throughout the US.

Jazzanova's *In Between* traversed metaphorical and spatial borders, bringing musicians across the Atlantic from Philadelphia's Afro-futuristic jazz scene to Berlin's electronic jazz collectives. There the influential King Britt introduced Jazzanova to such Philly-based artists as beatnik poet Ursula Rucker, DJ/producer Vikter Duplaix, and rappers Capital A and Hawkeye Phanatic. The project featured US jazz musicians including percussionist and marimba performer David Friedman (who played with Wayne Shorter and Chet Baker among others), and American drummer Doug Hammond (who played with Sonny Rollins, Charles Mingus, and Nina Simone). Its boundary-blurring proclivities were influenced by the transnational connections between the progressive hip hop of Grandmaster Flash and others working within Afro-futurism such as Parliament, themselves

FIGURE 3.2 Jazzanova record cover, *In Between* (Ropeadope Records 2002).

inspired by the technologically advanced recordings of German artists, notably Kraftwerk or the experimental tape pieces of Karlheinz Stockhausen.

Compiling the Remixes

Jazzanova released their first remix compilation in 2000, culminating in the jazz-house, trip hop, jazz rap compilation album *Jazzanova: The Remixes 1997–2000* (2000 JCR), containing remixes of artists from within other electronic jazz circles such as 4hero, Incognito, Azymuth, and Liquid Lounge. Writing for *All-Music*, Rob Theakston evaluated the combined aesthetics of jazz and digital sampling within Jazzanova's remixes, which he claimed elevated them above other more facile mixes:

> The discs assemble original workings from diverse artists … and morph them into well-produced bossa beat jazz workouts without forsaking the original intent of the composition; a refreshing concept.… These principles are no more evident than on the remix of Har-You Percussion Group's "Welcome to the Party". Originally a composition that appeared on Ubiquity's outstanding New Latinares compilation, Jazzanova turns this honest, simple piece into an extended workout, complete with a shimmering piano breakdown that would have the snootiest of jazz purists bobbing their heads and shaking their hips.
>
> *(Theakston n.d.)*

On the remix of the Harlem Youth Organization or Har-You Percussion Group's 'Welcome to the Party', Jazzanova combines the "participatory discrepancies" (Keil and Feld 1994) of this Afro-Cuban percussion jam within the unexpected digital reworkings of other recorded material. In this track, they alter the conventional approach taken by some remix producers, inserting the hybrid studio into the compositional and recording process.

Sampling Community and Love in 'L.O.V.E. and You & I' (In Between 2001)

In Between encapsulated the combinatory processes of artistic composition and sampling prioritised by the collective. Shortly after its release, DJ Alexander Barck claimed that the first track took six months to complete (Stein 2002). This process involved putting all of the samples together and then fitting them to a live sound. He summarised their creative goal as making a track "that had no limitations" and describing the whole project as a "multi-layered endeavour featuring myriad samples, live instrumentation and vocals" (Stein 2002). Such processes enabled the artful combination of various genres, performers, places, and soundscapes into Jazzanova's sample-based recordings with a self-conscious, backwards mediation on the social histories of particular Black music recordings. By connecting these recordings with living musicians from Philadelphia, Jazzanova linked the past to the present world of electronic progressive jazz and further extended the inter-cultural encounters of the Black Atlantic within the jazz and hip hop collectives of Europe.

According to the user-generated online database *Who Sampled*, the album's title track 'L.O.V.E. and You & I' samples fourteen albums, in particular the Philly funk and soul group Catalyst featuring keyboardist Eddie Green, bass player Alphonso Johnson and drummer Sherman Ferguson. Also included are rework-ings of samples from the Sylvers, a soul/disco family group from the Watts area of Los Angeles; as well as samples from the Five Stairsteps and Cubie, a Chicago-based sister and brother soul/R&B/disco group; and samples from various jazz instrumentalists, including vibraphonist Bobby Hutcherson, saxophonist Branford Marsalis, guitarist Antônia Carlos Jobim, drummer Les DeMerle, and the Australian Daly Wilson Big Band. Other songs sampled include the Motown single 'I'll Try Sometime New' performed by the Supremes together with the Temptations, 'Shop Around' by Canadian rock singer Neil Merryweather, 'Silver Child' by the Japanese Sadistic Mika Band, 'Jeansy' from the Polish Novi Singers, 'Agua' from the Brazilian singer songwriter Djavan, and 'Midnight Theme' by Manzel.[4] Most are from records made during the 1960s and 1970s, the exception being the Marsalis Quartet from 1990. Six of these are non-American groups and all others are American, of which the majority are Black groups recording the genres of especially funk, soul, and jazz.

Love, as an affective ideal, is easily mapped onto these recordings; Jazzanova's reconstruction of the romantic samples evoke dreamy soundscapes, linking this track to a particular historical and geographical moment in Black music history, embodying the dance-oriented genres of soul, disco, and fusion. By connecting the concept of family to a family of genres, Jazzanova's nostalgic conception of community recalls the places of Black music's strongest connections. The knowledge and exploration of these communal Black music spaces played a part in the musical growth and inspiration of Berlin's developing electronic jazz scene.

According to Tom Perchard, the 1970s form an important decade for the 1990s sample-based hip hop artists such as the Native Tongues collective. It was a period during which producers and sample-based DJs first experimented with the jazz-influenced recordings of Black music, especially those recordings contained in the collections of music-loving parents. Perchard understands the prevalence of 1970s-era fusion, funk, and jazz samples as a dialogical engagement of the youth-ful experiences of hip hop artists, who revisited record collections of (extended) family members while simultaneously participating in intergenerational debates about Black American culture and the aesthetics of jazz and hip hop – a practice theorised as "performative negotiations of historical memory" (Perchard 2011, 300). Perchard argues that the childhood exposure to such records contributes to a hip-hop-informed habitus for artists who incorporate more familiar interpersonal

musical references into sampled collages, while the overlying rap narratives promote the more common trope of citation as cultural memory.

If the interpersonal experiences of Black music recordings alongside the broader
conceptualisation of Black music as historical memory forged a connection to
Black aesthetic cultures for the hip hop collectives of the 1990s, what kinds of
connections are forged by Berlin's DJs to this music within the context of post-
reunification German culture? One possibility is that Berlin-based DJs sought to
encapsulate the innovative performative aura and the aura of place emanating from
these culturally compelling performances. Producers attempted to transmit this
within the particular sonic soundscapes afforded by the technologies and mediums of this period. As Mark Katz suggests, digital sampling offers the possibility
of 'performative quotation' in that samples cite the idiosyncratic performances
embedded within recordings (Katz 2004, 149). Yet such performances also evoke a
sense of place through the unique and technologically traceable reverberations and
ambient noise of these original recordings. In other words, not only are particular
instrumental styles recorded in these discs, but the unique affordances of particular
recording technologies are documented from the acoustics of studio spaces, to the
unique sounds of particular microphones, and to the original contributions of engi-
neers who experimented with technical effects (Horning 2015). Finally, these discs
retain traces of repeated listenings, articulated in the hisses and cracks of well-worn
vinyl – such traces lay claim to a Black Atlantic continuum evidenced since 1945,
which depended on the combined circulation of jazz recordings and performances
(Poiger 2000, Davenport 2013). Leisering and others emphasise that the combined
aura of such recordings offers something unique when reworked into new sample-
based recordings. Simon Reynolds would later postulate a science of haunting, or
hauntology (borrowing from Derrida), within DJ cultures as reconfigured recordings evoke a past which haunts our present even as samples offer only a trace of a
living original. Thus, recordings are only representations of something no longer
present (Reynolds 2011).

The title track of *In Between* opens with the vocal sample from Five Stairsteps
and Cubie from 'Something's Missing' (*Our Family Portrait* 1968) on the words
'something's missing', which is looped three times. Each time this harmonised
phrase is faded out with a delay, inserted four times over the arpeggiated piano
passage in a trace, recalling the past. The fourth time, we hear this phrase answered
by a male harmonised phrase modulated down a fourth, with the lead singer
Cubie from the Five Stairsteps answering the existential question with a nod to
the peace politics of the 1960s and 1970s: "Could it be love?" The 'love' sample is
taken from the Sylvers record 'Only One Can Win' from 1972. The single word
'love' sung by the Sylvers is cut up and modulated down chromatically to a minor
tonality and we hear the single female voice singing the word 'love' before the
Rhodes, guitar, and Latin percussion move towards vocal samples of images from
nature – reiterated in the poetic phrase "the sun, moon, sky", natural elements
which evoke a transcendental soundscape. Later, at 1.58, we hear a two-bar vocal

phrase from the Supremes and Temptations ('I'll Try Something New' *Diana Ross and the Supremes Join the Temptations* 1968) singing a rising arpeggiated diatonic scale before the next rhythmic transition. Then this vocal-dominant soundscape is folded into a funkier and more urbane drum loop, and the harp and guitar are modulated to a minor tonality before the full funk break. The bossa beat then reappears with the "sun, moon, sky" and "you and I" phrases. These are embellished with a sparse Rhodes-riff to a short jazzy brass refrain. Finally, a funky bass line drops in only briefly back to a bass line track. Around half-way through, the acoustic sound of the drum set predominates alongside a live-sounding string section which alters the sample-based sounding collage of the first half, leading to a more 'live' jazz soundscape.

This recording thus graduates from a nostalgic mix of old sampled records to something newly composed and performed, now mixed within a radically altered digital plus analogue 'hybrid' soundstage. Within this track, at 5.41, the aesthetic is fully transformed from a sampled collage to a live Latin jazz sequence with an improvised vibe solo, a live drum set, upright bass, and keyboards – the quintessential jazz rhythm section from the post-war period. This first theme is developed with a padded brass section. The samples used in the beginning of the track inspire an entire live jazz section based upon the concept, the sounds, and the aesthetics of the family-oriented soul-jazz fusion of the 1970s. The foundational theme of (Black Atlantic) love inspires and even fortifies this European artistic community by bringing into the present the poetic expressions attributed to the musical resilience of Black musical families often exploited by the dictates of segregated US cities where, despite such challenges, Black music flourished.

Sampling a Recorded History in PLOs (Producer-led Outfits)

Best, Leisering, and others have commented upon the highly personal role that jazz and hip hop recordings held for collectors and DJs during their formative years. For Leisering, Black music was always a culture that represented a certain profundity connected to groove, which for him superseded the more commercial aims of rock and pop in the 1990s (Stefan Leisering). However, the influence of new streams of hip hop, such as British trip hop, provided a more familiar and relevant aesthetic model for music experimentations and practices. Jazzanova bassist Paul Kleber (who has since performed and toured with Fink) also expresses his love of older music styles, especially the jazz, funk, soul, and blues of the 1950s to the 1970s, claiming:

> I am a real vintage retro guy. I love it. And also Stefan and all the guys. They are all into this old-school stuff and I love all kinds of jazz music from all the decades from the 50s to 60s and 70s and also the funk. Most of the music I listen to is from the 50s, 60s and 70s. Either it is jazz or

funk or soul and I love soul music and also now.… I am also obsessed
with the past. I still buy CDs sometimes but most of them are old ones.
(Paul Kleber, November 26, 2017)

Best similarly identified the retro obsession of crate diggers in 1990s Berlin.
Many of the early DJed events were informal gatherings for "like-minded
nerds" to commune, share recordings, and talk about newly found vintage vinyl
as well as new releases. Many conversations were preoccupied with sharing
discoveries of older genres of hip hop, soul, world music, and jazz. These early
gatherings afforded the display of one's passion for recordings of prior cultural
musical movements such as the Black American soul, jazz, disco, and R&B of
the preceding decades. But DJs also sought recordings from Latin America and
throughout Europe, in essence the groove-oriented recordings of prior decades
always provided a base for DJing, considering the dance roots of reggae, soul,
funk, and hip hop in general.

This *record archive to local café* process led producers to translate music mixes
from block parties or club nights into new musical works within the studio
context. Indeed, this process mirrored the earlier translation from the study of
recordings to the broadcast of big band jazz and swing on local radio[5] and eventually to recordings for jazz record labels; such trajectories form a foundation
for the translation of both artistic and aesthetic ideas from the live or communal
music environment to the recorded and broadcast jazz recording. Early live broadcasts via radio similarly translated dance-oriented music of local communities to
national radio audiences. Recordings of swing bands attempted to further translate recordings intended for dance culture to both radio broadcast but also for
more informal listening in domestic environments. Inevitably, this journey from
a 'live' or communal musical setting to a recording studio and to private listening sessions entailed a set of interactions within the music industry which were
socially and geographically grounded during the transition from an analogue to
a digital culture.

For Best and others within Jazzanova, the role of the recording is multifaceted;
it acts as the essential document of the music industry as well as the text which
stimulates intellectual discussion and evaluation. However, in the spaces of nightclubs and cafés, these records are reconfigured spontaneously and in response to
local communities with the primary goals of motivating enthusiasm for cultivated
listening and for dancing. For Jazzanova, this was accomplished when mixes combined contemporary beats and grooves with rare or unusual recordings. This ultimately motivated new music-making within the studio. Best compares the role of
vinyl recordings for jazz and electronic jazz history to the circulation of spoken
stories for oral histories. They form the evidence for a larger trajectory of cultural
influence, innovation, and transmission.

Within Jazzanova's hybrid sample-based live recordings, the album *In Between*
evidences a socially grounded conceptual work, where the poetics of love provide

the affective motif for the lead track, and where the combination of recordings reconfigures the social histories between families, cities, and genres into an entirely new historical moment within Berlin, a city symbolising late-twentieth-century reunification. Berlin naturally features as the centre of New Europe's new popular culture, and the emerging electronic dance music world (Rapp 2009). It was partly through the interactions of this collective, where notions of affect, camaraderie, and groove were intimately and socially mediated, eventually within the hybrid digital recording studio, where jazz records were studied, sampled, and reconfigured into something uniquely akin to the transitional culture of Berlin.

Archiving and Sampling as Musicking

In his chapter on the homosocial relations of record collecting, Will Straw reveals how collecting came to define certain forms of post-war male culture through the symbolic differentiation of forms of knowledge and power. Such bonding and discourse surrounding record-collecting facilitated the identification with particular forms of masculinity, such as the 'nerd' or 'hipster'. Record-collecting enabled forms of distinction and knowledge that simultaneously afforded a male-identified 'refuge' within the domestic space, while exerting exclusionary forms of bonding and knowledge-sharing, especially from the world of women and popular music, often situated in opposition to rock music and its perceived authenticity (Straw 1997).

As hip hop and DJ culture progressed, the more informal activities of digging in the crates and record-collecting led to the formalisation of networks for sharing knowledge about the recordings featured on DJ sets or mix tapes. The sampling of collections might be understood as a more performative extension of such masculine homosocial practices, where a recorded music collection is mediated for a group of similarly informed peers. This engendered an exclusionary discursive sphere (away from women) within which to assert cultural authority, and these discursive lines could then be redistributed within digital networks through the recognition of sampling practices within electronic jazz (and other sample-based musical genres) such as *Who Sampled*. Gavanas and Reitsamer uncovered the gendered nature of social, discursive, and training networks of DJ cultures in their study of DJing practices within Northern Europe in the 2000s (Gavanas and Reitsamer 2013). They discovered how culturally rehearsed conceptions of technology with masculinity, coupled with homosocial gendered networks within DJing networks, reinforced the gender divisions within these communities throughout Europe.

Within such gendered networks, *citation recognition* extended existing male collecting networks, which already during the 1930s were exclusively male-centred activities in Germany, such as the first Hot Clubs established in Berlin in 1934 (Zwerin 2000, 23). Eventually, the highly learned approach towards jazz recordings led to mediated discussions about the use of particular recordings within commercial sample-based digital platforms. Indeed, the process of record discovery, collecting, sampling, and re-identification resembles the pleasures of archaeological pursuits established within post-war male record-collecting culture, where record collectors hunt for rare or forgotten gems within the city (Straw 1991). For example, within the well-visited site *Who Sampled*, the shared contributions of DJs, producers, and avid record collections increase this site's archive of citations; their extensive knowledge of recordings allows them to contribute their insider knowledge to a collectively written recorded music history. Indeed, these data-mining sites naturally grew from the ecosystem of interactive digital landscapes where remixing was a creative outcome of this logic. Naturally, it is often the DJs and remixers themselves who quickly identify which material is sampled in new works. Such sites confirm Jenkins's proclamations about the value of participatory culture within digital networks (Jenkins 2006). Such participatory cultures appear continually bound by culturally rehearsed and particularly gendered forms of musical sociality and activities, reinforcing the technological associations and gendered expectations for recording music cultures. As Georgia Born discovered in her study of links between music technology and traditional music education programmes instituted in the 1990s and early 2000s, such cultural stigmas and gendered models are sometimes exacerbated within (neoliberal) pedagogical contexts seeking to promote progressive technological creative models (Born and Devine 2015). Recalling the logics of gender binaries within science paradigms, Born and Devine argued:

> The very epistemology of 'sound' that underpins the cultural origins of sound reproduction and manipulation – including today's digital music technologies – emerged from a historical conjuncture governed by a hegemonic rationalist masculinity locked in dualistic relation with its subordinate feminine Other.

In this dynamic, the neoliberal push towards innovation and entrepreneurship within technological domains only further promoted an existing bifurcation connecting masculinity to such traits and potentially yet unintentionally excluding young women from these emerging networks.

In discerning how recordings are sampled, listeners contribute to this gendered technological ecosystem, their continued involvement buttressing the basis of citation recognition as an important facet of sampling. One could connect this to the earlier record-collecting discourse in Europe, where knowledge of particular recordings, studios, and players enhanced the prestige of particular collectors, such as collectors turned producers Dr Jazz (Dietrich Schulz-Koehn) and Charles Delaunay, and later Brian Rust, who mapped out genealogies of recorded jazz musicians via their investigations of these musicians' participation within earlier jazz movements (Zwerin 2000, 35; Jackson 2003; Jordan 2010; Rust 1961). As DJs hear out the samples of these recordings, they continue this progression and similarly acquire cultural capital for their investigations. Furthermore, these iconic jazz influences are mapped onto genre and family trees of other recordings dating further back into recorded history. When listening to the original recordings listed on *Who Sampled*, participants deconstruct the mixes and share the listening and historical learning process of these producers. Such a process enables listeners to trace the sonic histories and fantasise about the lives of touring musicians, of race relations, and of the political potential of music in an earlier moment of exploration.

To some extent, the popularity of sites like *Who Sampled* confirm the archival/archaeological impulse underlying the pleasure of hearing electronic jazz remixes. Indeed, remixes remain unfinished products, always available for new iterations, and they stimulate new listening cycles always ready for recombination or reinterpretation. Sonic histories found in sample-based recordings therefore allow us to borrow inspiration from the past in order to proceed from the present.

Indeed, producers and DJs often respond to jazz-purist critics by claiming that their ways of interpreting, citing, and reconfiguring jazz recordings resuscitate earlier genres. They also claim that their remixes help revitalise forgotten gems of jazz history, and of cultural history in general. As Gunkel argues:

> As with writing, the inherent redundancy of remix can be validated as a kind of archival effort to preserve the memory of something that could be lost to the dust-bins of history by reanimating one's appreciation for the original and even creating new markets for source material and the artists who created it.
>
> *(Gunkel 2015, 50)*

While many reviewers appreciate the recombinatory logics of Jazzanova's remixes, others dismiss their artistic process as repetitive and unoriginal. However, such dismissals fail to recognise how sample-based recordings update a particular recorded music aesthetic or engage with culturally specific socio-cultural histories of German record-collecting communities. For example, in 2002, upon the release of *In Between*, Harold Petters of the Berlin newspaper *Die Tageszeitung* wrote:

> But how is now that these sounds are not so easy to determine. Certainly, there is that touch of jazz, which underlines the manicured charm of the album. There is this note of Hip Hop, decidedly mixed into the foreground beats. Thanks to some vocals of course there are still traces of recognisable Soul. Who seeks shall find snippets of bossa nova and Afro-funk, a little bebop rudiments, and, who knows, maybe even the last remnants of house. The main investigators will not emerge uninfected from their search for clues and references within 'In Between' which, however, point to nothing more than the album itself. Did they even have a meaning … Jazzanova thoroughly strips them [the record sample] to incorporate them into their universal club lounge sound that

[the record] no longer knows any regional conditions and codes; not
Berlin, where the sound ultimately arises, no Rio, New York, Tokyo, no
jazz club and no club. The rootlessness of the sound fits the certain face-
lessness of its authors: 'In Between' is known only by record collections
and archives, which are so extensive and large that they have nothing
more to say.

(Petters 2002)

Part of Petters' critique rings true as he reinforces the weight and significance of
the record archive for sample-based artists, but, by claiming a lack of profundity
to this recombining potential, he misinterprets the value of the broader processes
foregrounded by and culminating in such recordings. Here Petters' conservative
vantage point treats recordings as complete objects to be judged against a canon
of recorded albums as cohesive art works. This conception misunderstands the
ongoing and interactive circulation as well as the processual logics of sample-
based recordings and their connection to human bodies within electronic jazz.

In one regard, electronic jazz is driven by vinyl collectors seeking to combine
their accumulated knowledge in artful new ways. In doing so, they contribute to
the other social and aesthetic activities that constitute the 'musicking' activities
around records (Small 1998). Such activities occur in an era where vinyl recordings no longer occupy the primary medium for the music industry. Here, DJs
are less musicians or composers than curators who facilitate the elevation of prior
recordings into our participatory present. Furthermore, by transforming material
from recordings from our cultural past as source material for new compositions
within our present, sampling has fundamentally altered the way that we view the
notion of a composition, of an author, of a song, and of a recording as the object
which solidifies such unstable concepts solidified within modernity. As hauntolo-
gist Mark Fisher argues, "it is difficult to disentangle sampling from song writing,
impossible to draw firm lines between a cover version and an original song. Songs
are texturally dense palimpsests, accreted rather than authored" (Fisher 2013, 53).
In this sense, sampling and the remix force us to interrogate the assumptions
attributed to much of Enlightenment thought with regards authorship, composition, and cultural community in relation to larger structures of power and financial accumulation.

What Petters also fails to distinguish is the recognition of the connections and
meanings of these samples for both the DJs and producers, who combined them
as well as for those coming of age within Berlin during the 1990s, for whom
music-making was precisely about expanding the archive in a place where access
to international music cultures was sometimes difficult to acquire. Locating new
records, sharing them, evaluating them, and reworking them for new communities
within a profoundly transforming city were intensely social activities. By making connections to both modern and innovative sampling practices within the
UK, and by connecting these back to a mythically compelling community-oriented

Black music period, Jazzanova's music is metaphorical, musically, temporally, and geographically 'in between'. By combining the past with the present, their art builds community locally through a cosmopolitan but historically enriched attachment to Black music.

What Petters and other critics do understand is the role of the record archive for this process. Considering the insiders' knowledge shared by crate diggers within these informal sharing and playing spaces, it is not surprising that a digital sharing platform with similar aims and motivations would emerge to provide a space to discuss sample-based recordings and their recorded progeny. Like the physical gathering spaces of Delicious Donuts of the 1990s, the online platform *Who Sampled* provided a social platform for online camaraderie, where record archivists could share their insiders' knowledge about which recordings appeared on various sample-based recordings since the 1980s.

Of All the Things (2008, Second Production-based Album)

In 2008, the same year that *Who Sampled* was launched by Nadav Poraz, Jazzanova was taking a new approach in terms of record production, where the sound of discernible records was less crucial. Ultimately, the first wave of digital sample-based recordings had peaked, and some electronic jazz producers were looking to reinstate a more live-oriented music aesthetic, especially one connected to the live Black music genres of soul and funk, where the human voice is prioritised over the recorded instrumental sample. Jazzanova follows this revival in that this album features several male vocalists and recalls the live music aesthetics of 1960s-oriented soul and jazz fusion.

In the late 2000s, a number of popular recordings in the UK and continental Europe reproduced a sound that was decidedly connected to the vocal genres of soul and R&B. Duffy, Amy Winehouse, Maxwell, and others in the US were riding the live music and soul revival, partly responding to the over-saturation within the music industry of sample-based projects. Prior to this, Jazzanova contributed to the 'retromania' (Reynolds 2011) surrounding nostalgic soul singers mostly based in the US, including recording projects with Phonte Coleman, Paul Randolph (an American living in Berlin), and José James (from New York). Their soul-inspired album *Of All the Things* combines artists looking back to soul and jazz, and working forward within hip hop and production-based musical collages for a contemporary sound. This recording makes an explicit cosmopolitan connection to similar progressive electronic jazz scenes throughout the world, especially the UK, Brazil, and the US. It also affirms the last stage presented within DJ Chris Read's 'History of Sampling',[6] where the archive of recognisable sample-based albums has been uncovered to revive some of the community-based genres from earlier decades and especially jazz, funk, and soul.

Best remarked upon Jazzanova's transition from all sample-based material in the 1990s and early 2000s to works created, performed, and recorded in the studio with combinations of samples and acoustic instrumentations, and a greater number of original compositions featuring newly recorded vocals. This might be the third stage of this collective's musical development, where sampling is no longer the revolutionary sound of a late-capitalist remix aesthetic, but rather an established technological tool for the creation of new timbres, textures, riffs, and rhythmic loops for the soundscape of new compositions in the hybrid studio.

What remains constant in this development is the exploration of the aesthetics of Black music, which have reverted back to acoustic instrumentations and vocals saturated with the textures and phrasing of 1960s and 1970s-era soul and jazz. This producer-oriented stage has led to the compilation of an international network of artists and producers, many of whom have now returned to the 'live music' aesthetics of pre-digital genres. Interestingly, each of these musicians shared a commitment to long-term engagement and study of the recorded archive of soul, jazz, fusion, and now hip hop produced by community-oriented Black music artists.

Acoustic Orchestra Samples Sample-based Jazz – The Sonar Kollectiv Orchester

Aligning with the revitalisation of the acoustic sounds of jazz and soul alongside the incorporation of pre-digital-era vocal styles, Jazzanova, in 2007, formed the Sonar Kollectiv Orchester (SKO), a fifteen-piece ensemble of European musicians led by Volker Meitz, working closely with Jazzanova to materialise their studio recordings for live music concerts and tours. The orchestra features five vocalists, highly unorthodox for a jazz-style orchestra.

SKO's repertoire is depicted by the label as:

> a cross selection of tunes from the SK label back catalogue, the original styles of which cover a wide range from deep house and broken beats to reggae and experimental hip hop. The new arrangements for a 15-piece band, including many acoustic instruments, put the tunes into an orchestral context and provide a brand-new listening experience.[7]

By reversing the process of musical creation from the music collection to the hybrid recording studio, and then to the record label, the 'back catalogue' of sample-based recordings forms the source material to be mined for yet another sequence of musical adaptation, versioning, and presentation. Sonar Kollektiv's bassist Paul Kleber characterised this process of transcribing sample-based compositions:

> With Jazzanova you have two or three guys on stage. So, it is a big group on stage and we are nine people and it is like a whole live band with two guys with Stefan who plays percussion which is very nice and Axel is doing all the sample stuff and for their music it kind of makes sense

because they produce it like that and to show it live on stage makes sense. But first we see what we have, such as which instruments we have on stage played by musicians and what is missing from the recording. [We examine] the stuff which is important for the song with details like background vocals or some strings or something like that. The basis is the recording and then we see what we can add live. And we work on it and decide later who is playing which part and who is taking over the other one.

(Paul Kleber, November 26, 2017)

One interesting outcome of this process is the way in which especially Jazzanova's sample-based material, exploiting frequent groove, timbral, and tempo changes, is recreated in an orchestral setting – obviously a significant challenge. Extending the citation chain of influence even further, the Sonar Kollectiv released a cover version album in 2007 to commemorate Jazzanova's decennial. *Guaranteed Niceness* (2007 Sonar Kollectiv) featured cover versions of Jazzanova's sample-based recordings such as 'Fedime's Flight' (12-inch EP), and from *In Between* (2002), they recorded versions of numerous songs. SKO hadn't only looked to Jazzanova remixes of sample-based jazz, but also to other remixes of Jazzanova's material. According to the label, SKO's version of 'Boom Clicky Boom Klack' (SK094), was a "perfect blend of both the MR. SCRUFF remix flavour and the original JAZZANOVA arrangement".[8] They described the overall sound of the album as exuding "a genuine lounge feel with a tight horns section, lush strings, fender Rhodes and true-soul vocals".[9]

The newly arranged orchestral version of 'L.O.V.E. and You & I' is a purely instrumental track, opening with strings. These replace the vocal sequence, and are followed in the arrangement by tenor saxophone and flute, an orchestration combination which immediately suggests the 1950s Hollywood film studio orchestras, themselves invested in sampling exotic musical cultures. Meitz adapts the four-bar phrasing drops into percussive breaks before a more flowing bossa nova inspired 'cocktail-hour' rhythm section is introduced. Within this live-sounding jazz section, short motifs are traded between the string sections, keyboard, and reeds and brass. Throughout the second half, many of the breaks and drops are replicated by pauses or dynamic dips. Ultimately, the vocal excerpts from the music recordings of prominent Black community music scenes within the US are here abstracted into the trace of these communities, filtered through polished strings, reeds, and brass. The haunting of the past impregnates the timbres of acoustic instrumentals in this mixed-genre format.

Conclusion

DJ Spooky's conceptualisation of remixes as "dematerialized art objects", or "social constructions of memory" (Miller 2008, 51–53) aptly characterises the artistic processes of Jazzanova. Within their recorded oeuvre, the histories and memories of sampled subjects motivate new works, yet this process of reconfiguration also dematerialises vinyl recordings from their original context. By juxtaposing manipulated samples from the recording archive alongside newly recorded instrumentals, the producers reconfigure a range of sonic material, and in doing so, historical sounds merge with newly performed musical passages – bridging the recent past to the present. Finally, by creating unusual drum parts sequenced with great care to resemble the inconsistencies and dynamic textures of recorded 'live' drums, Jazzanova alters the aim of beat-making, drawing intimately from the signature sounds of live jazz, funk, or African (American) drumming.

Such dedicated study of the Black music archive has cultural and aesthetic implications for the contemporary hybrid studios of electronic jazz outfits working in new contexts of space and time, even as modern hybrid studios appear further removed from the social communities of these recorded musics' origins. However, music's potential to travel across spatial boundaries lends credence to the archival pursuit, as making music is always an unfinished project in the development of the human imagination. The DJs and producers of Jazzanova have brought forth the sounds of the Black past into their own transformative moment, forcing us to reconsider our own place in music history. When we study the recording archive, it encourages us to go deeper than extrapolating what we need for a clever beat or instant nod of recognition in the proverbial stomp treatment. Furthermore, in discursively evaluating and sharing the recorded output of Berlin's jazz-oriented PLO, we too can gain a more intimate knowledge of how music continues to enact symbolically both modes of exclusion and instances of community and resilience in the spaces that remain metaphorically and artistically, *in between.*

Notes

1   Within DJ circles, Attias highlights how these anxieties could paradoxically be reproduced as new technologies emerged which threw into question the skill and cultural capital attached to particular turntable skills such as beat-matching or mixing and fading, especially as new computer models more easily adapted to live music environments in the twenty-first century. Some examples are the beat-matching debates of the 2010s or the labelling of certain styles of DJs as 'controllerists' in recent years, as a younger generation of DJs incorporated computer equipment and programs such as Ableton or FruityLoops to sample and sequence sounds instead of mixing vinyl recordings in a social dance environment.

2   This song is often referred to as the first civil rights song, and it is one that explicitly referenced the racial violence in the South (the murder of Medgar Evers in Mississippi).

3   Other important presenters and curators of electronic or mixed-genre jazz are Jason Bentlye of KCRW in LA and Garth Trinidad in the US. Some of the important electronic jazz collectives outside of Berlin include the Twee Alkino and Prosanit scene in Japan, the 4hero electronic music collective in London, and the mixed-genre jazz scene surrounding curator, producer, and musician King Brit in Philadelphia (Daniel Best).

4   See "Jazzanova L.O.V.E. and You & I" on *Who Samples* (accessed July 10, 2018) www.whosampled.com/sample/50953/Jazzanova-L.O.V.E.-And-You-%26-I-Catalyst-Uzuri/.
5   Such translations from live music to broadcast media was already a feature of intellectual jazz inculcation during the 1930s such as within Seiber's *Jazzklasse* radio broadcasts beginning in 1929 in Berlin (Wipplinger 2017, 161–162).
6   *A History of Sampling w/ Chris Read (WhoSampled) at Point Blank London*. 2017. Point Blank Music School. www.youtube.com/watch?v=SZGobMX9I48&t=369s.
7   See the description of the album *Guaranteed Niceness* on the website of the label *Sonar Kollektiv*, accessed July 10, 2018, www.sonarkollektiv.com/sonar-kollektiv-orchester-guaranteed-niceness/.
8   Ibid.
9   Ibid.

4

OSLO'S JAZZLAND RECORDINGS

Finding Home in a *New Conception of Jazz*

In the early millennium years, Scandinavia had acquired a reputation as a jazz 'hot spot' across Europe.... In addition to Jan Garbarek, Jon Christensen, Palle Danielsson, Arild Andersen, Bobo Stenson, Terje Rypdal, Lennart Abert, and Per Henrik Wallin, who had established themselves on the European circuit, an exciting generation of young Scandinavian musicians were emerging who were beginning to make a reputation for themselves across Europe, each in their own way reflecting a distinct Nordic tonality in their music. Musicians such as Nils Petter Molvær and Bugge Wesseltoft enjoyed best-selling albums mixing jazz and rhythms from club culture and considerable success on the European jazz circuit.

(Stuart Nicholson 2005, 212–213)

NCOJ [New Conception of Jazz] isn't about any single musical concept; it's about the constant cross-pollination and integration of diverse musical influences, and the integration of acoustic instruments with increasingly sophisticated technology.

(John Kelman, All About Jazz, *2009)*

Throughout 2017 and 2018, I travelled to Oslo to meet musicians from the esteemed record label, Jazzland Recordings. During this period, next to my exploration of Oslo's transformative jazz labels, I witnessed massive building projects; between the giant Akershus Fortress and city hall, the noise of drilling and hammering perpetually echoed off newly constructed buildings. These mechanical rhythms alerted me to this city's current regeneration. Oslo's most extensive initiative, the Fjord City Project, aims to revive its waterfront district, part of which involved erecting the Oslo Opera House at the tip of the Bjørvika peninsula. Other projects included more modest cultural buildings such as the renovated Bårdar dance studio and the lane of high-rise buildings now occupying the Aker

Brygge area. These buildings provide housing and office space but also connect tourist routes and cultural spaces visited by travellers. They also symbolise neo-liberal capital and networks in Europe's post-industrial cities. Such projects brand the image of Oslo as a world centre of culture, capital, and advanced technologies.

The Fjord City Project originally considered plans for a new jazz centre, but this project was increasingly seen as too ambitious when combined with the estimated costs for the new opera house (Jan Ole Otnaes, Interview with the author, November 3, 2017). Thus, a more intimate and pre-existing space was chosen – the Victoria theatre near Karl Johans Gate, now aptly named the Nasjonal Jazzscene.

In November 2017, I spent an evening at the Nasjonal Jazzscene for a high-calibre concert of university jazz students. Before this concert, I'd attended the *Bårdar Danseinstitut* housed in the harbour area, on a newly refurbished block. The origins of this dance school date from before the Second World War, when jazz first appeared in Oslo, inspiring fanatical dance competitions. During the Second World War, the dancers and its jazz culture were forced underground. Apparently, Oslo had been a jazz city longer than some in Northern Europe. Since then, such grassroots, enthusiast-led activities were gradually incorporated into both national 'master plans' and urban rejuvenation projects, where cultural activities like jam sessions and jazz dancing shared spaces with highly prized international architectural projects.

After my jazz night out, I travelled back to my Airbnb accommodation in the Grünerløkka neighbourhood on a tram overflowing with people of various ages. The following day, I wandered past the Akerhus Fortress, beyond which I witnessed the massive cruise ships anchored at the temporary new docks. These ships were an impressive reminder of the scale and prestige of the contemporary Scandinavian tourist industry.

In this chapter, I explore Oslo as a reputed 'new' European jazz city, one which experienced the transformation from a socially organised Norwegian capital invested in supporting local cultural articulations of the nation, to a prosperous, cosmopolitan, global jazz city, boasting a highly mediated, technologically adventurous electronic jazz community. Within New Europe, Oslo's independent jazz record labels played a critical role in symbolically and aesthetically mediating this transformation through a discursive engagement with the ideologies supporting the Nordic tone, in part by modernising and embracing contemporary techniques. Through my case study, namely Jazzland Recordings, I reveal how Norway's jazz reputation and connection to the Nordic tone helped to spur the transformation of Oslo's surrounding post-industrial neighbourhoods through urban regeneration. Oslo's peripheral neighbourhoods afforded the sites for staging this transformation, forged through an increasingly transnational connection to cosmopolitan European electronic jazz and dance cultures. In particular, I highlight the Oslo-based electronic and polygeneric jazz community connected to post-Nordic tone musician and producer Bugge Wesseltoft and his Jazzland

Recordings, first established in 1996. I argue that two of this label's most success-ful and experienced musicians/projects, Wesseltoft and Beady Belle, necessarily contended with the established reputation of prior Nordic tone musicians, while simultaneously engaging with international currents in popular musical culture. Furthermore, these musicians adapted to the widespread changes in infrastructure of the music industry while also responding to and even precipitating local forms of urban regeneration.

Jazzland's international recording artists have collaborated with many ECM artists through intergenerational projects in the late twentieth century. Such familiarity with the musical practices and recordings of Nordic tone artists, as well as with the international reputation of Norwegian jazz within Europe and abroad, led to a reconsideration of local jazz and its role within contemporary Norway, in a moment of rapid transformation in terms of urban development alongside the growing influence of international capital and people as well as aesthetic and musical trends. Finally, by focusing upon these two artists as products of this highly revered label, as well as by connecting them to the unique late-capitalist envi-ronment of regeneration in Grünerløkka, I argue that the local connections of these jazz musicians to the performance spaces, musician networks, and aesthetic processes remain simultaneously driven by the pollination of jazz from continen-tal European electronic and popular music movements during the 2000s. I focus upon several recordings which emerge from this environment, each uniquely seeking to form a 'new conception of jazz' by rejecting the rules of jazz purism, but also breaking away from the label and associations of Nordic tone.

The chapter first traces developments within Oslo since the 1980s, which led to an environment of cultural and musical regeneration, especially through the processes of repurposing industrial spaces and remixing music styles. This period facilitated the transformation of Oslo from an industrial centre of trade and mobil-ity to a city primarily designed for living and working, with easier access to spaces of culture, entertainment, and tourism. The introduction includes a brief overview of the urban transformation embedded within long-term regeneration projects such as the Barcode Project and the Fjord City Project. It links these develop-ments to the high-quality jazz club the Nasjonal Jazzscene within Oslo's centre, and proceeds with an overview of the ecosystem which facilitated the organic experimentation and performance of electronic and polygeneric jazz within the surrounding neighbourhood of Grünerløkka in the early 2000s. Finally, I provide an analysis of the role of Jazzland Recordings for the musical output of two core musicians of this label, keyboardist and producer Bugge Wesseltoft and vocal artist and composer Beady Belle.

Nordic Tone Affiliations

In his provocative *Is Jazz Dead?: Or Has it Moved to a New Address*, Stuart Nich-olson argued that Scandinavia's widespread and committed institutional support of jazz helped create Europe's most innovative contemporary jazz scenes. By 2000, the international prestige of Scandinavian culture was often reflected by its acclaimed jazz networks. To illustrate, in 2004, Norwegian and Swedish jazz was described by the Edinburgh Jazz and Blues Festival as "One of the most exciting jazz scenes in the world today" (Nicholson 2005, 199).

Outside institutional support, the international acclaim of particular artists was also enhanced by key collaborations with American jazz musicians. Like European artists elsewhere, Norwegian musicians gained status from collaborations with cosmopolitan American stars. The most revered, saxophonist Jan Garbarek, first attracted critical appraisal for his melodic soloing style after recording with George Russell in 1967. Additionally, Don Cherry's contributions to George Russell's Norwegian band in 1967 Stockholm's *Gyllene Cirkeln* (Golden Circle) are frequently cited as foundational interactions, which during the 1970s coalesced around a perceived regionally bound aesthetic of jazz performance known simply as the 'Nordic tone'. Keith Jarrett's 1974 Belonging quartet featuring Garbarek on tenor is regularly cited as the pivotal exchange, birthing a compelling musical ideal – one considered distinct from the urban American aesthetic (Nicholson 2005, 207). These interactions are positioned by jazz writers as important precursors to the ascendance of an 'authentic' European jazz culture (Nicholson 2005, 206; Lewis 2009, 247). Dave Liebman even claimed that the Belonging quartet and the Nordic musician's fluid and melodic approach "had a major influence on the jazz scene worldwide as far as setting the tone of a style" (Liebman n.d.).

Despite this, few scholars have investigated the period that followed the progenitors of the Nordic tone (Holt 2016; Mäkelä 2014; Ward 2011), although most agree that Scandinavian jazz entered the international consciousness of the 1970s through a process of intensified cultural contact. Finally, in more recent studies of international and European jazz (Bohlman and Plastino 2016; Martinelli 2018), the cross-pollination of local and international live music aesthetics and influences are examined. Nicholson would depict this set of relations by incorporating Roland Robertson's (1995) theoretical frame of glocalisation, the cultural transformations stimulated through processes of global (universalising) and local (particularising) contact and performative reflexivity. For him, it was especially Garbarek's association with the Munich-based ECM label which brought the Nordic tone to a worldwide audience (Nicholson 2005, 207). ECM's founder Manfred Eicher also forwarded this ideal when he positioned Scandinavia's natural landscape and Norway's relative isolation as indirectly reflected in certain forms of jazz. Later, jazz scholar David Ake depicted the inception of the ECM label in the late 1960s as connected not to European movements but to the counterculture of the US. His examples drew from the corresponding American pastoral ideal as reflected in Keith Jarrett's ECM recordings but then extended to include an idea of 'open spaces':

> Concomitant with this ruralist turn in the arts, politics, and society the erstwhile bassist Manfred Eicher formed ECM Records. From its very

first release in 1969, ECM established a reputation as home to a serious and introspective brand of jazz ... artists explored styles reminiscent of or rooted in the folk music of their own native lands, the 'open-spaces' quality of their compositions and performances feeling even more capacious thanks to Eicher's predilection for a reverb-drenched sound.

(Ake 2010, 84)

Jazz historian George Lewis would declare the ECM sound and related commercial and international success as an indication of European jazz's "declaration of independence from hegemony" (Lewis 2009, 247).

By the 1980s, while Scandinavian musicians enjoyed their newly acquired accolades, a younger generation were admonishing the neo-conservative revival of older American styles. Finish percussionist and composer Edward Vesala commented in his 1989 album notes to *Ode to the Death of Jazz*:

This music is first of all about feeling and the transmission of feeling.... This empty echoing of old styles – I think it's tragic. If that is what the jazz tradition has become then what about the tradition of creativity, innovation, individuality, and personality?

After the success of ECM and subsequent Scandinavian progressive jazz movements, Norwegian keyboardist, producer, and Jazzland label owner Bugge Wesseltoft would later adopt this critique of a stagnating American jazz culture, claiming that it was in Europe where a "new conception of jazz" was unleashed (Nicholson 2005, 149).

Such criticism motivated a re-imagining of local forms of cultural heritage in a project not entirely indistinguishable from the nationalist musical adaptations of folk music in the late nineteenth century. Scandinavian jazz artists also sought to redefine their culture in relation to the jazz values of interpretation and improvisation through a corpus of culturally significant songs. During the 1980s, Arild Andersen's group Masqualero[1] (named after Miles Davis' *Sorcerer* LP) experimented with Norwegian folk tunes. An important progenitor of this folk music revival in jazz came from Norwegian vocalist Sidsel Endressen. After collaborating with Endressen and Andersen, electronic jazz trumpeter Nils Petter Molvær later recalled: "It was more like instead of playing blues we played Norwegian folk music ... playing around with it is what we did!" (Malvær, cited in Nicholson 2005, 211). Here the revision of conventional jazz practice, interpreting an established and recognisable jazz tune to promote one's unique style, is positioned in terms of adapting and interpreting local culture, especially folk culture with its romanticised connections to an authentic pastoral heritage.

Fabian Holt (2016) investigated the concept of the Nordic tone in his research on Scandinavian jazz, arguing that jazz's inclusion within expanding notions of cultural heritage inculcated new forms of belonging. For this affective jazz ontology, Holt suggested the concept of 'home', arguing that Scandinavian musicians sought to incorporate local sound repertoires into the cultural and existential realm of jazz exploration, in order to situate a sense of belonging within modern Scandinavian culture. While local jazz was increasingly understood as culturally authentic, the incorporation of a national jazz sound precipitated a perceived sense of shared values and cultural community. Holt underlines the founding tenants of the social welfare state for forwarding the values of national unity, consensus, and social equality. These values connected Denmark, Sweden, and Norway in their commitment to jazz in the post-war period, where a modern yet equanimous European landscape was positioned against the individuality, instability, and dominance of the growing American media industry (Holt 2016, 55).

While the Nordic tone image was in part predicated upon the practice of adapting local folk songs, by the mid-1990s, the next generation of Norwegian jazz artists sought to move beyond these ethnic jazz or 'glocal' fusions. A coterie of younger musicians, raised on an eclectic and faster-paced diet of pop music and electronica, looked further afield for their rejuvenation of home-brewed jazz; musicians like keyboardist and sound artist Wesseltoft and Beate Lech (later taking her stage name Beady Belle) adapted the timbres and textures of highly urban and cosmopolitan popular music styles. These combinations satisfied their desire to connect to expressly cosmopolitan streams of jazz. Having performed within the cross-cultural collaborations of Garbarek and Andersen, musicians including Wesseltoft and Malvær eagerly embraced popular musics while implementing new technical developments. By 2000, however, the Nordic tone had gathered cultural cachet, and was now broadly used to depict a variety of innovative Scandinavian musicians experimenting across genres in an expressive tone. Indeed, many of the younger generation of Norwegian jazz artists were reaching across the North Sea, connecting with their urban, rhythmic, and groovy electronic jazz peers, adapting more transnational and hardwire-driven techniques such as sampling and digital sound manipulation.

Oslo's Urban Renewal and Cultural Transformation

During the 1960s and 1970s, Oslo experienced significant renovation and rebuilding, in part because of Norway's prosperous natural gas and oil industry. After 1945, the period of urbanisation, carefully staged with urban planning integrated into the social fabric of expanding cities, offered initiatives such as the Building Act and the implementation of so-called 'master plans'. These plans ensured the full integration of social, economic, and urban growth. The government's integrated approach was supported by Norway's political system and welfare state.

Through the 1980s, Oslo undertook the massive construction of roads and tunnels connecting the harbour to the city centre. The waterfront, meanwhile, was designated as the centre of the industrial activities of its shipping, trading, fishing, and gas industries. Until the 1990s, transportation and port traffic dominated new infrastructure in and around Oslo, but in the twenty-first century, many of the harbours and prior industrial areas were reclaimed for culture, living, and work spaces in large-scale projects, such as the Barcode and the Fjord City Project. These were aimed at increasing the prestige, cosmopolitanism, and cultural appeal of Oslo. Naturally, some of these spaces were designated as sites for music (especially classical music, such as the extravagant and costly new opera house).

Barcode Project, the National Opera House and the Nasjonal Jazzscene

In the twenty-first century, a massive influx of capital facilitated building projects such as the Barcode Project, whose design reflected the international interest in the development of European cities. The project consisted of five high-rise buildings in the Bjørvika neighbourhood, an area which begins as an inlet of the Oslofjord situated between Gamlebyen and the Akershus Fortress. One especially important cultural institution is situated here: the new National Opera House, which opened in 2008 and cost over three billion kroner. Its impressive size and style lent itself for non-opera events such as outdoor cinema and urban games. In the same project, the city government approved the renovation of the new Oslo Public Library and the existing Munch Museum.

During the planning for the opera centre, bids were also made to build a new jazz centre, but the city instead chose to refurbish a local theatre, The Victoria, which was renovated into the Nasjonal Jazzscene, a respected jazz club run by prominent promoter and long-time Molde Jazz Festival director, Jan Ole Otnæs. Since the 1960s, Otnæs had worked in various jazz clubs and later as board member of the Norwegian Jazz Federation. In 1991, the Norwegian Jazz Federation was awarded three million kroner to connect a network of ten jazz clubs to cultivate such a scene. Despite this funding, the project required significant volunteer work, which was inconsistent. The large number of clubs throughout Norway was reduced to a smaller number in fewer cities. In the early 2000s, they narrowed their energies to four clubs, which succeeded until 2005, but this network also struggled financially. Finally, in 2006, they chose to focus upon the Oslo-based jazz club, Cosmopolite, a culturally significant theatre building with two attractive music rooms for local and international artists. While Cosmopolite was successful because of its innovative promotion of world music and contemporary jazz, in 2008, the venue was sold. The club moved outside of the centre into an old theatre in Torshov, north of the bohemian Grünerløkka neighbourhood. The artistic director, Miloud Guiderk, still programs predominantly jazz, world music, and mixed-genre projects and the musical offerings remain highly respected by the national jazz community.

With Otnæs' experience of programming and organising jazz events throughout Norway, by 2008, he committed all his efforts towards one prominent high-quality jazz club, the Nasjonal Jazzscene. This venue was built as a cinema in 1915 and was converted to a cabaret club in 1982. In 2008, Otnæs transformed it into a medium-sized jazz club in the heart of Oslo.

Nasjonal Jazzscene

Today a highly respected venue, the club programs predominantly Norwegian jazz, but also features international artists. The club is connected to others through the Europe Jazz Network. Otnæs promotes the club's role in both cultivating young Norwegian jazz talent and exposing Norwegian audiences and artists to international jazz; each year, he organises fifty concerts reserved for jazz students of the Conservatory of Oslo. This initiative successfully attracts younger audiences, while also cultivating a professional network between younger and older musicians. The club is the most successful in Oslo, able to program jazz four nights a week throughout most of the year.

While the new Opera House and Jazzscene both represent Norway's high culture, other spaces for jazz and popular music emerged amidst the more fragmented, post-industrial spaces within contiguous neighbourhoods such as Grünerløkka and Torshov, two working-class areas associated with industrialisation.

Since the 1990s, urban art forms – especially jazz – inevitably reflected aesthetic, philosophical, and physical connections to the cultural and (post)-industrial spaces of Oslo's centre and transforming neighbourhoods. While high art forms such as opera and classical music remained centrally situated in Oslo's most prestigious arts venues, electronic and polygeneric jazz inhabited the rather more peripheral areas.

Grünerløkka – Home of Electronic Jazz

Northeast of the centre lies Grünerløkka, formerly a working-class neighbourhood, which in the 1990s transitioned into a creative community of employees, professionals, and artists. It also offered an attractive milieu for jazz artists and electronic jazz projects, and benefited in particular from the existing industrial infrastructure, including disused factories and buildings which were transformed into cultural, artistic, and leisure spaces. However, contrasting with those top–down international building projects of the city centre, these spaces experienced a gradual transformation, driven by fragmented and grassroots forces.

Grünerløkka runs along the picturesque Akerselva river, winding south towards the city centre. It flows southwards, disappearing under the Barcode Project, surfacing just past the new opera house to flow out into the Oslo Fjord. The area was once home to textile manufacturing and factories for minerals such as the

Vulkan Iron Foundry. In recent decades, rather than demolishing these factories, locals sought to repurpose such culturally significant buildings for artistic and commercial endeavours.

Blå

In the heart of the Vulcan area alongside the west of the Alkerselva river is the Blå (Blue) Music Hall and Café, alongside other theatres, cafés, boutiques, and art studios within the bohemian environs of Grünerløkka. Blå is also the most important space for mixed-genre and electronic jazz. This café frequently showcased Jazzland recording artists during the 1990s and 2000s. Like other Grünerløkka structures, this building was once a (gold and diamond) storage and processing factory.[2] Especially in the 1990s, Blå gained a reputation for featuring progressive and mixed-genre jazz alongside other popular music styles. Because of the building's ideal location next to the river, during the summer months it features open markets and food carts enjoyed by visitors strolling along the waterfront. The combination of outdoor sculpture, the bohemian décor of local cafés, second-hand stores, and restaurants, as well as the emphasis on progressive jazz and world music at this club, meant that innovative, mixed-genre jazz became an important soundtrack for the revitalisation of Oslo's once working-class neighbourhoods. It looked back to its past and forward to the needs of growing cities with diverse cultural populations and environmental and infrastructural challenges. Since 2000, this neighbourhood also opened itself up to international capital, private investment, and moderate gentrification.

Because of spaces like Blå, some of the city's most progressive jazz artists sought to contribute to this scene. The jazz projects connected to this place helped forge the 'new conception of jazz', a name and aesthetic objective

FIGURE 4.1 Blå Music Hall and Café
Source: Photograph by Christian Brun.

attributed to pianist, producer, and label owner Bugge Wesseltoft. Wesseltoft has been actively performing and recording in various clubs in Oslo since the 1990s. His Jazzland Recordings evolved into a trans-locally relevant musicians' network, cultivating progressive and mixed-genre jazz collaborations and promoting an aesthetic emerging from the cultural mixing visible in this neighbourhood. Wesseltoft and those Jazzland artists that frequently played at Blå lend credence to both forward-looking and remixing (repurposing) of older materials to distinguish the new jazz of the last two and a half decades from its Nordic tone predecessors.

Bugge Wesseltoft and Jazzland Recordings

Wesseltoft began experimenting with jazz in the 1980s. Influenced by his father, a professional jazz guitarist boasting a healthy vinyl collection, he was always fascinated by jazz recordings, yet, as an avid technophile, he gravitated towards recordings heralding new techniques. He was especially enamoured with the recordings of Brian Eno, Thomas Dolby, and Steve Reich. However, the jazz and rhythm 'n' blues recordings of both American and Norwegian artists, including Miles Davis and Jan Garbarek, exerted a strong attraction. As a young musician, Wesseltoft lacked a piano, so he purchased a Fender Rhodes and a synthesiser, two instruments which accommodated his interest in improvisation. In 1984, he purchased an Atari computer with which he started experimenting with electronic music. This coupling of new computer and experimental, sound-manipulating hardware with his commitment to jazz improvisation would guide his aesthetic performance practice as well as his vision for Jazzland Recordings (Bugge Wesseltoft, Interview with the author, October 26, 2017).

In the 1980s and 1990s, he studied artists whose work displayed a wide eclecticism and progressive technological image – especially Herbie Hancock and Tangerine Dream. Eventually, the discovery of techno and house and "fabulous DJs like Stacy Pullen" in the early 1990s altered his perception of music-making (Bugge Wesseltoft). These combinations stimulated his desire to create an ensemble that could play live with sound artists and DJs while exploring the sonic possibilities of beats and dynamics in a more improvised way. Miles Davis's legacy and creative compositional approach informed Wesseltoft's penchant for musical experimentation in the jazz idiom. This dedication to improvisation alongside forward-looking textures, combinations of genres, and the experimentation with new technologies guided some of Davis's work during the 1970s (*Bitches Brew* 1970) and the 1980s (*Tutu* 1986, *Amandla* 1989). From this germinal period, Wesseltoft established his approach towards performing which always prioritised improvisation within various new technological contexts.

In Norway, the 1960s, 1970s and 1980s proved challenging for jazz musicians as rock, disco, and other forms of popular music dominated live music outlets. According to Wesseltoft, Oslo once had seven jazz clubs, but by the mid-1980s, only one remained. However, he remembers that the 1990s ushered in improvements for jazz culture, especially within the area of Grünerløkka. Ironically, part of this change occurred because of the influence of rave culture and the increased interest in world music alongside the growing prominence of the DJ in club culture. Reflecting upon this he recalled:

> the mid-80s was really a bad time for jazz music. But then it started to gradually grow, a lot of it was based around this kind of rave culture and then acid jazz … and people started to dance again and jazz suddenly became interesting again.
>
> *(Bugge Wesseltoft, October 26, 2017)*

Afterwards, two new jazz clubs opened: Jazid and Blå – the latter became the veritable home of the emerging electronic jazz scene. Blå currently remains an important venue for mixed-genre, experimental jazz.

Wesseltoft has worked as a professional musician for thirty-five years; he landed his first gig when he was nineteen. Then he was constantly "rehearsing, working and listening to jazz" but he did not "believe there was a way to live off it" until he performed with bassist Arild Andersen (who played with George Russell in the 1960s) and Jan Garbarek in 1990 (Bugge Wesseltoft). During the mid-1990s, he began working with other jazz musicians including Terje Rypdal (guitarist who'd also played with George Russell), Jon Eberson, and ECM vocalist Sidsel Endresen. For Wesseltoft, recognising that these artists supported themselves making their own music changed his perspective. After this, he began manifesting what would become both his long-term artistic vision and the title of his path-breaking first album, *New Conception of Jazz*, which he released on his new record label in 1996.

The most important model for Jazzland Recordings was Manfred Eicher's ECM independent jazz record company, which produced many of the foundational Nordic tone musicians. The Munich-based label supported experimental jazz musicians in a time when many felt that jazz was losing its relevance and vitality. While this label has since attracted some academic study (Lake and Griffiths 2007; Enwezor *et al.* 2013), those other smaller independent labels such as Oslo-based Rune Grammofon (temporarily distributed by ECM) founded by bass player Rune Kristoffersen furthered the reputation of Norwegians for their contributions to the world music sub-genre of 'ethnic jazz'. By 2000, attuned to these international technological developments and the local precedent of such recordings, Bugge Wesseltoft founded his Oslo-based electronic and mixed-genre label Jazzland Recordings.

ECM and Rune Grammofon provided important models for independent labels in Europe. As the 1990s progressed, the online sharing environment presented even more challenges. American music critic Lars Gotrich, working for the radio broadcast NPR, claimed that since the era of digitalisation, independent record companies were not only relevant for popular music, but increasingly also for jazz artists. During the 1940s and 1950s, jazz labels like Impulse, Verve, Columbia, and Blue Note had excelled by establishing consistent identities and maintaining dedicated buyers. However, the early 2000s marked a turning point for the jazz majors and especially with the release of Norah Jones' *Come Away with Me* (Blue Note 2002). Rather than adhering to the label's identity, larger record companies concentrated on promoting single stars, a strategy which put some crossover jazz artists back on the Top 40. It also signalled the re-emergence of some strands of jazz such as (nu) crooners into the mainstream of popular music. Simultaneously, independent record companies like London-based Ninja Tune, Chicago-based Thrill Jockey Records, and Wesseltoft's Jazzland Recordings, materialised to provide outlets for the most explicitly underground and experimental genre-crossing projects, representing a wider range of styles from electronic jazz to post-punk. These labels were often intimately connected to local music scenes.

Indicating the respect that Oslo (and Grünerløkka's) independent electronic jazz was gaining, in 1996, Wesseltoft and the other musicians were awarded a *Spellemannprisen* (the equivalent of a Grammy) for their album *New Conception in Jazz*. The album impressively sold more than 40,000 copies in Norway. Wulf Müller, the then director of Universal Jazz Europe, signed Jazzland to Universal during the late 1990s, facilitating the label's connection to international performance circuits including prominent jazz festivals such as the North Sea Jazz Festival from 1999 to 2006. Universal's support also enabled distribution of the label's discs throughout Europe and in Canada.

Retrospectively, Jazzland artists and their movements across Europe, Japan, and South America point to a growing international marriage of popular electronic music and club/dance culture, which have consistently captured new developments in live and recorded jazz. The UK jazz dance scene, for example, counted as part of this grassroots partnership flourishing despite a lack of interest from the mainstream industry (Cotgrove 2009). Some critics began to refer to this new music's growing popularity with younger audiences simply as 'new' or 'nu' jazz in the late 1990s, but the term remains contested by musicians grouped under this appellation.

Canadian music critic Marke Andrews (2003) wrote about the genre and about Jazzland's contributions to new jazz currents in the early 2000s. In his reviews, he linked the Norwegian movement to recording artists in the UK and the US such as "British guitarist Ronny Jordan, British saxophonist Courtney Pine, U.S. band Steve Coleman and Five Elements, Charlie Hunter Group, Medeski, Martin & Wood, and Canadian acts Bullfrog with Kid Koala". When interviewed by Anders, Wesseltoft recalled how the European progressive jazz movement was combining acoustic jazz and electronica and working across national borders. Some polygeneric jazz artists were also collaborating first in local electronic jazz scenes but soon explored continental borders to collaborate with other electronic jazz artists such as Erik Truffaz in France, who was popular in mixed-genre European clubs, where Jazzland artists had also consistently performed since before the millennium.

In Norway, Andrews stated that the movement began in the mid-1990s with Wesseltoft, trumpeter-composer Nils Petter Molvær, guitarist Eivind Aarset, and drummer Audun Kleive. Wesseltoft recalls how friendships between these musicians created a camaraderie and inspired shared performances and recording projects:

> We were all friends, and we started to go to these dance clubs. We became friends with people from the electronic music side in Oslo. Norway has some really good electronic artists. We talked about how we should play together.
>
> *(Bugge Wesseltoft, October 26, 2017)*

For him, this was the moment where the thriving electronic dance movement motivated listeners to explore the textures and sounds of improvised jazz, but in a dancing context.

Because of this synergy, Wesseltoft recognised a need for an outlet to record these innovative collaborations and so he decided to start his own label. He secured a distribution deal with Polygram (now Universal). Success was initially elusive, but after six months, he was contacted by an agent in France who was enthusiastic about the recordings; soon after, a tour of France followed. Wesseltoft's first album *Sharing* initially sold only 2,000 copies, but after his French tours, sales began to pick up with 25,000 records sold, "a bestseller in jazz terms" (Andrews 2002).

This strategy of releasing only a few albums per year by local artists similarly committed to touring abroad helped to establish Jazzland's reputation. Sales of recordings did not generate extensive radio play, but the label's distribution garnered a grassroots performance base as well as a transnational electronic jazz public. What further distinguished Jazzland artists was the creative spontaneity of live performances in the context of mixed-genre creativity and technological experimentation. Wesseltoft recalled:

> The music we do is not the kind of music that's heard on the radio a lot, and to play live is the absolute best way to promote the music. As far as my own group is concerned, I really like to play live. In a studio situation you can play, but it's more challenging to play live because we do a lot of improvisation. It feels more fresh when you do it live.
>
> *(Wesseltoft, in Andrews 2002)*

As dance-influenced jazz acquired more success, its popularity led to criticisms in more traditional jazz circles, where electronic jazz artists were often pressed to legitimise the knowledge of those DJs with whom they collaborated. Wesseltoft recalled:

> The DJs I know are really open to music. In addition to what they play at the clubs, their record collections at home would include Sun Ra and Pharaoh Sanders. What I liked about this culture was they are really into music, the same way jazz musicians are.
>
> *(Wesseltoft, in Andrews 2002)*

Eventually, Jazzland's label advocate Müller was dismissed from Universal and the support from the major diminished. This led to an amicable buy-back by Wesseltoft in 2016. According to Bugge, this ensured Jazzland Recordings once again independently owned the rights for all previous recorded material. One consequence was that Jazzland sold more albums in 2016 than they had through Universal in the preceding five years. This development betrayed the growing gap between the big stars supported by the majors and the regionally based independent labels that strive tirelessly to commandeer a buying public through the grassroots promotion of live recording artists.

Since 1996, Wesseltoft collaborated with Norwegian experimental jazz musicians as well as musicians of other genres. One long-time collaborator is esteemed vocalist Sidsel Andresen, an artistic partner for more than twenty years. They have since recorded several projects, including *Nightsong* (1994), *Duplex Ride* (1999) and *Out here. In there* in 2002. Andresen was first featured with Wesseltoft on the opening track 'Somewhere in Between' on his boldly titled *New Conception of Jazz* (1996). Other jazz musicians with which he has collaborated include Jan Garbarek (tenor saxophone), Beady Belle (Beate Lech, vocalist), Knut Reiersrud (American, guitarist), Dan Berglund (Swedish, upright bassist), Erik Truffaz (French, trumpeter), Joaquin Claussell (US producer), and Ilhan Ersahin (Swedish/Turkish tenor saxophonist based in New York).

Jazzland Recordings has also consistently supported both instrumental jazz artists as well as non-jazz artists, including 'world music' ensemble Maluca. In 2014, Wesseltoft produced a collaboration between Joyce and Maluca for their 2014 bossa nova album *Just a Little Bit Crazy* (Far Out Recordings). Another non-jazz-based collaboration occurred in 2014 with American blues musician Knut Reiersrud, a steel guitarist who improvised over ragas with sitarist Javid Afsari Rad for their release *Guitar* (Jazzland 2014).

Wesseltoft's eclecticism extends beyond technological exploration into a variety of genres. Of his twenty albums, nearly half contain solo piano works from styles ranging from jazz standards and melancholic ballads to Norwegian folk songs and Christmas hymns. These include *It Is Snowing on My Piano* (1997) and *Playing* (2009), which feature prepared piano, sound processing, and real-time looping. In 2012, he recorded a number of traditional Norwegian songs with internationally acclaimed violinist Henning Kraggerud on their duo *Last Spring*

(2012). In 2014, he released another solo piano album of jazz standards entitled *Songs* (Jazzland 2014) including 'Darn that Dream', 'How High the Moon', and 'Giant Steps'. This sheer variety of musical projects epitomises the Jazzland aesthetic – one that veers in and out of conventional jazz practice but embraces both national and international influences. By integrating styles reflecting Norway's traditional cultural heritage, Jazzland, and Wesseltoft's projects in particular, animate and update the so-called Nordic tone ideal which catapulted Norwegian jazz into the international jazz arena.

Jazzland's Electronic Jazz

Wesseltoft's commitment to acoustic piano music, electronic sound design, and live sampling led him to fluctuate from polygeneric projects to solo acoustic jazz albums, which some might describe as consistent with the melancholic, minimalistic aesthetic of the Nordic tone. But Wesseltoft's first recordings prioritised jazz soloing vocabularies transformed via the manipulation of timbres, performance techniques rendered through the use of experimental technologies such as sampling, the construction of new sounds through audio hardware applications, and finally through the construction of beats and sequences with drum programming software. The direction towards electronic

FIGURE 4.2   Bugge Wesseltoft record cover, *New Conception in Jazz* (Jazzland Recordings 1996)

jazz was first cemented in his award-winning *New Conception in Jazz* (1996), followed regularly with projects exhibiting influences from electronic music including *Sharing* (1998), *Jazzland Remixed* (2000), *Moving* (2001), and *Film ing* (2004). In 2014, Wesseltoft collaborated with Henrik Schwarz, a German producer and sound design composer who has persistently crossed the borders between classical, jazz, techno, and pop for the experimental *Schwarz Duo* (2014) album.

Remixing Electronic Jazz

In 2002, Jazzland's Universal representative Wulf Müller commented upon the growing trend adopted by the jazz majors in distributing independent recordings, and then releasing remixed compilations. For one, remixes helped the revival of the original jazz artists as well as promoting the current producers and DJs connected to the growing dance market (Müller in Lofthus). After signing a distribution and licensing deal with Universal Music Norway, Jazzland recording artists suddenly gained widespread exposure in international distribution networks, but also through international performance networks such as the European festival circuit. Usually, these corporate alliances were buttressed by hard-working individuals labouring for the musics they loved, such as Müller, Universal Music International's London-based VP of international marketing for classical and jazz (Lofthus 2002). Thus, Jazzland's connection to Universal reflected not only the label's self-conscious business strategy but rather a more personal and passionate advocacy by individual personnel working for the majors.

In the Norwegian press, Jazzland Recordings, alongside other prominent progressive Norwegian jazz musicians, was credited for rejuvenating jazz in a moment during which younger American jazz recording artists were increasingly viewed as conservative and imitative. Jazzland's many artists were perceived as enhancing the growing importance of the European jazz independents for cultivating new streams of jazz. Thus, nearly ten years after Jazzland's emergence onto the electronic jazz field, journalists were still claiming that Norwegian jazz was making itself known. Writing for Norwegian newspaper *Aftenposten*, Andersen reproduced some of these sentiments:

> Norwegian and Scandinavian artists continue to influence the interesting development of jazz, while the big jazz companies are happy to be safe, well-tried and polished.... New young musicians are still moving about, creating new musical tensions. The big companies are losing ground in this battle for innovation, while the small companies control much of the most innovative developments. In my view, it is first and foremost in Europe and not in the home country of America that the most exciting music is created today.
>
> *(Andersen 2011, translated from Norwegian)*

In the early 2000s, the idea of remixing existing jazz tracks aligned with the broader club culture and dance music movements in Northern European cities. In this milieu, extant recordings were conceptualised as flexible sonic material for further manipulation and exploration in the participatory environment of nightlife dance activities. On the *Jazzland Remixed* album released in 2000, several tracks from the *New Conception in Jazz* and *Sharing* album had been remixed including 'Somewhere in Between' (*New Conception*), 'Eve Nin' (*Sharing*), 'Existence' (*Sharing*), 'You Might Say' (*Sharing*), and 'New Conception in Jazz' (*New Conception*).[3] These tracks were remixed by both local and internationally reputed producers and DJs including Les Gammas (Germany), Andreas Dorau (Germany), Sternklang (Norway), Miss Catac (Norway), and Norwegian affiliate Jan Bang of the live remix festival Punkt.

Remixes combined ambient soundscapes with dark synth loops and minimalistic improvised piano phrases over minor tonalities. The layering of mixes sometimes featured European percussive textures connected to natural landscapes induced by shakers, rain sticks, or samples of waves or wind. On other remixes, an aesthetic evocation of northern natural landscapes was produced by the jazz drum tracks and live percussive textures. In other words, the generative and layering aesthetics of electronic, dance, and groove musics guided the construction of such soundscapes within a remix context. As Morey and McIntyre argue, sampling choices within modern compositions, rather than driven by harmonic and melodic material, are more often chosen because "aesthetically pleasing timbres and sounds [are] more pleasing than sampling a recognizable riff or melody" (Morey and McIntyre 2014, 46).

A secondary quality of such remixes was their visual and evocative filmic quality. Simon Reynolds (2011) and Mark Fisher (2014) would later theorise this aesthetic as one subsumed under the broader field of study as hauntology. As 'residual ghosts', sampled sequences often sounded as if they were taken from classical horror films or advertisements from the 1950s and 1960s. Sometimes ephemeral residues would give way to irony or post-modern fascination with the commodified or pop culture of earlier decades. An ironic stance towards the past was discernible in Jazzland remixed tracks featuring exaggerated upper-middle-class voices of (perceived) 'white' women, who proclaimed the wonders of high fidelity listening for (presumably male) bachelor pads and cosmopolitan record collectors. In the many cocktail compilations of these two decades, samples of 1950s-era voices presented a playful, post-modern stance – poking fun at one's parents' record collection and high-fidelity stereo equipment but also repurposing these objects within contemporaneous musical practices. Such ironic voices are also sampled and treated in the remixes of Wesseltoft's 'Eve Nin'.

'Eve Nin', Sharing (1998)

From Jazzland's and Wesseltoft's breakthrough electronic jazz recording, *A New Conception of Jazz*, the opening track 'Eve Nin' evokes the pared-down, acoustic bass and drum textures of Medeski, Martin, and Wood. In the opening sequence, the bass line jumps an octave to the minor third and back to the fifth. The same ostinato riff then repeats a half-step higher in the second measure. This track then features a funk drum pattern in the chorus heard after the original jazz funk bass line over the minor seventh chord. The keys provide a funky four-bar riff which complements the bass line. We hear occasional 'whah' effects before the sampled 1950s-era female voice, admonishing her captives with the phrase "most men fear me, they suffocated my spark" with an exaggerated slur on the s's which gives the sample a cartoonish ("suffering succotash") yet sensuous quality. A Latin percussion sequence builds up over the bass line, followed by two layers of keyboard riffs. In short, this is a highly funky and danceable track which generates layers of grooves while sonically referencing the past and present.

Halfway through the track, we hear an intensification of the drum sequence with live-sounding drums or a live-sounding computer drum sequence and long deeply reverberated 'ahs' in the female vocal sequence with heavy delay. This leads to an enhanced synth solo reproducing the texture of an electric guitar. Finally, the vocals are chopped, cut up into short syllables and with breathy sighs, effected with heavy reverb and delay. This sequence seems to pay homage to the acoustics of the reggae sound system or perhaps the funky psychedelia of Parliament's Afro-futuristic P-Funk.

'Eve Nin' (Les Gammas Remix), Jazzland Remixed (2000)

'Eve Nin' was remixed by Les Gammas on Jazzland's remix album from 2000. Les Gammas, a nu jazz group active during the early 2000s, consisted of Bavarian drummer/singer/DJ Marc Frank and Rhodes keyboardist/singer Jochen Helfert. The duo was instrumental in mixing many jazz tracks during the early 2000s. This remix begins with a text sampled from a vinyl disc of DJ Olle Abstract animated by a quavering dissonant string run followed by a Herbie Hancock-inspired synth riff with flute aftershocks and an acoustic bass paired only with percussion. After a few measures, an alarm tone slides up the octave in a classic EDM soar culminating in the first drop – as the percussion and synth briefly disappear. The acoustic bass is gone, but rather a half-tone funk ostinato repeats three times (in place of the alternative G to A flat minor riff) with a harmonic change of the fourth measure to the seventh, in the upper register. After the drop, the track recapitulates the bossa-nova-like pattern, this time pushed higher in the mix over the bass and looped Hancock-inspired keyboard. Finally, we hear the original keyboard riff from the *Sharing* LP. The track features a funky bass-heavy track with synth sequences looped over a prominent funk bass line and sound-scape inspired by a 1970s-sounding percussion track. One sequence features a jazz flute with a padded mellotron-sounding keyboard riff. The flute phases in and out in rhythmic counterpoint with a peddle-tone whahed keys, bass, and unison string tracks. References to Herbie Hancock's 'Future Shock' as well as the soundtracks of 1970s Blaxploitation films emerge within short passages of strings and an increasing layering of Latin-inspired beats and percussion. There are several drops and breaks with short solos on keys of flute, for example. The wirery bass loop and congas sequence close the track with one final syncopated string riff. This remix then offers intertextual references to European electronic jazz, but also to Black popular musics from earlier decades such as funk and Black action cinema soundtracks.

Through collaborations across musical and geographical borders as well as the continual reworking of electronic jazz through the remix, Jazzland alters the practices associated with jazz recording and the recording object. With the constant reconfiguration and collaboration with producers and creatives across European electronic jazz cities, Wesseltoft transformed the role of independent jazz labels within European jazz culture. By consistently collaborating with musicians working in other genres and introducing techniques driven by popular music genres, Wesseltoft connected contemporary jazz to modern production aesthetics as well as modern transnational networks. Naturally, these collaborations depended upon the local networks and reconfigured spaces of Oslo's post-industrial neighbourhoods, spaces where electronic jazz could first experiment and refine such remixing proclivities for live and often dancing publics.

Beady Belle

> Something dark and exciting has been stirring in the backwaters of Norwegian music in recent times. It's not often that Norway reaches out and shakes our collective musical consciousness, but when it does, the results are usually memorable. There are metaphorical as well as physical mountains to climb to make your voice heard, so what gets out is pretty special. The latest in that line are Beady Belle, a band of four musicians who are the musical outlet for the creative muse of Beate Lech, a young woman of singular musical, vocal and lyrical talents.
>
> *(Keith Shadwick, the Independent, London, 2003)*

Beate Lech grew up listening to the music of her father, a Polish jazz violinist, and her mother, a singer. As a child, she was immersed in music; studying violin, singing at home and in choirs, and composing. Her early vocal and instrumental training augmented her abilities as a composer and producer later in life. Her passion for composing was predisposed from various multifaceted formative experiences. In an interview in 2003, she recalled her earliest music memories:

> My first strong memory of music is my mother singing lullabies to me when I was very small. She would sit on my bed and sing these old

Norwegian songs to me, and she would sing for hours ... I was embraced by it. It was very intimate and intense, and it has stayed with me.

(Shadwick 2003)

Echoing the topographical analogies of the Nordic tone, Lech claimed that her music likely reflected the combined intimacies and intensities of Norwegian life created by cultural disposition coupled with extreme weather variances:

I was born in a town in western Norway with a population of just 9,000. Norway has only five million people; Oslo is just 500,000.[4] The people keep their distance, like the country, until you know them well. Not like Italians, who are expansive, throw their arms in the air and exclaim over everything. Here it's dark and cold, people hurrying along in the snow with their heads down and going to bars or cafés to meet friends. No great show of emotion.... But these places, they're very intimate, too.

(Shadwick 2003)

British journalist Keith Shadwick connected the extremes of climate to the contrasts of Norwegian culture, claiming "that is what Lech's music epitomises: a surface coolness that conceals a surprising turbulence and an utter lack of sentimentality. Her music is all about contrasts: taking disparate elements and making them work together, so redefining them" (Shadwick 2003). In these evocations, the Nordic tone surfaced as both cultural *dispositief* and a musical propensity for affective contrasts.

In the 1990s, Lech studied vocal jazz performance and composition at the University of Oslo and the State Academy of Music. Here she intensified her connection to both soul and jazz. Within this period, she developed an important and long-lasting creative partnership with fellow student and bassist Marius Reksjo, who would later perform and co-produce tracks with Lech. Together Lech and Reksjo would become Beady Belle.

In 1999, Lech was invited by Wesseltoft to record an album for Jazzland Recordings for which she was given total autonomy. She composed, arranged, programmed, wrote the texts, and produced all of the songs on her Macintosh computer in her six-metre-square studio apartment in Oslo. Instrumentals, including vibraphone, drums, and strings, were later recorded in Bugge's room. As the project developed, Reksjo was invited to develop additional grooves and bass lines. This collaboration proved fruitful and inspiring, so Lech abandoned her solo title to pursue Beady Belle. The various creative roles of the two were clarified on the Beady Belle website: "He [Reksjo] took care of the groove elements while Beate composed the melodies, harmonies and lyrics, with some exceptions both ways. The product of this work, done in their private surroundings, would be entitled 'Home'".[5]

With the increased flexibility and adaptability of both computer software and sound design hardware, 'bedroom producer' Lech (with Reksjo) created a sonically compelling and multifaceted album. The 'bedroom studio' remains a weighted term, one conventionally imbued with masculine subjectivity or, as Peter Whelan argues: "the term conjures the bedroom of the teenage boy in the family home, a backstage place, loaded with meaning as a specific masculine domain" (Whelan 2008, 18). However, bedrooms or residential flats can easily transform into important creative spaces for under-funded jazz musicians, or for women who may lack industry connections and resources to finance expensive studio albums. With Lech's training in jazz, composition, and popular music alongside her unique creative and compositional voice, she gathered important 'polygeneric' jazz musicians to materialise her personal artistic vision. The title of this album then reflects not only the domestic and creative partnership unfolding between bassist/groove designer Reksjo and Lech, but also the creative musical compositional affordances of the home environment, which has always provided important spaces for younger musicians, and especially women.

The album succeeded internationally, attracting critical acclaim in Australia, Germany, the UK, and the Netherlands. One journalist in Australia suggested that the album corresponded with the growing fragmentation of genres in the late 1990s:

> We've had old skool, nu skool and nu metal (not to mention ambient glitch and acid croft), so perhaps it was only a matter of time before nu jazz entered the hipster's dictionary of musical mumbo jumbo. That said, this newly monikered movement boasts one duo who have just released a very exciting album. They're young, they're Norwegian, they're called Beady Belle and their record is called Home (Universal/Jazzlands).
>
> *(Jones et al. 2003)*

The opening track, 'Ghosts', quickly became a radio single in Norway. Later that year, Universal gave this album 'European priority' status, and it was released across Europe, and in Japan, Canada, and Korea during that summer, and in Australia a few months later. From this successful first album, Beady Belle engaged upon a rigorous touring schedule. Since then she has recorded eight albums and toured internationally for nearly twenty years.

'Ghosts' combined the stylistic aesthetics of drum 'n' bass with electronic jazz, requiring that performers deliver the phrasing conventions inherited from electronic samples combined with the technical skills of modern jazz drumming (performed by Eric Holm), while maintaining the freedom to depart from both for short sections of well-chosen but efficient improvised phrases. 'Ghosts' begins with a lyrical string synth loop (sixteen measures), mixed with backgrounded sound effects followed by the sound of sirens panning right to left and other percussive sonic textures. After eight measures, the vocals call out three repeated phrases followed by an answer in the combined bass, vocal oohs, and trap set with airy and light cymbal work for eight measures. Then a full-fledged stop ensues giving over to the break beats under the first verse, "I fall into your trash bin once again … same kind of story … I know what's happened every time before, still I want more". These three phrases are followed by an altered fourth phrase. The chorus takes the upper octave, doubled with lower improvised responses in the lower octave again over a rich and densely orchestrated drum and string track, with more fills and breaks into the second verse where the drums largely drop out leaving only the high hat. Then a second break of two beats is followed by the full trap set. Acoustic piano riffs fill the breaks on the last phrase of the second verse. A second chorus builds with harmonised 'oohs' and short improvised interactions between piano and jazz drums with a freer bass approach. Then a fully orchestrated bridge section unfolds, the voice further compressed before a final string chorus – this time singled out before an open piano section improvises over drums and bass alone. This track particularly epitomised the seamless merging of pop, electronic, and jazz aesthetics through its pop vocal song structures, through the alternation between live jazz and programmed electronic beats, and through layering acoustic and electronic textures.

CEWBEAGAPPIC

Beady Belle's second album, CEWBEAGAPPIC (2003), featured the duo with many important Oslo-based jazz musicians. The liner notes promoted a range of dichotomies which betrayed the duo's desire to bridge older-genre conventions with contemporary soundscapes and recording practices, reflecting the collective's philosophy. The album's title, a new term coined to reflect this range of musical properties, also privileged creative principles intrinsic to European electronic jazz. Each of these dichotomies is given two letters:

> CE = Complex + Easy
> WB = White + Black
> EA = Electronic + Acoustic
> GA = Groovy + Ambient
> PP = Played + Programmed
> IC = Improvised + Composed

From both the title of the album and the sounds of the recording, a modern take on the jazz tradition is proposed, inheriting traditional jazz values of improvisation and performance, and combined with the modern musical possibilities of electronic compositional tools and popular music song conventions, rendered through complex electronic mechanisms. Finally, the race-based understandings of hybrid musical categories are proposed, as these two white Norwegian jazz musicians engage with the heritage of Black American jazz, updating a racialised matrix projected by European musicians since the arrival of touring American Black musicians in the nineteenth century (Gilroy 1993). Such fascinations with musical and cultural hybridity have long preoccupied not only European jazz musicians but the early critics and enthusiasts of jazz such as André Coeuroy and Alfred Lion (Jordan 2010, 102–140; Wipplinger 2017, 2). However, current interactions with Black music often occur through intensive study of phonographic works which have become central in the development of new musical genres for jazz-based European musicians. Knowledge and study of recordings of critically acclaimed Black artists from soul, hip hop, jazz, and funk remain important precursors for collaborating and creating in this environment. This relationship to Black music recorded genres is then referenced in Belle's reception as reviews of the project's 2001 album described Belle's music as Norwegian soul (Beady Belle (Beate Lech), Interview with the author, October 25, 2017).

A review from the *Independent* (London) also highlighted the polygeneric sound of this album, again an indication that these artists were less interested in creating 'straight ahead' or folkloric Nordic tone jazz than producing new music relating to their own personal experiences of music (PJ 2001). A subsequent review of *Home* from the online magazine *Groove.no* highlighted the idea that a particular mix of electronic genres, pop hooks, and improvised jazz characterised the so-called [Grunn] Løkka Sound, claiming:

> Beady Belle can be said to have its musical anchoring in jazz structures, with a somewhat distorted eclectic spirit hanging over the spices from drum 'n' bass, living-funk and some peep soul. The temptation is great in terms of linking them to the highly used concept of 'Løkka Sound', which has both become geographically and musically most frequent to catch headlines like Folk & Røvere and D'Sound. Yes, there are the airy, sophisticated and golden urban sound images that meet us, but what impresses me is Beady Belle's ability to pull the association towards the house and soul of the daunting 90s … 'Home' reveals an experimental rapping from two lifetimes listening to the more refined part of the musical highlights of the last 20 years….
>
> *(Nygaard 2001)*

Lech's musical trajectory is evident in her musical development throughout the last two decades. She viewed especially her first electronica-driven records performed locally as pivotal for this process of connecting to Jazzland's post-Nordic tone aesthetic. She reflected on this path from playing at the home of electronic jazz at Blå in Grünerløkka to the various projects created since then:

> When I started the first Beady Belle album, there was a lot happening around a club called Blå, which means blue. This was a scene with jazz music and DJs. People went there to listen, dance, and drink beer. It was

an old rusty factory and people just opened their minds when they came there. I think that was important for the kind of music we created in that period. For me to work with Bugge was also very important because in Norway it is a very small country and the music scene is very small but there was a lot happening. Musicians like Bugge, Nils-Petter Molvær, and Jan Garbarek in the generation ahead of them, showed the way to break rules and to cross genres…. Jazz is an old American tradition, which you have to respect, but they said – 'I'll put in some Norwegian folk songs and some jazz and electronic'. This created a trend and a caste for us who were younger and we thought, yeah there is a path here, there are many options…. This kind of base that they created was very important and a lot happened at Blå. I think I played fifty times at Blå in that period.

(Beady Belle (Beate Lech), Interview with the author,
October 25, 2017)

From the project's first album *Home* (Jazzland 2001) to their recent album *Dedication* (Jazzland 2018), Lech has exhibited a pattern followed by other electronic jazz musicians. This included experimenting with the important dance and rave scenes of the 1990s to adapting to the creative possibilities afforded by the digital recording studio, and finally working back to more acoustic and pre-digital genres such as soul and cool jazz. Belle's last album situates her artistry more squarely within soul, pop, and jazz than electronic jazz. There is even a philosophical and spiritual tone to this album, especially on tracks like 'My Religion', which provide the soundscape of the airy crossover jazz of the 1970s with the characteristic Rhodes tracks, bass, and piano supporting Belle's vocal wanderings at an easy, relaxed tempo. Tracks feature influences from reggae, soul, and pop jazz. Lech's song-writing skills are expertly exhibited on this album, which has something nostalgic and original in the way melodic lines are combined with subtle textural effects. Ergo, the soundscape of this album prioritises simplicity, with only a few choicely selected effects from phasing to panning and dramatic changes in the mix.

Reflecting upon her representation by critics and agents, Lech struggled to define own her role in the jazz world, preferring to represent herself as a soul singer. However, she admitted the importance of jazz for her personal artistic development. For her, Stevie Wonder, Aretha Franklin, Ella Fitzgerald, and Billie Holiday all feature prominently in her stylistic development. Since the early 2000s, she has avidly followed similarly polygeneric artists, especially those who bridge the genres of soul, jazz, and pop as she has in her career. Lech (Belle) cites Alicia Keys, Erika Badu, James Blake, and D'Angelo as important models of musicians who also attempt to bring jazz into the centre of contemporary (Black) musical practices. When speaking of other contemporary artists to which she shares the strongest affinity, she stated:

The most famous is perhaps Alicia Keys. She is one of the artists that also plays with genres.… She is a soul singer, she makes pop music, and she puts dangerous chords into it. She stretches the genre and there is a lot of jazz in her music as well. Since she is a famous artist, she is allowed to play with it in her own way, and still be accepted and embraced for it … I therefore think she means a lot to that kind of 'in-between-music'; between jazz and soul and pop.… When these artists dare not to follow the fashion, it makes it much more interesting.

(Beady Belle (Beate Lech), October 25, 2017)

Beate's compositional process betrays contemporary generative methods, especially since she often begins not with a piano but rather with a 'machine'. She depicted this process as one driven from her desire to experiment with different tempos and textures to find the right ambiance and soundscape for a particular melody's sound and sentimental qualities. She described the ways of both composing and recording as organic, yet cemented by experimentation:

When I create music, I use the computer, and the program Logic, actively by finding sounds, programming grooves and moves. I don't sit at the piano and write songs and then record. I often change instruments and settings, because if I create something for one type of instrumentation and then I change it – the atmosphere changes and I get new inspiration. I use the computer not only as a documentation of ideas, but for *producing* ideas. For me the computer is an instrument, for changing sounds and settings to find new atmospheres.

(Beady Belle (Beate Lech), October 25, 2017)

Lech's compositional process shares some of the process-oriented creativity of other remix artists:

When I make music I experiment a lot with the instruments, the arrangements, the sounds, the grooves and the tempo. Actually, my way of creating new music is like I somehow remix myself during the process. So this makes the bridge from remixing old stuff not so far away because this is what I do when I compose.

(Beady Belle (Beate Lech), October 25, 2017)

For her more conventional 2016 jazz album *On My Own*, Lech recognised how her work has developed to less digitally mediated genres. She understands the various musical projects as reflections of her own psyche, age, and experience. Such experiences as motherhood too have impacted how she has composed, recorded, and performed her music. For example, the last three albums (*Cricklewood Broadway* 2012, *On My Own* 2016, *Dedication* 2018) have returned to a more acoustic sound with genres firmly rooted in the history of both popular music and jazz from country to soul, jazz, and pop. She recognised this transition as important and necessary for her own integrity and autonomy. She viewed this transition away from electronic genres reflective of her changing physical and musical maturation:

> I've always felt an urge to express the kind of music that is me. And this *me* has changed over the years.… You know, life changes.… After making three albums with some electronic influence, then I became a mother. So this hormone stuff, I don't know, my music made a change into a more countryish style. I think my booking agents were frustrated because they thought they couldn't book me in any of the places we used to play before.… And the line-up in Beady Belle has changed over the years too. In 2008, Beady Belle went from being a duo to a trio. And in 2015 we decided we shouldn't work together any more. I was suddenly on my own. And then when I should make the sixth album I just felt, for the first time: I am *not* going to produce this myself. I felt alone. I am just going to write the music and lyrics and I am going to have someone else producing it. So I asked Bugge to produce it. That was the first time I put my baby into someone else's hands, and it felt safe and extremely risky at the same time.
>
> *(Beady Belle (Beate Lech), October 25, 2017)*

Such lifecycle changes corresponded to aesthetic transformations within her recording projects. But these life changes also corresponded to aesthetic and technical transformations within the music industry in the last decade.

On My Own (2016)

After disbanding the trio, Lech agreed to do a full jazz album *On My Own* (2016 Jazzland Recordings) with Norwegian and international musicians including Joshua Redman (saxophone), Gregory Hutchinson (drums), Reuben Rogers (bass), Fran Cathcart (guitar), and Bugge Wesseltoft (keyboards). Backing vocals were recorded by Anja Martine Mørk and Torun Eriksen (with Lech). The collaboration with such established New York jazz stars as Gregory Hutchinson, who had played with prominent artists including Joe Henderson, Joshua Redman, Betty Carter, Ray Brown, Johnny Griffin, and Jimmy Smith, betrayed the level of respect both Wesseltoft and Lech had acquired in the international jazz community. Joshua Redman features on two tracks of this album, 'Incompatible' and 'On My Own'.

Within this album, not only these established musicians and Lech's compositions adhere to a more restrained jazz sound, but the manner of recording prioritised a more traditional aesthetic. The entire album was recorded in two days

FIGURE 4.3   Beady Belle record cover, *On My Own* (Jazzland Recordings 2016)

with few overtakes so as to reproduce the so-called 'live' sound. Lech recalled this interaction as exciting and intimidating:

> I had never been to New York and I had never met these people. Giants! I felt like a child. I just came with a suitcase of my songs and said; do you really want to play this? But it was amazing! The whole album was made in two days. That was Bugge's idea. We're gonna make it the jazz way, and it's gonna be free and alive, he said. And it felt really nice.
>
> *(Beady Belle (Beate Lech), October 25, 2017)*

The *On My Own* album crosses the boundaries between singer-songwriter pop and gospel inflected acoustic jazz. It shares the darker and stark quality that is often used to describe Nordic jazz, which is typically described as sombre, melancholic, yet expressive and lyrical. The track 'Marbles' opens with Belle declaiming two poetic verses, after which a gospel-like rhythm section gradually unfolds. The verse seamlessly transitions to the sung chorus. At the end the first chorus, trumpet player Mathias Eick (who often performs with Jaga Jazzist) takes a short solo. His playing is slightly enhanced with reverb. The title track 'On My Own' features a long solo by Joshua Redman. His playing is imbued with a soulful gospel sound, and the minimalistic folk quality of Belle's voice complements such acoustic numbers. The track 'Bury' features a rock jazz track which veers from a slower rock beat to fusion textures, and the doubling of vocals during the chorus and the breakdown in the bridge, accompanied by a loosely played bass line and clap track. Here the classic 1960s rhythm 'n' blues section is featured after the first chorus. The track fades out during the synth solo. Throughout the album, Wesseltoft's playing appears reserved and subtle.

Within these last two albums, Belle's evolution seems to correspond with her thoughts on the traditions of jazz and music as open-ended creative forces for both highly sophisticated electronic experimentations and organic acoustic melodic lines. Belle's transition from electronic jazz to other related genres depended upon the web of relations and musical tastes of her musical upbringing and professional network within Oslo, but always conditioned by the climate of 'breaking the rules' as articulated by Jazzland Recordings.

Conclusion

Jazzland's success and transnational reach owed its connection to both the preceding Nordic tone musicians and newer, more electronically inclined creative labels responsible for Norway's millennial reception within international jazz. The pre-dominance of romanticised images of home, the use of local song repertoires, and the imagery of Nordic landscapes gradually succumbed to technologically mediated iconographies and disparate sonic aesthetics, an artistic move which resonated with popular music's de-territorialisation. Keenly aware of both local and transnational aesthetic developments, Wesseltoft initiated his Jazzland Recordings to explore musical influences and techniques from a variety of sound cultures from jazz to electronic and world music. His first release on this label *A New Conception of Jazz* (1996) discursively and aesthetically staged a rejection of the regionalism of the so-called ethnic jazz of Nordic tone, but it also presented an implied and perfor-mative critique of what some considered the growing conservatism of mainstream American jazz.

Increasingly during the 1990s, it was the jazz and mixed-genre independent labels that facilitated and stimulated the promotion and careers of electronic and polygeneric jazz musicians. The Norwegian press was eager to highlight this trend in stressing the growing gap between the jazz majors, depicted as increasingly polished, conservative, and risk-averse, and the local independent labels, admired for their innovation and long-term commitment to jazz artists' careers. Reflecting the latter, Jazzland and other independents, such as Runne Grammofon, embraced adventurous artists and were lauded for their ability to rejuvenate international jazz.

By 2011, the perspective persisted that Scandinavian artists were responsible for altering the direction of jazz as well as establishing prominence for the European jazz independents. Jazzland's most established artists, Bugge Wesseltoft and Beady

Belle, embody the pioneering fusing of techniques and aesthetics within their recordings. However, in their commitments to local scenes in local post-industrial neighbourhoods, their expansion of trans-local musician networks and communities, and their connection to polygeneric jazz, they embodied the Nordic tone ideals of both 'rule-breaking' and simultaneously sustaining an ideal of home and belonging. This localised sound ideal lasted even as the creative techniques of electronic jazz depended upon the cosmopolitanism and technical sophistication of digital production aesthetics and electronic dance communities. For Jazzland artists, the progressive legacy of Miles Davis provided a critical point of departure for musicians labouring outside of the canonised borders of American jazz. However, as Wesseltoft's 'Somewhere in Between' riffed upon this metaphorical jazz border, a Norwegian independent record community landed firmly 'Home' within current streams of transnational jazz. From the regeneration of music and arts attributed to the 'Løkka' sound within Olso's renewed and cosmopolitan Grünerløkka neighbourhood where DJs and jazz artists found their first fruitful encounters, Jazzland Recordings' Bugge Wesseltoft and Beady Belle forged ahead from this moment into an expanded European jazz network, pursuing a transnational sonic aesthetic through their perennial search for a new conception of jazz.

Notes

1   This group too came to be associated with the Nordic tone, yet jazz critics would hear influences from both local Norwegian musicians such as Garbarek as well as American saxophonist Wayne Shorter. The band consisted of Jon Balke on piano, Jon Christensen on drums, Nils Petter Molvær on trumpet, and Tore Brunborg on saxophones.
2   See 'Om Blå' on their website: www.blaaoslo.no/om-bla/ (accessed June 10, 2018).
3   From the *Jazzland Remixed* compilation in 2000, 'Superstring' performed by guitarist Eivind Aarset was remixed by Chilluminati Remix, 'Existence' was remixed by Chilluminati, 'Eve Nin' was remixed by Les Gammas, 'You Might Say' was remixed by Andreas Dorau, 'Newborn Thing' was remixed by Sternklang, 'Driveline' performed by Audun Kleive was remixed by Motion Control, 'Fast Forward' was remixed by Pia Myrvold, 'You Might Say' by Miss Catac, and 'Somewhere in Between' by Jan Bang.
4   There are now more than 600,000 people living in Oslo proper.
5   See 'Biography' on Beady Belle's website, accessed December 26, 2018, www.beadybelle.com/biography.

5

PART ONE: THE 'REVIVAL OF THE REVIVAL' OR A SWING DANCE CONTINUUM?

Mediascapes, Time Machines, and Intercultural Encounters at the Herräng Dance Camp

> New York can be a seductive vampire as well as sweet as fortune and fame: vulgar for a beginner, satisfactory for an intermediate, and maybe heavenly for an advanced. New York once had what it took to receive and develop the culture of jazz: it had the momentum to transform this old-school Louisiana sound into something sparkling, vivid and new. Some thirty to forty years later, it all collapsed under the turmoil of changed preferences and cold winds. A handful of veterans kept the traditions alive, still dancing cheek-to-cheek and holding hands at midnight, while the future revivalists waited in the wings, biding their time, unaware of all that was to come.
>
> *(Lennart Westerlund, 'The Revival of the Revival' –*
> HDC Weekly Magazine, *Week One, 2018, 14)*

Since the birth of the Lindy Hop in Jazz Age Harlem, numerous jazz-related dance movements have erupted, faded, and resurfaced again, evidencing something of a *swing continuum*, a term inspired by Amiri Baraka (Jones and Baraka 1963). Such a continuum was stressed by Rikard Ekstrand, a performer with the Stockholm-based Harlem Hot Shots troupe and an established teacher at the Herräng Dance Camp, asserting: "we do have a beautiful jazz culture here in Sweden; I guess now it is almost a hundred years old … and I think that is why it is so strong". In Sweden, Ekstrand and many other Lindy Hop dancers lay claim to a long history of swing dancing. In 2018, Ekstrand informed me that he is "a third generation of [swing dancing] Swedes" and further stated "my parents and their parents [did it], so I think it is quite a deep thing we have here … it is not just about the revival and remembering, but here the past is a living thing" (Rikard Ekstrand, Interview with the author, July 4, 2018). Thus, Europe's professional Lindy Hop dancers experience jazz dance as neither entirely foreign and temporally distant, nor exclusively Swedish. Instead, they recognise social dancing to jazz as embedded in Swedish culture, albeit dynamically responsive to encounters with jazz dancers, American films, and jazz-oriented media within Europe in the early twentieth century. This complex relationship could now be understood as encompassing both long-term physical intercultural contact and transnational initiatives by local actors who examined performances by those African American professional dancers having first created and transmitted the dance in ballroom culture and within various entertainment media[1] (Brown 2008; Fry 2014; Zwerin 2000; Jackson 2003; Jordan 2010; Wipplinger 2017).

Within this continuum, the dance developed in particular places because of the specific quality of regional, national, or place-based jazz cultures. Moreover, within Europe, swing dance has persisted and later flourished because of the unique forms of interest of passionate individuals within their communities, such as in Stockholm and later in Herräng, Sweden, during the 1980s. Here, swing dance acquired a prominent position within the international swing world and its development parallels those of other cosmopolitan musical cultures (such as hip hop) now firmly established in centres throughout Europe (Mitchell 2001).

This chapter marks a departure from established jazz scholarship by prioritising not a recorded musical corpus, but a jazz culture focused upon the dancing body. This is partly motivated by a desire to intervene in dominant jazz narratives from the Frankfurt school onwards, which often reject corporeal engagements with jazz as insignificant and anti-intellectual. Further, while the revival of swing dancing in Europe may seem too remote for consideration in a book focused upon remix, the perspective of this research looks in particular at the role performed by jazz-oriented media as influential in the dance's adaptation, alteration, and forms of sociality and performance. From this perspective, dancing is positioned as an essential facet of contemporary European jazz culture, even as its present is deeply informed by an intimate and complex relationship to prior jazz and dance-oriented media.

Within the chapter, I explore the late twentieth-century jazz dance revival in Sweden as it acquired its recent reputation as the focal point of European jazz dance culture, namely the Herräng Dance Camp. In particular, I investigate how the long-term relationship established between the original Savoy Lindy Hop dancers and the contemporary Swedish and international Lindy Hop community has led to Herräng's prominence in the international swing dance community. While this has been discussed in existing studies (Sékiné 2017; Wells 2013), which similarly uncover Herräng's role in reviving Lindy Hop, this chapter foregrounds Herräng's contemporary musical community and especially their transmedial practices, extending and transforming connections with the earlier revival from the mid-1980s to the profoundly transformed engagements in the digital sphere. From such 'media pilgrimages' evolved complex relationships between many of the old-timers and European dancers. In this era of intensified migration routes and communications networks, a modern Black Atlantic route took shape which ultimately precipitated original yet more diffuse and sophisticated mediascapes (Appadurai 1996). These mediascapes have transformed not only the values and discursive engagements with the dance within Herräng, but have led to greater self-reflection concerning how the revival impacted the identity formations, power hierarchies, and global routes occupied by participants of this revival. The confluence of media networks and embodied encounters forms a unique feature of the current Lindy Hop transnational community. Ultimately, I argue that as a result of the combined, conservationist commitment to the earlier legacy of the old-timers, with a more flexible adaptation of performance routes, dance styles, and media promotion tactics, the Lindy Hop scene in Sweden has positioned itself as the most advanced and versatile community internationally, while maintaining connections to the perceived authentic (while mythologised) roots of this Harlem-based dance.

In the following, I explore developments within Sweden related to the Lindy Hop and Herräng especially since the first revival in the late 1980s. First, in the Introduction I offer a historical overview of the original Black Atlantic passage and intercultural encounters between the celebrated Savoy dancers and Lindy Hop recruits in Europe during the foundational three decades of the 1920s to the 1950s. I then historically contextualise the Swedish revival of the 1980s and 1990s (with related contexts elsewhere). Here I focus upon the African American 'old-timers' transnational relationship to the camp and the broader Swedish community. I also analyse how media played a prominent role in cultivating and enhancing this relationship, additionally cementing particular values and discourses at Herräng. Within this chapter, the camp's role is explored as both a platform for jazz preservation and education. I reveal how the historical, cultural, and aesthetic context which positioned this camp's prominence within Europe from the 1990s to the present proved critical for establishing both the prestige and trans-locality of this expanding community. In particular, I examine the camp's important relation to the old-timers who have visited the camp since the late 1980s. Finally, I zoom in on various facets of this camp, especially the night-time *daily camp meetings* which through their 'time machine' character helped to fortify this socially dynamic community.

Introduction

The Herräng Dance Camp and the Swedish Lindy Hop Continuum

Within Herräng, what began as a local initiative in the 1980s eventually grew into an international dance movement connecting people from all over Europe.[2] Since the 1990s, the Herräng Dance Camp has earned its reputation as the leader of contemporary jazz dance inculcation, mentoring, and instruction in Europe. As Herräng Lindy Hop ethnographer Christopher Wells argued, by 2000, its reputation elevated the camp's position to the international 'cultural broker' for Lindy Hop dancers, teachers, and participants throughout the world (Wells 2013, 391).

The camp takes place annually from July through the first week of August, attracting some 5,000 dancers, musicians, old-timers, and teachers to share in aspects of jazz dance culture. In this village of 450 residents, professionals and enthusiasts forge cultural and social bonds, and the camp provides the highest quality of dance instruction alongside a committed presentation of historical jazz perspectives. According to camp founder Lennart Westerlund, Herräng not only teaches participants Lindy Hop, but also offers knowledge about jazz dance heritage, where participants can discover the unique culture of swing[3] dance and this dance's roots within Black American dance culture of the first half of the twentieth century. While the camp is an important institution for immersion into this history, it also exposes one to the means by which the dance was adapted in Sweden, such as through the rock 'n' roll dances which were popular in mid-century Sweden.

As in other cultural revivals, Swedish jazz dance underwent a period of legitimisation through personal contact with living dancers next to intense study of dance movements represented in a corpus of early jazz dance media. Such jazz dances were recorded by the American film industry in the 1920s such as the 'first' documentation of the Lindy (origins) in the film *After Seben* (1929), featuring Harlem dancer George 'Shorty' Snowden. With the expansion of sound films in the 1930s, jazz-based musicals and comedic studio productions such as *A Day at the Races* (1937) featured the dazzling Whitey's Lindy Hoppers. Later films in the post-war period filtered into new Lindy-inspired dance forms such as the jive in the teen rock 'n' roll films of the 1950s.

Europeans came into contact with these films since the First World War in a number of unusual and serendipitous channels. Some of the earliest included Cab Calloway's *Jitterbug Party* (Paramount 1935) in local theatres in the 1930s and 1940s. Many of the 1980s-era 'revivalists' discovered jazz dance sequences through local television programmes or in theatres featuring old American films (Lennart Westerlund, Interview with the author, July 5, 2018). These films inspired European dancers to investigate such documented dance cultures, and enthusiasm for such films motivated dancers to seek 'undiscovered' films. They subsequently connected with dedicated collectors who located and revived footage not available officially. Since 1945, particular collectors earned fame in the dance community, including Bill Savory and Ernie Smith, who actively preserved films, especially those featuring jazz musicians accompanying the spell-binding dances of the Charleston, the Lindy Hop, and later the jive variants found in movies of the 1950s, like *Rock Around the Clock* (1956).

Now a widely circulated, intensely studied, and pedagogically canonised dance-driven media became paramount for guiding how the Lindy Hop revival has taken shape since its recent 'discovery'. Such study and enthusiasm organised in affinitive communities reflects what Lindy scholar Sékiné, following Foucault, depicted as the "will to knowledge" foregrounding the ideologies of Herräng's Lindy Hop community (Sékiné 2017). Furthermore, this media would become the catalyst for a number of profound relationships between American (mostly Black) jazz dancers and European (mostly white) leaders and/or revivalists. These pivotal relationships would engender a discourse for preserving jazz dance within digital, globalist Europe.

In the new millennium, the 'swing revival of the revival' occurred as European popular culture and related broadcasting industries became increasingly connected and beholden to American media entities. Eventually, the liberalisation of the European broadcast networks hastened the influence of the American-dominated transnational media industry (Wickström 2009, Rutten 1999). Interestingly, the ubiquity and accessibility of mainstream popular musical media served to enhance the cultural capital of such locally produced pre-digital, 'vintage' dance numbers. Furthermore, this recently canonised dance media would inspire 'jazz pilgrimages' to New York, where travellers experienced the genesis of jazz dance culture. As Nick Couldry argues (2004), the circulation and valuation of a particular body of media informs the affective connections to particular historical places conceived and mythologised as the origins of important cultural movements, such as the Harlem Renaissance in the 1920s and 1930s. For many of the examined revivalists, such documentations proved foundational for the ways the dance was transmitted at the end of the century. This media also inspired the meeting and collaboration of dancers across a *new* Black Atlantic in an altogether different set of cultural and artistic relations (Gilroy 1993).

The Original European Black Atlantic Lindy Roots/Routes

Like many enthusiasts, I first discovered Lindy Hop performances after viewing the famous dance scene from the film *Hellzapoppin'* (1941), featuring numerous second-generation Whitey's Lindy Hoppers. Each began as social dancers in Harlem, but quickly advanced to competing professionally at various clubs throughout New York, especially the Harlem Savoy Ballroom during the 1930s and 1940s (Miller and Jensen 2001; Manning and Millman 2007, Stearns and Stearns 1994). Different combinations of this troupe formed under the guidance of Herbert White ('Whitey') and some also travelled extensively during the 1930s and 1940s, first to cities throughout the US such as Chicago and Boston, but also abroad to Australia, England, France, Switzerland, Ireland, and Brazil (Manning and Millman 2007; Miller and Jensen 2001). Some of Whitey's original members continued dancing the Lindy Hop well after the Swing Era, either together in smaller troupes such as Manning's Four Congaroos or individually during the 1940s and 1950s (but others have occurred in nearly all decades since). Of these documented dancers, choreographer and dancer Frankie Manning became the leading figure of the Swedish revival. Manning's growing reputation as Lindy originator, performer, and choreographer would motivate a number of European groups to invite him to their home countries. Indexed as "ambassador of the Lindy Hop", Manning had renounced dance-retirement to transmit his own prior routines at the encouragement of some of the very young but persistent jazz, boogie, Lindy, and jive pilgrims.[4]

However, Manning was not the only individual to transmit the dance to Europeans in this decade. Others such as Dawn Hampton were frequently invited as guest teachers from the mid-1990s until 2015 ('Dawn Hampton Post Memorial Service'). Especially important for the European revival of boogie-woogie and the Lindy Hop was the under-recognised role of Mama Lou Parks, a third-generation Savoy dancer who continued to dance and teach the Lindy from the 1950s to the 1980s to African American youth in Harlem. Parks was one of the first to revive the dance after the disintegration of partner dances in the 1960s. During the 1970s and 1980s, she also brought members of her Harlem troupe to England and Germany, where they performed for jazz festivals, competitions, and workshops (Monaghan 2015; Sékiné 2017). Despite such stalwarts as Parks, Manning would assume a leading position in the Swedish and later broader European dance revival. Since the 1990s, Manning connected frequently and deeply with Swedish and later other international jazz dance communities until his death in 2009 at the age of 94. Manning's paternal role within the Swedish revival especially symbolised the long-standing relationship between the Harlem-based jazz dance and Swedish jazz culture in general. This relationship was strengthened by the intimate dance interactions between Manning and other 'old-timers' including Dawn Hampton, Al Minns, Chazz Young, and Norma Miller within Sweden throughout the last three decades, a period of persistent jazz dialogue, encounters, dances, and the inculcation of new performance styles.

By 1999, many of these documented professional dancers acted not only as 'ambassadors' for the dance, but occupied a leading role in teaching it, following increased communication and alternative modes of travel across the 'Black Atlantic' (Gilroy 1993). This metaphorical and physical route only partially resembled Gilroy's oft-cited 'routes versus roots' of Black American and Caribbean musicians and performers travelling to Europe after a period of reconstruction, or during the massive cultural and technological transition from the nineteenth to the twentieth century. As Dinerstein observed, early African American originators of the Lindy Hop were instrumental in aesthetically interpreting the contemporary modernist technologies. These fast-paced, highly rhythmic dancers concocted a "survival technology", a corresponding aesthetic, cultural expression, and corollary to the rapid developments of urbanisation (Dinerstein 2003). Moreover, as Unruh and Hunter remind us, dancing the Lindy Hop provided a form of resistance from mechanised forms of labour imposed by white society as well as source of physical and sexual freedom and joy, especially for women, whose bodies were increasingly subjected to disciplining as well conditioned by the politics of respectability in urban communities during the 1920s, 1930s and 1940s (Unruh 2011; Hunter 1997).

In 1935, as the dance's popularity and prestige began to spread, the revered French modernist architect Le Corbusier keenly understood the connection between this new 'technologically' advanced dance style and the advanced technologies of urban America when he first came to New York, claiming: "Jazz, like the skyscrapers is an event … representing the forces of today. The jazz is more advanced than the architecture. If architecture were at this point, it would be an incredible spectacle" (Corbusier, cited in Dinerstein 2003, 3). Corbusier and other Europeans who travelled to New York, including French modernist composer Darius Milhaud, were inspired by the jazz created by African Americans. They proclaimed that both big band swing and the Lindy Hop were two of the most advanced and technological driven aesthetic forms (Dinerstein 2003; Jordan 2010, 74–77). Le Corbusier was perhaps the first European to make the connection between the architecture of modernity and the machines and modernity of jazz. For many Europeans, skyscrapers and jazz were the two most significant cultural contributions of Americans to the modern era.

This European perspective partially departed from the racially charged dismissals of Black art forms within American critical discourses.[5] However, the fetishisation of jazz and cabaret culture of the interwar period as simultaneously "hybrid and primitive" is well explored in recent work, especially by Brown (2008), Fry (2014), and Wipplinger (2017). Nevertheless, these representations alerted international audiences to the virtuosic and highly modern dances of Whitey's Lindy Hoppers, partly countering the primitivist, othering, and essentialising representations of African Americans in both dance discourse (Gottschild 2003) and major American Hollywood films (Bogle 1973). As Dinerstein argues, big band swing and the Lindy Hop were two aesthetic forms that fit squarely into the artistic milieu of modernism, because of the fast tempo of swing performances, the mimetic representation of modern technology (trains and city noises), and the combination of collective and precise streamlined sections with individual mastery. Indeed, the creation, advancement, and perfection of the Lindy Hop was something of a 'survival technology' against the unrelenting demands of a racially stratified society.

As representatives of America's most modern and impressive art form, Lindy Hoppers crossed the Atlantic, performing for Europe's cultural elite, and teaching this dance to French and British audiences from the 1930s (Miller and Jensen 2001; Manning and Millman 2007). The dance had appeared in musical revues as early as 1931 in London such as in Charles Cockran's Revue when African American dancers introduced the Lindy Hop to British audiences. Other Black American performers provided examples of the Lindy Hop in music revues in other jazz-loving cities such as the 1930 Black Flowers Revue in Paris (Heinila 2018). The Savoy's Whitey's Lindy Hoppers travelled to Europe twice during the 1930s: first in 1935 when members sailed for England, France, and Switzerland (Miller and Jensen 2001, 88–97). A second iteration followed in 1937, this time as (Whyte's) Hopping Maniacs, who toured the ballrooms and theatres of Paris, London, Dublin, and Manchester (Manning and Millman 2007, 135–137). Ultimately, the Lindy Hoppers re-enacted the dance's namesake, crossing the Atlantic and performing for awe-struck Europeans in the new and increasingly democratic spaces of European jazz culture.

The inculcation of jazz dance throughout Europe could also be understood as concretely connected to local performance cultures driven by particular performers, record companies, dancers, and musicians in various jazz spaces, and also importantly through European dance societies and schools formed since the 1920s. Examples of such societies include the earlier and well-researched Hot Club du Jazz in Paris (Jordan 2010, 141–184), but also lesser historicised enthusiast clubs, including the jazz dance society in Oslo subsumed within the Bårdar Danse Institute, initiated by early jazz enthusiast and swing dance teacher Bergljot Bårdar Nordal. In the pre-war period, Nordal had organised informal dance instruction and promoted jazz dance club nights for locals. These Norwegian 'swing' dances were considered subcultural affairs, especially during the repression of jazz and Black American culture, which was often depicted as degenerate during the 1930s and 1940s (Stendahl 1991; Zwerin 2000).[6]

Other more recent examples include the boogie-woogie dance clubs which flourished in the 1970s and 1980s such as the Pop Club in Munich, and the more recently institutionalised competing federations such as the World Rock 'n' Roll Federation launched during the 1970s. These dance federations forged international consortiums which provided spaces not only for competition but for instruction and social dancing in the rock 'n' roll and boogie-woogie styles (Marcus Koch and Bärbl Kaufer, Interview with the author, July 3, 2018). Such clubs also engendered the appreciation and study of jazz and rock 'n' roll recordings and films, as dancers tried out and often modernised and improvised upon the popular social dances connected to these earlier performances first erupting in the dance halls of the US. These mythological places became important for European jazz dance cultures and especially within Berlin, Munich, London, Paris, Stockholm, and Oslo, cities emerging as important centres for jazz, boogie-woogie, and Lindy Hop since the 1930s. Derivatives of these dances would emerge continuously in Sweden since the First World War, proving that swing dancing, despite the lack of attention to this important artistic and cultural movement within historical jazz studies, constituted part of a jazz continuum.

By the 1980s, many of the so-called 'old-timers' were still teaching classes to swing devotees until around 2010 (the 'Queen of Swing' Norma Miller was still teaching in 2018). The most celebrated throughout Europe remains Frankie Manning. Other star Lindy dancers, like Norma Miller (also of Whitey's Lindy Hoppers), Al Minns (also of Whitey's Lindy Hoppers and of the Cotton Club and Radio City[7]), and even famed tap dancer Fayard Nicholas of the Nicholas Brothers (who stunned audiences with 'Jumpin' Jive' with Cab Calloway in the Hollywood black cast film *Stormy Weather* in 1943) too would cross the Black Atlantic to teach, preside over courses, and be interviewed by dancer and later camp founder Lennart Westerlund during his famous Herräng Dance Camp meetings. This trajectory mirrored the routes of other American jazz dancers connecting with European dancers and teachers, staged for enthusiastic, young (international) dancing publics. Through such contact, Minns, Manning, Miller, and others spread Lindy Hop to cities all over the world. Moreover, such contact led to overdue recognition of these pioneers within the European context.[8] These international mentorships helped to cultivate a prominent and thriving European Lindy Hop culture in the twenty-first century.

The 1980s Swing Dance Revival in Sweden

Sweden's 1980s swing dance revival is often connected to the Swedish Swing Society, a dance society formed in 1978. This society evolved via the European competition and performance style, including social dancing styles such as the jitterbug (and related 'bugg' dance), rock 'n' roll, and boogie-woogie, as well as the more professional forms that expanded throughout Europe during the twentieth century. At this stage, competitive dancing became popular throughout Northern Europe, with strong bases in Germany, the Netherlands, and Sweden. Concomitantly, in the 1970s and 1980s, Mama Lou Parks' Lindy Hop Troupe became active on European jazz festival circuits. Additionally, in the early 1980s, she initiated her Mama Lou Harvest Moon Ball in Germany and the UK. This was partially motivated by the popularity of more formal ballroom dance competitions in the post-war period (Monaghan 2015; Sékiné 2017). Similarly, the Swedish Swing Society formed its association with the American old-timers as well as established networks with the New York Swing Dance Society (Crease 1996). Unlike the largely competitive jive and jitterbug schools, these societies grew out of an alternative desire to highlight, research, and preserve especially the social dance styles (and not those varieties seen in competitions) from the 1920s to the 1940s. Like their New York sibling, the Swedish Swing Society remained a non-profit group dedicated to social dance styles and informal events, especially the Lindy Hop. Within this larger society, an important performance troupe emerged during the 1980s, the Stockholm-based Rhythm Hot Shots, later renamed the Harlem Hot Shots.

Lennart Westerlund, a leading figure in the first revival of the European Lindy Hop, had been dancing the jitterbug in Stockholm in the early 1980s. Many of the professional Swedish dancers and teachers began dancing bugg, a competitive style often taught to children. Bugg is a word derived from the somewhat pejorative appellation 'jitterbug', a term which Al Minns and other old-timers used to describe especially white dancers, in resembling jitterbugs, who "just went wild" and lacked control of their bodies.[9,10] However, in Sweden, the bugg evolved out of the 1940s Lindy Hop, and was further transformed when danced to the rock 'n' roll music of the 1950s. By the 1970s, it had solidified into a serious competitive four-count dance. Today, bugg is distinct from both Lindy Hop and boogie-woogie in that it is understood as containing Swedish roots, and performed to modern Swedish music. During the late 1960s, the competitive facet of this dance style coalesced around the formation of municipal schools where the dance was taught. From here, an official state federation further streamlined the competitive networks for young and experienced dancers. The *Svenska DanssportForbundet* (Swedish Dance Sport Federation) was formed in 1968, but only in 1984 did The Bugg and Rock 'n' Roll Federation become a member of the Swedish Dance Sport Federation.[11]

For young Swedes, grounding in the foundational steps of bugg enabled them to transition to the more complex rhythmic patterns of, for instance, Lindy Hop. Typically, those who graduate to Lindy do so because they develop a taste for jazz music. The well-travelled Swedish dancer Nils Andrén admitted that some Lindy dancers eventually find the bugg 'a little bit corny' (Nils Andrén, Interview with the author, July, 2018). Because dancers start so young (Nils began at age nine), the culture of dance in Sweden is quite advanced, earning it an international reputation throughout Europe.

While dancing in Stockholm, Westerlund and others made contact with Anders Lind of the Swedish Swing Society, the first to 'discover' the Harlem-based roots of the bugg and boogie-woogie dance. They established a rapport, eventually cultivating an affective and aesthetic community. Collaborations were dedicated towards learning more about the roots of Black American jazz dance. A small group of dancers began learning the dance from films and books, and were even invited to perform with the New York-based Harlem Blues & Jazz Band for the Stockholm Jazz Festival in 1985 (Lennart Westerlund, Interview with the author, July 5, 2018). This same band had frequently performed with Mama Lou Parks Lindy Hop Troupe in Harlem (Monaghan 2015). Parks was one of the last generation of Savoy Lindy Hop dancers who had danced there until its closing in 1958. She was also the one most responsible for keeping the dance alive; her troupe lasted twenty-nine years, the longest period of any Lindy Hop dancers (Monaghan 2015). Inspired by Parks' troupe, as well as the many film clips studied, in the summer of 1985, these three Swedish pairs decided to form a dance company, the Rhythm Hot Shots, in preparation for the upcoming return of the Harlem Blues & Jazz Band to Stockholm.

This project emerged partly because of this fortuitous exchange with the Harlem Blues & Jazz Band, but additionally after some of these members had actively sought out various Lindy dancers seen in jazz films from the 1920s, 1930s and 1940s, especially *A Day at the Races* (1937) and *Hellzapoppin'* (1941). As Lennart Westerlund recalls, he, Anders Lind, and Henning Sörensen (Secretary for the Swedish Swing Society) travelled to New York in 1984, seeking dancers from these films, including Al Minns – rumoured to be teaching in New York. Al Minns' name was discovered in Marshal and Jean Stearns' important history *Jazz Dance: The Story of American Vernacular Dance* (1968/1994). After finding Minns, Westerlund and others invited him and members of the New York Swing Dance Society to Stockholm to lead dance courses. Minns travelled to Stockholm in

1984 to teach various Lindy Hop courses during one month, including a five-day workshop that included the future dancers of the Rhythm Hot Shots: Lennart Westerlund, Catrine Ljunggren, Anders Lind, Lena Ramberg, Eddie Jansson, and Eva Lagerqvist. Lennart recalls the profundity of this first interaction, particularly regarding how Minns expressed the dance's relationship to jazz, which was apparently very different from their musical enculturation. The Swedish dancers had relied upon imitating the dances studied on films by mapping them to the musical structure with corresponding counts. He recalled how Al Minns admonished them for trying to dance by numbers, calling out "stop counting and start feeling the music" (*HDC Weekly Magazine*: Week One 2018, 2).

This series of events occurred also after this first trip to New York, and coincided with the memorial for Count Basie, who died in April 1984. Having heard of this memorial at the Red Parrot nightclub, the three Swedes (Lind, Westerlund, and Sörrenson) decided to attend. Here, they met Al Minns, who was dancing at this memorial. During their stay, they eventually introduced the idea of inviting him to teach in Sweden. In New York, Lind also met and "attempted to dance" with Norma Miller, one of the original Savoy Lindy dancers, where he established an important connection which would later evolve into a long-term relationship with her, motivating other dancers to travel to Sweden (Lennart Westerlund, email correspondence, January 1, 2019). Naturally, this would *not* be the first time American Lindy dancers had travelled to Europe to perform and teach. Indeed, Norma Miller, Frankie Manning, and others had embarked upon ground-breaking excursions between 1935 and 1937 to perform the Lindy Hop in British, French, and Swiss theatres and night clubs (Miller and Jensen 2001, 90–98).

As the Rhythm Hot Shots became more established in Stockholm, they invited Minns to return in the summer of 1985, but Minns sadly died shortly after. Through Minns, they learned of Frankie Manning, who at that time was a retired postal worker. In 1986, Westerlund invited Manning to visit Sweden and work with the company. Here he worked with the troupe for two weeks, one in Stockholm and the second in Herräng. This proved a mutually rewarding experience, and so Manning was asked to return, this time to the Herräng Dance Camp in 1989, which had existed since 1982. Since 1989, Manning returned every year to the camp until his death in 2007 (*HDC Weekly Magazine* Week One, 2017). The year 1989 was the same year that the Rhythm Hot Shots also became more involved in organising the camp, together with the Swedish Swing Society. During the 1990s, the troupe performed the Lindy Hop internationally, reproducing numerous routines, including the now famous *Hellzapoppin'* Lindy Hop routine, originally choreographed by Manning (Manning and Millman 2007, 172).

It was also during the 1990s when the dance revival stimulated interconnected networks within Europe. Parallel to grassroots interactions between locally active societies was the increased mediation, popularity, and commodification of various facets of jazz and swing culture, which adapted, commercialised, and even remixed the Lindy Hop for a mainstream public. Popular music theorist Simon Reynolds would argue that such digitally and transnationally mediated engagements with the past were symbolic of the larger 'retromania' sweeping late-capitalist societies. Furthermore, with the neo-swing movement, the 1990s witnessed an explosion of mediated swing representations of the Lindy Hop in films, television, and commercials including the films *Stompin at the Savoy* (1992), *Swing Kids* (1993), *The Mask* (1994), *Blast From the Past* (1999), *The Talented Mr. Ripley* (1999), and ad campaigns such as Gap's 1998 'Khakis Swing' commercial featuring the neo-swing band Brian Setzer Orchestra (Hancock 2013, 787).

According to swing dance scholar Black Hawk Hancock, such commodified mediascapes created a kind of 'cultural amnesia' of the Black cultural roots of the dance. This was part of a larger commodification and streamlining of the dance especially for white mainstream audiences, particularly given that "with the exception of African American dancers in *Hoodlum* and *Malcolm X*, all of these representations featured exclusively white dancers" (Hancock 2013, 787). William Given also argued that the Lindy's broader commercialisation in the 1990s was enabled by removing it from the socially mediated and interactive practices of the dance floor such as the circle jam (first situated in the Savoy Ballroom) and treating it rather as a commercial performative spectacle. He argued "this discon-nection … transformed the meaning of the dance from one that had an inclusiv-ity of community at its central core into something that now had a liminal space that created a distance between observer and participant" (Given 2015, 2). Others, including Usner (2001), would similarly argue that mass-mediated presentations of the revival created a homogenised and commodified version of the Lindy Hop, now depicted as 'swing dance', which further filtered out the important social and collective participation engendered by the African American participatory dance spaces of the Harlem ballrooms.

Germany and the Subcultural Revival of Rock 'n' Roll Dancing

In Germany and Sweden, however, this social adaptation had occurred before this widespread and mediated commodification. For instance, in the first decades of Herräng, an important alliance had been forged with the German boogie-woogie dance community, represented by the now experienced dancers and teachers Marcus Koch and Bärbl Kaufer. It was also in this period during which other Black music dances were incorporated into local swing dance classes. These additions became especially important for the social dancing occurring at parties in 1990s Germany. As Marcus and Bärbl recalled, most of the German dancers learned 'swing dancing' not through study of steps, but through social dancing within the more subcultural nightlife spaces such as Munich's Pop

Club. Here, a long-lasting rock 'n' roll dance scene evolved through a combined study of dance films, informal collecting of rock 'n' roll recordings, and lots of 'stealing steps' (Stearns and Stearns 1968/1994) on the social dance floor. Because of this practice, Koch recalled how the Swedes were surprised by the Germans' versatility on the dance floor:

> … when we came [to Herräng] we just danced. And we said – we never dance routines…. And for them it was strange. "You can just dance – you don't do a routine". And so we had a competition and we won the first week – the Harvest Moon Ball. Just busting out and every night Lennart said, "Hey these Germans they wanted to dance the whole time. They wanted to dance all through the night". Because there [at Herräng], they went to their fitness studio to work out for their aerials and it was more of a sports idea.
>
> *(Marcus Koch, July 3, 2018)*

German boogie-woogie dancer/teacher Bärbl Kaufer also remembered these early clashes, stating, "for us it was like okay yeah let's have a good party" (Bärbl Kaufer, Interview with the author, July 3, 2018). Marcus claimed that the competitions of the various federations were important for boogie-woogie in the 1980s and 1990s, but that the culture in Germany was perhaps more connected to social dancing. For him, Munich was an important centre of boogie-woogie competing *and* night life:

> It was party time for us and in the old days a lot of people were drinking a lot. When we had competitions, a lot of the cool dancers were at the bar and when you heard your number, 'number 57', you went to the dance and came back drinking again.
>
> *(Marcus Koch, July 3, 2018)*

This alternative path to the Lindy Hop in Germany during the same period reveals how different dance communities inculcated different values and practices relating to social dance.

While dancing at parties formed the locus of the social dance scene, boogie dancers like Marcus and Bärbl were similarly seeking out the old-timers and inviting them to give workshops in Germany. Eventually, these pursuits led to partnerships in Germany with Herräng. They also invited Norma Miller, Dean Collins, and Frankie Manning to Munich and elsewhere to give workshops during this earlier revival period (Marcus Koch and Bärbl Kaufer 2018). Marcus and Bärbl recall that after the Germans started attending Herräng in 1993, the influx of foreign dancers increased to a plethora of nationalities (Marcus Koch 2018). Today dancers come from virtually all parts of the world including South Asia, Africa, and Latin America.

Part One

HDC as Time Machine: A 'Brain Wash' in Jazz Culture

The Herräng Dance Camp (HDC) was first organised in 1982 by the Swedish Swing Society as an informal camp to teach the jitterbug and later Lindy and other swing dances. Taught by John Clancy, a white dancer from New York, the first editions were followed by Swedish participants exclusively. Years later in 1988 and 1989, there were two competing dance camps held, one organised by the Swing Society and one by the Rhythm Hot Shots, who actively invited not only Manning but other old-timers from the US to teach courses, lead workshops, or simply act as guests during camp meetings. In 1991, the two groups organised their first joint camp, and from 1994 when SSS stepped down, the dance camp, now organised by the Rhythm Hot Shots, grew in scale and reputation throughout the 1990s, following the revival of Black social dances throughout the world (Parish 1999; Sékiné 2013; Unruh 2012; Usner 2001; Wells 2013). As Christopher Wells wrote in his recent study of this camp, camp organisers gradually shifted their energies from literally reconstructing dance routines to more freely embodying the "creative, improvisatory spirit" of the dance through interactions with the original practitioners. Through such interactions, Wells argued, Herräng's partici-pants cultivated a swing dance subculture through "a shared pool of embodied knowledge" and "a common history built from traces of film clips and the vivid personal accounts of aging African American dancers". Ultimately, such activities crystallised the organiser's current role "as cultural brokers constructing and nur-turing a global network of dancers … to reinvigorate and advocate for this form of African American popular culture" (Wells 2013, 391).

Increasingly, dancers from countries all over the world attended the camp, although Northern and Western Europe remained prominent regions represented by both teachers and campers (Sékiné 2017). According to Anais Sékiné, in 2016, about 37 per cent of participants were Swedish and about 80 per cent were from Northern Europe (including the Swedes); about 58 per cent were women and the majority were white, middle class, cisgendered, and heterosexual (Sékiné 2017, 104). Furthermore, most were able-bodied. Sékiné describes this camp public as "relatively homogeneous, active, urban", and part of the international "cosmo-politan" economic class, in its capacity for mobility, leisure, and "participation in global capitalism more generally" (Sékiné 2017, 104).

In 2001, the camp digitalised, transitioning from a paper to an online regis-tration process, and subsequently its international composition grew exponen-tially; it also increasingly adopted digital media, while also retaining some of the Swedish and local traditions that developed from its origins such as the meetings, Swedish food traditions (like the Swedish coffee and cake known as '*fika*'), or the second-hand markets or '*loppis*' in which many dancers find vintage clothing, and the particular style of humour expressed especially by Lennart Westerlund. Since the 1990s, various traditions developed, including the weekly cabaret on Thursday nights, the Masquerade party on Friday nights (and also Thursdays), and the Savoy Night on Fridays. The Daily Camp Meeting Chorus Line is also a relatively new tradition, initiated in 2012 to stage original creations and re-creations of historical and primarily African American chorus line performances (Sékiné 2017, 100).

In 2018, the camp hosted some 900 participants weekly, during five weeks in which dancers enrolled for courses in boogie-woogie, balboa, Charleston, solo jazz, tap, and collegiate shag next to the staple of Lindy Hop courses. During the camp, dancers sometimes stay for multiple weeks and others register for the parties only. Some of the best dancers often take no classes, but loiter near the tents to watch instructions and practise independently.

The camp boasts unique opportunities to take lessons with the current leaders of both the local Swedish and international swing dance community. In the four years that I attended from 2015 to 2019, I took lessons with competitive dancers from across the globe. In 2018, students and teachers arrived from over sixty countries. Many of Herräng's teachers frequent international competitions through the worldwide dance federations, and also participate in the party-based competitions such as those staged for the famous Rock That Swing Festival in Munich or the annual London-based European Swing Dance Championships. These competitions mirror the kinds of enthusiastic and highly promoted Lindy contests staged at the Savoy, especially the Harvest Moon Balls, which first featured competitions between the best teams of Lindy Hoppers and other dancers. This includes the Savoy Ballroom's Whitey's Lindy Hoppers, who famously competed against other New York social dance teams. Following Miller, the Harvest Moon Balls were not only celebrated events in the African American community, but they also attracted New York's arts set (Miller and Jensen 2001, 65–82).

Herräng's Immersive Jazz Culture

During my first day at Herräng in 2016, a group of so-called 'swing kids' raced towards the school on their bikes; one did a wheelie while another blasted the music of Count Basie (from his make-shift boom box within his vintage bike basket affixed). This international group, dressed in baggy pants, flat caps, and plaid shirts, rode around doing tricks with 1930s-era big band jazz pumping out of their portable (vintage CD) players. A few playfully chided and hollered at the stylish adult dancers walking by. This scene, where an imaged jazz culture was made present in the habits and attitudes of its community, would replay itself multiple times throughout the camp. At Herräng, an embodied jazz culture clearly manifest as part of daily life, one embraced by its international participants first through a process of dislocation from national identities and modes of living, and second through location and connection to this temporal spatial community, through a process theorised by Christopher Wells as "the creation of a temporary physical space for a community otherwise defined by a fractured multiplicity of remote scenes" (Wells 2013, 395–396).

Elsewhere, participants are inundated in jazz music and culture, with documentaries and films shown nightly, as well as jazz music seeping through sound systems at all hours in the various camp buildings from the Ice Cream Parlor to the Café Blue Moon, and the Bar Bedlum in the old school. As Lennart revealed during a camp meeting in 2016, the Herräng experience is something of a 'time machine'. Furthermore, he argued, it constitutes a "brain wash in jazz".[12] Gradually, other facets of the camp, such as the history lecture, library talks with the old-timers, or the special programmes geared towards the 'Harlem Roots Track' reveal the important role of 1930s Harlem and in particular the Savoy Ballroom for the organisation and aesthetics of the entire camp, but especially during the meetings and educational programmes. As Lindy Hop scholar Anaïs Leï Sékiné argues in her dissertation on this Lindy Hop community, the "will to knowledge" and the desire to foreground this particular historical period, inscribed a particular ideology relating to how this moment is recreated within this unique location (Sékiné 2017).[13] Furthermore, the elevation of one particular Harlem Savoy dancer, Frankie Manning, determined the particular style and values of the dance's preservation and re-creation, prioritising this prominent performer and transmitter over others. However, the camp continually invited new old-timers from all three generations of the Savoy Ballroom, and thus enabled a broader interaction with numerous dancers.

The nightly camp meetings particularly became an important facet distinguishing this camp from other swing dance centres, with highlights of the (Harlem roots) of jazz dance within an entertaining and interactive format. Over six nights, camp founder Westerlund chooses films from his extensive archive to present to campers. This fascination with jazz-informed films began in the 1980s, when Lennart and others first aspired to learn about the dance culture of Harlem. He recalled how important these films were for his exposure to the origins of swing dance culture:

> I remember I sat at my job at the time, because they had a VHS player and a good TV, and I sat there at night time watching these movies and I know I came home very early in the morning after watching them. It was this time machine aspect of it. And I also liked to get the entirety of the culture around this and I was not only interested in the dance, the dance was priority number one, but I was interested in everything that kind of took place in Harlem at the time so it was about getting the feeling of what the Harlem Renaissance was like. What was the context of where everything was? It just took over my life … it was very much a love affair from my side. I wouldn't say I idolized it, I've never done that really. I really looked up to many of these African American performers that I could see in many of these old movies and so I got closer and

closer to that culture and being a Swedish person with my background, my way of being was far away from how I think being was back in Harlem in the days, it was really far away. But something pushed me back to that even though I could never dance like those people. Because I think the cultural barrier was too big somehow.

(Lennart Westerlund, Interview with the author, July 5, 2018)

From this early study, Lennart evolved into an avid collector and expert on jazz dance and jazz media. These films would become paradigmatic for the Herräng dance experience and especially during the meetings, in which clips from films remain a critical facet of this 'time machine' experience.[14]

Collectivising a Jazz Sociability at Herräng

Daily Camp Meetings

These nightly meetings help to inculcate the total jazz experience at Herräng.[15] Meetings originally began as more of an informal administrative gathering, but Lennart eventually professionalised them, sometimes joining with others such as Calle Johansson, who added humour and music. After 2000, the meetings' format solidified and quickly required a full team of producers, technicians, dancers, and others – a group of up to twelve people who work full-time in the summer only producing the evening meetings (Lennart Westerlund, July 5, 2018). Lennart claims that the meetings serve the purpose of group cohesion; they provide a "good start of the evening" before the parties. For him, the meetings offer a mix of entertainment, necessary administration, and a sense of history and education. Ultimately, these meetings help to create community while highlighting the roots of the dance in this faraway contemporary setting.

After the showing of film clips, as the campers settle into the darkened theatre of Folkets Hus, a spotlight rotates around an elevated stage. Campers are enveloped in big band revue music as the curtains are cast open to reveal a single stool in the spotlight. Typically, Lennart walks out to this stool, dusts it off, and then sits down with notebook in hand, always well heeled in his fashionable vintage suit and wing-tipped shoes. Often the meetings begin somewhat informally with announcements about camp business, or to provide tips about sleeping and laundry or where to eat and how to navigate the camp on a bike.

In the years I attended, meetings often developed particular themes, in an interactive 1950s variety television-like format, where the community audience would become part of the proceedings. In 2018, the theme revolved around old-timer Sugar Sullivan, a third-generation Savoy Ballroom dancer. In a humorous bit, she was awarded her favourite ice cream treat (rum raisin ice cream) on a silver tray as she sat in the special spot reserved for guests. While in the spotlight, Sullivan was asked to taste it. She responded with a slow hum of approval followed by a humorous quip, claiming ice cream was one of the last 'legal highs' she'd allowed herself. Lennart retorted, "what was the last *non*-legal high that you allowed yourself", to which she responded bluntly, "men". This elicited an immediate laugh in the audience. Then during the next evening, as a response to her last remark, Lennart had one of the male teachers and dancers perform a slow drag for Sugar, which amused her immensely. Eventually, the other guest dancer Barbara Billups (also a third-generation Savoy dancer) became disgruntled over the special attention paid to Sugar, and so Lennart brought out an ice cream sundae for her, which apparently was *her* favourite. The next meeting, Judy Pritchett (dancer, former companion, and partner to Frankie Manning), was given her special ice cream treat – a root beer float. Finally, the whole ice cream theme was turned into a competition for the best ice cream dessert to be judged by none other than Lennart's well-trained pit bull (amstaff), who proceeded to taste each of the desserts on stage to the wild laughter of the public. These old-world antics helped to instantiate a sense of group solidarity and also provide topics for conversation during the courses and parties. More importantly, they highlighted the role of the special guests and old-timers for the dance while engendering a feeling of informality. To encapsulate and cement this connectivity, the last meeting of the week often ends with a group enactment of the shim sham dance and then a nostalgic 1930s sing-along to the song 'We'll Meet Again' (sung famously by the British Vera Lynn in 1939) during which everyone sings while waving handkerchiefs in the air. These moments indeed reinforced the 'time machine' feeling of camp life in Herräng. They did so by simultaneously positioning the prominence of the old-timers for the rebirth of the dance in Europe since the 1980s.

Camp Films

Because both historical films and newly created camp media were an important facet of the meetings, sometimes short commercials were produced on site during the day and staged on the camp premises to highlight or satirise particular camp personalities. One year, I even featured in one of these films as an announcement to the library talk which I would give after the meeting. Other films highlighted important moments of jazz dancers' lives, such as in 2017, when a film from the 2000s of recently deceased Dawn Hampton was shown in which she danced joyously to some Bhangra music for a group of youngsters in Harlem. During the meetings, Lennart also incorporated segments featuring a small group of 'experts' such as the camp's cinephile, who would introduce the films to be shown with important background information. During camp meetings, Westerlund would ceremoniously hand over the films chosen for viewing, revealing his role as the chief archivist and curator. Finally, the meetings provided space to encourage participants to attend the many historical events such as the daily library talks.

Music and Dance Acts at Daily Camp Meetings

Many of the camp personnel were featured in the meetings, from the music booking agent Meghan Gilmore, to the professional dancers, who were often charged with choreographing small numbers. These dance numbers often featured as the star acts of this variety-like show. Sometimes dancers performed hilarious drag burlesques of social dancing etiquette, such as in 2016 when two very tall, male, Norwegian professional boogie-woogie dancers dressed in 'old lady' vintage dresses and danced to a boogie-woogie number, each vying for their 'heartthrob', camp founder Lennart Westerlund. They staged a dancing fight to win his affection, and eventually aggressively forced him into a fast-paced and very physical Lindy performance, each one pulling one half of Lennart to the opposing side of the stage. This was both comic and virtuosic as it revealed the dancers' finesse in burlesquing gender and generational roles, while also riffing on foundational steps of the Lindy Hop.

The meetings also often featured the Daily Meeting Chorus Line consisting of professional women dancers from the jazz and Lindy Hop dance world. Other numbers featured competitive Lindy pairs dancing famous routines from Lindy

FIGURE 5.1   Herräng's Daily Meeting Chorus Line, July 2015, Herräng Dance
                Camp, Sweden. Dancers from front to back and left to right: Larisa Vivas
                Kurbatova, Vassia Panayiotou, Matty Phelan Miller, Hanna N'diaye, Elin
                Rhodiner, Frida Häggström Gerdt, Marie N'diaye (creator, choreographer,
                producer, and artistic director), Alexandra Alhimovich
Source: Photograph by Tamara Pinco (www.groovy-banana.com).

films or newly choreographed numbers. Finally, solo jazz and tap dancers, such as the revered Chester Whitmore, Josette Wiggan, and Daniel Larsson, were featured in individual numbers with recorded music or a small live music ensemble. The mixture of informal repartee, historical jazz documents, and contemporary professional performances set the stage for the kinds of expectations and interactions present. Essentially, they replicated and adapted the informal and interactive cabaret jazz culture of Harlem but also of Europe's interwar jazz period.

Old-timers

The role of the old-timers is essential for the camp meetings, providing an embodied and intimate connection to the past. Lennart emphasised the critical role performed by the old-timers for swing dance at Herräng in 2018:

> The old-timers, all of them, they have added so much as dancers but also because they know the history, but even more so they were willing to share things all of the time. They were very, very generous with the dance and so we had a very good connection with many of them. And I think they liked to come to this little village. There was something relaxed about it. It was not the big city life or anything like that. It was really to come somewhere and maybe to step back in time a little bit. Because here Herräng was very much like a time machine.
>
> *(Lennart Westerlund, July 5, 2018)*

Such a close bond was poignantly revealed in 2017 during which parts of the cremated remains of the dancer Dawn Hampton were dispersed into the nearby Singöfjärden Bay after a procession of New Orleans-style jazz. Hampton was a multifaceted cabaret entertainer who sang, danced, composed music, and played saxophone in a variety of platforms. At Herräng, she was still active as special guest, representative old-timer, and Lindy dancer until 2016, the year of her death. This celebratory march musically and affectively enacted the special bond established and maintained by the early innovators of the dance and the Swedish revivalists.

Much of Herräng's organisation was driven by the 'will to learn' from, but also honour and credit, the old-timers. No old-timer was more important than Frankie Manning for the dance's revival in Sweden. As Lennart recalled, Frankie's visits were central not only for his artistic life but for the entire ethos of Herräng. When he died in 2009, his loss was deeply felt by Westerlund and others running the camp. Lennart soberly recalled:

> I remember when Frankie passed away, some of us we felt why should we do this camp any longer when Frankie is not here. And it sounds weird maybe to say that, but some of us really felt we did this partly for him because we liked what he stood for and who he

was…. So, it was something that was just an empty room in front of us suddenly. And it was very weird for me to sit at the meetings for a long time and look a little bit to the right and Frankie was not there, because he had been sitting there. He had never missed a meeting. He was always there. And then he was gone. And who should I ask all those questions like – well "how was it at the Savoy in 1934?" There was no one to ask any longer. It was very empty.

(Lennart Westerlund, July 5, 2018)

As illustrated, the role of the old-timers cannot be understated, especially the connection between Frankie Manning and Herräng.

Library Talks as Embodied Jazz Discourse

After these meetings, there are numerous events in which to participate in Herräng's 'brain wash' in jazz culture, from the library talks to the documentaries and single crash courses in particular jazz dance steps. The library talks commenced nightly after camp meetings, often featuring the honoured guests in a more intimate and engaged discussion. Prominent guests and dancers include current teachers, as well as old-timers Norma Miller, Dawn Hampton, Fayard Nicholas, Chester Whitmore (protégé of Fayard Nicholas), Sugar Sullivan, Chazz Young (Frankie Manning's song and long-time dance partner), Sonny Allen, and Barbara Billups. Sometimes evening guests would be interviewed by Westerlund about their experiences dancing in New York during the 1930s, 1940s, and 1950s. Other evenings, current dancers would be interviewed about particular topics such as their experience and knowledge of jazz and dance culture. These talks thus highlighted the connection between the old-timers and Harlem-era jazz dances to contemporary practices.

While relationships with old-timers were generally amicable, sometimes talks during meetings could also provide opportunities to reflect upon the racial dynamics of the European Lindy Hop revival. In 2017, when American dancer Sonny Allen guested during week one, his interview during the library talk broached both diverse and contentious subjects. After Allen proclaimed (with some irony), "Europeans discovered jazz, then Blacks moved on", there was significant discussion. During this honest observation, Allen claimed the Lindy Hop was "a kind of gift". He also commented upon contemporary Black dance, claiming, "now they have new dances and hip hop is still popular but then they don't know how to entertain – like on a stage in an all-around format". One man asked Sonny how he managed to make a living dancing and he retorted – "If you could go out and dance at Carnegie Hall would you give up your high-earning job", signalling the disparities between the economic status of the old-timer dancers versus many of the middle- and upper-class participants of the dance classes at Herräng.[16]

In order to highlight the racial politics of the American music and film industry, he talked about the differences between popular vocal styles and how the superficial naming of white singers as pop singers and Black vocalists as R&B singers indicated the persistent racial divisions. For him, Tom Jones exemplified a man who cultivated a Black sound and earned more money due to his race and ethnicity. He also pointed out how the cake walk was a dance invented by Blacks that became popular for Europeans. He even pointed to the audience and asked, "how many Black people do you see coming to this camp?" Allen had witnessed first-hand the wide transformation from a vernacular participatory culture to the transnationally mediated musical recordings and dances of the post-war period. He had danced in all styles from tap, swing, and Lindy to mambo and Cuban styles. He also had groups of women with whom he toured as chorus lines. The dancers of Allen's network maintained challenging work schedules while often caring for children while on tour. Such recollections of these experiences reminded campers of the realities of Black dancers as racial divisions and exploitations persisted. This library talk with Sonny Allen in particular enacted the very kind of intercultural communication and reflection which typified the camp as it engaged with the dance's past while also self-reflexively interrogating the present dynamics for contemporary European dancers, even if such reflection led to critique.

A second example of the sometimes-contentious dialogue facilitated by the camp relates to the meetings and interactions between Black and white old-timers of the dance. Marcus Koch, German boogie-woogie dancer and teacher and one of the first wave of revivalists responsible for inviting both Black and white old-timers to Germany in the 1980s and 1990s, remembers one particular incident wherein such resentments and contested values were staged. In 1996, Koch invited Jean Veloz, Ray Hersch, Norma Miller, Chazz Young, and Frankie Manning as special guests in Munich for the Boggie Bären Festival (Marcus Koch 2018). Los Angeles-based Veloz had danced with Arthur Welsch, Dean Collins, and other white dancers in various Hollywood films. These film clips earned her the reputation as Queen of Hollywood, while Norma Miller was known in Europe as the Queen of Lindy (or Swing).

Marcus relayed the story of Norma (Miller) meeting Jean (Veloz) in Munich and of accusing her of stealing the Lindy Hop, to which Jean demurred, claiming she was completely unaware that Black dancers had invented it. Further, Veloz protested that she had never seen any of the films where Whitey's Lindy Hoppers had danced. Marcus mimicked Veloz's voice, emphatically claiming, "you know we just did what we loved and what we thought was the Lindy Hop. I never knew about the Black dancers there. We never saw the clips, we never saw anything". According to Marcus, it was not until Jean was in Munich for the first time that she saw these important clips. After seeing these films, she said to Norma, "we really thank you for what you gave us". According to (Marcus) Koch, such a pronouncement assuaged long-standing feelings of betrayal and resentment by the Black creators of the dance. He claimed, "Boom! From this moment on they were best friends". However, Koch depicts this interaction from Veloz's point of view, acting out her sentiments upon seeing these films: "'hey it was from you … wow it is amazing what you did. We thought we were good, but we didn't know the dance'" (Marcus Koch 2018).

This anecdote encapsulated the long-standing grievances and power dynamics of the Lindy Hop as its representation was transferred from the Harlem-based ballrooms to the centres of the film, theatre, and music industry during the 1940s, which predominantly featured white dancers and actors often engaged in Black vernacular culture, such as the now well-studied and cited Lindy Hop scene from *Groovie Movie* (1944). Furthermore, Veloz's cultural amnesia about the Black roots of a dance she performed, which by the 1980s was generally referred to as the 'jitterbug', as it was in MGM's *Groovie Movie*, belied significant dynamic and institutional racism. Such films as *Groovie Movie* elided the Black roots of the dance while generalising their appeal for mainstream American teenagers. Unlike Mili's 1944 *Jammin' the Blues*, a contemporaneous art house film, which featured a rather unorthodox group of well-known jazz musicians (white and Black) jamming together with a rather straightforward Lindy Hop presentation, *Groovie Movie*, intended for the mainstream, featured a comical dance instruction bit with music by the Jimmy Dorsey band playing 'One O'clock Jump'. The narrator mentioned only one dancer by name, the award-winning white jitterbug dancer Arthur Welsh. The film sanitised, satirised, and de-racialised the dance as it 'misrecognised' and misplaced the dance's roots within various spheres such as square dancing, ballet, and other old-fashioned dances. Furthermore, the film's narrator satirically uttered and appropriated Black-inflected lingo. Further demonstrations of 'peckin', boogie-woogie foot-work, and 'the Hesitation Shorty George' (named after Black dancer, George 'Shorty' Snowden, considered the first Lindy Hop dancer by many), reveals the complex cultural relations of such mainstream presentations of the Lindy Hop even as these dance steps and phrases all aimed to imitate and gain pleasure in their adaptations of Black expressive culture.[17]

As Black Hawk Hancock argued with regard to dominant dance media, "In the case of the Lindy Hop, the decontextualisation of the dance is a process of symbolic violence whereby the dance is deracialised as it is erased from its historical and cultural context and racial identity" (Hancock 2013, 790). Within Bourdieu's conceptual framework, MGM, their creatives, and those who consumed this dance enacted symbolic power. Moreover, when such power dimensions are unrecognised or even denied, a symbolic violence is enabled which occurs through the transferring of ownership into elite European cultural forms. Finally, a misrecognition occurs as this dance performance, and its former racial power dynamics, is forgotten and re-contextualised into the 'colour-blind' contemporary swing revival. The jitterbug is further mediated as the more amorphous and racially neutral 'swing dance'. As Hancock reminds us, "Symbolic violence occurs not through techniques of manipulation or strategic deception but through a process of dehistoricising our taken-for-granted categories of thought that reinforce the dominant social order" (Hancock 2013, 789).

Within the context of the European swing dance revival, this meeting enabled both a staging of such power dynamics, and offered these dancers a chance to share their more personal experiences of the dance with each other and with the revivalists. In this sense, Veloz was made aware, after decades, of the Black roots of the dance she performed commercially and professionally; and for the old-timers who created this dance, they were able to air their grievances face-to-face to the dancers that once profited from adapting their dances. Such intercultural and inter-racial interactions were an important part of the swing dance revival of the 1990s, which eventually led to more sophisticated and knowledgeable debates in the twenty-first century.

In a more recent online Lindy Hop dance forum, a white female dancer depicted Norma Miller as an example of what Sékiné theorises as a "killjoy" or "angry black woman" (2017, 201–218): the African American female old-timers who are sometimes excluded from events because of their politicised comments. In this sense, knowledge of the racial appropriation and exclusion of African Americans, and especially Black women, to the most profitable and visible commercial enactments of the dance, led to a certain type of engagement with the old-timers, often only those who would present their experiences in more positive terms. These would be favoured exemplars of the old-time tradition. Yet at Herräng, these difficult questions and assertions were accepted and sometimes encouraged through the discussions with old-timers and the revivalists. In several instances, it appeared that airing such grievances was allowed, even if perhaps everyone would feel more comfortable with Frankie's manner of enthusiasm for the dance and making participants feel welcome and emboldened to dance, without allusions to the broader socio-political context. During her time at Herräng, the recently deceased Norma Miller was reluctant to do this, considering her long and complex history with this dance. It appears that Herräng has accepted her point of view, as Miller was even filmed in one of Herräng's promotional videos cursing at some of the (white) dancers for "not getting it right god dammit". While Herräng has chosen Frankie Manning as the ambassador and leader of the Savoy-inspired dance revival in Sweden, other perspectives were facilitated, lending a sometimes contradictory and complex enactment and entanglement with theory as embodied on the dance floor and in the other platforms of the camp.

Part Two of this chapter explores how the current values precipitated by this now long-term relationship with the old-timers alongside the interactions with vintage dance media have impacted the performative and mediated lives of contemporary professional Herräng-based dancers. Attention is focused upon a group of current dancers active within Herräng, but also within the international Lindy Hop dance community. Their performances and professional lives are explored in relation to both the community and ethos of Herräng and to the increasingly prominent role

of audiovisual media and vintage jazz recordings within the digital environment of
Lindy Hop in the 2010s.

Notes

1   Zwerin references the Zazous in his book *Swing Under the Nazis* and their devel-
     opment of a swing culture during occupied France in the Second World War. With
     their unique style of dressing, collecting records, and especially dancing, they were
     perceived as excluding themselves from the culture of war. See especially Chapter 17,
     'Zazou Hey!' pp. 147–162. Jackson also discusses the jazz dance rages in 1920s Paris
     because of a variety of cultural developments from the increased tours of travelling
     Black American jazz bands to the increased tourism industry to Paris to the number
     of travelling theatrical revues and especially the *Revue nègre* (1925) starring Josephine
     Baker and to the dance halls and cabarets offering exotic cocktails, dance lessons, and
     dance bands. France also developed its own film and music recording industry which
     too incorporated the figure of the jazz dancer into its Golden Twenties films such as
     Le Danseur du Jazz (The Jazz Dancer) (Jackson 2003, 49).
2   I'd like to thank the many dancers and participants that offered interviews for this
     chapter. These interviews took place from 2016 to 2018 during week one at the
     Herräng Dance Camp in Herräng, Sweden. Interviewees Marcus Koch (Germany),
     Bärbl Kaufer (Germany), Bianca Locatelli (Italy), Nils Andrén (Sweden), Mimmi
     Gunnarsson (Sweden), Fredrik Dahlberg (Sweden), Rikard Ekstrand (Sweden),
     Felix Berghäll (Sweden), Hasse Mattsson (Sweden), Marie Nahnfeldt (Sweden), and
     camp founder, dancer, and first-wave revivalist Lennart Westerlund (Sweden) are all
     included in this chapter. Camp course participants interviewed include Jessica and
     Mats Oldin (Sweden), Sven Dupuits (Netherlands), and Kersten Bengtsson Gavander
     (Sweden).
3   This is a contested term in both practice and in the literature on the Lindy Hop as
     swing dance is sometimes understood as a white-washing of the more specific jazz
     dances innovated and created by Black dancers in the 1920s and 1930s and especially
     the Charleston and the Lindy Hop. Swing dancing is often understood as connected
     to the mainstreaming of jazz music in the 1930s and the resulting 'dilution' of the
     dance for white and eventually international audiences and participants. See Black
     Hawk Hancock's book *American Allegory: Lindy Hop and the Racial Imagination* (2013
     University of Chicago) for a broader discussion and argument about this discourse
     and the ideological and power dynamics informing the naming of the dance.
4   As some of the older jazz dance revivers revealed, in the 1980s and 1990s, the dance
     was referred to with many different names depending upon the local dance cultures
     of those regions or cities. Some versions of jazz-inspired social dancing referred to it
     as the jitterbug, boogie, or even bugg (in Swedish) and others called it rock 'n' roll,
     boogie-woogie, or the jive depending upon the particular style of music used for
     dances.
5   See for example Adorno and Horkheimer's cultural critiques of jazz and mass culture
     in the chapter *The Culture Industry: Entertainment as Mass Deception* (1944) in which
     he dismisses jazz as a standardised form of mass entertainment which further com-
     modified musical works and led to more passive responses to modern music such the
     oft-cited 'false differentiation', 'pseudo individualisation', and the emasculation of
     music subjects from more serious cultural contemplation of musical works.
6   According to the Bårdar Dance Institute, in 1937, Bergljot Bårdar Nordal opened a
     'Swing Dance Institute' with courses in swing dancing for students, youth, and adults
     with "private lessons all day", every day of the week. This dance school thrived until
     1939, when it was banned during the war. After 1939, swing dancing continued but
     went underground as it did in many occupied nations (Zwerin 2000). In 1945 at

the end of the war, founder Bergljot Bårdar re-opened the dance school at Kristian Augustsgate 15, where the institute has since functioned. According to Lennart Westerlund, even Frankie Manning had visited Bårdar a few times during his trips to Europe. During the 1990s swing dance revival, the institute regained its status as a swing dance school and social club to host a 'swing dance marathon' with the record-breaking 110 hours of dancing. See "Bårdar feirer 80 år!" ("Bårdar celebrates 80 years") on the Bårdar Dance Institute website: https://baardar.no/2017/12/bardar-80-ar/, accessed June 5, 2018.

7   Interview with Al Minns by the Swedish Swing Society in 1985?, accessed February 4, 2018, YouTube: www.youtube.com/watch?v=npONjnioOmI.

8   This pride and recognition was warmly conveyed in an anecdote retold by Judy Pritchett at Herräng in 2018. Pichette was Frankie Manning's late-life partner and dance collaborator. Here she relayed how Manning would become ecstatic when hearing that he had been invited to an international city that he had never visited before, for it provided a chance to spread the dance ever further while also cementing its role as one of the most internationally influential of all popular culture forms of the last century (Judy Pritchett, History Lecture, Herräng Week One, 3 July 2018).

9   Interview with Al Minns in Sweden 1984 entitled "Al Minns Part I", Accessed October 10, 2018, YouTube: www.youtube.com/watch?v=-6DlmqOWBlg.

10 There is also the anecdote that after the Benny Goodman concert in LA at the Palomar in 1935, as the young dancers went wild in the aisles, Benny Goodman remarked to the other musicians that they looked like jitterbugs.

11 See the Swedish Dancesport Federation website at: www.danssport.se/English/Swedish DancesportFederation/DSFHistory; Marcel Gomes – https://marcelgomessweden. wordpress.com/2011/04/02/bugg-the-swedish-swing-dance/.

12 Lennart Westerlund, Camp Meeting, July 4, 2016, Herräng Dance Camp.

13 Sékiné investigates the current Lindy Hop world of Herräng and the Cats Corner dance school in Montreal as case studies to examine how this African American dance vis-à-vis its Harlem origins during the 1920s and 1930s has been culturally transmitted in these locations. Through the lens of Foucault, she uncovers the "will to knowledge" pursued by revivalists as well as the ways that a particular homogeneity overturns the particular gendered and racial power structures present during this dance's original cultural context. She looks at the story of discovery retold by current dancers/teachers as well as the particular networks which facilitated the Lindy Hop's instruction and performance in Sweden and in Canada. She also uncovers the particular role that the old-timers and especially Frankie Manning held for the revivalists in creating this idealised place, one expressed in terms of conviviality, openness, and inclusivity, despite the general homogeneity of the dancers that attend HDC. Finally, Sékiné pays long overdue attention to the women Norma Miller and Mama Lou Parks, who were equally responsible for transmitting the dance abroad after the Savoy Ballroom closed in 1958.

14 Films shown at camp meetings might range from humorous jazz-tracked cartoons (*Betty Boop*) to jazz or dance-based shorts from the sound film era to dance clips from Hollywood musicals and even Swedish jitterbug dance films from the 1950s.

15 Sunday, July 2, Camp Meeting, Week One, 2017.

16 Library Talk with Guest Sonny Allen, Week One, July 2–8, 2017, Herräng Dance Camp.

17 In the film, there are two African American dancers, who dance as children in a brief passage before a very tall woman dances with a short male lead, again borrowing and adapting the famous routine of the Lindy Hop's progenitors such as Shorty George, who famously performed a comic yet virtuosic routine with Big Bea at the Savoy and in other theatrical presentations.

5

PART TWO: JAZZ RECORDS, DANCE MEDIA, AND SURVIVAL TECHNOLOGIES WITHIN HERRÄNG'S PROFESSIONAL JAZZ DANCE NETWORK

Part One of this chapter examined the emergence of the Swedish Lindy Hop revival, embodied especially by the Herräng Dance Camp, particularly through its connection to the transnationally mobile American old-timers alongside the study and passionate engagement with vintage jazz dance media. This part, however, examines Herräng's *contemporary role* for European jazz culture through a close reading of the musical, aesthetic, social, and media-centred values and patterns rehearsed during camp parties as well as in spaces external but related to camp life. At Herräng, it is not only the 'place-making' and social activities that cement new forms of cultural heritage, but also the community's connection to a highly mediated, historical music repertoire amplified through both physical forms of interaction and through online spaces of discursive contestation and evaluation. Especially important for this sub-chapter then are the ways that jazz music from prior decades stimulates contemporary jazz values, which in turn instantiate a live, interactive, corporeal jazz dance culture within Herräng, as the current centre of swing dance's transnational dance community.

In the following, I examine the camp parties as an essential facet of the current European Lindy Hop dance culture. I'll first trace the embodied histories and related forms of heritage connected to the prominent dance spaces within Herräng. I'll then offer an ethnography of camp parties and their media-related aesthetics and practices. Part of this ethnography entails uncovering some of the social and cultural dance rules enacted and negotiated during social dances. It also involves an analysis of the role of vintage jazz recordings for Herräng's dancing DJs. Finally, this ethnography and practice-based study focuses upon the highly mediated and mobile lifestyles of a select group of professional dancers and teachers active internationally and at Herräng to make connections between the camp and the development of a particular trans-local cultural and aesthetic dance community.

Within the chapter, I'll argue how the combined worlds of Herräng, with its preservationist and academic values of knowledge dissemination, and the more diffuse and unpredictable sphere of online media, have engendered newer forms of 'survival technology' for the most dedicated millennial dancers. Further, this chapter illuminates these dancers' virtuosic and artistic contributions, while also examining the role of digital media and vintage recordings for the style and aesthetics of the dance. Through recent examples, I illustrate how Herräng's professional dancers contribute to this embodied affective community, while also establishing 'media power' (Carroll 2008) via the online circulation of new films. In this ecosystem, these dancers variously acquire prestige, visibility, and income in a precarious economy. Through active engagement with such media and related forms of visibility, this chapter posits the existence of critical self-reflection as a feature of both Herräng and the shared mediascapes constructed and disseminated by the international jazz dance community. Finally, I argue that as a result of the combined, conservationist commitment to the earlier legacy of the old-timers, with a more flexible adaptation of performance routes, dance styles, and media promotion tactics, the Lindy Hop scene in Sweden has positioned itself as the leading Lindy Hop community, while able to maintain connections to the perceived authentic (while mythologised) roots of this Harlem-based dance. Ultimately, this chapter attempts to prioritise the Herräng's current Lindy Hop professional community to elucidate their broader relation to contemporary European jazz culture.

While the 'survival technology' developed by the original Lindy Hop dancers occurred in a moment of massive upheaval, industrialisation, and modernisation, the contemporary international Lindy community also engineer their own strategies to maintain careers as professional jazz dancers against new forms of instability. Part of this path relates to their contribution and participation in Herräng as their aesthetic and geographical centre. Herräng remains an attractive site for this international community, partly because it affords an escape from modern urban life. The camp thus functions as a form of retrograde, romanticised 'survival technology', looking to the past for models of aesthetic freedom and solace, especially regarding the ubiquity of modern digital technologies and environmental crises. The small town of Herräng aids in creating this total 'brain wash/time machine' experience. Given its remoteness, it provides a "reduction in alternatives", and, as camp founder Westerlund argued, it "pushes a little bit in the direction of 'step into the world of swing for a while and leave ordinary life behind'" (Lennart Westerlund 2018).

Place-making at Herräng

Within the camp, the historical spaces of African American dance are animated through the place-naming of spaces after iconic dance sites. For example, the five outdoor dance tents honour and animate an affective connection to particular New York dance spaces – the Savoy Ballroom tent, the Roseland Ballroom tent, the Alhambra tent,

Smalls Paradise tent, and the Palladium Ballroom tent. While these 'place-namings' (Alderman 2008; Cohen 2007) promote a mythological relation to the jazz dance past for experienced dancers, for newcomers, they more concretely educate campers about the historic spaces of early jazz dance. Yet next to these mythologised place-markers, other specifically Swedish dance spaces emerge as part of Herräng's current heritage. For instance, current dancers often casually mention the famous Swedish dance floors of the Folkets Hus Ballroom and the Dansbanan, renowned Herräng spaces which interchange from dance studios by day to Lindy Hop and boogie-woogie dance floors by night. In terms of the swing revival, both of these spaces have accrued decades of important intercultural interactions since the 1980s – acquiring both cultural capital and forms of trans-local heritage.

Equally important to the camp's dance instruction, workshops, and evening crash courses are the evening parties offered within the two dance floors of the Folkets Hus. For example, during the first camp meeting of week one, 2016, Lennart Westerlund revealed that some of the camp buildings were constructed in the early twentieth century for the Swedish labourers who worked in the local iron mines. These buildings were erected by the workers as (left-wing) gathering spaces for education, meetings, and leisure. Apparently, the school and lake were part of these provisions (HDC Week One Camp Meeting, July 2, 2016). In this early-twentieth-century building, the education and leisure goals of the building are upheld as live music unfolds during the parties featuring Swedish jazz bands as well as international DJs specialising in jazz and other related music genres.

Dance Parties and Contemporary Swedish Jazz Spaces

Herräng's evening parties are perhaps the most important facet of the camp for this international community's embodied performance of jazz culture. Such dances provide numerous social dancing opportunities, but also offer spaces within which to cultivate new jazz aesthetics, to forge collective bonds around jazz culture, and to perform jazz dancing. Social dancers are important in that they feature both formalised and informal interactions such as through competitions, or within the circles materialising around improvising couples.

Herräng's annual week one 'Fast Feet' competition in particular acts as a prestigious event for international boogie-woogie dancers. Many arrive during week one to compete with the best dancers from throughout the world, but especially Europe. This competition is an endurance test of speed and agility, and dancers are required to prove their versatility with different partners in songs gradually increasing in speed. Additional competitions staged during the meetings include the boogie-woogie couple competitions taking place during the first and last parties of week one. For this competition, six couples 'dance off' to a boogie-woogie or fast blues, each taking two choruses, followed by one chorus, then eights, and finally dancing simultaneously, much like jazz musicians competing in cutting contests during jam sessions. The skill and speed of these dancers is a testament to the seriousness with which contestants approach this dance.

The other more informal competitive spaces emerge during parties as featured pairs enter informally marked 'jam circles' for short periods. In this space, new couples enter and attempt to one-up previous pairs. Such combinations of both informal and formalised competition attract not only amateur social dancers but many international Lindy and swing performers and teachers. This combination also mirrors the kinds of interactions taking place at the Lindy Hop's most important dance club, the Savoy Ballroom in Harlem during the 1930s, at least as relayed by the old-timers during camp meetings and in autobiographies of celebrated dancers (Miller and Jensen 2001; Manning and Milman 2007).

Regenerating the Jazz Past on the Herräng Dance Floor

An essential facet of swing dance culture at Herräng is the knowledge of American jazz recording history. Consequently, dancers pride themselves on their recognition of particular jazz artists from the Jazz Age and Swing Era. Thus, it is common to see professional dancers also DJ at evening parties; many have acquired extensive jazz record collections while progressing within the scene. Some of the DJs are hired expressly by the music coordinator, Canadian Meghan Gilmore, who has been programming Herräng's DJs for several years. Some DJs come specifically for this gig, while others are established teachers and dancers who divvy their time teaching courses and spinning for evening parties. These DJs generally don't engage in turntablism but rather act as 'selectors'. However, they are required to display skills in collecting and choosing the best selections for dancing.

The evening parties feature both bands and DJs, but occasionally the upper smaller theatre room plays mostly jazz styles from before the late 1940s, while the lower Folkets Hus ballroom features diverse styles. The music played from the various sound systems at the camp is an essential component of the immersive, 'jazz brain wash' experience. Many participants eventually learn the songs they repeatedly hear on Lindy dance floors. Favourites are recordings by Count Basie, Duke Ellington, and Ella Fitzgerald, but Louis Armstrong, Cab Calloway, Erskine Hawkins, Benny Goodman, and Fletcher Henderson are also staples of Herräng's ballrooms. For boogie-woogie dancers, R&B artists including Ruth Brown, Louis Jordon, Freddie Jackson, and Joe Williams remain dance floor staples.

Next to teaching and dancing, camp DJs, such as dancer and teacher Felix Berghäll, a frequent DJ at Herräng, participate in the larger network of DJs that has emerged specially at the camp. Here DJs share playlists and discuss the tunes that are most effective on the dance floor. Person-to-person and online discussions stimulate debates about particular recordings for various styles from Charleston to balboa and of course Lindy and boogie-woogie. For Berghäll, every summer particular tunes become popular with campers. The collective recognition and enthusiasm of such tunes creates a shared musical experience; such tunes often become yearly anthems. This occurred recently, when 'One O'clock Jump' was not only a favourite, but it prompted an exercise for DJs to riff on the playlist. Felix had decided to test the limits of the tune by playing multiple versions of the song for over one hour on the dance floor. This nerdy challenge might not progress well on less specialised dance floors, but in Herräng, where dancers are musically literate, the enjoyment of comparing and dancing to different versions of the same tune was clearly appreciated.

In 2018, Herräng's dance floor anthem was 'Buck Fever' (1951 Regal Records) by Freddie Jackson, a riff-based R&B tune which bridged the transition from swing to rock 'n' roll during the early 1950s. Apparently, dancers were requesting it after it was used by international Herräng pair Remy Kouakou Kouame (France) and Laura Glaess (USA), who performed a captivating routine to the track for the 50% & 50% Festival Showcase in Buenos Aires, Argentina in 2017.[1] Respected Lindy Hopper and teacher Sharon Davis (UK) had also choreographed a jazz routine to the song for the Swing Train Festival in 2016. As these versatile performances were filmed and then circulated through YouTube, the songs quickly acquired accompanying 'media power' for both the recordings and dancers. First the tunes are heard in festivals and competitions, then they circulate online, where the routines are studied and appreciated. After acquiring cultural capital and familiarity, the dance floor expectations too are impacted and subsequently colour the kinds of social dance interactions taking place during parties. In the summer of 2018, whenever the song was played, according to Berghäll, the dance floor exploded.

Favourite tunes could also be taken from other dance festivals or even social media documentation and representation of such events. For example, the rockabilly song 'Hey Baby' by Bruce Channel (1961 LeCam Records) was viewed a million times on YouTube when choreographed and danced to by Herräng teachers and international competitors Nils Andrén and Bianca Locatelli for the Rock That Swing Festival in Munich in 2018.[2] The song opens with a harmonica solo and an arpeggiated acoustic guitar ostinato as the intro transitions into the first verse of the countrified, rock 'n' roll crooning of Channel. I often heard this tune at the camp, both during lessons and a few times on the dance floor during the parties. Through international digital networks, but also locally within Herräng's DJ network, music playlists would circulate informally between DJs on their online dedicated platform, but also through the more diffuse circuits of international dance competitions. Such performances would later circulate through online media for the now rather large international swing dance community. This trans-local community interacts discursively through their connection to mediated routines and tunes, which gain important media power for the songs, artists, and competing dancers. These "disjunctive flows" (Appadurai 1996) breathe new life into lesser-known tunes such as this one by Channel, sometimes anachronistically inserting old tunes into this contemporary transnational dance culture. Such tunes are then re-introduced within the scene, and become new favourites of modern European swing culture. While newer yet lesser known artists and songs might emerge in particular moments, the staple of swing recordings of Basie, Ellington, and Goodman, however, remain the most important artists that dancers acknowledge in the various revivals.

At Herräng, an appreciation for music from especially before 1960 predominates, and is even included in the guidelines for camp DJs. Such rules provide an authentic swing soundtrack for those learning the roots of social dancing. They also educate dancers on the important jazz and swing bands active during the decades of the 1920s through the 1950s. One disadvantage for local Swedish jazz culture is that recordings of contemporary swing bands are rarely featured in the scene. This focus upon early jazz, swing, and R&B, or upon a predominance of Black American music-oriented genres connected to paired social dancing remains the focus of the camp. Not only does the study of the old dances next to mentoring from the old-timers enable a corporeal and historical engagement with the past, but the musical sounds heard help to preserve an already canonised tradition, while also guiding the interactions expected during more informal moments. However, digital media networks complicate the ways that we understand preservationist cultures who not only explore, but re-mediate the past.

DJs at festivals and camps are sometimes dedicated swing music collectors. They also may combine this pursuit with dancing. Dancing is a skill which elevates and assists in swing music record-collecting; as versatile and perceptive dancers, they are more knowledgeable and capable DJs. Because becoming a capable DJ often entails translating knowledge about dancing into the music sphere, and because the swing community attracts a large number of women, equal numbers of women and men often DJ for such events. As Herräng grew in reputation and size, the role of music became increasingly important for successful parties. In 2018, twelve women and fifteen men (and potentially one transgendered DJ) from eighteen countries were invited to DJ during week one. That year, DJs represented nationalities from across the world, with only Africa un-represented. This relatively even ratio vastly counters the ratio of DJs in other popular music genres where women typically represent less than 10 per cent of the total number of festival performers (Gavanas and Reitsamer 2013; Farrugia 2012; Friedlander 2016). Therefore, the Lindy Hop scene is not only immersed in the musical culture of the past, but contemporary values and hiring practices have influenced this historicised space.

As Sam Carroll discovered in her research on the gendered ratios of DJs in Australian swing dance communities, women were as equally represented as men in especially the lower-level swing dance events, yet this was not true for the more prestigious and larger events, where "men are by far over-represented" (Carroll 2007, 146). In these lower-tiered networks, women breached the barriers of other musical cultures such as EDM, where women DJs were heavily under-represented in all tiers. However, even in the progressive swing dance community, women (and non-binary DJs) failed to acquire the highest status and highest paid positions. Here too in Herräng, a (tentative) feminist disposition was enacted by music programmers, who openly sought to represent more "boobs in the booth" (Carroll 2007, 146), or women in the DJ stands, even as such organisers often eschewed more radical feminist politics.[3]

Carroll understands DJing in the swing community as an "authoritative performance of swing music fandom" (Carroll 2007, 141), one that could convene a sense of cultural capital and power within the larger Lindy Hop community. Further, as 'textual poachers' of Swing Era recordings, DJs curate songs for particular dance styles. Thus, the logics of DJing in swing dance events evolved its own set of etiquette and values, such as finding original and lesser-known recordings of Swing Era musical groups. For example, playing Glenn Miller's 'In the Mood' was considered the mark of a lesser DJ. Displaying one's fully developed knowledge by spinning the best and most suitable tracks for the varieties of swing dancing was one way to establish scene credibility. Finally, DJs were often looked down upon if they played the same recordings used by other DJs in the same event (Carroll 2007, 144). In Herräng, DJs also adapt modern technologies to expand their record collection and to continually renew their sets for innovative dance nights. This could pose particular challenges for DJs engaged in showcasing musical recordings drawn from a finite musical past.

DJ and dancer/teacher Felix Berghäll revealed some of the challenges and contradictions arising because of the historical and experiential gap occurring when dancers become acquainted with vintage recordings. For example, as dancers learn additional styles from different sub-periods, they sometimes develop expectations about what music they should hear during dances. Felix relayed one interaction that occurred while DJing for a festival during which collegiate shag had been taught. Following the dance, a few dancers complained that they didn't enjoy the music. When Felix asked for examples they would have preferred, they listed musical selections popular during a later period than when the shag was actually danced. He recalled how this conversation evolved into an extensive discussion on Herräng's chat site because of the cultural differences occurring between social dancing 'then' and today as a result of new dancing contexts. In some sense, this mediated reception reverses the process experienced by the original Swing Era dancers. As Berghäll suggested, the differences between the current swing dance jazz music culture relay specific historical knowledge of the dance, but "back then" you just accepted the music because there was only "one main popular style" in the clubs. He argued:

> One thing that I think we need to remember is that during that time they just had one style. Of course, it evolved during the time but they danced the dance because of the music and today it feels like the dancers want to have a specific type of music to the dance instead of understanding that it was all jazz music and some things swing and some things didn't. If you want to dance, maybe you pick the thing that swings.
>
> *(Felix Berghäll, Interview with the author, July 5, 2018)*

This complicated and ahistorical interaction between past musical recordings and the modern teaching styles of particular dances can sometimes create false expectations, or alter the intimate relation between (live) music and dance. Naturally, as Sarah Thornton revealed in her study of the variable and creative use of recordings in discotheques of the record hop and rave eras, the ways that music recordings have been used in live dance spaces remains fluid and subject to the changing aesthetics and desires of individuals in particular places and times (Thornton 1996).

Herräng's DJs expand their playlists through internal online chat networks, but they also acquire knowledge through more established sources, such as Tom Lord's Jazz Discography site – likely the largest digital reference site for jazz recordings from the twentieth century (Lord). In addition to sharing songs through the dance DJ networks, DJs also study and gather new releases of Swing Era recordings. The Lindy Hop scene has thus inspired the circulation and popularity of many swing tunes that were generally not recognised or canonised in extant swing music histories or compilations. Herräng's focus on prior Harlem dance venues, and especially the Savoy Ballroom, also conditions how and which older recordings are re-released by current jazz labels. Indeed, swing dancers' and DJs' knowledge and desire to play these big bands likely motivated the recent remastering and re-release of various recordings considered lost or simply forgotten.

One important recent compilation was released in 2018 by the preservationist label Mosaic, entitled *The Savory Sessions*. It features six CDs and 108 tracks of the Swing Era, especially bands featured at the Savoy and other prominent dance clubs active between 1935 and 1940. Many of these recordings were largely undocumented until the long-time collector and studio engineer Bill Savory released his private collection to the National Jazz Museum in Harlem. Mosaic depicted this phenomenal find this way:

> The Savory Collection … locked away for more than 70 years and finally available on CD for the very first time anywhere. The recordings are from the personal collection of Bill Savory, a quirky and secretive studio engineer in New York whose day job in the late 1930s and early 1940s was transcribing radio broadcasts for foreign distribution, and whose nighttime passion was turning on the disc recorders to pull in and preserve what was happening in the clubs of New York City and other cities.[4]

The continued interest in swing spaces provides a counter to the more official and sanctioned jazz histories, which frequently paid only passing attention to these interactive spaces. As Lindy Hop DJs purchase, study, and then spin such newly released Savoy era recordings, a new 'look, listen, and dance' with the past is engineered within such 'time machine' spaces. Dancers look to the well-known and well-worn standards, but they too dig out 'new' authentic recordings for modern inspiration from the jazz dance past.

Social Dancing at Herräng in Folkets Hus

The two Folkets Hus dance floors are designed to attract both boogie-woogie and Lindy Hop dancers. During week one, the lower ballroom is intended to attract boogie-woogie dancers and the upper Dansbanan spins music designed to attract the Lindy Hop dancers, but both groups of dancers can be seen travelling between the two dance floors. In fact, many of the dancers are so proficient that they effortlessly transition from boogie, Charleston, and Lindy styles to even earlier dance styles derived from the music genres of ragtime and early blues.

The best dancers and many of the teachers territorialise spaces on the dance floor. On the larger Dansbanan floor, the space near the DJ is taken by the competitive boogie-woogie dancers and dance teachers. On the first-floor Folkets Hus ballroom, the space closest to the stage is dominated by the Lindy Hop dance teachers and competitors. This territorialism mirrored dance values of earlier cultures. Original Whitey's Lindy Hopper Norma Miller recalled how the best and most competitive dancers territorialised the 'Corner' near the first (most prestigious) bandstand at the Savoy,[5] and only the most daring and competitive dared enter this space (Manning and Millman 2007, 65–67; Miller and Jensen 2001, 107).

As an intermediate dancer, I knew to maintain some distance from this space, but I watched as dancers 'owned' their moment to riff during the breaks or to show off their advanced swingout variations. While the joy of dancing was clearly evident, sometimes advanced dancers (usually not the teachers) would become irritated or even aggressive on the floor. Once a younger American dancer yelled at my lead for getting in his way, and not 'keeping the line'. In 2018, another very established Lindy dancer even pushed my lead as she attempted the difficult and fast-paced shag step. Both of us were intermediate dancers, and our inexperience and lack of efficiency clearly upset both the spatial and the social expectations of expert dancers. In short, many of the proclamations about the harmony and joy of social dancing, or the "politique de la joie" (politics of joy), as theorised by Herräng ethnographer Anaïs Sékiné (2017), could quickly turn to disappointment, rejection, and embarrassment for newcomers.

Conversely, other unspoken but quickly learned rules related to the generosity of the space. As a dancer, you were encouraged to say yes even to inexperienced dancers when invited on to the dance floor. Furthermore, you typically were expected to dance two songs, as the first song was usually necessary to establish a dancing rapport. Finally, the dance floor was intended as a safe space, so drinking and overly sexual invitations were discouraged, although flirtations and sexual innuendo were common and part of Herräng's dance culture. Despite these rules, dancers would sometimes reject invitations if the partner was deemed too inexperienced, for instance. I learned quickly that followers needed to be extra assertive if they were to gain experience on the social dance floor as the number of followers to leaders (which usually were men and women but not always) was sometimes two to one. This imbalance remained a frustrating part of the social dance interaction for followers, who could typically only accumulate half of the potential dance hours when trying to improve their style.

However, the generational divide characterising conventional society much more easily dissipated on Herräng's dance floor as older, experienced dance partners are keenly invited by younger dancers, and vice versa. I also observed many parents bring their kids to the Swing Kids programme. As one regular camp attendee Mats Oldin claimed, he felt "one hundred percent confident" that Herräng was a safe place for his daughter to wander around and dance with new partners. His partner Jessica Oldin also felt that passing on the dance to their children was an important way to teach them values you couldn't acquire elsewhere. She explained that by dancing with people from all over the world of different genders, ages, ethnicities, and races, you allowed your children to communicate and create in a shared space with no ulterior motive but to enjoy the rhythm of jazz music, claiming:

> It's about meeting people from different countries, you can connect without having to share details, but still you can get to know someone since music is like a world language and you are able to feel relaxed in that environment and know how and what to do with it, to *use it*. Not just listening, but for *something else*. I think that would be something good to have in life. That we have given them something, shown them something, a way to meet people. You don't have to just sit in a bar and get drunk. I mean what do young people do nowadays? A lot of drugs and alcohol and stuff when kids get together and this [music and dancing] is another way. I really like that we can do this as a family. In my class, someone is over 60 and Emma is turning 15 and we can all dance together. It is a mix of following and leading and colours and languages and it doesn't matter. It is a human activity and we can share feelings in the way we listen to music.
>
> *(Jessica Oldin, Interview with the author, July 6, 2018)*

Here Oldin expresses not only the joy of the dance, but the ability to communicate despite cultural barriers. Yet she points to something else, something performative and poetic; the ability to *use* one's body to engage the rhythms of jazz music, and this seems an essential component of the social dance experience, the cultivation of an affective embodied community. For Lindy Hop dancers, it is not simply a form of communication but a creative expression of the rhythms and poetry of swing music, through the semi-improvised movement of one's body. Especially for women, who have often been excluded from instrumental jazz culture, dancing provides an active, performative, and embodied connection to the music that they love.

Dancing Gender on the Herräng Dance Floor

Next to social dancing rules, other kinds of performative and cultural enactments could be observed on the dance floor, such as more neutral or fluid gender positionings between the leader and follower. This might take the form of same-sex dances, in a varying degree of leading and following and therefore allowing relationships to be staged performatively. As Lisa Wade (2011) argues, the modern Lindy Hop community in particular facilitates progressive networks which often favour feminist and gender-neutral habits. During her participatory research in the United States, Wade observed "a community of dancers who, in the process of attaining a Lindy Hop habitus, are socialised – both cognitively and corporeally – into an alternative, feminist gender regime" (Wade 2011, 224). Here Wade reminds us that the Lindy Hop was derived from the Charleston, "a jaunty dance that accompanied the first wave of the feminist movement". Ultimately, the Lindy Hop inculcates a gender aesthetic enacted by contemporary dancers to "challenge and usurp masculine domination" (Wade 2011, 224). Techniques such as disconnection, alternating following and leading roles, light-handed leading, and improvisation can encourage a more fluid partnership in social dancing. At Herräng, such fluid gender or androgynous styles of Lindy Hop were also discernible, especially for the most advanced Lindy dancers, who could easily switch roles from leading to following and who could subtly accept or reject the suggested movements of leads during social dancing.

In some European Lindy communities, committed same-sex couples or same-gendered friends take lessons and dance with each other. More often these are women who dance with other women, but recently and more frequently same-sex male dancers have been emboldened to dance together. The politics of a more gender-fluid dance style is not everywhere present and some dance scenes are unexpectedly conservative. But, for example, within the LGBTQ+ spaces of the west coast of the United States, the Jack and Jill competition, where random leads are paired with random followers, were renamed to the gender-neutral 'Pat and Chris' competition. These randomly paired competitions were first staged in the 1950s by the famous and now 'Hall of Swing' indoctrinated California dancer Jack Carey to encourage more people to enter swing dance competitions (Blair 1994). However, this competition practice has now grown to accommodate new versions of swing dance as well as new ideas about the traditional gendered proscriptions for leading and following. During one party conversation in Herräng's Bar Bedlum, I asked a parent and regular Lindy dancer about how her kids liked the courses. She recounted how after asking her son what he had learned from the day's lessons, he stated "both following and leading", which he enjoyed "about the same". She shrugged her shoulders and said, "see, times are changing" (Herräng Week 1, 2018).

Next to the growing normalisation (although still mixed-gender couples predominate) of same-sex partners are the more theatrical and aesthetic facets of performing gender on the dance floor. Some same-sex interactions are clearly intended to satirically reinforce heteronormative dance roles, such as humorous or flamboyant burlesques of the expected lead and follow (or male and female) moves of swing dancing. Humour, however, could be used to critique the rigidity of roles, or to reinforce gender norms. In 2018, I was impressed when watching famed boogie-woogie dancer and first-wave revivalist Marcus Koch as he danced with a younger but highly proficient male boogie-woogie dancer to an early 1950s rock 'n' roll song. Each reacted dynamically to the other's steps with exaggerated turns, kicks, and quick falls, and spins to the ground. It was clear that the code switching enabled by the follow and lead to this up-tempo song were the basis for improvisation and humour. Their dance frequently erupted into laughter when the timing perfectly gelled – these two were answering each other's jokes. Such same-sex dancing, therefore, could be motivated by a variety of gendered and aesthetics goals – to riff humorously on leading and following or to engage in more serious romantic expressions between same-sexed couples.

The Third Generation of Herräng's Transnational Lindy Dancers

Bianca and Nils

Sweden's reputation as the leading Lindy Hop community in Europe motivates many dancers to attend the dance camp and even move to Stockholm to be

FIGURE 5.2   Bianca Locatelli and Nils Andrén, 2017, Herräng Dance Camp, Sweden
Source: Photograph by Tamara Pinco (www.groovy-banana.com).

closer to Sweden's established dance network – this was what motivated award-winning Italian boogie-woogie dancer Bianca Locatelli to move to Sweden. In 2015, Locatelli had won the Euro Star Award at the European Dance Championships in London. Together with Swede Nils Andrén, she also recently won the Advanced Lindy Hop Couples competition. Inspired by her older sister, Locatelli started taking courses in hip hop in her home town of Imola, Italy, but after trying her first class in boogie-woogie, she decided to follow this style. She soon became serious about dancing on a competitive level. Still a teenager, she was invited to perform with the local boogie-woogie group, practising four times a week, and competing throughout Italy. As Sweden had a reputation for an established boogie-woogie and Lindy Hop scene, Locatelli decided to enrol as an exchange student there during her high school studies. This experience convinced her to transfer to Sweden to finish her studies and participate in the local boogie-woogie competitions. After receiving a pass to the Herräng Dance Camp for her winning performance at the Rock That Swing Festival in Munich, she discovered the community of Herräng, and returned several times before being invited at age nineteen to teach Lindy Hop and boogie-woogie courses there in 2017 (Bianca Locatelli, Interview with the author, July 4, 2018).

Andrén followed a somewhat similar path as a young teenager. When he was nine, he was invited by a friend to try some bugg courses in his hometown of Falun in Sweden. He recalls that he wasn't particularly motivated to learn boogie-woogie or any form of swing dancing, but he merely acquiesced to his friend's encouragement. He enrolled in the local 'fiscal dance education programme', where his friend's step-dad taught bugg courses. Here he experimented with other styles from salsa to ballroom and later Lindy Hop and boogie-woogie. He was predisposed to dance and music early on by a very musical mother, who played piano and sang popular songs, and his uncle, who was an avid 1950s rhythm & blues and rock 'n' roll fan. His other uncle played violin in a professional orchestra and his great grandpa had sung and tap-danced professionally in a touring Swedish jazz band during the Swing Era (Nils Andrén, Interview with the author, July, 4, 2018).

Nils and Bianca met on the competition scene but didn't start dancing together until 2014 after Locatelli had moved to Sweden. Both shared the experience of learning the dance as pre-teens and both excelled in the competitive environment. Now they live in Borås and tour the same festival and teaching routes as many of the dancers at Herräng. Such a lifestyle requires schedules that allow only occasional weekends at home. Their intense touring and performing schedules remind one of the industrial touring of the old-timers, such as Norma Miller, who travelled most days of the year. Norma Miller vividly recalls the physical stress and endurance required of such performing schedules. One example occurred during New York's 1939 World Fair ('The World of Tomorrow'), where Whitey's Lindy Hoppers 'exhibit' 'The Savoy Ballroom' was the most popular attraction, positioned within a larger platform which fetishised technology and progress. During several weeks, dancers were required to perform in an assembly line format, producing highly acrobatic routines eleven times daily from noon to midnight (Miller and Jensen 2001, 133–148). Current professional dancers may not be required to perform eleven hours a day, but the combination of teaching and competing plus social dancing could sometimes average ten hours daily during festival weekends.

FIGURE 5.3   Marie Nahnfeldt and Hasse Mattsson
Source: Photograph by Groovy Banana.

Marie and Hasse

Swedish dancers Marie Nahnfeldt and Hasse Mattsson are one of Herräng's beloved and established teaching couples, having taught at Herräng for over two decades. Like many of Herräng's teachers, Marie too began dancing as an adolescent in Stockholm. She was eleven years old when she enrolled for folk dancing, but soon she attended classes at the local bugg school under Lasse Kühler. In 1984, she was already competing in bugg and later boogie-woogie. She recalls that two of her early competition judges were the famous Al Minns of the original Whitey's Lindy Hoppers and camp founder Lennart Westerlund.[6] Because of her natural talent, Marie began competing throughout Sweden. Like many of the current and past teachers at Herräng, she enrolled for classes there to improve her dance, when in 1998, she was invited to teach boogie-woogie with her partner and future husband Hasse Mattsson. It was in Herräng that the two learned to dance Lindy Hop. They began performing and competing in Lindy Hop in 2004. For Nahnfeldt, her attraction to the Lindy was more about the complexity and flexibility of the dance. Yet her love of jazz music increased as she inundated herself into the culture of the dance. She recalls the combined benefits of couple dancing with the improvisation and freedom afforded by Lindy Hop:

> It was the fascination of couple dancing … and after trying a lot of couple dancing styles, I found Lindy Hop the one dance that never gets old. I've never been done with it. I feel like every time I learn something, there is so much more for me to learn and that is interesting to me. But I know that for some other people – their entrance into this dance was music. Or some had clothing that they wanted to dress up in, like during the 40s, and that is their entrance. So I think we are many people coming into this scene with different goals. It is also about the social scene around it, not only competition.
>
> *(Marie Nahnfeldt Mattsson, Interview with the author, July 2, 2018)*

Like Marie, Hasse Mattsson enrolled for the local dance society as a teenager, but in the town of Ostersund in the middle of Sweden. He was cajoled to enrol by his parents. Initially he wasn't especially interested in bugg or swing dancing to old jazz records, but rather he preferred typical adolescent pastimes like cars and sports. Nevertheless, he kept dancing and as a young adult, at the age of twenty, he moved to Stockholm where he enrolled in the dance society Eba Dans. There he met Marie, and the two quickly established a partnership and began performing and competing in boogie-woogie platforms throughout Europe. Soon they travelled to Herräng to improve their boogie-woogie, but also to learn the Lindy Hop. Because they were well-versed in the foundations of swing dancing, the Lindy was a natural progression. Hasse recalled how their training in these other styles made it quite easy to adapt and mix boogie with Lindy:

> We started to do shows with Lindy Hop so we learned the steps by
> doing shows and then they (Herräng) asked to teach us and then we
> had to study it a little bit and we took many classes up here in Herräng
> like you traditionally do – you take all the styles and you just make it a
> mix because we were already experienced dancers so we can adopt the
> style and the thinking of Lindy Hop. I think that is what we liked – the
> organizational part of Herräng. And then we have travelled the world
> with Lindy Hop. It is just fantastic.
>
> *(Hasse Mattsson, Interview with the author, July 2, 2018)*

For Marie and Hasse, Herräng became an important centre for mastering a variety
of jazz dances but also for building important bonds with international dancers.
Further connections to the prestigious jazz camp buttressed their international
performing careers while enabling them to travel worldwide.

Frequently, dancing pairs combine teaching with full-time jobs while others
dedicate themselves full-time to dancing. Marie and Hasse eventually decided to
treat dancing as their hobby. This decision presented both rewarding experiences
but also extremely taxing lifestyles. Marie recalls that some years, they were travelling more than thirty-two weekends per year. This was an incredibly demanding
schedule for a couple that held full-time jobs.[7] In 2001, they decided to stop competing to dedicate themselves entirely to teaching and social dancing, "enjoying
the mechanics and the dynamics that happens between two people enjoying the
same song" (Hasse Mattsson 2018). Some of the committed second-wave teachers
and competitors connected to Marie and Hasse's Herräng-based dance 'family'
have also danced full-time and travelled these international circuits. They include
the respected Ramona Straffeld, Joanna Stillman, Naomi Uyami, Soochan Lee,
Hyunjung Choi, Sharon Davis, Skye Humphries, Sylvia Sykes, Peter Strom, Asa
Heedman, Egle Regelskis, Memanja Lazovic, Isabella Gregoria, Caisa Weinemo,
Marej Dujakovic, Pontus Persson, Frida Segerdahl, and Daniel Heedman. These
last two dancers, Segerdahl and Heedman, are not only celebrated international
dancers and teachers of the second wave of the Lindy Hop revival, but they are
now two of the prominent organisers of the Herräng Dance Camp, supporting
long-time camp founder Lennart Westerlund. Of these many dancers and teachers, like Marie and Hasse, some work full-time as dancers/teachers and others
teach and also compete while working full-time jobs.

Competing and Dancing as Lifelong Careers

In 2015, first-wave boogie-woogie revivalist and long-time competitor and social
dancer Marcus Koch from Germany, together with second-wave Lana Mykhaylyuk (from the Ukraine) won first prize in the balboa competition at the European
Swing Dance Competition.[8] Marcus and long-time partner Bärbl Kaufer were
involved in the 1980s revival of boogie-woogie in Germany during the late 1980s

before learning of the Herräng Lindy community. The versatility of many of the first- and second-generation Herräng dancers is evidenced by their long-term engagement in learning the related styles of the Swing Era. Especially for those involved in the 1980s revival, many quickly expanded their interests in other dance forms such as balboa after coming to Herräng.

In this earlier revival moment, the combination of competing and first-hand instruction from the old-timers in Sweden and elsewhere (e.g. Germany or the UK) led to a more professional swing and boogie-woogie dance culture throughout Europe with a strong focus on regional, national, and eventually international competitions. Teacher and former boogie-woogie competitor Hasse Mattsson believes that the large number of young competitive dancers who later become teachers, or as he refers to them "travelling inspirers", have spread the dance outside of Sweden. For him, this trajectory led to a passionate and strong dance culture within Sweden and beyond in various places throughout Europe. He claims:

> I think a good part of the stamina is the young people that have grown up with the revival, including myself. We were maybe the second generation that had the stamina to keep going, teaching the dance and showing the inspiration. It was not just me, it was the amount of young people that became good dancers and teachers and we started to travel the world either via competition or via show groups or just going from social dancing to teaching and it is all of the above.
>
> *(Hasse Mattsson, July 2, 2018)*

Just as younger African American dancers spread the dance from Harlem to other cities in the US and then abroad, these cosmopolitan dancers too spread their unique style to dance scenes throughout the world. Although the racial and power dynamics differ quite obviously as European dancers spread the dance in the twenty-first century to other European dancers (who are not necessarily white themselves).

The intensity of such schedules nevertheless takes a toll mentally and physically on dancers' lives. In 2018, most dancers teach in their home cities while also travelling to festivals to offer weekend workshops. Others attempt to combine the demanding worlds of competing, social dancing, performing, and teaching. When asked to reflect upon both the advantages and disadvantages of this international lifestyle, Mimmi Gunnarsson, Herräng Lindy Hop teacher and member of the Stockholm-based Harlem Hot Shots, admitted that travelling was exhausting and that sometimes you would "lose your sense of a home base" (Mimmi Gunnarsson, Interview with the author, July 6, 2018). Long-time dancers and teachers Marie and Hasse also reflected on the international teaching circuits as both rewarding but also exhausting and difficult on one's body. These gruelling schedules were exacerbated by the intense schedules programmed during weekend festivals, which according to Gunnarsson could range from eight to twelve classes a weekend with expected performances and appearances during evening parties. This twenty-four-hour schedule is both physically and mentally demanding for professional dancers, who then retain only a few days during the week to rest and also train for upcoming performances and competitions (Mimmi Gunnarsson, July 6, 2018).

The intensity of this lifestyle allows little room for private time. Bianca Locatelli recalled that after such a weekend, during which dancers must maintain a public personality, she often longed for a quiet room with "no talking for five hours" (Bianca Locatelli, July 4, 2018). Dancer, musician, and DJ Felix Berghäll felt that such intensity and the constant need to work meant that one had no time to "rest your mind" (Felix Berghäll, July 5, 2018). This could lead to a loss of creativity or motivation for the social dance, which was often what first attracted competitive dancers to the scene. Furthermore, the dancers of the revered Stockholm-based Harlem Hot Shots maintain a frantic schedule of teaching for festival weekends, rehearsing during the week, performing at various events from corporate gigs to yearly theatrical shows, and then organising and executing special projects such as period-based films and music videos.

Despite such drawbacks, many competing dancers value the intensity of the Lindy Hop lifestyle as it affords participation in an invigorating jazz dance culture. Almost all of the dancers/teachers interviewed glowed when they talked about the friendships and experiences they gained. Marie and Hasse both reflected on how the friendships formed at Herräng especially motivated them to return year after year to see their so-called 'second family' of dance friends. The more mature dancers like Bärbl and Marcus, two founders of the boogie-woogie movement in Germany and Western Europe, continue to dance and teach because of their love for it. These experienced dancers maintain optimal physical shape and this community feeds their passion for imparting the dance on to both younger and older generations who come to Herräng as novices or more experienced social dancers.

Intercultural Dancing and Cross-cultural Exchange

While the intense mental and physical demands of a dancing lifestyle can be severe, dance-related travels often afforded metamorphosing events such as rec-ollected by Berghäll, who claimed that travelling around the world was the only way to mature into a well-rounded, compassionate person. He remembers his trip to Mozambique as a life-changing experience. Here the troupe collabo-rated with the Afro-Swing troupe Maputo Afro-Swing, who later also came to Stockholm to perform with the Hot Shots. In Maputo, the Afro-Swing troupe hosts a festival every year which provides the occasion for cultural exchange. Felix recalled this as one of one of his "best experiences" touring (Felix Berghäll, July 5, 2018). This trip resulted in a mutual exchange and reinforced the idea of dance as a core facet of particular aesthetic cultures, but one which could benefit from exchange, diffusion, and mutual collaboration. One thing shared by these two dance communities was their desire to explore and preserve the roots of Harlem-based Lindy Hop from the 1930s. A dedication to learning about this period, but further to enacting it in their dance, created a common ideology between these groups.

In his analysis of the Ciroc dance movement in the UK and France beginning in the 1990s, a dance derived from the jive and rock 'n' roll styles of earlier periods, dance scholar Jonathan Skinner (2012) conceptualised the globalising and intercultural processes supporting the spread and streamlining of this dance as "disjunctive flows", a concept borrowed from Arjun Appadurai's oft-cited account of cultural globalisation. Furthermore, the spread and diffusion of this dance through the specific media-, ideo- and technoscapes conditioned the ways that the dance took shape in the UK at the end of the century (Skinner 2012, 36). Skinner identified many forms of vernacular dance as intimately connected to an earlier period of globalisation, which first enabled various swing dances to spread throughout the world, claiming:

> the history of swing (including jive) is an account of the Americanization of dance taking place in the key globalization period between the 1880s and 1925, when global cultures were emerging.... It is a tale of mobility, creolization and disjuncture.
>
> *(Skinner 2012, 37)*

While the processes of increased mobility and cultural contact stimulated a long-term and sometimes disjointed popular dance culture in Europe, it also motivated an interest in continually discovering its roots and historical antecedents. Anaïs Leï Sékiné, in her writing about the Lindy Hop revival in Sweden and Montreal, revealed how such modern dance revivals shared the basic instinct to understand and publicly revere the African American historical roots of the dance; they share the "volonté de savoir" to discover and preserve the dance within a new participatory cultural context (Sékiné 2017).

In Mozambique, the 'will to knowledge' was further motivated by the desire to create more visibility for the African and African American cross-cultural connection to the Lindy Hop from the twentieth century, especially as the most recent revival is so often represented in Europe. The Afro-Swing project was similarly motivated by the desire to connect the Black swing dances of Harlem to their African roots. This revivalist group too then engages in performance-based research, as is evidenced in their mission statement:

> For us, Afro Swing is the beginning of a movement connecting Swing and Lindy Hop with its African roots and this is how far we have come in our research: Already in the 1950s inspiration from Louis Armstrong and other Jazz musicians came to the Township Sophiatown in Johannesburg which

was even called "Harlem of South Africa". This was, just like Harlem, the first place where people of all colors came together and danced a South African predecessor of Afro Swing called "Township Jive" to the music of Miriam Makeba and Hugh Masakela and jazz inspired music style Kwela.

('What is Afro Swing?')

Here, the role of the Lindy Hop in inspiring young dancers to investigate their cultural past acquires special meaning, because of the complex and exploitative histories of Africans' forced expulsion to the Americas, where the dance fulfilled an essential role as collective cultural expression as well as a "survival technology", and also a rebellious and life-affirming act (Unruh 2012).

A further impact of this exchange was the inclusion of African dance courses at Herräng. In 2018, campers participated in courses in traditional African dances with African drummers. Such exchanges potentially push the limits of the camp's ethos – preserving the dance from Harlem in an unadulterated fashion. Yet this exchange not only revisited the roots of African dance, but also modernised them by encouraging the cross-cultural pollination of styles. Interestingly, at Herräng, the Black roots of the dance then become the common link for the Lindy Hop's transmutation. Moreover, this exchange highlighted African and African American dancers who are often less visible within the international Lindy Hop community. Improving this visibility is a stated goal on their online mission statement:

> Spread Lindy Hop in Africa; Bring in Africans into the Lindy Hop world as teachers and social dancers; Create awareness of the African Roots of Lindy Hop and its challenges; Create opportunities for professional African dancers to share their rich culture and expertise; Bring Lindy Hop to African young people and children that can enjoy these dances with high energy.[9]

Given these goals, many of the dancers of the Swedish Harlem Hot Shots recalled with great enthusiasm the exchange they had with the Mozambique Afro-Swing group in 2014. This connection led to performances by both the Hot Shots in Mozambique and the Afro-Swing group in Stockholm and thus increased the visibility of African dancers abroad.

Gunnarsson also recalled the various benefits travelling to other countries to teach and perform, such as in Brazil, where dancing with the locals was an "eye-opener" into how other cultures embed dance as something quite ordinary into daily life. She recalled a visit with dance partner Fredrik Dahlberg to a party, where everyone at some point entered the jam circle, just to strut a single move, but with "lots of attitude and style". This alerted her to another way of thinking about dance – not as something codified one way, but as something individualised and shared by many in a community (Mimmi Gunnarsson 2018). The experience of travel forced others to acknowledge the large cultural differences between various communities engaged in the dance. For example, dancer Felix Berghäll experienced this significant cultural gap when he travelled to Tokyo with a dance troupe. He reflected upon these differences after dancing there and teaching the Lindy Hop:

> Tokyo was really interesting. I really enjoyed it but the cultural differences are so strong. Maybe in my age group, the people are more liberal and they are opening up but you clearly can see in Asian culture how they are controlled by their history, like how you are supposed to live your life. You are supposed to get married at a certain age. Me as a Swede from a super liberal country, the way that I have been growing up – for me it is really different. But I mean, that is something in the pros, the life learning, that part of how I live, you can't get that from anything else but travelling. There is only one way and that is going to see cultures, meeting people, talking and reading and understanding and experiencing bad moments as well and be like, okay you can learn from that too.
>
> *(Felix Berghäll, July 5, 2018)*

Other forms of travel for the Harlem Hot Shots included participating in Frankie Manning's 100-year birthday celebration in 2014 at the Apollo Theatre in New York, performing some of the Whitey's Lindy Hoppers routines for live audiences

FIGURE 5.4 Film still from the Harlem Hot Shots' 'When Rhythm Moves Us – First Stops' (2016) featuring Fredrik Dahlberg and Mimmi Gunnarsson

(Rikard Ekstrand 2018). Those who knew Manning had wanted Sweden's role within the dance's revival to be staged during this historic memorial performance. Harlem Hot Shots dancer Ekstrand claimed he'd learned more during this performance than in any other of his twenty-five years dancing. Thus, each of these cultural interactions led to renewed recognition of the dance's diversely accumulating cultural meanings and values in different geographical and cultural contexts. Such contact also increased an understanding of how the African American roots of the dance came to be culturally significant in different historical periods and places outside of the United States.

The Harlem Hot Shots and the Stockholm Swing Dance Scene

Many of the Swedish dancers at Herräng share a background in the municipal dance societies. Other dancers come to Lindy Hop later in their lives after seeing performances in films, through social dancing, or through performances of local performance groups such as Stockholm's Harlem Hot Shots. Fredrik Dahlberg, who teaches at Herräng, also performs with the Harlem Hot Shots in Stockholm. He came to swing dancing when he was nineteen, cajoled by a friend to attend social dancing courses at the Stockholm school Chicago run by camp founder Lennart Westerlund. At first, Dahlberg gravitated towards the musical culture of hip hop, having grown up during the 1990s and listening especially to those hip hop groups sampling jazz records of the post-bop and soul era, such as A Tribe Called Quest or Digable Planets. He was also an active jazz trumpet player, and currently plays with a jazz band, the Kunstgarten Ramblers, consisting only of Lindy dancing musicians. This band has already enjoyed prestige not only within the Lindy Hop community but has been invited to perform jazz festivals where musicians will intersperse moments of Lindy dance within the musical tunes. Fredrik's hybrid jazz position began when he was a kid as a player and avid listener of jazz and Black popular music, so his relationship to various jazz was well entrenched by the time he began dancing (Fredrik Dahlberg, Interview with the author, July 4, 2018).

Gunnarsson was first inspired to learn the dance after seeing it performed on a Swedish competitive reality TV dance programme, *Floor Filler*, in 2006. Soon after, she began taking lessons at the Swedish Swing Society in Stockholm. Eventually, she moved to the Chicago studio, and soon became influenced by the professional dancers of the affiliated Harlem Hot Shots. After this period, both Mimmi and Fredrik trained very hard, attending camps and workshops to evolve into highly respected professional dancers. In 2011, Mimmi and Fredrik auditioned for the Harlem Hot Shots and were invited to perform with the troupe.

In Stockholm, the Chicago swing dance school is a space to train, meet new dancers, and recruit members for the highly respected performance troupe the Harlem Hot Shots. While the Lindy Hop has evolved into a variety of modern forms in the twenty-first century, the goal of the Harlem Hot Shots is to preserve the dance as it was performed in Harlem during the golden age of swing. Indeed, their website even promotes a preservationist view of the dance:

> Harlem Hot Shots is a group of Swedish dancers whose specialty is entertainment authentic to the Swing Era. With the deepest appreciation and passion for dance styles that originally derived from Harlem, their mission is to keep spreading knowledge and the tradition of swing dancing. Dances such as the Lindy Hop, Charleston, jazz and tap make up the company's repertoire which also includes acrobatics, singing and comedy.
>
> Harlem Hot Shots is artistic, professional and re-creative. All of the company's activities are inspired by the ideals of the Swing Era, focusing on both faithful reconstructions just as original choreography with a framework that is true to the period. High energy, improvisation and tight rhythms. No modernizing. No compromising. Instead, the music, dances and overall presentation all emanate directly from genuine sources, such as authentic material from old film clips as well as many meetings and collaborations with dancers and musicians who were active during the 1930s and 40s. No intermediaries or distortions. No superficial adaptations or transparent clichés. Simply pure swing.[10]

The ideology of the Harlem Hot Shots evolved directly from the founders of the earlier performance troupe from the early 1980s, the Rhythm Hot Shots, who laboured to preserve the dance at a moment when some feared its disappearance. Westerlund and others had created this group as a way to research the Harlem origins of the dance and preserve it. This goal has remained consistent with the newer iteration of the Harlem Hot Shots.

According to Mimmi and Fredrik, the Harlem Hot Shots remain active in a variety of performance venues and media forms. Their gigs range widely from birthday parties and corporate events to performances at jazz festivals and for their own yearly theatrical shows. Recently they were featured in the 2018 film *Dansa Forst* (Dance First), a fictional romantic drama inspired by the Lindy Hop dance community. Even today, many of the projects are driven by purely artistic goals. Hot Shots dancer Rikard Ekstrand reinforced the aesthetic and artistic goals of the group's particular projects, such as filming a particular dance sequence in a single long shot as "they might have done" in the 1930s. This artistic exercise helped to foreground the dance, especially in light of the many digital editing techniques currently used to promote popular dance. By recreating these older dances as well as presentational technologies, the troupe attempts to authentically engage with and represent the jazz dance past.

Other preservationist projects initiated by the Hot Shots entailed learning the original routines of celebrated swing films such as the highly demanding Whitey's Lindy Hop routine from *Hellzapoppin'*, which they recreated for one of their performances with the original film playing in the background. Additionally, the group has also made various dance videos, some inspired by film maker and photographer Gjon Milli, who had filmed *Jammin' the Blues* in 1944, a short black and white art house film featuring celebrated jazz musicians (Lester Young, Jo Jones, Harry Edison, and others) and revered dancers Marie Bryant and Archie Savage Lindy Hopping in a minimalist set with prominent shadows, smoke circles, and close-ups of musicians and dancers. Other films, including *The Spirit Moves* (1950) produced by Mura Dehn, inspired recent films, such as *When Rhythm Moves Us*. Ekstrand explained how two recent projects came about:

> Two years ago, we had a project called *When Rhythm Moves Us*,[11] which was filmed with one camera, one angle, one shot, because nowadays you can edit and you can make everything look very nice but maybe in the 30s and the 40s, you just had one shot so you couldn't go back and rewind and change things. So we did the same thing there, but also we did it because we wanted to make a historical mark; so 50 years from now we can see − "what did swing dancing do this year?" Then six, seven years ago we had another project called *The Call of the Lindy Hop* … the idea was to record the Lindy Hop just like they did in the film *Hellzapoppin'* from 1941, and then Whitey's Lindy Hoppers filmed and performed one number and it is filmed from let's say five different angles with one front camera so they had to dance this routine over and over again. So, we did the same thing with one camera and different angles and the performance is really heavy duty with air steps and a super high tempo, over and over again just for fun but also to see what it is like to have the same challenge, one camera like you would have had in 41. So, we are doing weird things, but it is for us to get a better understanding of the dance.
>
> *(Rikard Ekstrand, July 4, 2018)*

In this film, each dancer offers their own interpretations of dances inspired especially by various dancers from Whitey's Lindy Hoppers, including Frankie Manning, Esther Washington, Leon James, and Norma Miller. These include a number of rapid swing outs, Charleston steps, aerials, jazz foot work, apple jacks, ballin' the jack, truckin', and the Suzie Q, all staples of the Jazz and Swing Era. By presenting young, third-wave revivalist dancers re-enacting Harlem-based dances as first mediated in Hollywood or New York art house studios, the troupe draws attention to an under-recognised corpus of jazz media from the last century. Furthermore, the troupe is engaged in practice-based research as they dance to better understand the aesthetic, corporeal, and technological limitations of the intersecting dance and film worlds of the 1930s and 1940s.

Another Hot Shots video features dancers Fatima Teffahi and Gabriella Rosati re-enacting their version of the Shim Sham. The same vintage style of

FIGURE 5.5   Film still from the Harlem Hot Shots' 'When Rhythm Moves Us – Jam Session' (2016) featuring Gabriella Rosati, Fatima Teffahi, Jenny Deurell, Mimmi Gunnarsson, Rikard Ekstrand, Sakarias Larsson, and Fredrik Dahlberg

the dance is recreated with one shot in muted tones. The video simply features the accomplished dancing of Rosati and Teffahi. The notes to the video on YouTube reinforce the idea of paying tribute to Manning as well as educating viewers on the dance's origins with the 'liner notes': "Common knowledge is … that the original Shim Sham was created by Leonard Reed & Willie Bryant".[12] Here they give credit to the pioneers of the dance while regenerating history and keeping the tradition alive, in their own performative style.

Conclusion

The second- and third-wave revival driven by the dancers and participants at the Herräng Dance Camp in the twenty-first century evidence a transformation and re-evaluation of the earlier 1980s-era revival in Europe. Through these decades, the first wave dancers, 'explorers', and archaeologists have evolved to develop more complex understandings and discursive relationships with the original Black American dancers, especially those who participated in the prolific and vital Lindy Hop dance culture of the Savoy. This occurred through a now nearly four-decade interaction with such dancers in various formats, from competitions, to ad hoc workshops, interviews, and discussions during the 1980s, to the intense study of jazz dance media and histories, and more recently to the practice-based research and interaction with the now nearly canonical jazz dance media preserved, studied, and circulated within the international Lindy Hop dance community.

The longevity of these relationships persisted while a new generation developed an even more extensive knowledge of the jazz dance media of this period. Further in the millennium, the power dimensions and debates surrounding the dance's adaption, internationalisation, and revival developed and expanded as such knowledge about cultural transmission and racial hierarchies increased within the international dance community. This knowledge and critical reception of the dance was partially accepted and later more actively encouraged within the platform of Herräng's "will to knowledge" ethos (Sékiné 2017). Further dancers came to the camp with greater access to theoretical approaches through both academic resources and online, and discursively through expanded debates within social media.

The second-wave revival in Sweden and especially in Herräng has not rejected the recent and consistent critiques levied by both old-timers and newer dancers of the appropriation of the dance and of the persistent racial and class, and now gender, hierarchies surrounding the dance's expansions in the late twentieth century. Rather, the widespread politicisation of various debates about culture, race, class, and gender via especially academic and digital platforms have indirectly seeped into the various platforms of education, discursive debate, and embodied dance within the dance classes and dance floors of Herräng. Such debates could be enacted through swing playlists and hiring practices of DJs or through the more fluid styles of leading and following on the dance floor. Further, this newer generation of young Lindy dancers, who now travel international Lindy Hop dance circuits of festivals, competitions, and workshops, appear more prepared to recognise the complex dynamics of cultural transmission as well as admit how they have benefited from their own (privileged) class and cultural background because of an earlier moment of 'cultural amnesia' and misrecognition as symbolised by the anecdote about Norma Miller and Jean Veloz in Part One of this chapter.

At Herräng, while the revival of the revival forges ahead in our current moment of intensified virality, environmental crisis, and online mediated polarisation and cultural contestation, at least newer dancers can prepare themselves for an ongoing and deeply embodied engagement with the *jazz dance past*. While a critical self-reflection continues to occupy a place within the preservationist, 'brain washing', and 'time machine' ethos of Herräng's re-enactment of the jazz dance culture of Harlem, it will be up to the next generation of dancers to discover how our bodies will adapt new survival technologies to the challenges presented by changing technologies and aesthetics within the broader European jazz music industry. Enabling young African American and African European and all other Black diasporic dancers more visibility and connection to this now international community would be the most productive and happy development of the revival of the revival so that Lindy dancing, like Baraka's blues continuum, could be productively incorporated into a more engaged and long-term dance culture, where the Lindy Hop could reposition its role as a survival technology for a variety of cultural groups and specifically the Black and Brown races, those who created the dance, and those perhaps still waiting in the wings to take their place in the spotlight within this global community.

Notes

1   You can view this dance video of Remy Kouakou Kouame and Laura Glaess on YouTube at www.youtube.com/watch?v=B9xnQJudrwE, accessed August 20, 2018.
2   You can view this dance video of Nils and Bianca on YouTube: *RTSF 2018 – Nils & Bianca*, accessed February 11, 2018, www.youtube.com/watch?v=N-J_Mgx7eNc.
3   After reading a draft of this chapter, camp founder Westerlund proclaimed that there is no feminist ideology represented at this camp, yet this chapter argues that even disavowed or unarticulated, a feminist vision can be enacted by the act of creating more gender parity while also supporting women financially and artistically.
4   See "The Savory Collection 1935–1940" on Mosaic's website: www.mosaicrecords.com/The-Savory-Collection-1935-1940/productinfo/266-MD-CD/.
5   Later historicised as the supposed Cat's Corner, although this is contested by current historiographers including Sékiné (2017).
6   Nahnfeldt has a VHS of this competition wherein both Minns and Westerlund appear as judges.
7   Hasse Mattsson holds a demanding job in the aircraft industry.
8   You can view this performance of Marcus and Lana at "ESDC 2015 – Balboa Couples – Finals – Marcus Koch & Lana Mykhaylyuk" on YouTube: www.youtube.com/watch?v=Rwg_OJEDm7g, accessed February 20, 2019.
9   See the home page of the Afro-Swing website: https://masx.org/what-is-afro-swing/.
10 See the home page of the Harlem Hot Shots: www.harlemhotshots.com/, accessed November 19, 2018.
11 You can see clips from this project on YouTube here: "When Rhythm Moves Us – Jam Session", www.youtube.com/watch?v=P00bBKkTXYM, accessed July 18, 2018. The dancers featured in this video are Fatima Teffahi, Fredrik Dahlberg, Gabriella Rosati, Jenny Deurrell, Mimmi Gunnarsson, Rikard Ekstrand, and Sakarias Larsson.
12 See the video performance of the Shim Sham by Rosati and Teffahi at "Harlem Hot Shots: Shim Sham – Frankie and Chazz – Gabriella Rosati and Fatima Teffahi" on YouTube at: www.youtube.com/watch?v=IFH3waV26Uo, accessed July 18, 2018.

6

PART ONE: CONFIGURING CRISIS AND SAMPLING SWING IN VINTAGE FESTIVALS AND ELECTRO SWING

On June 24, 2018, as the sun disappeared behind the Saumur castle, I crossed the Cessart bridge to arrive at the Place de la Bilange, the historic entrance of Saumer, France, nestled between the Loire and Thouet. I had come for the Anjou Vélo Vintage festival, featuring electro swing and other vintage music genres. That evening, I was invited to the opening reception at Le Dôme, an eighteenth-century theatre. The reception took place on the roof balcony, affording a panoramic view of the entire village and the Loire river. Local wines were offered with aperitifs, and a wandering trio (a vocalist, upright bassist, and acoustic guitarist) played a combination of 'gypsy' jazz and chanson. They offered intimate and humorous cabaret songs to party-goers in polka-dotted skirts and high-waisted slacks. From one end of the balcony loomed the imposing medieval Saumur Castle and below the picturesque if dilapidated buildings punctuated its banks. From this perspective, you might imagine a vacated village, but if you ventured behind this historic lane, a bustling square with many restaurants and modern businesses would appear.

This festival not only promoted the historic architecture of this medieval town, but the surrounding region during long bike rides, winding through the scenic vineyards and pastoral landscape of the Loire Valley. Such participatory activities were combined with a vintage market of retro clothing and local foods. At either end of the market were two stages for the music festival featuring a variety of vintage music genres from electro swing to more 'trad' genres from cabaret to chanson. During the two days that I visited, musical acts included a gypsy jazz group (The Hot Swing Sextet), a trio of female swing singers with a chanson-influenced repertoire (Les Nanas dans l'Rètro), and a quartet performing jazz in a New Orleans style (The Sassy Swingers). The headliner of the closing day was the UK-based Electric Swing Circus, a high-energy group featuring two vocalists, an electronic sound artist, a full rhythm section, and a versatile drummer who sometimes switched to synths during their hyperactive, polygeneric set. The days' music programme was concluded by the electro swing set of the French DJ Tagada, one of the featured artists of the Electro Swing and Vintage Reboot events promoted in Paris.

Such 'vintage' festivals have become more common throughout Europe, especially those providing visitors cultural transport to another era in which music was perceived as an interactive activity providing a "survival technology" (Dinerstein 2003) against larger forces of transition or turmoil. Recently, this retro music festival circuit organised itself into a professional consortium, as advertised in the accompanying brochure listing 'vintage festivals' throughout Europe. Each highlighted their own particular connection to vintage arts and culture, naturally including swing music mixed through combinations of electronic music and live instrumentations.[1]

Introduction

It seems fitting to close this book with a chapter that investigates the current neoliberal environment and its connection to the mediatisation and festivalisation of popular and jazz music culture. Prior intersections of jazz and pop depended upon visual media for promotion, but since the expansion of configurable culture (Jenkins 2006) within digital platforms, jazz-inspired media has assumed a more prominent role within particular remix cultures. This is nowhere more evident than within the electro swing genre, which prominently reframes pre-1950s jazz recordings and discursively stages facets of Depression Era jazz culture. Symbols of this era include the spaces, corporeal rituals, and performative arts of jazz culture from the cabaret theatres and music halls, from the 'Zazou' clothing and celebrated jazz dances to the black and white musical films of the 1920s and 1930s, and finally to the carnivalesque atmosphere of European popular music and mixed-arts festivals. Like other electronic music spheres, electro swing finds centres of production throughout Europe, but depends upon a transnational network of music performance spaces often within mixed-arts events and cultural festivals for its economic, social, and artistic viability.

This chapter explores the genre of electro swing as it developed from the mid-2000s within Europe in both 'live' music festive spaces and the related online spaces of digitally mediated participatory networks. Furthermore, it situates the genre within the broader vintage remix culture. In this context, electro swing's reconfiguration of music has become a foundational component of both small-scale swing-inspired events and large-scale popular music festivals. These range from the small-scale city festivals such as Anjou Vélo in Saumur, to the largest pop music festivals in Europe, such as Sziget, where nearly 500,000 visitors come from all over Europe.[2] Even in these mass-mediated settings, electro swing makes the jazz past audible for today's popular music youth culture. Although the degree and form of audibility remains contingent upon the desires and modes of interaction within these more generalised, typically escapist festival spaces. Finally, this chapter anticipates the frequent 'but this isn't jazz' comment by arguing that electro swing engages meaningfully with past jazz cultures, even if the outcomes and forms of engagement dramatically depart from more orthodox understandings of jazz music recording aesthetics and performative spaces of prior decades.

To illustrate, the 2018 edition of Sziget featured Austrian electro swing DJ Parov Stelar, one of the founders of the genre, in a ninety-minute headlining set for tens of thousands of mostly younger people. During his performance, Stelar interacted with live musicians, including cabaret-styled Viennese singer Cleo Panther, who intermittently acted as master of ceremony when not riffing over Parov's swing-sampled tracks. His three-piece horn section of trumpet (Marc Osterer), saxophone (Sebastian Grimus), and trombone (Jakob Mayr) performed sectional arrangements and improvised solos interwoven between thick layers of jazz sequences and electronic beats enhanced by the percussive grooves provided by a live rhythm section of trap drums (Willie Larsson Jr) and bass (Michael Wittner). Each of these musicians responded to Stelar's alternating mixes of 'musica gitana', klezmer, gypsy jazz, hot swing, and even classic blues within the aesthetics of electronic music; and each rearranged instrumental parts within the layered sequences of gradually accelerating tempos, industrial textures, and the aesthetics of acid house, techno, and of course electro swing (now exhibiting its own conventional tempos and textures).

Within this culture, an imagined jazz past (McGee 2016) drives the artistic and philosophical connection to prior European jazz culture, and the dialogical mediation of this past enables artists and participants to engage performatively with contemporary cultural frames such as neoliberalism. Since the arrival of electronic music, this stream of European jazz had long vacated the free, collective, and avant-garde spaces of the countercultural years, arriving in the centre of popular music through electro swing (and other sub-streams). Consequently, its large-scale popularisation demands a new examination of how swing *and* pre-1950s jazz culture matter for contemporary culture. Within this chapter (Part One), I thus examine a variety of swing-inspired arts events. These range from retro club nights to vintage festivals, and from smaller community-oriented dance events to the circulation of online jazz-inspired music videos. Special attention is paid to those heavily symbolic responses which connect the last century's Depression Era jazz arts culture, which witnessed the restructuring of social and cultural groups within the urban environment, to this century's economic and environmental crises. As the current organisers/DJs of the Electro Swing Club events (based in Paris) claimed on one of their promotional videos, electro swing incorporates "the classic sounds of the first depression with the cutting-edge technology of the second".[3] Thus, while some might dismiss the 'vintage' impulse of such mixes as yet one more example of Reynolds' 'retromania', I contend that in the context of mixed-arts festivals and participatory culture, electro swing signals a performative and aesthetic engagement via a reworking of twentieth-century crisis-inspired aesthetic movements, especially with the 'Golden Age of Jazz', as is often referenced in European histories of the 1920s through the 1940s (Zwerin 2000, 12).

By discursively engaging the perceived resilience and artistic virtuosity of jazz culture from this period within the present culture, electro swing provides an immersive, corporeal, and interactive response to the current crises. It is therefore clear that this culture extends beyond the "analogue effects" (Katz 2004) of 1990s-era electronic jazz, and instead places greater emphasis upon an entire gambit of artistic and mediated forms from the early jazz and Swing Era. Beyond early jazz recordings, other corporeal arts prominently feature within electro swing from the burlesque and social dancing styles, to comedy and cabaret performances staged in theatrical revues, to the jazz and dance performances documented in early sound films. Ultimately, electro swing is a culture that actively mediates and engages with the entire ethos of World War-era jazz. That an earlier age, which too managed economic and socio-political turmoil alongside massive transformations resulting from new industrial and reproduction technologies, is then reconfigured into the contemporary electronic and popular music milieu of mixed-arts events and festivals within Europe – events which explicitly aim to regenerate cities while also re-evaluating the value of regions and local cultures in light of contemporary challenges – should be less perplexing for contemporary scholars of jazz culture. Furthermore, it is apparent that vintage remix appeals especially to younger people, those most likely to suffer the consequences of current crises. Their presence remains important for linking past jazz and the 'jazz past' with contemporary culture. Finally, the far-reaching role performed by digital and social media for how youth culture engages and interacts within electro swing proves critical for understanding the unique quality of such a historical reconfiguration. In this context, the hybrid economies optimistically characterised by Lawrence Lessig (2008) must be reconsidered as we investigate the labour structures and digital promotion strategies undertaken by current artists and performers within vintage remix cultures.

Within Part One, I first contextualise these case studies with a review of the antecedents of electro swing, especially through the resurgence of the sounds and images of jazz culture within broader media such as electronic jazz, film, and recent jazz-influenced television series. I then examine new contexts for vintage jazz performances and remixes, especially within the medium-sized 'vintage' festival space – the Anjou Vélo Vintage Festival in France, and the transnationally organised Paris club nights known as the Electro Swing Club events in France and the UK. I provide contextualisation of these spaces and of how musicians and dancers interact in vintage festivals by examining the performances and recordings of the vintage remix group Electric Swing Circus from the United Kingdom. I then contrast and configure their 'live' music performances to the audiovisual promotional material circulated, supporting their engagement with the past and with broader understandings of prior and present moments of crisis.

Finally, in Part Two, the dance and vintage era inspired electro swing videos and recordings of particularly active groups within this transnational network are examined. Their promotional videos drive the multi-arts and highly eclectic aesthetic of electro swing and other electronic music combinations. It is through and within such audiovisual texts that the symbols of Europe's jazz past mingles with the current virtual world of modern technology and mixed-arts participation. As case studies, I consider both concert performances and promotional videos and recordings of the Dutch PLO group Caro Emerald, the UK-Birmingham-based live music/electro swing outfit Electric Swing Circus, and the French electro swing group Caravan Palace.

Electro Swing and its Antecedents

Electronic DJ and producer-led collectives active since the 1990s and early 2000s share a connection to a corpus of instrumental jazz recordings from various eras. However, the electro swing revival of this century expanded the archival influence of DJs and producers beyond jazz recordings to other jazz-era-related media and activities. Especially important for the electro swing movement were not only the largely male artists featured on canonised jazz recordings, but the entirety of pre-Cold War era jazz culture from the female chorus dancers and leading stars such as Josephine Baker working in theatres and jazz clubs, and finally to the travelling entertainers of fringe culture circuits, the 'freaks', magicians, and circus performers populating the margins of entertainment before the expansion of a transnational film and music industry was fully under way. It is not surprising, then, that the gendered make-up of electro swing generally displays more parity than other genres of instrumental jazz. This multi-gendered constituency of the genre might also have contributed to its absence in existing jazz studies. Part of electro swing's large-scale popularity relates to its inclusive gendered engagement and performance types from this pre-Cold War period. However, like many popular music revivals, white Europeans appear to dominate this genre.

Within the international party and festival circuits, the rapid growth of electro swing mirrored other kinds of electronic music trends within mainstream popular music. Experimentations with jazz-inspired remixes occurred as part of the impromptu rave phenomena of the 1990s and within local electronic music parties. In one interview, electro swing's 'Manouche'-inspired jazz violinist Hugues Payen of Caravan Palace fondly recalled attending such parties in the early 2000s. In particular, he admired their open and bohemian spirit (Beaudoin 2016). Before the large-scale promotion of EDM events, the free-party scene depended upon DIY networks and encouraged combinations of electronic music with local artists. While electro swing too appeared in these impromptu spaces, it gained additional momentum in the field of audiovisual media circulated on the internet after around 2006, especially through the distribution of music videos on You-Tube. However, the rise of electronic jazz in the 1990s, as well as the swing revival within dominant media during this decade, provided an important precedent for this musical culture's growing dependence and engagement with audiovisual media. The most spectacular and commercialised facets of swing culture had already been staged within dominant media prior to the eclectic 2000s. Swing-centred films such as *Swing Kids* (1993) drew their aesthetic from the contemporaneous 'New Jack Swing' culture animated within local live music scenes such as London or Chicago with artists such as the Squirrel Nut Zippers, the Mighty Blue Kings, and the Cherry Poppin' Daddies driving the revival of local swing dances.

While the film industry has often depicted the jazz-age speakeasies of New York and Chicago in period films, the European stages of transnational jazz have only emerged more recently in this century of transnational film and television series. In the new millennium, nostalgic images of particularly European culture were incorporated in contemporary media, such as the dance numbers and live jazz sequences set against the resorts of the Mediterranean in the film *The Talented Mr. Ripley* (1999), or the Paris cabaret culture of *Moulin Rouge* (2001), as well as more recent series including the BBC's *Dancing on the Edge* (2013) set in 1930s London, and the recent Netflix television series celebrating Berlin's multicultural Weimar culture, *Babylon Berlin* (2017), which offers fictional but historically inspired suspense narratives celebrating swing and jazz spaces. European-style electro swing would have convincingly 'soundtracked' the remixed Jazz Age film *The Great Gatsby* (2013) by Baz Luhrmann, as its bass heavy beats, sped up shuffles, and throaty saxophone wails perfectly fit this director's aim to modernise the look and feel of the past for contemporary spectators.[4] Luhrmann, however, chose modern electro, rap, and hip hop for his soundtrack.

Beyond audiovisual media, swing recordings had also already featured in the more underground circuits of local parties or for electronic music productions, such as the many jazz electronica hybrids offered by the electronic/jazz hybrid label Ninja Tune based in London. An early example is Mr Scruff's 'Get A Move On' from 1999, which combined Moondog's 1969 'Bird's Lament' saxophone riff and a muted trombone blues lick in an early jazz style sequenced over strings and computerised drum tracks.

Electro swing, however, largely evolved within the rave, nightclub, and later EDM European festival circuits, as DJs sought more novel sounds and genres for mixing and sampling. Veit Erlmann investigated the mid-1990s integration of world musics into new contexts and especially within dance and hip hop to argue how such reconfigurations signalled a truly "global aesthetic" or rather "a new aesthetic form of the global imagination, an emergent way of capturing the present historical moment and the total reconfiguration of space and cultural identity characterising societies around the globe" (Erlmann 1996, 468). Drawn from this global aesthetic, the precedent for incorporating distant cultural and historical sounds was well established within these nightlife spaces before the new millennium, especially as an accelerated globalisation altered our consciousness of the processes of historicity, while stimulating new modes of "mimetic representation" under digital culture (Erlmann 1996, 470). Before 'vintage' jazz featured in such mainstream popular music festival spaces and commercial films, it was through the middle layer of festivals and local club nights where particularly spectacular and bohemian enactments of Jazz Age culture were staged in combination with the technologies and aesthetic dispositions of contemporary electronic dance music. Electronic swing currently appears connected to this middle layer of arts entertainment, the local mixed-arts festivals and audiovisual media within the digital landscape.

During the 1980s and 1990s, driven by the expansion and incorporation of world music recordings within rave culture, the 'Balkan Beats' remix style had proven popular in dance spaces. European DJs, and most famously DJ Shantel, appropriated and remixed Romani musics into what Carol Silverman coins a "contested commodity;" such performances reified the cosmopolitan tropes of hybridity and multiculturalism while simultaneously absenting Romani musicians from the stages of electronic dance music (Silverman 2015). Such combinations established an interest in incorporating Eastern European instrumental styles and other syncopated 'Old-World' sounds into cosmopolitan, hybrid new mixes. In such reconfigurations, such as the Balkanised electronic mixes of DJ Shantel, Szeman and others would argue a "Balkan cosmopolitanism" positioned as alternative to a Western modernity. However, such performances also proffered a "nestled Orientalism" which ultimately served to erase actual Romani musicians from mainstream musical performance spaces as well as further Orientalise Balkan identities via an exoticised image of Gypsies within such remixes (Szemen 2009, p. 100).

One of the acknowledged progenitors of the electro swing sound, the Austrian DJ and producer Parov Stelar (born Marcus Füreder), had successfully mixed hip hop with jazz and other Eastern European styles such as gitana and Hungarian folk music in his first electro swing compilations.[5] The ecstatic responses to such mixes pointed to the broader taste for old-world instrumental dance music with strong connotations to such stereotyped Balkan dance cultures through the reoccurring East and West European dichotomies (Szeman 2009, 100), either pre-modern peasant cultures or conversely pre-digital yet highly cosmopolitan European cabaret and dance cultures, which often promoted the duo and contradictory tropes of urbanity and primitivism or earlier European jazz cultures (Fry 2014). Stelar developed his pan-Austrian programming career during the 1990s in nightclubs throughout Austria but soon emerged as a global DJ.

While many EDM scenes developed in European cities with strong local music networks including Berlin or Vienna, electro swing DJs rather gained their following in the more diffuse spaces of online networks or within the annual music festival circuits (Mazierska 2018, 77). They therefore increasingly gained status in connection to these placeless musical cultures of electronic music and their international festival communities. Stelar's national reputation grew after his

FIGURE 6.1   The cover of the electro swing compilation *The Electro Swing Revolution* (Lolas World Records 2011) featuring the track 'Baska Brothers' by Parov Stelar

mixes were featured on the Austrian popular music station FM4. In 2007, his LP *Shine*, which reconfigured the sounds of swing recordings from before 1939, was widely understood as one of the first electro swing recordings. Upon this release, the BBC named Stelar one of the "most promising European DJs of electronic music" as well as the founder of the genre electro swing (White 2008). Stelar established the genre's characteristic sound and cultivated an appeal for Jazz Age recordings in the amplified and electrified environment of contemporary dance music. Tracks including 'Little Lion' reintroduced nightclub and festival audiences to the fast shuffles of Jazz Age rhythm sections, but more often it was the muted trumpets and the female 'classic' blues vocalists in muffled 1920s-era soundstages that signalled a conversation with the past. This aesthetic favoured European references, such as the gypsy jazz guitar of Django Reinhardt and the violin riffs of Stephane Grapelli, or the fuzzy blasts of Louis Armstrong or the bluesy, full-chested calls of Bessie Smith's 'talking back' Jazz Age poetry, all musicians who established connections to European jazz culture via the Black Atlantic before the Second World War (Gilroy 1993).[6]

Sonically Signifying Swing

Moreover, within early forms of electro swing, the sound of 1920s and 1930s-era jazz rhythm sections were important aural and cultural signifiers. In electro swing mixes, sampled clarinet riffs were juxtaposed alongside the 'jungle' beats of swing age drummers. The exoticised jungle aesthetic, heavily debated by European critics during these decades (Jordan 2010; Wipplinger 2017), which became a characteristic aesthetic within Jazz Age cabaret culture, features prominently also in the visual imagery of contemporary music videos, as Jazz Age dancers from black and white films are sampled into contemporary videos or modern dancers perform the feminist-inspired Charleston in shorter, fringed dresses for jazz-aged theme parties. As Parov Stelar's reputation expanded, this genre increasingly appeared in both popular music and jazz festivals, but electro swing was more likely featured in popular music festivals with carnivalesque themes such as Wonderland in Cologne or Sziget in Hungary.

Within the broader genre of vintage remix, those that experimented with Jazz Age aesthetics ranged from single DJs to live music groups, such as the Paris-based Caravan Swing, a once producer-led outfit that quickly developed into an improvising instrumental group offering highly energetic and hybrid digital/acoustic live performances. The electro swing wave inspired multifaceted combinations of live music ensembles with electronic sound artists such as the UK's Electric Swing Circus, an eclectic touring band within the festival circuits of vintage fairs and mixed-arts events. The group also organises their own yearly festival in Birmingham, the Swingamajig Festival, featuring electro swing groups within a festive mixed-arts environment, where other circus and fringe arts performances offer interactive multi-arts theatrical experiences such as daytime workshops in swing dance and aerial circus acrobatics. Often electro swing acts adapt such strategies of casting their performances within their own self-organised vintage events such as the Electro Swing Club consortium led by several established European DJs. This transnational consortium boasts over eighteen clubs in Europe and North America.[7]

On these same festival and vintage party circuits, DJs mix both little-known Swing Era recordings as well as established swing hits – lesser known swing recordings are partly sought to capture the patina of 1920s-era jazz recording soundstages. Slowly the blending of the electronic DJ aesthetic with the performative and improvisational expectations of swing, early blues, and jazz have motivated both formats to collaborate in live music settings so that electro swing events rarely feature only single DJs anymore, but rather offer a combination of acoustic, sampled, mediated, and programmed music tracks.

Festivals as Immersive Spaces for Vintage Remix Jazz

Since the 2010s, festivals have become the most important context for experiencing electro swing. Rashad Gregory, sample and sound artist of the Birmingham-based Electric Swing Circus, claimed that vintage festivals offer the required atmosphere for electro swing bands to satisfy the cathartic urges of crisis-weary festival-goers. He argued that many fans seek escapist music in which to immerse themselves, just as the crazed Charleston dancers, and the African American zoot-suiters and 'zoot girls' (Unruh 2011, 222) sought outlets to physically relieve the pressures of the Great Depression. He claimed:

> Our music, it is the escapism of the 1920s and 1930s that make people just want to enjoy it. I mean people like to dress up as well ... and other times the music is not such a simple thing to do but it brings everyone together and everyone puts on the same kind of outfit, there is something about that. It is the escapism I think. If you have always wanted to do that Great Gatsby jazz revival thing, you can.
>
> *(Rashad Gregory, Interview with the author, September 14, 2018)*

In such immersive spaces, it is unsurprising that electro swing groups thrive in the festive and temporary 'time out of time' medium (Delanty *et al.* 2011), where participants celebrate the seasons and collectively gather before the winter months. However, the overt connection to jazz and other pre-digital musics, and especially those historicised as intimate musical cultures deeply connected to particular musical cities, remain prominent features of these group's audiovisual and performative output. Moreover, the festivals that most explicitly promote vintage remix styles also do so to connect particularly with local cultures and industries.

By providing a connection to this corporeal past, festivals privilege the localised cabaret or dance hall jazz cultures of the interwar period. In turn this connection buttresses the reputation and flavour of local regions and forms of heritage. Electro swing or vintage remix provides a fitting escapist yet celebratory soundtrack for the various regional festivals erupting throughout Europe, which seek to counter the hegemony and power of large-scale festivals, often sponsored by multinationals and programmed by the big players of the global music industry. Instead, these festivals promote not the big headlining acts of summer pop festivals, but the regional or transnational acts who often perform niche genres and make connections to local cultural fields of production. In this sense, the cottage industry of vintage festivals throughout Europe affords collaboration and sharing of promotional resources and bands who travel and re-populate genres such as trad jazz, electro swing, or gypsy jazz.

One of the most representative 'slow' festivals, which presents modern culture as deeply connected to a long tradition of the past, is the vintage bike and music festival Anjou Vélo Vintage hosted in Saumur, in the province of Anjou, France.

Anjou Vélo Vintage – An Escape into the Jazz Past

The Anjou Vélo Vintage festival, first launched in 2011, attracts some 8,000 cyclists for two days of curated scenic tours, and some 30,000 visitors to its vintage market and music/arts festival. During these picturesque regional bike tours, festival participants sample local regional wines from the dry Chenin grape of the Savennières to the sparkling Crémant de Loire wines. The musical programme offers a variety of genres presented within two stages situated at either end of the vintage market. Styles span the vintage remix category from cabaret and gypsy jazz to chanson and electro swing. Isabelle Montanier, director of L.E.O. (Loire

Événement Organisation), is the founder of Anjou Vélo Vintage. She claimed that this festival was inspired by another vintage festival in a mountain village of Italy, a "charming festival" which combined the exhibition of local cultural and epicurean products with an "old-world" flair (Isabelle Montanier, Interview with the author, June 23, 2018). For this festival, Montanier wanted to organise something fun, small-scale, and regional, but also an event that looked back into history. For her, the vintage bikes and old styles of dancing seemed to offer something physical and collectivising for contemporary participants, offering a festive break from what she depicted as their "high-paced plugged-in lives". The slow regional food, the intimate musical settings, and the many acoustic and modern/vintage mixes, she argued, attracted those who wanted to experience this particularly celebrated region, and to regain "a style of living" (Isabelle Montanier, June 23, 2018). More importantly, the festival offered a way to highlight the region's local traditions and agricultural products, especially as it eschewed all things mass-produced, overly commodified, or fast and cheap.

On June 23–25, 2018, Anjou's thousands of cyclists dressed up in vintage clothing for three days of routes chosen from seven different courses including the 'Authentic 1868', 'Abby Cyclette', 'Les Freres Dondroit', and 'Anatole Laguibole' routes, many of which offered wine tastings from local vintners. The various routes were poetically presented within the festival programme in terms of the historical sites, panoramic views, and the riches of local wines and cultural heritage, such as the 'Anatole Laguibole' route:

> Between vineyards and the Loire, cross the valleys in the direction of the famous territorial victories. In front of the singularity of the touristic and historical summits, the view of this excursion takes shape under your eyes.... Domaines winegrowing, exceptional panoramas, the Troglodyte patrimony: discover the riches of the *Saumurois*. A refined course, sparkling, fruity and gourmand.[8]

By highlighting the region's connection to a rich historical past, the festival promotes local culture's continued embeddedness within the landscapes, agriculture, and especially local vineyards. Furthermore, the connection to ancient cultures provides the setting for vintage music performances. Finally, because this vintage market and music festival is situated in the heart of Saumur, visitors' immersive experiences are affectively enhanced, engendering an ambience of eclecticism, conviviality, and '*décalé*' (offbeat quality). The marketing of the festival highlights this facet of the experience; the combination of time travel facilitated by one's festive and participatory corporeal interactions (swing dancing and biking), and the indulgence in local and regional delights, set against the impressive cultural heritage of this region:

> For three days, this time machine transports you to a 100% vintage world thanks to the many animations in this large program. Musicians, singers

and swing dancers, peddlers and street hawkers; a selection of unusual and *heteroclite* artists will transport the public to another era. Shows, initiations and ambulatory exhibitions; a total immersion for an indelible memory. In terms of the *soirées*, there is no early retirement. The *guinguette* on Friday and Saturday nights and the grand swing ball on Sunday afternoon invite festival-goers to come and dance to the jubilant airs of jazz and swing. Fine Loire Valley flora and local products will accompany the glamorous and convivial decor of this timeless rendez-vous.[9]

The market next to the restored cultural centre and theatre featured many hand-made vintage crafts and fashions, such as: La Vie Est Belt, an artist designing belts and accessories from recycled materials such as bike tires; Frenchoui, an artist making accessories in especially a French vintage style; a vintage hair coiffeur booth; and Le 'tech vintage' "tangible items to take you away from the digital age". Within the vintage market, the hand-made items and accessories are combined with an exhibition and tasting of especially local and regional products, namely wine, cheese, and brioche, which, as many of the market sellers explained, have been made in that manner for centuries.

Through the discursive connection to this region's past combined with the economic support of local economies, and through the artistic participating in vintage music styles, Anjou Vélo encapsulates the participatory and immersive goals of local European vintage arts festivals. The organisers commit to mediating notions of a European past, where grassroots cultural products supported local economies, and where collectively binding activities symbolised the social cohesion and resilience of communities combatting global economic pressures or local socio-political unrest.

During this festival, participants registered for day-long bike tours, adorning clothing from a variety of styles from before 1970. Within the international cycling community, this festival was known for promoting a celebration of cycling from 'bygone eras' and especially the 1930s to the 1950s, centred on "dressing up and having fun" (John 2013). Cyclists chose their attire from their favourite retro decade. Participants were required to ride bikes manufactured before 1980, and so this wave of 'slow' traffic blurred the boundaries marking one vintage era from the next. However, the majority of participants chose clothing and even bikes from before 1960, with the 1920s, 1930s, and 1940s favourite decades. Women displayed fishnet stockings and brightly coloured silk scarfs in their hair, and men sported suspenders and woollen caps with breathable white linen shirts. Some explored the professional or labour positions of pre-war France, with nurses' uniforms or farmers' overalls worn and peddled with a comic flair and sense of bravado as they raced by the intersection of Anjou and the Cessart bridge. Others wore less glamorous outfits such as turn-of-the-century military attire, or vintage hospital gowns. Some dared to bike in heavy, ruffled vintage wedding and party dresses with flowers protruding from their woven straw bike baskets. As they

FIGURE 6.2   Cover of festival programme, Anjou Vélo Vintage, 2018

launched their first ride, they all blinked and buzzed their bike bells and soaked in the hollers of the crowd, kicking their heels up with gleeful laughter as they rode past amused spectators.

Next to this starting point, the small vintage fair was in full swing, where visitors could buy large straw hats from a high-quality chapeau stand or handmade vintage clothing of the 1920s through the 1960s. Other specialties included local delicacies such as crepes or peanuts, roasted on the spot in an antique cast-iron stove fuelled with coal. These old-world offerings within this historic centre aided the experience of meandering into some mythical but visceral past, one where the music of jazz, the sun-ripened wines stored in local *caves*, or the crooning and old-time intimate performances of cabaret permeated the atmosphere.

Vintage Remix and Electro Swing at the Anjou Vélo Festival

The festival's vintage musical genres presented a cumulative image of modern cosmopolitanism and nostalgic regional musical cultures. This occurred through the combination of vintage remixes to the more acoustic local genres such as chanson or gypsy jazz, sung in French with inviting melodies to encourage audience participation. *Les Amaruex du Dimache* provided chansons '*a l'ancienne*' and *Les Compagne Arts* combined genres to produce a 'neo-retro rural soul'. Other, swing-inspired acts were *Les Nanas dans le Retro*, a vocal trio filtering the close harmonies and synchronised melodies of the Andrew Sisters but sung to tunes with lyrics in French. *The Gipsy Jukebox Allstars* sextet performed a largely acoustic set directly inspired by Django Reinhardt's quintet. They performed a medium-tempo version of 'Sweet Georgia Brown' with a captivating violin solo. In addition to the swing- and jazz-inspired acts from before 1950 were other retro-musical genres such as the neo-soul duo *Same Soul* and a Beatles cover band.

On Sunday, June 25, the headlining act was the Electric Swing Circus (ESC), who entered the stage and immediately established a professional air with their complex hardware and acoustic set-up. During their eclectic, high-energy set, Rashad Gregory, the sound artist, triggered various samples and synth pads from his keyboard, playing it live as a percussive instrument rather than as a pre-recorded back track. The group also highlighted the theatricality of their performance by changing instruments or dancing in a comic style. The band's highly versatile and energetic drummer, Chadra Savale-Walker, also sometimes switched to playing keyboards so that electric beats could be foregrounded in the mix. Two lead vocalists, Vicki Olivia and Fe Salomon, fronted the group, projecting boisterous chest-heavy vocals and sometimes more intimate solo cabaret songs in a chanteuse

FIGURE 6.3   Electric Swing Circus promotional photo, 2018
Source: Photograph by Summer Ameen.

jazz style. Their 'uniforms' added to the air of festivities, each wearing a hybrid punk/Charleston costume with black sequins and flapper fringe, white and black striped tights, and elaborately feathered Mardi Gras ornaments. The guitarist Tom Hyland was also the 'head master', wearing a tall black gentleman's top hat and baggy black trousers, and a white shirt with suspenders. This British guitarist spoke excellent French, in a highly theatrical, circus-like, ringmaster voice. Their arrangements evolved from dub breaks to break beats and from Charleston rhythms to jungle beats. No one danced swing or Lindy, but a number of younger people were doing something like Charleston knee-swaps or more EDM-inspired shuffles, bounces, and hand waves.

In contrast to ESC's international make-up, the festival's organiser, Isabelle Montanier, confirmed that the majority of acts are French and are chosen for their convivial, festive musical styles inspired by musical mixes of the past. Other acts featured burlesque and street performers such as the stilt walker comic *Kevin, Dylan, Velours*. ESC (Electric Swing Circus) proved the exception to these purely revivalist acts with its modern-hybrid live music act, but this group also forged a strong link to past cosmopolitan musical genres by incorporating both samples from this era as well as performing contemporary references to prior jazz styles. During Electric Swing Circus's set, the sounds of the 1920s were audible in the various samples used, including especially cuts from Fletcher Henderson or Sidney Bechet. Other jazz-era references occurred mimetically as evidenced by the sometimes Django-inspired hard-hitting rhythmic comping style of guitarist Tom Hyland. Additionally, the full-voiced musical theatre or cabaret style vocalising of Vicki Olivia and Fe Salomon also provided a link to the styles of the 1930s and 1940s.

In short, the musical offerings of this festival provided a convivial mix, allowing immersion into the past, but also in the present, with modern sounds mixed with Swing Era instrumental performance aesthetics. These vintage–modern combinations offered an effective backdrop for consuming local Loire delicacies and enjoying the local scenery; here these pastoral villages and their cultural heritage contribute to the city's regeneration. Such festivals also remind France's visiting urbanites of the Loire's regional value for France's national cultural heritage. In fact, according to Montanier, some 900 Parisians visit the festival to sample the local wines and to cycle through the local villages. A connection to both past popular musical cultures and genres such as Parisian swing or chanson, as Isabella confirmed, contribute to the *bon enfant* experience of the festival, a welcoming and convivial environment where participants are asked to take part in reviving the past rather than passively consuming the present (Isabelle Montanier, June 23, 2018).

Mikael Bretagne of Bordeaux Swing, who arranged the swing dancing performances presented during the festival, claimed that such festivals' connection to older jazz genres remain important for showcasing the existing and distinctive styles of French swing dancing, which he claimed flourished in Bordeaux after 2015, because of the establishment of a swing dance school there. For him, by showcasing the live music of European (and Black Atlantic contributions to French jazz) jazz musicians in the outdoor festival environment, dancers could effectively present social dance to those not yet initiated into this participatory corporeal culture (Mikael Bretagne, Interview with the author, June 24, 2018). Furthermore, as the dance became more established in Bordeaux, his dance troupe was increasingly solicited to exhibit the ecstatic swing dance culture of this particular region within vintage festivals and other social events. He believes that the popularity and linkage of swing dance to outdoor vintage festivals is owed in part to the desire for more engaged social interactions, as the solo dancing that became prominent after disco in Europe after the 1970s (was felt to have) left a rift in corporeal musical cultures. Bretagne articulated the paradox of going to a discotheque but then feeling alienated by the increasingly individualistic dancing styles of electronic music. For members of the vintage dance community, the modern EDM style no longer satisfied the desire of some to connect physically to music in social spaces. The swing revival and especially the Lindy Hop revival, with its association of a modern, urban, and spontaneous dance style facilitated current gender values and conventions which allowed spontaneous movement but simultaneously offered a form of enjoyable communication and physical integration. However, the more dedicated swing dancers typically did not dance to the hybrid electronic mixes of electro swing or vintage remix, but rather preferred the more traditional preservationist acts of gitana swing, jazz hot or 'trad' (New Orleans) jazz. Nevertheless, the swing dances shared the dance floors with the younger or older dancers of electro swing in a mixed-generational platform as both aided in the mediation of the jazz past into the current interactive spaces of the present.

Within the electro swing stages, the combination of modern musical tastes such as electronic textures and sound sequences such as swing music samples with especially festival musical genres such as punk, reggae, funk, or disco enhanced the immersive atmosphere for festivals, which generally did not attract only the specialist Lindy Hop dance community, but rather a more polygeneric music-loving crowd. This music provided brief moments of 'authentic' paired swing dancing but also enabled and encouraged other types of collective or individualised movement to the modern mixes of old and new.

Between programmed acts, DJ Tagada filled in the breaks as well as ended the day with a set inside a local club. His sets, committed to the techno and electro tempos and timbres of electro swing, featured sampled swing records and early jazz from both the New Orleans and New York repertoire and the early Paris-based jazz bands. While he played, many young kids came out to jump around and a small group of middle-aged women in more psychedelic clothing danced in a circle. But the younger, more fastidiously vintage-attired dancers waited for the acoustic 'gypsy' jazz group to play acoustic swing and shuffle beats before they entered and then completely occupied the small dance floor. The Bordeaux

Swing demo featured three couples, exhibiting impressive footwork, fast swing-outs, and jazz acrobatics to swing recordings, but they remained dancing during the New Orleans inspired jazz of the Sassy Swingers Quartet set immediately after their swing demo. Many of the mostly French families, groups, and individuals clamoured to see these impressive dancers, exclaiming as they watched: "Oh I love this style, look how fast they are. I want to learn that". One older couple, perhaps in their seventies, wore clothing from the 1920s and had practised synchronised leg movements, which they practised on the side of the dance floor.

The promotional video[10] of the 2018 edition of the Anjou Vélo festival imbedded Electric Swing Circus's title track 'Empires' from their LP *It Flew By* (2017) as the soundtrack backing a collage of images of vintage bike riders, retro clothing, swing dancers, acoustic musicians, and the beautiful architecture of Saumur and panoramas of the Loire Valley. This song perfectly encapsulated the past-made-modern ethos of this vintage festival.

Electric Swing Circus and the Swingamajig Festival

Because festivals have become important performance networks for musicians, many groups organise their touring schedules around the European festival circuit and season. Electric Swing Circus's longevity and financial viability depends upon this circuit. Realising the potential of festivals to stimulate the interactive reception of their vintage modern music, ESC launched their own inter-arts vintage festival, the Swingamajig Festival in Birmingham, beginning in 2013. After two years of refining their outdoor festival performances, Electric Swing Circus decided they wanted to create their own mixed-arts festival in their hometown of Birmingham, which, according to guitarist Tom Hyland, is a difficult place to play such mixed-arts music events. The first edition in 2013 offered an array of acts, and within the festival market, participants could sample street food, browse a vintage market, and have their hair styled in Swing Era styles. Furthermore, they scheduled their festival during a yearly UK bank holiday in order to connect this festival to the yearly rites of British culture. Their promotional video described the festival as a global romp from traditional to modern popular music genres and places: "From vintage swing and rock 'n' roll to hip hop & jungle, Balkan big bands to floor filling music from around the world, Swingamajig is a festival of supreme acts".[11] At the time of writing, ESC is currently planning their 2019 edition, which they claim should be their most immersive, partly owing to the historic venue acquired: a 1920s-era botanical garden outside of Birmingham (Tom Hyland, Telephone interview, September 19, 2018). By connecting the architectural spaces of pre-digital culture and architecture, this festival too connects Birmingham's historic past to the present music and arts moment. Hyland claimed that the venue was a central element in achieving the immersive atmosphere of vintage events. He also believed that vintage remix festivals allowed people the "chance to dress up, have a bit of fun and imagine an alternative world" from what they currently experience without "taking themselves too seriously" (Tom Hyland, September 19, 2018). Additionally, he explained how he wanted this festival to expose local audiences to other remix groups from mainland Europe while also cultivating a festive atmosphere for interactivity and cultural escape within Birmingham.

The Electro Swing Club Consortium

During the 2010s, vintage festivals, club nights, and electro swing clubs gained popularity throughout Europe. These were mostly smaller events in historical theatres or nightclubs which featured electro swing DJs and performers. Eventually a dedicated coterie of prominent electro swing DJs, who also worked as party promoters, organised a consortium of electro swing clubs, describing them as "an international chain of clubs spanning the European and North American continents".[12] The consortium sought to professionalise electro swing events as well as expand their reach within a network intended for both corporate clients, audiovisual media, and city-based arts initiatives. They promoted their concept as a comprehensive music platform:

> The A–Z global home of 'Electro Swing' and the 'New Swing Generation'. The original and largest multimedia entertainments company, offering the ultimate 'Electro Swing' experience to promoters, venues, festivals, party people & music fans worldwide. ESC has its own in-house events management, booking agency and record label.[13]

Furthermore, they advertised their professional events within the now familiar rhetoric of bridging the past to the present:

> The ESC [electro swing club] events bring back and evoke the feeling, nostalgia and fashion of the 1920s and early 1930s to the audience & dance floors of today with a modern twist and concept, delivering a whole evening's exciting and dynamic entertainment for your 21st Century venue.[14]

The Electro Swing Club consortium soon managed over eighteen electro swing clubs in Europe and North America. Moreover, the promo video displayed swing dancers and the burlesque performers of *La Cabaret des Filles de Joie de Juliette Dragon* (a Paris-based troupe) with a musical soundtrack that transitioned from a 'trad' jazz rhythm section to more conventional house beat, culminating in an electro swing track. Their promotional video boasted the global reach of their events as well as the style of electro swing by making connections to especially the golden era jazz culture with the catch line, "Incorporating the classic sounds of the first depression with the cutting technology of the second", followed by the naming of the "dynamic ESC DJ team" of Max Pashm, Chris Tofu, Typoboy, and Mirk Oh. Some frames featured instrumental jazz artists including established Vancouver bassist Jen Hodges.[15] The promoters thus viewed the ESC events as the international home of the new swing generation, replacing the old promoters of both the 1990s-era electronic jazz culture and, further back, the jazz aficionados of the Swing Era and cabaret culture.

On their website, this management/creative group explored the history of swing music and its relevance for the current electro swing movement:

> By the early 1990s swing samples & influences were becoming popular and were beginning to appear on 'Acid Jazz', 'Nu-Jazz' & 'Lounge' tracks. In 2004 Parov Stelar released the first 'Electro Swing' on his own label, triggering a boom of 'Electro Swing' DJs, producers & bands like 'Caravan Palace'. Between 2008–2010 Wagram (France), Freshly Squeezed Music (UK) & other labels associated with 'Electro Swing' released a succession of very popular compilations, including tracks from some of the freshest & brightest talent. 2009–2010 saw the first 'Electro Swing Clubs' opening in London, Paris, Zurich, Utrecht & Antwerp with further clubs opening in USA, Canada & Asia as a new 'Swing Generation' was born.[16]

One journalist even described this international spread of electro swing as a truly global movement but mediated on a small scale with the phrase "*un concept du soiree global*". The intimate associations of the *soiree* with the market-driven business-oriented reach of global expansion pointed to some of the contradictions implicit in expanding vintage musics and retro festivals to a global commercial network for inclusion within broader and more streamlined events for non-swing specialists.

In addition to the Electro Swing Club events organised globally, in Paris the electro swing genre attracted a special reception with audiences who sought not only live music experiences but the total immersive experience of engaging with the jazz past, but with the harder textures and faster tempos of the electronic music present. This desire to connect the past with the present was exhibited in the titles of special events and club nights often promoted in old warehouses or theatres with an old-world ambience. One example was *The Vintage Reboot Soiree*, a "neo retro experience" organised on June 9, 2018, at the renovated La Bellevilloise[17] in Paris. This event provided the context for connecting the founders of the electro swing genre with the more recent acoustic and electronic sound samples and hybrid mixes featured in large-scale festivals and EDM nightclubs. The three well-known and respected DJs Typoboy, Kid Supreme, and Brotherswing headlined this event after a variety of acoustic jazz acts and workshops.[18] The promotional text from their Facebook page highlighted this genre- and epoch-mixing eclecticism:

> The Neo-Vintage spirit now has its own soundtrack, such as a semi-disorganized journey through the most prominent epochs of pop culture, or rather as the Doc would say, an auditory distortion of the spatio-temporal continuum or electronic sounds, the most current [of which] are intertwined with the most famous retro melodies. Swing becomes Electro-Swing, Disco-Funk grooves and Soul voices contaminate Hip-Hop and House, Rhythm 'n' Blues and Rock are dynamited by relentless Breakbeats. It's James Brown with a Daft Punk helmet, Elvis in top-of-the-head mode, the Beastie Boys singing Surfin USA.… It's Vintage Reboot, it's irresistible. We also advise all travellers in our retro-futuristic corridor to detach their belt and let go as never during unwanted bass drops.[19]

These events relate to the neoliberal context of contemporary music, where the responsibility of local clubs to secure a paying public have been transferred to local event organisers through club nights. Here, promoters shoulder the burden to curate local artists, find spaces, and collaborate with other event planners to expand their reach and share their resources for promotion, recording, and distribution by collaborating with small musical entrepreneurs in other cities to offer events featuring a core group of DJs and live music ensembles. Thus, these mid-layer clubs, promoters, and collectives offer medium-sized festive electro swing events outside of the more expensive and large-scale pop music festivals promoted by the global live music industry.

The Electric Swing Circus: Live Performance within Vintage Remix

Electric Swing Circus established their reputation before electro swing had acquired extensive genre recognition in the UK. Indeed, Tom Hyland recalled that he was first inspired by this new sound after hearing the track 'Deep Henderson' by Nick Hollywood around 2006, which mixed samples from Fletcher Henderson with modern electronic drum sequences. The sampling of the audio past was supplemented by visual collages of clips from black and white silent and musical films. He recalled that hearing this track deeply inspired him: "It was the track that got me into electro swing and I bloody loved it … and so I heard that and had the idea to form the band" (Tom Hyland, September 19, 2018). The track also encapsulated the aesthetic goals and alliances of the genre – the deep beats of modern electronic music combined with old swing and jazz samples put into an innovative sonic and visual context. After this hearing, Tom and others, including drummer and keyboardist Chandra Savale-Walker, began informally jamming in their Birmingham neighbourhood, after which Rashad requested to join the jam. Rashad was also a guitarist but since Tom was already playing guitar, he switched to experimenting with samplers and midi keyboards. Rashad embraced the concept and sound of electro swing and quickly transitioned to mixing new and old sounds with a sampler and midi-keyboard in which he could trigger old samples but also create new, 'heavier' sounds and textures.

The band was given their first gig by DJ and booker Chris Tofu in London for an electro swing night,[20] secured prior to ever having performed in Birmingham, so for three months, they feverishly explored the possibilities of the electro swing sound to create new tunes. They sought to extend its boundaries, mixing old jazz samples from the Swing Era, but also developing into a 'real' live band, one described by Tom as "not perfect and polished but live and fun", adding that they favoured a dirtier and unpolished sound, hoping to achieve that raucous live energy of other UK punk bands from earlier decades (Tom Hyland, Interview with the author, July 8, 2018). He contrasted their live band sound and performance aesthetic to the mainland European electro swing sound. As the sound developed in the UK, he claimed that audiences and producers seemed to prefer the bass-heavy genres of dub and drum 'n' bass over house and techno. Electric Swing Circus too would incorporate much of the bass-heavy aesthetic of other familiar UK genres such as dub step, ska, two tone, rock, and punk.

Since 2011, the band has especially profited from the festival climate, where the carnivalesque ambience of seasonal outdoor celebrations, coupled with the escapism and immersive quality of annual festivals became one of their main attractions. Hyland preferred the term vintage remix, as it afforded the band the ability to draw from a wider variety of genres and periods. Nevertheless, the band's dedication and connection to especially these periods continually inform their listening habits and use of particular samples. Both Gregory and Hyland cited Fletcher Henderson, Sidney Bechet, and Django Reinhardt as the three most important early influences on their music, three musicians with strong ties to the European swing culture of the 1920s and 1930s.

Not only the recognisable solos of such musicians, but the timbres of Swing Era recordings also influence the band's recording aesthetic. Gregory claimed that they incorporate a wide variety of samples from this era which are sometimes time-stretched, effected, edited, and stitched together from such sources as "Sidney Bechet, Fletcher Henderson, Cab Calloway, Henry Allen, and Artie Shaw" (Rashad Gregory, email correspondence, September 21, 2018). Unlike other electro swing groups, where horn players learn riffs from jazz tracks, in Electric Swing Circus, rather, their brass section, who rarely tours with the group, compose new passages to complement the newly composed charts and especially the guitar and keyboard lines. This way, they argued, the ensemble sounds more natural in live shows. Further, by separating the role of samples with the performances of instrumentalists, they allow the especially distinctive sound of, say, Sidney Bechet or Artie Shaw to be audible above the lines delivered by live musicians. This provides a more organic integration of the horns while not overshadowing the samples carefully selected as the inspiration for particular tunes. ESC has recorded and performed with professional jazz instrumentalists in the studio and for high-profile gigs. According to Hyland, however, the cost of paying professional wages to horn players is prohibitive. The group aspires to expand their line-up for bigger gigs in mainland Europe with their so-called *ESC Grand Band*, a group featuring three horns (trombone, saxophone, and trumpet) in addition to the full band.

Hyland claimed that it was his exposure to electro swing that motivated his study of early swing and jazz. Because of this, ESC spends hours listening to old tracks to find interesting samples. Unlike some remix genres, where the extreme manipulation and de-familiarisation of samples constitutes the aesthetic end, for many electro swing artists, the recognition of the unique timbral quality of particular players on these recordings remains critical. Hyland claimed:

> Sidney Bechet has loads of great examples – those clarinet and alto sax wails that are just absolutely killer and there is no way to reproduce that – you hear it and you think – what was that noise! And how do I get it again. It is so *so* good and you just know it is absolutely audio gold and that is the bit that we want, we don't want the notes played by somebody else – we want Sidney and we want Sidney in the 1920s.
>
> (Tom Hyland, September 19, 2018)

Thus, the band engages dialogically with the jazz past; each interaction and reworking of these recordings makes audible the signature sounds of 1920s-era jazz performers, especially those with the most distinctive timbres on their instruments.

If samples are manipulated, it is generally to alter the time-feel or sense of syncopation. This altered time-feel becomes the subject of heated debates in the electro swing and wider jazz community and especially in discussions about the nature and meaning of swing. Indeed, Hyland and others understand vintage remix not as a particularly swinging genre, at least in their approach to the quaver and semi-quaver. In swing, the rhythm section established the syncopation especially between the snare and high hat. In electro swing, drawing from faster tempos of electronic music or other acoustic genres such as punk or ska, the tempos rather place the emphasis upon the bass drum and the semi-quaver and at faster tempos, swing's typical syncopation sometimes becomes secondary, or disappears altogether. This discrepancy confuses not only musicians when comparing the two genres, but the 'trad' swing and Lindy Hop dancers who perceive tempos in terms of larger partitions. Such confusion sometimes leads bands to play strange tempos when called out by swing dancers. Indeed, many Lindy dancers don't enjoy dancing to electro swing, missing the vital relation between the drummer, guitar, and bass that is accentuated in early swing recordings (Day 2012). Yet ESC incorporates a wide range of tempos and approaches towards syncopation including faster songs suitable for dancing the Charleston and others driven by modern electronic dancing styles, including the shuffle (the modern electronic solo dance style).

When asked why there is more recent interest in combining swing recordings with current music styles, Hyland noted that the swing revival began some 25 years ago with groups such as the Squirrel Nut Zippers and Big Bad Voodoo Daddy, live bands interested in the style and aesthetic of live dance music from the 1930s and 1940s. He continued:

> What we are talking about is some of the best musicians of all time playing some of the best arrangements of all time – of course it's gonna sound good. Right! You know it shouldn't be a surprise that the very best music from two decades still resonates with people now. And we are not gonna be surprised if people in 40 years are still listening to the Beatles and you know if something is absolutely incredible then people love it.
>
> *(Tom Hyland, September 19, 2018)*

Recognising this period as exceptional, one where musicians laboured to create something new, resonates not only with the musicians but with dancers and listeners who recognise the excitement of this earlier musical culture.

In order to survive the challenges presented by the current music industry climate, the group must tour constantly to make ends meet. Neoliberalism entailed not only the vast consolidation of the recording industry in the 1990s and 2000s and the fragmentation of musical styles, but the transformation of distribution and production outlets from analogue to digital channels. Such transformations impacted the modes of financial remuneration for performing bands. In this eco-system, ESC must play nearly every weekend of the year in order to make a living. A large part of their tour circuit depends especially upon festivals organised in warmer months. ESC performs two types of festivals: popular music festivals with a strong inter-arts and theatrical dynamic, such as Shamballa, Boomtown, or Glastonbury, or vintage festivals, which tend to be smaller, mixed-arts events offering interactive workshops and vintage markets, such as the Twinwood Festival ("The Ultimate Vintage Festival for Music and Dance") which takes place at the Twinwood Farm Airfield near the Glenn Miller Museum in the UK.[21] ESC has played this festival many times, which attracts about 8,000 people. Like other vintage festivals, this one highlights many aspects of interwar jazz culture such as cabaret, burlesque, comedy, and circus arts.

Like many electroacoustic mixes, ESC relies especially upon videos, more so than recordings, for their exposure and breakthrough to international audiences. To date, they have released five videos, and the three of these that were professionally produced have all acquired more than one million views, something unimaginable in pre-YouTube platform decades. While the band makes no money from this visibility, it has become their main 'calling card' for gaining more gigs and exposure in the international live music sphere. Further, the videos provide a visual image and idea of what the band and the broader genre are about. Two of their videos, *Penniless Optimist* (2011) and *Empires* (2017), have led to gigs in festivals all over Europe.

Penniless Optimist (2011)

In 2011, ESC released a 'demo version' of their single 'Penniless Optimist',[22] which presented an early version of the band performing in a disused warehouse within Birmingham. This post-industrial scene was enlivened with graffiti and steeped in old-world atmosphere. The band performing within this video consists of founding member and vocalist Eleanor Dhattani and various actors/musicians (including Ellie Williams and Jo Newman on vocals and Sarah Farmer on violin), but their presence and performances already signalled the theatrical, mixed-gendered make-up of contemporary electro swing. The video too progressively staged jazz dancing as a part of electro swing culture. In this video, a young professional dancer, Peggy De Lune (Caroline Amer), is filmed performing classic vaudeville-era jazz steps and wearing an androgynous three-piece suit and top hat, which she dramatically exploits with pantomime steps and comedic jazz slides. The musicians too dance throughout the song in a more modern, informal manner – eliciting an invitation to partake in the song's festivities and utopian sentiment as they sing "got no money but he's got his song". The two lead singers hold domestic objects of women's depression-era culture, a tea pot and a rusty soup pan. On the side of the smoky dark stage, another woman performs a ribbon-twirling routine and the violinist provides short improvised phrases throughout the bridge and between the chorus refrain. The video positions young people making music as a form of revelry by way of nostalgic symbols of prior jazz-era cultures.

Empires (2016)

In front of 'Valentine' (2013) and 'Penniless Optimist' (2011), ESC's most viewed video from their second album, *Empires*, also staged a performative engagement with depression-era jazz culture. The video questions "What's the point in building empty empires?" in between intermittent sections of double-time jazz and a musical theatre inspired two-beat march sequence. The video takes a simple photographic concept – the View-Master – to showcase various members of the band singing, dancing, or playing their instruments for this up-tempo, existential anthem. Within each frame, the viewer gets a quick rhythmic peek into their 'party like it's 1929' dance hall. Further, the timing of each frame enhances the rhythmic structure of the verses and the chorus; a four-beat measure is held during the verses (with slower-moving harmonic motion) to the more punctuated two-beat frames of the choruses – here the shorter frames emphasise the energy and propulsion of this call to dance against end-of-the-world ennui. The bright colours throbbing in time to the quaver against the white and black yet festive vintage-inspired clothing also reinforces the idea of partying and revelry as a modern survival technology. The song invites listeners to sing and dance away their cares in light of the futility of building "empty empires" or of forging hegemonic structures in an era of disappearing resources – "Can you hear the call, I can see it in your eyes – what's the point in building empty empires now".[23]

Both videos adopt themes which speak to the current economic and cultural crisis by conversing with the past through lyric references or through images and sounds of the golden age of jazz. Both offer mixes of acoustic jazz, recorded swing samples, and modern live popular music to showcase this local band currently headlining middle-layer festivals throughout Europe. These audiovisual and concert performances within club nights and vintage festivals reinforce the "global aesthetic" (Erlmann 1996) yet provide a mediated connection to cultures of crisis within the specific transnational nexus of European golden age of jazz culture, even if symbols of African American jazz and of the Great Depression are often interwoven into such highly mediated configurations of the current remembering of Europe's jazz past.

Conclusion

Within the broader culture of electro swing, and through the more complex forms of mediality engendered by the interactions between musicians, DJs, sound producers, and festival and event organisers, the current crisis is enacted and performed through a number of interpretive, citational, and aesthetic practices. Through sampling the swing past either in live performances or within audiovisual enactments, a dialogical reworking and 're-versioning' offers participants a way of re-imaging and experiencing the present. Within the context of small-scale niche festivals, the enjoyment of vintage musics also provides a mode of escapism. Finally, both festivals and the interactivity connected to such audiovisual medialities provide alternative modalities of consumption connected to but as alternatives to more traditional jazz festivals where an improvisation with more familiar settings of canonical works and instrumental practices predominate. By encouraging a re-imaging of the past, with its broader incorporation of dancers, theatrical presentations, and the unique patinas of the interwar jazz culture, electro swing and vintage jazz festivals offer an alternative, albeit escapist, forum for promoting contemporary polygeneric jazz culture, especially in its most audiovisually, electronically mediated form. Here, new media provide the locus for those less connected to jazz orthodoxies as represented by large-scale festivals and specialised jazz performance routes and recordings.

In the following sub-chapter, I examine the role of vintage production aesthetics, of swing dancing, and of the unique retro visual aesthetics of music videos as primary media for the promotion of contemporary vintage remix and electro swing groups. The case studies featured in this sub-chapter, the French group Caravan Palace and the transnational Dutch-based PLO Caro Emerald, exhibit an engagement with the jazz past through the production aesthetics of recordings, through the incorporation of live improvisation in vintage jazz styles during concerts, and through a visual iconography with references to particular periods of the imagined jazz past.

Notes

1   The appearance of such vintage and smaller-scale mixed-arts festivals is evidenced through a consortium of so-called vintage festivals in various regional or transnational travel and tourism brochures. Some of these were shared with me during interviews with the organisers of the Anjou Vélo Vintage festival in Samur in 2018. In the UK, vintage or retro festivals are promoted by tourism agencies or event agencies such as the Retro Festival organisation, which helps to promote, organise, and book acts for retro festivals in the UK. See their website www.retrofestival.co.uk for a list of festivals connected to this agency. Sometimes vintage festivals are referred to as traditional festivals. See for example a review of 'traditional festivals' listed in the *Guardian* in 2018, "Twenty Great Traditional Festivals in Europe", June 2, 2018, accessed December 20, 2018, www.theguardian.com/travel/2018/jun/02/20-great-traditional-festivals-europe-france-spain-greece-sweden.

2   Highlighting its carnivalesque atmosphere, Sziget presents over 1,000 concerts on five stages, and features other ancillary events such as an electronic music party train and a 'warped' amusement park.

3   You can view this promotional video "Electro Swing Club 1st Official Trailer" on their website: www.electroswingclub.com/.

4   Rather Luhrmann chose rap, EDM, and hip-hop-related genres produced under the executive supervision of Jay-Z. Artists featured include will.i.am, Florence and the Machine, Lana Del Ray, Fergie, and Beyoncé, among others.

5   See for example Stelar's Balkan beats releases on compilation albums such as the *Feel Good Productions presents Balkanica vol. 2* in 2012 (Green Queen Music 2012).

6   Although I don't mean to argue that European DJs and vintage remix artists engaged exclusively with Black Atlantic or European jazz culture and not with American artists who remained within the US during these decades.

7   On their French website, you can see the DJs and hybrid artists/groups promoted by this consortium: http://electroswingclub.fr/artistes/.

8   This is translated from the French on the "Anatole Laguibole" page of the Anjou Vélo Vintage website from 2018:

> Entre vignes et Loire, sillonnez les paysages valonnes en direction des celebres wins du territoire. Devant la singularite des hauts-lieux touristiques et historiques, l'esquisse de cette excursion se dessine sous voy yeux.... Domaines viticoles, panorama exceptionnel, patrimonine troglodytique: decouvrez les richesses du saumurois. Un parcours raffine, petillant, fruite et gourmand"
>
> www.anjou-velo-vintage.com/fr/randos-retro/
> parcours, accessed June 18, 2018

9   This is translated from the French:

> Durant trois jours, la machine à voyager dans le temps vous transporté dans un univers 100% vintage grâce à de nombreuses animations en une large programmation. Musiciens, chanteurs et danseurs de swing, colporteurs et crieurs de rue; une sélection d'artistes insolite et hétéroclite transportera le public dans une autre époque. Spectacles, initiations et shows déambulatoires; une immersion totale pour un souvenir indélébile. En matière de fête,

aucune retraite anticipée. La soirée guinguette du vendredi et du samedi soir et le grand bal swing du dimanche après-midi invitent les festivaliers à venir guincher sur des airs enjoues de jazz et de swing. Fines bulles du Val de Loire et produits du terroir accompagneront le décor glamour et convivial de ce rendez-vous indémodable.

> From the page "Le Festival Programmation" on the Anjou
> Vélo Vintage 2018 website: www.anjou-velo-vintage.com
> /fr/festival/festival-musical-retro, accessed September 10, 2018

10   See the promotional video "Anjou Vélo Vintage 2018" on *YouTube*, www.youtube.com/watch?v=J_C4p_7v_cg, accessed June 26, 2018

11   See their 2017 promotional video on the festival's homepage Swingamajig, https://swingamajig.co.uk/, accessed July 4, 2018.

12   This is the home page of the Electro Swing Club website: www.ElectroSwingClub.com.

13   See the homepage of Electro Swing Club, www.ElectroSwingClub.com, accessed July 4, 2018.

14   This is the home page of the Electro Swing Club website: www.ElectroSwingClub.com.

15   Hodges had also performed at the Herräng swing dance camp in July 2018.

16   This is taken from the home page of Electro Swing Club: www.ElectroSwingClub.com.

17   La Bellevilloise was once a leftist-leaning centre for political meetings, educational workshops, visual art studios, and cultural and music performances in the late nineteenth and early twentieth centuries. See the "Histoire" page on their website: www.labellevilloise.com/.

18   These included a Charleston workshop and a forum led by the *Welcome to My Flat*, a DJ collective which mixes house, disco, and electro swing. The event was hosted by the Paris *Gatsby Night* series. All of these pointed to the interwar Jazz Age fascination of organisers and workshop orchestrators.

19   See the Facebook event *The Vintage Reboot Soiree* here: www.facebook.com/events/1989064541407775.

20   Chris Tofu has DJed with Nick Hollywood and continues to DJ in the electro swing scene around London. He is also a booking agent for many popular music festivals within the UK, including for Glastonbury (Rashad Gregory, Interview).

21   This is the home page tagline from the Twinwood Festival 2019 website: https://twinwoodevents.com/.

22   This video "The Electric Swing Circus – Penniless Optimist" can be viewed on YouTube: www.youtube.com/watch?v=hkwLO44IQN8.

23   You can view "Electric Swing Circus – EMPIRES" on YouTube: www.youtube.com/watch?v=u2uHgIqc5jo.

6

PART TWO: (RE)GENERATING THE JAZZ PAST IN THE VINTAGE REMIX OF CARAVAN PALACE AND CARO EMERALD

> The Caravan Palace band takes its inspiration from the pre-World War II era. This music has a strong (unintelligible) 1930s swing running through it and it produced one of the top records in France last year. But the band didn't find its popularity among nostalgia fans … Caravan Palace has found its niche, or is that a niche, in dance clubs.
>
> *("Swinging to Electro Beats")*

This sub-chapter explores the phenomena of electro swing and vintage remix as musical cultures driven by contemporary audiovisual practices, such as the promotion and interactive reception of the music video medium. In particular, it examines two vintage remix groups – the Paris-based Caravan Palace and the Amsterdam-based PLO project Caro Emerald (and their various digitally mediated sources) – to illustrate their symbolic and aesthetic value for modern European jazz culture. Each group draws inspiration from recordings and films documenting Europe's early jazz decades as well as contributes, through performances and related audiovisual output, to a more asynchronous, globally circulated mythology of Europe's jazz history. Part of this exploration focuses especially on the intersections of vintage remix, jazz, and pop music within the context of music videos featuring footage of live concert venues. My analyses focus especially upon the circulation and reuse of audio and visual iconography, in connection with recorded soundscapes within music videos for mediating and manifesting a particularly dialogical engagement with Europe's jazz past. As Andy Fry argues, jazz musicians (re)configure themselves alongside extant (written) histories so that the combined impact of verbal articulations and musical performances constitute forms of remembering, which are at once "generative and regenerative" acts (Fry 2014, 261). Here too through reconstitutions of the jazz past, contemporary electro and vintage swing groups (re)generate a version of the past, re-signifying it for the current aesthetic aims and cultural predilections of convergence, participatory culture embodied by vintage remix.

In the following, I examine in particular how this jazz past is crafted within various digitally circulated performances of Caravan Palace and Caro Emerald. This examination begins with contextualising the rise of electro swing within Paris during the mid-2000s in relation to Caravan Palace's development as a group. My focus illuminates how the imagination of a French jazz past connects the pleasures, performance styles, and aesthetic practices for cosmopolitan artists working across music genres. Finally, in the second section of this chapter, I examine the music videos of both Caravan Palace and Caro Emerald to reveal how the mediated circulation of electro swing informs its reception in more traditional jazz spaces. Here the sampling of an interwar European jazz culture compels a dialogical participation by both performers and participants, even as the level of engagement varies in scale and degree from intertextual references to festive and theatrical jazz culture, to a performed embodiment of prior jazz practice through the staging of choreographed jazz dance or insertions of 'trad'-styled improvisation during concerts.

The French Wave of Electro Swing

That Paris would emerge as French electro swing's cultural capital is unsurprising considering its central place both within popular imagination (filtered through Hollywood and European film culture) and academic historical accounts. Furthermore, Paris and its related jazz critics, musicians, hot clubs, cabarets, and revues have been culturally historicised and codified as embodying the quintessential French jazz milieu with origins in interwar Paris. Here, the Hot Club Du Jazz as well as the culture of 'Harlem in Montmartre' (Shack 2001), and the many other jazz cafés inspired by Black theatrical revues such as Josephine Baker's *La Revue Nègre*, provided an earlier moment for intercultural contact and the rehearsing of new cultural identities and alternative political spectrums (Jordan 2010). The dance and cabaret culture of Paris profited from the celebrated and mythologised performances of jazz musicians such as Sidney Bechet and Mitchell's Jazz Kings. However, the historical prominence of Django Reinhardt's quintet and subsequent recordings with African American musicians of hot jazz have since anchored Paris as the perceived progressive centre of European jazz in the interwar period, and despite considerations of the political posturing surrounding racial encounters, which reveal entrenched yet under-recognised anxieties about cultural mixing and fears regarding the excessive spread of commercial mass-mediated musics from the United States (Fry 2014, Jordan 2010).

In France, a growing number of electro swing events which specifically catered to this particular imagination of an exciting and progressively intercultural jazz past erupted in the late 2000s. During this decade, both the physical spaces of

prior jazz cultures alongside audiovisual media played a prominent role in mediating the virtual and celebratory events of this vintage movement. Around 2008,
a number of DJs, promoters, and record labels actively cultivated interest through
a creative and expanding integration of various sources into contemporary performances, including promotional artworks and a body of audiovisual output
from the music video, to the hybrid music performance of electro swing groups
during music festivals and club nights. In particular, the role of music videos
increasingly proffered attention for electro swing DJs and hybrid groups, ultimately leading to increased performance opportunities for electro swing artists
and organisers within the transnational Electro Swing Club consortium. Through
this network, artists were invited to create, perform for, and promote electro swing
events in Paris in culturally relevant historical spaces, such as La Bellevilloise, one
of the first multi-arts cooperatives, opened in 1877. This unique space originally

FIGURE 6.4   Poster for La Nuit Electroswing, June 8, 2014, La Bellevilloise, Paris,
France[1]

supported the ideals of collaborative education, political action, and avant-garde artistic endeavours. In later years, it hosted the first cinema as well as a library and meeting rooms, and a café for local workers and participants.[2] Recognising the historical, artistic, and cultural relevance of rejuvenated jazz-era spaces, many electro swing and jazz revival events have chosen such venues to host inter-arts events. Prior electro swing balls also chose culturally relevant spaces such as La Bellevilloise or La Java (an art deco venue where Edith Piaf and Django Reindhardt once performed) to program local electro swing DJs and artists, especially those most active with the Electro Swing Club consortium including vocalist/rap artist Lyre le Temps and electro swing DJs Typoboy, Kid Supreme, and Brotherswing.

One of electro swing's most widely acknowledged performance groups, particularly in Paris, is Caravan Palace, a seven-piece group featuring vocals, violin, clarinet, trombone, guitar, bass, drums, and vibraphones, with several instrumentalists doubling on electronics, percussion, synthesisers, and samplers. This group is often credited for birthing the genre of electro swing, and it has been material in advancing the prior instrumental sound and dance-driven facets of French interwar jazz culture within a modern electronic dance-oriented context.

Caravan Palace and Electro Swing

Since the mid-2000s, Caravan Palace has grown from an electronic producer-led outfit to a live instrumental group whose recordings, videos, and performances incorporate contemporary music compositional aesthetics from hip hop and house, yet also exhibit early influences from French swing and jazz, especially from the body of recordings by Django Reinhardt and Stéphane Grappelli and their intercultural collaborations with various musicians including Louis Armstrong. The group also takes inspiration from contemporary electronic music techniques. Within their many promotional outlets, band members cite the French electronic artists Daft Punk and DJ Vitalic as equally important stylistic influences.

The group began in 2004 as a project of violinist Hugues Payen and double bassist Charles Delaport, after he was commissioned by Canal Plus to create a soundtrack for a silent porno film (or 'blue film') from the 1920s. At the time, he was playing with the guitarist Arnoud Vial and violinist Payen (then a musicology student from the Sorbonne) in a local jazz Manouche-inspired band in the style of Reinhardt's hot quintet. Although the French influence of interwar swing is strong, as Payen reiterated, Reinhardt was a "Belgian-born French guitarist and composer of Romani heritage" (Grennen 2014). This part of Reinhardt's musical heritage is often negated in references to electro swing, which rather privilege the Parisian and Black American roots of early French 'hot jazz'.

After composing the soundtrack together, this duo felt they had crafted a compelling, modern-vintage mix with potential as a performance style; thus, they soon began a rigorous rehearsal schedule. He recalled:

> We did our first album quite blindly, and began touring for a year before the release of the album. People immediately loved it in France (jazz Manouche is a long, long love story with the French), and we decided to tour abroad very soon, because we felt that it could work in a lot of countries!
>
> *(Grennen 2014)*

By 2007, with their newly combined electro swing sound, they embarked upon a busy touring schedule across Europe.

Payen recalls that Parov Stelar had also initiated his DJ sets which sampled the Swing Era, and thus journalists often credit these two acts as forging the electro swing sound around 2006. Despite the attempts by the media to codify the progeny of such electronic jazz remixes, Payen admitted that combinations of modern electronic sequences, textures, and grooves layered with swing and jazz samples had already occurred in the 1990s with tracks like 'Doop' (1994) by the Dutch electronic group of the same name (Grennen 2014). 'Doop' featured a Charleston-based sample from Sidney Berlin's Ragtime Band set to a techno track.

While DJs and producers had long experimented with mixing jazz and swing from the interwar period, Caravan Palace was one of the first to transform the genre into a more acoustic, improvisational style. They have performed as a full 'live' acoustic ensemble coupled with the thick and machine-sounding textures of their remixed samples. Artists often sampled by Caravan Palace include the Andrew Sisters, Django Reinhardt, Stuff Smith, Count Basie, Cab Calloway, Spike Jones and His City Slickers, and Chick Webb. Their live improvisations reference the styles of important Black and popular American artists for France's interwar jazz culture as well as now celebrated European jazz artists of various backgrounds. The ensemble features the improvised clarinet solos of Camille Chapelière, the cabaret vocal style of Zoé Colotis, the Django-inspired guitar of Arnaud Vial, the percussion and Swing Era jazz vibraphone solos of Paul-Marie Barbier, and the prolific Manouche-inspired violin solos of Hugues Payen. Their hot jazz sound is modernised by the darker techno-inspired sound collages pre-programmed or triggered in real time by the original members Hugues Payen, Arnoud Vial, Charles Delaport (who doubles on upright bass), and Antoine Toustou (who doubles on trombone).

Equally important for Caravan Palace's music performance and online mediated reception is its promotion of jazz-era dancing with steps referencing the Charleston and the Lindy Hop. They are thus revered both by the electro swing and swing dance communities (Rikard Ekstrand 2018). The role of jazz dancing has remained an important facet of how the group promotes its audiovisual material as well as how it composes and performs. As Arnoud Vial stated, the group's incorporation of swing music was not only about the swinging sound of these records but of their connection to prior swing dance communities, including the fanatical 'Zazous' of the Second World War period. From a 2010 radio interview with band members, NPR presenter Arcos reiterated this facet of the group's aesthetic: "After all, back in the 1930s and '40s, people danced to swing music, so combining swing and today's dance makes perfect sense", to which guitarist Vial responded, "We come back with this old stuff, with modern electronic beats, and so people just think, oh, I'm swinging, I'm swinging. Just they needed more bass". The modern-day proclivity for a fuller bass spectrum updates the danceable rhythms of the Swing Era for contemporary ears and modern dancing bodies ("Swinging to Electro Beats"). In the larger context of revivals and remixing, Caravan Palace (and other electro swing acts) regenerate sonic and corporeal artefacts of the past not as hauntologists but rather as popular mediators who especially borrow those bits which stimulate the corporeal facet of interwar jazz culture within the newer context of electronic dance music festivals.

During the early 2010s, in addition to releasing studio albums and promotional videos, the group toured Europe, appearing especially within the pop music and jazz festival circuits. Their first festival appearance occurred in 2007 at the Django Reinhardt Jazz Festival. Following this appearance, they were signed for the Paris-based Wagram music label. Their self-titled album, *Caravan Palace*, peaked at number eleven in the French album charts in 2009. They were also one of the few popular French acts to tour the US and Canada in the last decade with much success. Representing the range of their music's reception, in 2010, they performed for the Montreux Jazz Festival in Switzerland and then in 2014 they played Coachella in the Colorado Desert in California (Beaudoin 2016).

Because of their versatility in improvising in swing and interwar jazz styles as well as modern electronic popular musics, Caravan Palace frequently performs various festivals throughout Europe. Fans and critics have praised live shows for their highly theatrical presentations with dramatic combinations of jazz dancing, 'hot' instrumental solos, jazz-era costumes, eclectic electronic soundscapes, and moody, spectacular lighting. The group also captures mixes of acoustic and electronic music styles from electro and current electronic timbres to the Black-music-inspired grooves of funk and disco with modern sound textures inserted from glitch to the electro timbres and beats of deconstructed swing recordings. In addition to live DJing, many of the eclectic soundscapes are configured with the benefit of various electronic techniques and devices.

The challenge of sampling old jazz records from 78s proved difficult for a group dedicated to high fidelity. In one interview for *Music Radar*, guitarist and sound artist Arnoud Vial emphasised these challenges:

> It was difficult at first trying to make the music sound good with crap samples, mainly taken from very old records. At first, we were using old 78s and vinyl, but more lately we've been using samples from YouTube or Spotify – less sexy, but still very effective. We sample ourselves too, so when we do a demo we are recording all together in the studio. That way you also get the sound and the spirit of the music and better-quality samples.
>
> *(Turner 2016)*

Unlike the preferences of Electric Swing Circus, who expressively favoured the recognition of particular artistic voices, Caravan Palace favoured the music of this period but filtered through the improved high fidelity of contemporary dance music recordings.

In terms of their composition style, the trio develops new material both independently and collectively. Members share tracks digitally and then add melodies or bridges over tracks or sampled sequences. They also remain conscientious about how they record acoustic instruments such as the piano and guitar in order to capture the correct timbre of these jazz instruments originally mixed with the limited frequency spectrum of vintage soundstages. For example, they use the Neumann U87 microphones for piano and guitar and the Audio-Technica AT4050 mic for an enhanced 'vintage' sound. In the studio, their compositional style bypasses the computer with the use of buttons and filters, which stimulates a more tactile, physical mode of composition. Both Payen and Vial espouse reverence for vintage synths, favouring the sound of older synthesisers such as the Roland Jupiter 8, which has the 'arpeggiator' feature, or the Minimoog or Korg MS-20. In 2016, bassist Delaport claimed he favours the Little Phatty Moog for its unique sound and sample manipulating capabilities. He also uses other plug-ins such as the Nexus virtual synth plug-ins to enhance the vintage sounds of old samples such as by adding "reverb and delay on the presets to make plain samples sound powerful" (Turner 2016). Payen too prioritises the sound of the "old machines" for Caravan Palace's unique vintage/modern sound, claiming,

> I need to be surrounded by all those old machines, like the ARP Odyssey and the Korg PolySix, but my favourite is my Memorymoog because I like to put the live mode on it and for me it's the best polyphonic synthesiser possible.
>
> *(Turner 2016)*

The group's knowledge of both acoustic jazz performance techniques and the vintage and modern recording and editing hardware and machinery is a unique facet of Caravan Palace, contributing to their particular combination of modern and vintage musical aesthetics.

After the group's first festival appearance, Caravan Palace signed with the Paris-based label Wagram Music, specialising in genres including vintage remix and electro swing. Since then, they have released three albums; the self-titled *Caravan Palace* (2008), *Panic* (2012) and *Robot Face* < | °_° | > (2015). With their videos, LPs, and performances, Caravan Palace is one of the few electro swing acts to reach international audiences outside of Europe. For example, their most recent album < | °_° | > sold more than 100,000 copies in the USA.[3] The title of this album was named by their fans, *Robot Face*, which Payen depicted as the mascot that accompanied them through their musical evolution:

The public was allowed to give it a name. And they nicknamed it 'Robot Face'. It is actually the robot that followed us from the beginning and has since become an album. And then, it was important for us to be part of modernity and play with the current codes, to let people take ownership of this record.

("Caravan Palace va faire swinguer Art Sonic" 2016)

In connecting their most recent recording to the configurable culture of the digital ecosystem, the group immerses their work and creative processes into contemporary aesthetic practices while fostering participatory culture.

During performances, Caravan Palace transform their sample-based electro swing material by adapting various (sampled) jazz recorded riffs and progressions as the basis for extended arrangements of improvisation. An example is their performance of the track 'Rock it For Me' from a 2012 engagement at the Trianon in Paris. Here the group highlighted not only improvised instrumentals and vocal riffs by Colotis, but an impressive jazz dance act in the middle of their set.[4] For this live performance of 'Rock it For Me', the original sample from the recording 'Jungle Fever' (Decca 1934) by the Mills Brothers is first introduced. The recorded track also samples Stuff Smith and his Onyx Club Boys' 'It Ain't Right' (Vocalian 1936) and Duke Ellington's 'Topsy' (Decca 1937).[5] Their concert performance begins with the Mills Brothers sample of an eight-measure ii-V-I progression. The band then introduces a new theme on the vibraphone followed by Colotis singing the sixteen-bar verse before Colotis and others sing the Stuff Smith sample 'It Ain't Right' on the chorus. For this chorus, the drummer stood up, playing only snare with brushes, 'stirring the pot', as the original track's electronic drums punch through the live mix. This chorus is followed by a bridge during which short samples are traded with brief improvised riffs by the clarinetist and guitarist while Colotis does a few jazz steps, a four-pattern side to side Charleston step punctuated by a short kick.

The performance's bridge section delivers a modern–vintage combination of stop-time and modern breaks; all of the instrumentalists but the clarinet and violin abruptly stop, before playing in unison with the sampled riff from the original Smith sample. As the two (clarinetist Chapelière and violinist Payen) play facing each other, the vibraphonist (Barbier) descends to the side of the stage. Colotis then invites him to centre stage when, in a dramatic move, he begins to dance jazz steps over the break. He first introduces a few broad Charleston steps (the 'black bottom'), and Colotis then joins in with her own version of the step until they both Charleston together in a brief but dynamic choreographed routine. The dance segment ends with a few spacious Lindy swing-outs and in perfect timing, a technician from the side of the stage runs to centre stage and tosses a mic caught by Colotis on beat eight of the swing-out, in perfect timing. This fast and unexpected move results in massive cheers from the audience. The song then gains intensity as the improvised clarinet riffs fill out the final chorus vocal riff from Smith's vocalese, "It ain't right babe, No … Mama don't do that you

FIGURE 6.5   Zoé Colotis and Barbier dancing swing in 'Rock it For Me' live in 2012 at the Trianon in Paris, film still

know, It ain't right, boy boy". Colotis sings this callout in conversation with the clarinetist before the abrupt ending – after her final phrase "boy boy" – she falls quickly to the floor as the lights are dramatically extinguished. The crowd erupts again. Through the theatrical staging of this performance and the layering of electronic soundscapes with Swing Era riffs, Caravan Palace regenerates especially the musical versatility and theatrical facets of the Swing Era. Through their interactive and performative antics, Caravan Palace integrates some of the most engaging and entertaining aspects of Jazz Age culture into their vintage modern live sets.

Liveness and Spontaneous Jazz Acts within Electro Swing

Part of Caravan Palace's characteristic sound emerges from the production of studio recordings which predominantly combine electronic sequences of sampled records with mixes of vocals and other constructed soundscapes, interspersed with improvised instrumentals. However, concert performances often depart from these to emphasise new arrangements with the full acoustic band. In order to accommodate more spontaneity and improvisation, rather than pre-programmed sampled sequences, during concerts, midi-samples or electronic sounds are incorporated in real time by the sound artist/DJ. This can be seen in Caravan Palace's festival performance of 'Brotherswing' from the Phénix concert in Bourges, France on April 16, 2010.[6] 'Brotherswing' likely references various facets of vintage and modern swing culture, including the B-side 'Swing! Brother, Swing!' (Vocalian 1939) performed and recorded by Billie Holiday and her orchestra featuring Charlie Shavers on trumpet. 'Brotherswing' is not only the name of one of Paris's most prominent electro swing DJs, it is also the name of the Paris-based swing dance school to which Colotis and others have participated. Furthermore, many of the dance school's parties and balls are given at the Bellevilloise, the same location where Caravan Palace has performed for Vintage Reboot soirees, often co-organised by DJ Brotherswing.

This performance epitomises the group's mix of jazz gitan/Manouche, electro, and swing. It also highlights the hybrid electronic jazz improvisations of the band's musicians. Within this performance, the propulsive electro grooves slowly build with short vocalised riffs by Colotis in two-bar breaks with the rubbery synth bass lines, played, not sampled, over the original swing sample of Stuff Smith's 'It Ain't Right'. Colotis increasingly incorporates scat singing and improvisation on the simple phrases "swinging boy, oh my brother swing, come on, let's swing again, don't stop, swing again". With each new phrase, she delivers a more dramatic extension of her range with stylised cabaret theatrical textures in the peaks and valleys of the sudden falls and drops. As the song increases in texture and intensity, she too pushes the timbral capabilities of her chest and head voice. This passage occurs over the IV-VI-i-iii (F, D, A, C) in A minor. First the clarinetist begins with a short two-beat response to Zoé's calls in different registers with a pedal tone sustained with an octave bass line. This non-syncopated bass line allows more rhythmic freedom in the vocal lines, which complements the buzzy, reedy texture of the clarinet.

After one minute of a slow build to the first soar and then drop, the full acoustic and drummer-less quintet takes over, with the live contra bass walking in double-time and the Django-style rhythm guitar strutting forward. This electro section soon dissipates into a 'hot club' quintet sound (though here a trio) with acoustic guitar, upright bass, and vocal verses sung by Colotis. She sings,

> Boys and girls shake your knees, clap your hands, snap your fingers and sing, popeil, popeil; Here comes swinging boy, dancing ring, looking for the king, the king of the swing; So clap your hands, snap your fingers and sing, brotherswing.

These Gitan-inspired acoustic verses follow a more typical VI-(iv)-ii-V-i (in A minor) progression of popular swing and French jazz of the hot interwar period, what many critics began to refer to as the 'trad' influence of jazz within electronic music during the 2010s.

After the first jazz hot section, the electro band hook and chorus is reincorporated, in a fast electro disco groove with octave bass lines moving step-wise over the same progression. A short eight measures later, the Kraftwerk-inspired robot voice is sung by the trombonist with the robotic flanging effect layered over the increasingly dense clarinet riff, full of chromatic notes over this four-bar progression. Two minutes into this performance, the clarinetist and violinist perform a rapid-fire extemporisation of the original clarinet riff, like a bebop extraction from the original popular song, in harmony over a clipping hot tempo, before a final trill over the first stop-time (or drop, in EDM nomenclature) with only the disco bass line pushing time forward. Another triggered sequence interrupts this trill as the clarinet stutters on the highest part of the last phrase, repeating it several times in a kind of feedback loop, and the liveness of the clarinet and violin duo infuse this technical glitch with a visceral excitement – as machines and old world, yet cosmopolitan instruments are welded together. At three minutes, the jazz trio of upright bass, guitar, and vocals emerges before a second drop with sampled jazz trap set before the full acoustic takeover by the two programmers and sound artists, who trigger live bass lines, grooves, and modernistic deconstructions of timbre and texture. However, this is accomplished without relinquishing the steady swing beat, even as a number of historically disparate grooves provide a link to standard acoustic jazz or groove music practice. The final soar is enhanced by the darkened stage as strobe lights gradually pierce the stage over the rubbery sirens and eight-note bass line, working the minor triad in an acid fashion. The song ends with the quintessential Django chord, an arpeggiated A minor sixth/ninth-chord hanging unresolved in the steamy night air. This live performance fully embraced the modern visual and sonic technologies to effectuate a hyper-modern sound, but one imbued with references to France's unique jazz past. Caravan Palace achieved this through their jazz improvisations in the style of hot jazz as well as their references to the recorded history of interwar jazz and finally by incorporating Jazz Age dances into their concert performances.

Like other electro swing groups, this group samples both well-known and internationally travelled musicians, especially Cab Calloway and Count Basie, but others including the Washboard Rhythm Kings ('Pirates' 2012), The Mills Brothers ('Dramophone' 2012), Spike Jones and his City Slickers ('Wonderland' 2015), the Golden Gate Quartet ('Clash' 2012), Lucky Millender and his Orchestra ('Wonda' 2015), Fats Waller ('Maniac' 2012), and Chick Webb and Ella Fitzgerald ('Maniac' 2012). Because most of the musicians perform various roles from playing, singing, and dancing to programming and DJing, the mix of electronic soundscapes and performed Swing Era jazz occurs in a complex and heavily rehearsed format.

The samples chosen by the group provide a thematic connection between electro swing and the Swing Era, but they also motivate the visual and narrative themes of videos and lyrics. For example, 'Maniac' samples the intro of Ella Fitzgerald and Chick Webb's 'Rock it for Me', with Fats Waller's characteristic chromatic piano runs over a stride left hand from 'Ain't Misbehavin' (1938). On the same album (*Panic* 2012), they feature 'Rock it for Me', which later becomes the title of another track about robots, jazz, and the apocalypse. By 2012, many of the 'trad' jazz recordings resided in the public domain, and thus the sampling of this material became simpler and less expensive.

Because electro swing was a genre with origins in electronic studio production techniques whose sonic material drew from recordings of the 1920s and 1930s, the incorporation of performed jazz instrumentalists was a natural way to make shows more engaging and improvisational. By the late 2000s, well-known DJs increasingly worked with instrumentalists and vocalists who often reproduced the material constituted within samples. Sometimes these samples were cut into prior releases and compilations – many had already circulated on dance floors and at festivals. This added a challenge to shows, as instrumentalists had to exhibit the required stamina to repeat sometimes highly demanding instrumental passages over a number of sequences, therefore disrupting the normal phrasing and breathing patterns executed on the original jazz recordings. Sometimes instrumentalists would sample themselves live or take breaks for freer improvisation during the B sections of performances.

Caravan Palace adapted this practice further by building new arrangements to highlight and accentuate the technical skill and musicality of musicians, including violinist Hugues Payen and clarinetist Camille Chapelière, who arranged full phrases from the original sampled material of the various swing riffs from French jazz and gitana sources as well as swing riffs from American jazz artists, especially Benny Goodman, Chick Webb, Cab Calloway, and other recordings. In this fashion, Caravan Palace was able to integrate both the produced sound sequences and aesthetics of live DJing and studio productions with trad and 'gypsy' jazz harmonic improvisation, and a swinging approach towards rhythm. This was accomplished by alternating the more modern yet syncopated grooves such as disco or jungle to acoustic swing sections. It was the extension and incorporation of 'live' instrumentalists as well as the freer approach towards electronic tracks which enabled Caravan Palace to acquire a large international following at both the contemporary popular music and French jazz festival circuit.

Critics of the group recognised the sophisticated manner in which they had merged the electronic aesthetics of contemporary popular music with the sound of traditional jazz. *Pop Matters* critic Jedd Beaudoin spoke of how the group's appeal owed to the combination of electronic sequences coupled against the high musicianship of acoustic instrumentalists:

> Songs such as 'Dragons' and 'We Can Dance' demonstrated perfectly the direction the group would take on future releases while 'Ended with the Night' paid closer attention to tradition while enveloping the listener in a blanket of almost hallucinatory sounds. Payen, guitarist Arnaud Vial, and bassist Charles Delaporte had struck upon something with a deeply theatrical twist that didn't compromise musicality. "We were serious musicians at the beginning", Payen says, "and we never forgot about this. It's most important for us to focus on playing our instruments as much as putting energy into the show. We just wanted to play good music, although that's something very subjective.
>
> *(Beaudoin 2016)*

It seems likely that the group's status as both an improvising instrumental French jazz group and innovative sample-based electro swing group continues to attract listeners and dancers from a variety of vintage remix cultures.

The Music Video as the 'Calling Card' of Vintage Remix

While the recordings and performances remain essential for CP's (Caravan Palace) career and economic viability, it is their many music videos that garnered the most attention and increased their invitations for festival performances. Indeed, the media platform of YouTube quickly superseded radio for the promotion and mediated reception of electro swing. Since 2008, of their fourteen singles produced, CP released nine videos, which have acquired from three million to 120 million views. Part of the success of these videos are their high-quality production values, especially in comparison with other electro swing groups. Caravan Palace is able to finance these videos in part because of government subsidies. They also receive funds which enable them to record new material, while rehearsing in between tours. Such financial assistance makes these musicians' lives less precarious than other touring jazz and popular musicians within Europe.

FIGURE 6.6 Caravan Palace record cover, *Panic* (Wagrum 2012)

'Rock It for Me' (2012)

In 2012, Caravan Palace released one of their most successful videos, 'Rock It for Me', featuring a single from the *Panic* LP (2012 Wagram). The video neatly encapsulates the electro swing ethos with its animated science fiction scene set in Paris circa 1889. The story begins as 'vintage' space ships threaten to take over Paris and ultimately the whole world. With its combination of vintage futuristic scenes, centennial architecture and robot images and music samples, the video presents a Parisian homage to two asynchronous sources: the natural cultural symbols of late nineteenth-century French empire; and the more modern futuristic funky jazz fusion inspired by Herbie Hancock's music video 'Rock It' from 1983. However, it also aestheticises the unique historical and cultural heritage of Paris as a modern cosmopolitan European city, and of France's empire at the turn of the last century. This *mise-en-scène* reinforces the group's relation and remaking of French heritage, set at the Parisian world fair with the Eiffel tower featured at the centre of the pavilion, alongside La Galarie des Machines and the large open space near the Champs de Mars where the band plays. Further by positioning the Exposition Universelle, which itself commemorated the 100-year 'Storming of the Bastille', Caravan Palace enlists electro swing to humorously re-enact this prestigious historical moment.

The music video looks akin to a 1920s-animated black and white film. Within the narrative, Caravan Palace plays their acoustic set within the open space in front of the exposition buildings as the first retro-futuristic spaceship hovers above. Their set is interrupted by this terrifying alien invasion, and soon Paris is under siege as spaceships drop their chequered vintage, marble balls onto the ornate cement structures of the fair. Parisians respond with panic and bewilderment, yet soon an organised and accelerated response is under way with the government's production of 'super' robots assembled in Paris's machine age factories. However, as the video presents the efficiency of this factory and its commodified labour force, one of the musicians-turned-factory workers throws a jazz trombone onto the conveyer belt. This instrument, metonym for the resourcefulness, resilience, and freedom of Jazz Age culture, ultimately lands in the robot's head. This subversion transforms the super warrior into a gigantic animated, dancing robot whose swing steps and jazz music produce a glitch in the space ships' flight patterns. Subsequently, the jazz-dancing robot causes the other ships to crash to the Earth's surface. The city's leaders respond with a plan to accelerate production of super-charged jazz-dancing robots. Ultimately, Paris is saved by this 'king of jazz' robot, who dances his way to the top of the Eiffel tower to survey the city with his protective far-reaching robot vision.

The soundtrack of this video begins with a hybrid swing/bayou beat and a familiar (I-iii)-ii-V-I progression followed by a walking descending bass line (I-vii-VI-V) back to the original ii-V-I riff. The verses are often paired with the bass alone, in the original bass drum beat and then over the chorus, the clarinet and brass are gradually layered in increasingly textured counterpoint. The moment the trombone is furtively thrown onto the conveyer belt, we hear a breakdown of the rhythm section in the most Django-inspired section – an acoustic trio – walking bass, guitar, and a full swing beat. As the robot reaches the final stages of production, the track is dampened, with a compressed vocal verse heard singing softly over the comping rhythm guitar (the ii–V–I progression) before the 'big reveal' of the super robot. As the huge factory gates open, the track features the full big band blasting into the city as the robot struts over the threshold. In the classic sectional writing of Fletcher Henderson, the atomised brass sections alternate with the rhythm section in contrasting registers of high and low. Occasionally these riffs are glitched by the robots' improvised hard-wiring, but as the robot dances into the city, the music builds in texture, intensity, and volume to the final and heavily layered shout chorus. As the robot finally reaches the top of the Eiffel Tower, the music recedes into its artificial, compressed sample, a quick fade intimates the feeling of peace and stability – electro swing has come to the rescue. In this audiovisual collage, France's musical past is modernised to accommodate contemporary tastes, especially for a younger generation accustomed to mediating music within the digital ecosystem of YouTube and other user-generated platforms. Intertextual knowledge of the musical aesthetics of these two cultures – the architectural spaces of Paris's pre-war culture and of contemporary aesthetics for electronic music – enabled Caravan Palace to connect with participants of both electronic and jazz culture.

In response to inquiries regarding the radical changes of the musical environment since 2005, Caravan Palace violinist Payen stated:

> Electronic music is the real living music today, for it has penetrated almost every other style. As a living thing, it always evolves. In 2005, when we began, dubstep didn't exist, even our own genre didn't exist!! And at the same time, the economic environment has radicalised through the Internet and the digital way of consuming music.
>
> *(Grennen 2014)*

CP was clearly aware of the centrality of digital technologies to many forms of contemporary music experience and influential promotional platforms. From 2008 on, they embraced the digital and visual environment of YouTube, and indeed this electro swing group has released more music videos than most other electro swing acts within their transnational community.

Since 2012, Caravan Palace committed itself to releasing multiple videos every few years, many of them offer humorous or science fiction inspired stories often featuring fantastical pre-digital yet futuristic themes. These videos include 'Suzy' (released on February 28, 2012) with 4.2 million views, a video in which Suzy (with the face and stature of Zoé as a Jazz Age Zazou) dances combinations of the Charleston and slightly more modern moves such as 'the robot' with the 'amazing dancing machine' (a 1920s-era robot-like man). The video takes place in art deco meets science fiction Jazz Age spaces with references to the 1930s film *The Wizard of Oz*. The same year, an animated video featuring stop-time animation figures modelled from the posters and detritus of the band's gigs are featured dancing to lyrics of 'Jolie Coquine' (February 29, 2012). This was followed by 'Rock it For Me' video (March 1, 2012), "an alien space ship attack of the world" scenario staged at the turn of the (last) century within Paris's World's Fair. CP's most-viewed video is 'Dramophone', released in October 2012. This video departed from the vintage swing machine/robot theme to highlight modern swing and jazz dancing in a 1980s-style music video narrative combined with 1930s-era modern jazz compositions. These videos were followed by several more in 2015 and 2016, with 'Lone Digger' (November 12, 2015) featuring an animated swing dancing cat 'about town', followed by the video 'Comics' (June 30, 2015), and then 'Mighty' (August 6, 2015), a 'lo-fi' collage of several robots from pre-1960 black and white films, and then 'Wonderland' (June 14, 2016), an animated short with characters modelled after the musicians and featuring a more hip-hop-oriented track and dancing by a swinging Colotis as the main character. To date their most recent video is 'Midnight' (November 2016), a modern-day scene set in LA's Compton neighbourhood with stoic images of Black urban culture narrated through the course of one day (and night).[7] This last video incorporates a more modern 'urban' soundscape, yet enhanced with blues-oriented vocal samples from the 1930s and 1940s. The signature sounds of the Roland TR 808 drum sequencer modernise the typical electro swing mix. The sonic signifier connecting this video to electro swing is the single baritone saxophone sample of a slow bluesy line performed with thick vibrato.

Of all of these hybrid videos, the 'Dramophone' video was one of the most viewed, helping launch their European-wide success. The filmic video features some of the current competitive European Lindy and jazz dancers who, in this video, perform a variety of steps from the Charleston, the Suzie Q, and the Lindy Hop to contemporary shuffle dance steps and hip hop moves. To date, this promotional video has accrued 2.3 million views since it was published.

'Dramophone' (2012)

The soundtrack for 'Dramophone' evokes a European jazz flavour with a trio of female vocalists, a Reinhardt-style guitar comping pattern, a four-beat muted trumpet riff, then a clarinet call-out riff answered by the violin. The track also samples the Mills Brothers 'Swing it, Sister' from the LP *Four Brothers and a Guitar* (Decca 1934) in 'Get Happy and Lose Control'. The trap set is pared down to snare with brushes and minimal bass bumps in a combined funk and disco style. After a minute, the bass turns to a walking bass line with the refrain "Sassy sisters, come and taste the sweetest candy". This lyric provides the enjoinder for a 'dance-off' between two rival fractions – but this time not between rival gangs of the urban environment, but rather between the two genders and classes of electro swing, the Lindy Hop revival and the lower-class, male motorcycle crew patronising this dusty off-road highway café.

The video foregrounds the role of dance as a light-hearted, participatory antidote for cultural conflict in a manner reminiscent of Michael Jackson's theatrical dance-offs in his iconic 'Beat It' (1982) music video. A group of campy bikers trail these carefree cosmopolitan women in their vintage automobiles to *L'Ecole*, a local road-side dinner in a non-descript place. The young but gregarious, attractive blond woman follows the bikers into the café. After entering, she confronts the lead biker head on – ripping his denim patch from his leather jacket, an act demanding a challenge. Everyone stares in shock and fear – the soundtrack is briefly suspended to dramatise this daring act. The savvy and more mature waitress (played by CP's Zoé Colotis) breaks open the safety box (fixed on the wall where the fire extinguisher should be) and pulls out a white-label vintage vinyl disc titled simply "jazz record". She tosses the disc to the cook near a DJ booth/table, who quickly sets it up as the dancers begin their competition. The women battle the men in a number of comedic and catchy jazz and contemporary moves. Naturally, the rhythmic compulsion of this hybrid vintage/modern music eases the tensions between the 'rough' motorcyclists and the trendy retro adventure seekers. Eventually the party washes out into the street for a large-scale collective community dance before the climax of the song builds to a drop, whose subsequent climax leads to an improvised jam circle. This improvised dance section also occurs during the most recognisable soundscapes of jazz recordings with short improvised riffs on the muted trumpet and clarinet and a full swing or rather jungle-style trap set break. Short stutters of the electro sound world punctuate this old jazz track until the bass is fully present during the last thirty-two measures.

After the dance-off between a white, trashy motorcycle gang and the young 'sassy' dancing woman begins, the 'gypsy' jazz guitar break ensues with a IV-ii-V-I progression. Four choruses of the instrumental breaks (clarinet, violin, saxophones) are danced to in a hybrid Charleston/shuffle style, and then the drums transition to a conventional swing beat. This is the moment that the dancers break into the jam circle with a Krupa-inspired jungle beat while a variety of young and old dancers take short solo breaks on the floor. Others do impressive jumps in the air into the final drop before the last refrain, while the line "sassy sisters" repeats over and over to the accompaniment of the stride style, out-of-tune barrel house piano. The big finish to the dance-off occurs outside in the streets and features breaks of Charleston, four-beat aerial Lindy tricks (in the style of Whitey's Lindy Hoppers), and a number of modern individual solo shuffle dancers – symbolising the merging of contemporary electronic dance and more traditional social swing dancing styles. Furthermore, the mixing of contemporary sampling and bass aesthetics and timbres with more fully audible samples of traditional swing and jazz provide the appropriate sonic invitation for such intergenerational and corporeal improvisations. With their movements, this dancing group too understands the

(a)

(b)

(c)

FIGURES 6.7(A–C) Caravan Palace music video, 'Dramophone' (2012) featuring
Colotis as a dancing waitress; the street dance scene; and two cooks
dancing in a jam circle

iconic *La Poumpe* sound of Reinhardt's guitar, and his quintet in general as well as the stride-piano style of 1920s-era 'piano professors'. In this track and danced video performance, the typical gypsy jazz combination of I-VI-ii-V-I over the *pompe* rhythmic attack perfectly fits this modern retro remix style, a polygeneric music not only intended for the recording studio but for the dance floor and music hall.

Within these videos and live performances of Caravan Palace, the instrumental training and interest in interwar instrumental Parisian jazz culture contributed immensely to CP's performative and music video aesthetic. This combination of electronic sequencing, vintage musical aesthetics, and live acoustic popular music compositions proved successful for other jazz pop acts within Europe after 2010, and especially for the producer-led outfit of Caro Emerald. Like Caravan Palace, the Caro Emerald project worked through various audiovisual media ecologies to promote their vintage aesthetic. This landscape enabled vintage remix groups to draw a transnational public to their performances through the promotion and circulation of music videos on YouTube and the creation of soundscapes which drew from a particular mythology of the European jazz past. Such mediatisation combined with a generative approach towards the jazz past also informed the performance and recording aesthetics of Caro Emerald in the 2010s.

Caro Emerald – Reviving Europe's Jazz Past within Convergence Culture

One of the headlining artists of the 2012 North Sea Jazz Festival was Caro Emerald, a talented artist and songwriting team whose music was quickly popularised across Europe partly due to the project's adept navigation of various media forms, including performances on syndicated television talent shows such as *Idols* and *Strictly Come Dancing*. Like other vintage remix artists, Caro Emerald's music videos and recording projects adapted images of and sonic references to an earlier European jazz culture. However, the reference point for Caro Emerald was not exclusively the jazz and Swing Era, but in particular the late 1940s and 1950s period, wherein the American production styles of exotica and 'space-age' jazz composers such as Martin Denny and Les Baxter became prominent. Interestingly, the many recordings and videos of Caro Emerald also incorporated contemporary pop music aesthetics, betrayed by digital samples of iconic lounge and jazz instruments and riffs layered amongst hip hop drum sequences within accessible and well-crafted pop music song structures.

In 2009, the producer-led project known as Caro Emerald[8] materialised after the fortuitous meeting between Dutch producer David Schreurs and Canadian songwriter Vince Degiorgio. The former Vice President of International A&R at RCA Records, Degiorgio was a seasoned music professional who had overseen dozens of popular groups, most famously N' Sync. As part of the record industry's consolidation, RCA released Degiorgio from his contract in 2005. In search of new projects, he contacted Schreurs. Their interactions began with digitally shared tracks, which each augmented and reworked before Dutch hip-hop producer Jan Van Wieringen programmed beats for these tracks. From these first compositions, they sought a capable vocalist to record their first song, entitled 'Back it Up'. Schreurs suggested local vocalist Carline Esmeraldo van der Leeuw (later adopting the stage name Caro Emerald), a professional singer and vocal coach from Amsterdam, who trained at the Amsterdam Conservatory of Music where she followed a vocal jazz programme. Schreurs and Degiorgio presented their first arrangement to Van der Leeuw, and according to Emerald, she immediately clicked with both the melody and ambient references of the track, which for her recalled the glamorous lounge singers of the 1940s and 1950s (Carline Esmeraldo van de Leeuw, email correspondence with the author, October 6, 2012). Her jazz training worked well in this crossover style, as did her experience and skill in performing new currents in pop music, from 'nu' soul to R&B. The song's vintage/modern hybrid perfectly suited her eclectic musical tastes and talents.

Soon after the single's completion, Schreurs and Wieringen shopped it to local labels, although interest was scarce. Undeterred, they promoted the song through visual media, first on local television, and soon after they staged a playback performance at a Dutch brown bar in Amsterdam to broadcast on YouTube in 2009. Both the television and YouTube performance triggered rapid word-of-mouth attention, going 'viral'. Soon after, national Dutch commercial radio stations including 3FM promoted the single.

Within 'Back it Up's' contemporary aesthetic, the song references exotica conventions from the 1940s and 1950s, such as the opening growling tenor saxophone blues lick, the rolling vibraphone sample, and thick brass horn lines. The electronic hip-hop beat, the backbeats, and the call-and-response chorus layered over Emerald's main text, though, point to modern electronic pop conventions. The bridge also features dub elements, such as the phasing of the offbeat horns, the scratching, and the deep resonance of the bass. Dense polyrhythmic textures build before the last voiceless refrain during which the iconic, but here, a generically sounding DJ's voice is sampled over a muted speaker effect.

The original YouTube promo video for 'Back it Up' reinforced 1950s crime jazz scenarios. The first sequence is set in a dingy, low-budget film-editing studio, poorly lit with dark shadows and smoke-stained walls. Film footage rolls to the ground amid pin-ups of Emerald propped against the wall. In the next scene, the projector spotlight suggests an illicit adult pictures theatre, with battered footage in sepia tones. Visually the track also juxtaposes 1950s lounge against contemporary, gentrified racial signifiers in European hip hop and nu jazz; the final sequence highlights the young, handsome, white DJ mixing two 45s prominently positioned to showcase the Grandmono record label. Here, vintage technologies promote notions of authenticity to reify particular media within the history of recorded sound. The spatial incongruities of reel-to-reel projectors compete with the street credibility of two turntables, each fashioned within the subterranean, subcultural spaces of after-hours editing studios. Conspicuously absent, however, are the computers and their flexible digital software.

As 'Back it Up' rose in the charts, breaking number one records for multiple weeks in the Benelux region, the Emerald outfit constructed a full album similarly inspired by jazz and cinema from the 1950s. For the next recording, the project mined vintage audiovisual sources to meticulously integrate the sounds and recording aesthetics of the great producers of the so-called golden era of Hollywood exotica, from the hybrid Cuban American dance music of Perez Prado to the space-age exotic lounge odysseys of Martin Denny. For Schreurs, the music of this period represented an apotheosis of musical quality coupled with expert production values, and visualised with the necessary glamour and spectacle that surrounded the Rat Pack appearances in Las Vegas (David Schreurs, Interview with the author, November 3, 2011). This music's live and mediated reception privileged the visual aesthetics of musical films and television series over live European cabaret culture of the Swing Era. It was these vintage images that inspired the style and design of the promotional video for the group's second video, 'A Night Like This', in 2009.

When asked about the significance of this 'American' inspiration, Schreurs reflected upon Europeans self-fashioning against the model of post-war American prosperity. For him, this period particularly resonated wealth, prestige, and optimism for the future:

> Well in the 1950s everybody was looking at America weren't they – I mean the Dutch were covering the Americans as were the Germans. A lot of the hit music came from America and it wasn't until the 1960s that more hits came from Europe.
>
> *(David Scheurs, Interview with the author, November 3, 2011)*

Emerald highlighted the more ephemeral associations with this era, from the prominent role of the 'American dream' to the glamorous popular music culture of Hollywood crooners (Carline Esmeraldo van de Leeuw, Email correspondence with the author, October 16, 2012). These were powerful images for the post-war Dutch nation, deeply invested in conceptualising its own traumatic past through the escapist and soothing routes of popular culture.

The album's second single, 'A Night Like This', surpassed the popularity of 'Back it Up', but did so outside the usual channels of radio promotion. This led to several bookings for Emerald within festivals. In January 2010, the twelve-song album *Deleted Scenes from the Cutting Room Floor* on Schreurs' Grandmono label was released. After the success of the second single, Schreurs and Degiorgio took over the project's business aspect, initiating their own record company and establishing distribution deals with international labels in over seventeen countries.

While the single ('A Night Like This') stormed the Dutch charts, it wasn't until Zazou Mall (a young vocal contestant on Germany's *Idols*) performed her

(a)

(b)

FIGURES 6.8(A–B)   Caro Emerald Martini Moments promotional video 'A Night Like This' (2009) featuring Emerald singing with full band and close-up with vintage mic

version in 2011 that German audiences began buying the album.[9] Soon after, performances of the song appeared on other reality-based syndicated programmes, including the UK's *Strictly Come Dancing* and *The Voice of Poland*. These interactive TV platforms provided unprecedented opportunities for the song's promotion. The current promotion of European popular music stars through syndicated mainstream European talent contests reanimated prior historically established relationships. Since the 1950s, the industry promoted the spectacle of professionalism by appropriating the promotional potential of television to publicly mentor young talent. In the audiovisual climate of both participatory culture and media consolidation and integration, Europe's transnational entertainment industry dedicated national media for exposing music stars to an expanding European audience. Such a relationship had seldom been symbolically spectacularised since Abba's rise to international fame after their first *Eurovision* song contest appearance in 1974. This adaptation of prior European media formats points to globalisation's flexible routes of transplantation and 'de-territorialisation' in the expanding media landscape of television and other digital media (Appadurai 1996).

Soon after, Emerald was invited as one of the headliners for both the 2012 and 2013 North Sea Jazz Festival (NSJF) editions. Audiences were now familiar with the act's presence and recorded singles, signifying both popular and crossover engagements with Northern Europe's unique jazz past. Furthermore, audiences were so familiar with the song's melody, lyrics, and post-war dance production aesthetics, they could respond similarly to global stars in large pop music venues. The crossover appeal of popular music stars who re-enact the fantasies of collective memory, such as the image of carefree, jet-setting, European jazz lover, prominently coloured the pleasures of Emerald's public, who danced and sang along in full voice the romantic, euphoric chorus of 'A Night Like This' during the height of her 2012 NSJF set. In a dramatic but well-rehearsed moment, Emerald pointed the microphone to the large festival audience, who crooned:

> I have never dreamed it
> Have you ever dreamed a night like this
> I cannot believe it
> I may never see a night like this
> When everything you think is incomplete
> Starts happening when you are cheek to cheek
> Could you ever dream it
> I have never dreamed, dreamed a night like this

Such images of romantic encounters betray the enduring longing of European jazz soloists to be included in the great jazz cannon. Moreover, these popular, trans-historical, creative musical tropes encapsulate the fascination and desire for the romance and passion of Europe's early jazz festivals, as beautiful, natural sites where romance, the scintillation of hot jazz, and uncommon cultural and racial encounters were coveted experiences (McGee 2016).

Since Caro Emerald's breakthrough into the European jazz and popular music festival circuit, the project has released two more albums inspired by European (and American-influenced) cultural movements and trends. For example, *The Shocking Miss Emerald* from 2013 explored the French 1960s Parisian fashion, music, and photography movement with images and sounds which corresponded to this post-war moment. In 2017, the Emerald project released a four-song EP with a video to accompany the song 'The Ghost of You', a lounge-inspired track whose visuals embroidered the decorative flora and fauna of a sensual and exotic botanical scene. These vintage remixes could be sonically located to the cinematic style of 1960s' soundtracks composed by Ennio Morricone combined with

(a)

(b)

(c)

FIGURES 6.9(A–C) Film stills of 'The Ghost of You' (2017)

Hollywood's post-war exotic dance and lounge rhythms. Together, these afforded cultural time travel, a revisiting of the romanticised voyages offered through post-war sound cultures. Within Caro Emerald's most recent recordings and music videos, this soundscape and visual style is welded to another era, the 1920s with the classic blues sounds of Black American female jazz singers, whose voices haunt this modern electronic acoustic track. Emerald's recent video 'The Ghost of You' anticipates this recapitulated past by interjecting, sonically, a long-lost lover's eternal discontent, this time taking the form of the classic blues singer's (probably Bessie Smith) agencied voice.[10]

'The Ghost of You' (2017)

Caro Emerald's recent video adopts the classic blues voice as metonym for the haunted spectre of the past. The video's vintage cinematic scene is established by the sombre setting of a dimly illuminated colonial-era mansion. The sound of the vibraphone and theremin invokes a classic haunted soundscape of 1950s-era television and film. From this brief soundscape, the broken sample of a classic blues singer's haunted voice filters through to the foreground, and the vintage setting is visually established by the colour palette of an old-fashioned sci-fi or horror film. The video sonically synchronises such melancholic recollections via a bedevilled dance (in a classic 3–3–2 clave pattern) with a lost lover ('the ghost of you'). The soundtrack of vintage horror and crime is later reinforced by flutes and strings, a nod to crime jazz soundscape, such as Mancini's late 1950s series *Peter Gunn*. The song, however, takes the form of a tango with the guitar, drums, and bass prominently playing the tango rhythm, before the strings provide counterpoint to Emerald's chorus, where she sings:

> I dance with the ghost of you
> What else can I do?
> You seem too far from view
> So I dance with the ghost of you

After this first verse, the ornamental wallpaper transitions into a luscious green-house scene animated with delicate butterflies, nocturnal birds, and a distant blue moon. These decorative features are animated as projections of the memories and psychological states induced by the song in a disorienting dream-like sequence. In one sequence the wallpaper butterflies come to life as the 'ghosted' portrait begins to sing. The theremin solo during the chorus also reinforces the mysterious othering of the tune as the chorus fades out to return to the original blues sample – here Smith's voice of pain and pathos as signified within Black music provided an affective feminised 'surrogate' for this modern ballad of lost love in this vintage remix (Brooks 2008).

The video 'The Ghost of You' (2017) from the EP *Emerald Island* offers a highly romantic and nostalgic ballad whose narrative stages the ephemeral longing for the past through the spectre of a lost lover, a metonym for "imperialist nostalgia" (Rosaldo 1989). The use of the sample and of soundstages associated with prior historical moments also speaks to our longing for lost sonic and visual cultures. Contributing to the romantic cinematic sound, which many YouTube users identified as a James Bond track,[11] are rather the early influences of pop music and jazz which were so ingeniously composed into mainstream film music practice by Hollywood and film producers, including Henri Mancini and later Ennio Morricone within their television and later cinematic crime soundtracks of the 1950s and 1960s. This well-crafted popular song, arranged with 1950s-era instrumentation, set the scene of these later noir soundscapes: the luscious unison strings, the grand piano's acrobatic runs, and the rolling vibraphone riffs. The track also features a minimalistic strummed Flamenco guitar, sparsely implemented vibraphone chords, and Emerald's nostalgic languid vocal, which in the bridge is effected by a vintage microphone. By making audible this vintage recording hardware, the song dialogically engages with the human musicians of the past, but equally with the sounds of recording technology of past colonial music cultures. These technologies of love and loss seep through to the present. With this brief sample bookending the video and song, the classic blues voice acts as a vintage surrogate, this time disrupting our sense of (lost) time as the ghost (Emerald) sings from (but also to) the past in response to the classic blues singer's culturally symbolic voice.

The last sequence of the video frames a gramophone with a 1920s-era blues song as the more intimate cabaret sounds of the violin and trumpet play sombrely, interwoven between Emerald's nonchalant phrases. The sound of classic blues artists singing "you can't read my mind" features as the lyrical motive for the track and video, and this brief descending blues line provides the opening and closing motif of the song – a symmetrical convention within pop and classical music.

Emerald sings, "So I dance with the ghost of you", as her image is inserted as a 'passed' relative within an ornately and highly stylised family portrait. Her portrait is variously framed by ornately carved tropical wood designs and stained and corroded mirrored glass – decorations which stage European and American colonial history. These framings haunt the present both sonically and visually as palimpsest, sonic and visual frames eroding and metamorphosing the passing of time through the faded patina of wallpaper and picture frames, but also the scratchy echoing distortions of the vintage microphones and amplifiers enhance this haunted visual past dream world.

The scene's sartorial references, such as the beret and cigarette held by Emerald, elicit various periods from post-war Paris. Her cynicism about both men and smoking is evident – both are addictive and 'dangerous', akin to unhealthy obsessions and attachments to the past. The smoke and black walls provide the setting for an ad hoc art cinema. And still another stylistic period is referenced as Emerald's visage is framed with a flower in her hair in high black and white contrast, reminding one of Kahlo's famous self-portraits.

Throughout the video, we are invited to experience this nostalgic dream sequence in which the old instruments of Paris's cabaret tango culture are mixed into other periods, from the colonial Mexican art world of Frida Kahlo to the intimate music joints of the Chicago blues singers and finally to the 1950s noir crime detectives of Hollywood cinematic practice. All of these stages provide the disorientation presented by fetishising the past through musical instruments such as pianos, drum sets, marimbas, and finally a single gramophone (which plays the original classic blues sample). These are not simply tools for performing a song, but semiotically charged symbols of faded arts cultures. Within these videos, remix culture enables their summoning for contemporary arts communities and their obsessive excavating of the sonic and visual past. Vintage remix and electro swing lay bare their obsession with the past through this audiovisual time travel. By staging such asynchronous trips in both 'live' music and digitally mediated platforms, vintage remix allows an open-ended conversation and a generative staging of European jazz history and its relation to our eminently haunted future.

Conclusion

These two sub-chapters have proposed an alternative to generalised critiques of electro swing and vintage remix as superficial instances of retromania (Reynolds 2011), or of a more ahistorical "global aesthetics" (Erlmann 1996). Instead, by providing close readings of the recorded, multi-arts, performed and visually mediated work of these three groups, I have revealed how this corporeal, visual, and sonic conversation with the past reflect creative strategies undertaken by contemporary musicians and other arts participants within this culture to make sense of the future. However, while the pleasures and playful remembering gained and inspired from these vintage encounters do not necessarily yield politicised solutions to such crises, they do provide immersive transport to a mythical conception of the past. While the pleasures afforded by fetishising the sonic, technological, corporeal, and visual symbols of the past offer collectivising and sometimes participatory escapes, for the vintage remix musicians committed to sampling the past, this conversation offers more than pure escapism. The arts participants of vintage festivals and electro swing admit their love of past musical cultures, for the 'audio gold' contained within the recordings of some of the jazz era's most prolific, resilient, and creative artists – but their connection and reworking of this material also stages a plea for current musical participants to become more involved. By performing a conversation with this past, the musicians of Caro Emerald, Caravan Palace, and Electric Swing Circus attempt to revive especially the most interactive and resilient facets of this prior jazz culture to motivate greater participation in the future.

The role of outdoor festivals in reanimating an interactive corporeal jazz culture through a unique conception of Europe's jazz past has in some ways ameliorated the dislocation of communicative bodies from the public sphere as digital culture threatens to overtake our daily activities with "sound bubbles" and privatised public spaces (Bull 2008). Ironically, it is this digital landscape which has afforded the most intense alignment with not only the recordings of jazz culture but the sartorial symbols of prior interactive bodily cultures, the fashion, the decorative arts, and the highly physical and interactive jazz and swing dancing of the Swing Era.

Finally, this chapter lays bare the features of contemporary music praxis, a practice which disregards rigid boundaries for the flexible reconfiguration of audiovisual arts worlds. From the recording studio to the vintage festival stage and to the music videos circulated as calling cards for the modern/old sounds of electro swing, this pop jazz practice depends upon the integration of sampling and electronic soundscapes within acoustic music stages to one where vintage recordings are woven into modern tracks through the electronic dance sets of headlining DJs of popular music festivals. Within this remix culture, the so-called jazz tradition has not yet been fully evacuated as the riffs and improvised choruses of violinists, the propulsion of Django-inspired comping, the ii-V-I harmonic structures, and the blue notes and talking back phrasing of jazz queens and chanteuses is easily audible in each of these multi-mediated acts. The spectres of European jazz pasts are here made audible and danceable within the participatory and corporeal spaces of vintage remix.

Notes

1 This event is promoted on the venue's website: www.labellevilloise.com/la-nuit-electroswing-7/ (accessed November 28, 2018).
2 See the page "Histoire", from the venue's La Bellevilloise website: www.labellevilloise.com/la-bellevilloise/ (accessed November 28, 2018).
3 From Caravan Palace's Facebook page post from Le Clan Records from October 25, 2017: www.facebook.com/CaravanPalace/, (accessed November 1, 2018).
4 This performance is from 2012 at Le Trianon and the video is produced by MAÏTO PROD. This performance can be viewed on YouTube: www.youtube.com/watch?v=-7JOa3dISg0 (accessed December 15, 2018).
5 These samples are identified on the sample-based music archive *Who Sampled* under the track "Caravan Palace – Rock it for Me": www.whosampled.com/Caravan-Palace/Rock-It-for-Me/ (accessed November 27, 2018).
6 This concert was filmed on April 16, 2010 at the Phénix in Bourges. The video can be seen on YouTube: www.youtube.com/watch?v=7YR-AvTDctk (accessed November 15, 2018).
7 This YouTube commenter wrote: "To those who don't know, there is a horse stables in Compton. It's ran by the Compton Jr. Mounted Posse. This is in Los Angeles and gangland territory rounds up these rebellious and possibly gang affiliated black teenagers" (Jwargod Da Hedless 1 year ago). Some might find this video essentialising and criminalising of Black (music) culture, which is reinforced by this seemingly innocuous comment.
8 Consisting of Dutch vocalist Caroline Esmeralda van der Leeuw, Dutch song writer/producers David Schreurs, Jan van Wieringen, and Canadian lyricist Vince Degiorgio was released as a promo video on YouTube.

9   Zazou Mall performed 'A Night Like This' on April 9, 2011, during the episode "America vs. Europe" on *Deutschland sucht den Superstar* broadcast on media channel RTL.

10   Schreurs could not confirm which record this sample was taken from as he has worked through several jazz-era recordings and made brief samples several years ago and since worked them into new manipulated sonic material (David Scheurs, email correspondence, December 20, 2018).

11   See the comments to the official video of Caro Emerald's 'The Ghost of You' published on YouTube in 2017 at: www.youtube.com/watch?v=bYp-opz6jHA, (accessed January 4, 2019).

EPILOGUE

In May, the town of Hamar, Norway, welcomes visitors to AnJazz, a small annual festival held in this scenic locale, situated 130 kilometres north of Oslo near lake Mjøsa. This region is home to well-preserved medieval log houses as well as fifteenth-century ruins. Since the nineteenth century, this city's combined natural, architectural, and artistic attractions made it a popular tourist destination for both Norway's elite and wealthy internationals, hoping to experience the beautiful ruins, picturesque pine trees, and snow-covered lakes. In this historical setting, festival concerts are programmed in the Hamar Teater, a building completed in 1927 at the height of Norway's Jazz Age culture. During the festival, the small theatre, café-salon, bar, and adjacent exposition hall host both concerts and interactive social spaces. The style of this theatre, hotel, and its music and café spaces affords visitors a vestige of early twentieth-century forms of leisure and music-making within Norway's bustling villages peripheral to its cosmopolitan centre of Oslo.

While researching this book, I visited many such festivals and historical spaces throughout Northern Europe, seeking to acquire a sense of the breadth of contemporary jazz performance practice. However, I had attended this festival expressly because of its headlining act on May 11, 2018 – the trio of Norwegian jazz musicians known as GURLS featuring Hanna Paulsberg on tenor saxophone (and vocals), Rohey Taalah on vocals, and Ellen Andrea Wang on bass (and vocals). In recent years, GURLS had gained a reputation for both their compelling live performances and for the originality of their newly composed material as represented on their last album *Run boy, run* (Grappa 2018). The compositions and lyrics of this trio, composed primarily by saxophonist Paulsberg, reflect these relatively young musicians' collective experiences of jazz labour, music, desire, media, and global culture in the new Europe. During the festival, these themes were

FIGURE 7.1 CD cover to *Run boy, run* (Grappa 2018)

performed with personal style and versatility by the young but quickly emerging Norwegian jazz star Rohey Taalah.

This concert took place in the theatre's recital hall, an 'endstage' theatre, which hosted some 300 festival-goers. GURLS entered the stage from behind a vintage velvet curtain in casual streetwear. Without introducing themselves, they began their set unceremoniously. Taalay sang four measures of sustained vowels in harmony with Wang's upright bass; this duet constituted the exposition of the song 'Oui'[1] from their recent album. Her mellow, lower-register voice (with the harmonised bass) punctuated the vocables "hum, ee, yo, yo, ee (oui)" in slow-moving harmonic rhythm and with a methodical, reverent attack. After this first phrase, Paulsberg's saxophone harmonised the other two voices to form eight minor triads progressing from tonic to dominant and back to tonic in F sharp minor. These slow-moving triads (followed by quarter rests) provided a plaintive, cyclical motion which highlighted the timbre of this modest trio – the bass, alto voice, and tenor saxophone – as three jazz voices which were variously configured throughout the set as human voices, instrumental voices, and combinations of both.

The ensemble's arrangements took full advantage of the unique timbres and colours afforded by no drums, piano, or guitar. Sometimes Paulsberg and Wang sang backup harmonies to Taalah's main vocals, and other times only one voice was cast in harmony with the bass or tenor saxophone. As band leader and composer, Paulsberg fluently adapted her instrument to reconfigure the quintessential and expected 'jazz voice' of live instrumental jazz culture. In particular moments, the saxophone momentarily relinquished its role as the solo instrumental object to become a harmonised supportive and mimetic human voice. At other moments, Taalah adapted her vocal timbres and textures to promote her instrumentalism as established within jazz performance practice.

Throughout the set, Paulsberg's solos captured the moody, millennial malaise of her jazz aesthetic when arranged and filtered through Taalah's lyrical voice, and although Paulsberg exhibited much virtuosity and technical control, her improvisational approach resisted an unbridled, indulgent style of an earlier Northern European jazz collectivism (Heffley 2005; Rusch 2015). Sometimes she veered into the altissimo range, and other times rested on single-note riffs syncopated by the back beat of funk or soul. Most of the songs performed were in English, apart from one Norwegian song, 'Syngedam'.

The group incorporated no major electronics or digital remixing, but rather depended upon the versatility of their three voices within well-crafted arrangements, traversing the boundaries of popular music and jazz while prioritising the textures and performance style of neo-soul and modern jazz. Wang too provided lead vocals on one song, but since there was no drummer, she generally sustained the groove and tempo. Her impeccable feel provided the perfect counterpart for Paulsberg's solos and Taalah's wide-ranging melodies. Cumulatively in this set, these musicians' three voices resonated with and realigned the modern polygeneric and texturally attuned consciousness of young jazz musicians occupying the spaces of Europe's twenty-first-century jazz culture.

After the trio's last tune within this intimate but exceptional set, GURLS' Norwegian audience quickly shifted from clapping to a collective quarter-note pulse – an old-fashioned custom with its collective synchronisation. Paulsberg, however, satirised this practice as she led the trio back onto the stage while hopping in time from left to right. Soon she was stomping around the stage in a military fashion to the 'authoritarian/collectivist' beat produced by the audience. The trio then refocused their antics to prepare for their last blues-based ballad, 'Blues for T', a sombre, melancholy tune which nevertheless inspired one older couple to dance romantically in the aisles near the front of the stage.

After their performance, I had arranged (I thought) an interview with Rohey and Hanna, but while waiting in the bar for the musicians to finish selling merchandise, Hanna hurried past me to leave, effectively snubbing me. However, in a brief conversation, Taalah offered to share a few ideas about contemporary European jazz. In a cramped hotel room, she reviewed her musical training and influences. She started singing at a young age in the collective music groups in which all Norwegian children participate as part of their primary education. Recognising her vocal talents, she was early encouraged to forgo the classical and folk ensembles in order to perform in jazz groups. She soon transferred to a special arts high school and then earned her degree in music performance at the prestigious Trondheim Music Conservatory, which offers one of the most competitive jazz education programmes in Norway. Here she studied jazz and vocal performance. Her early influences ranged from canonised jazz instrumentalists and vocalists including Fitzgerald and Holiday to soul singers Erykah Badu and Jill Scott (Rohey Taalah, Interview with the author, May 11, 2018).

Bassist Ellen Andrea Wang also had studied jazz performance, but at the Oslo Conservatory for string bass. As a child, she was constantly inundated with music from her parents, both professional musicians. She also studied classical violin and sung in choirs. Her expanding role as a duo-jazz instrumentalist, rhythm section bassist, and vocalist was not unprepared when she entered the live music world (Ellen Andrea Wang, Telephone interview with the author, December 15, 2017). Wang listed important musical influences as fusion, rock, and pop. Favourite recording artists included American artists Herbie Hancock and Michael Jackson and Norwegian jazz artists, especially those featured in her father's record collection. A foundational early album frequently played in her home was European Quartet's *Belonging* (1974 ECM) with Keith Jarrett, Jan Garbarek, Palle Danielsson, and Jon Christensen. In addition to playing bass with GURLS, Wang also fronts her own combo with Jazzland Recordings, with which she recently recorded her critically acclaimed *Break Out* (Jazzland 2017), which garnered some traction on national radio.

GURLS' name betrays a connection to third-wave feminist movements (the riot grrls of the 1990s or the contemporary European riots of political punk movements, e.g. Pussy Riot in Russia). Furthermore, it provides a performative link to their unique jazz voices as they variously implement their vocal chords and instruments to growl, flutter, as well as dulcetly harmonise in live performances. Their particular approach towards orchestration, the jazz voice, and to modern cultural themes thereby performatively asserts their presence within Europe's twenty-first-century jazz spaces. They also engage a reworking of European jazz culture by embracing the many audiovisual opportunities now exploited and adopted by musicians within the landscape of global media, digitalisation, and transnational performance networks.

As represented on their recent 2018 *Run boy, run* album, the trio's music has acquired transnational critical acclaim, but many listeners have heard and seen their compositions and performances especially through live performances within small or middle-sized European jazz festivals such as this one. The second primary platform for their music is of course the many digital platforms for listening and viewing jazz performances. Like many modern jazz artists, GURLS has also produced their own professional videos of original music material, such as their video 'Dis Boy' (2018), an informal music video which dramatises the trio in jazz-related states of waiting, walking, commuting, and playing in urban settings. The video also features a brief appearance by their former vocalist Emilie Nicolas performing a short chorus during the bridge of the song. After gaining a reputation as a vocalist and composer with GURLS, Nicolas went on to record and tour as a solo artist in the experimental margins of pop and electronica.

The 'Dis Boy' video was staged in the modern urban setting of Oslo's underground subway stations. Here the musicians loiter in dark passages amidst soot-covered tiles and gum-soiled concrete. These underground spaces evoke a familiar setting for many large-scale post-industrial European cities. The video reminds one of the black and white, mundane urban scenes filmed for the realist and music-inspired French films *La Haine* (The Hate 1995) directed by Mattieu Kassovitz or *Bande de Filles* (Girlhood 2014) directed by Céline Sciamma. Here in this dreary setting, these three everyday street-smart musicians wait for forms of mass transit, in route to their next gig. Taalah delivers her post-modern ode, veering from blues riffs to a full-voiced yodelling over a back beat. Within the verses (composed by saxophonist Paulsberg), she asserts a growing infatuation with a boy ('Dis Boy'), with lyrics drawing on Black parlance of contemporary mediascapes from hip hop lyrics to representations of street culture as reified within European media. The concept of the hard-working, gigging jazz musician juxtaposed against the dull, yet incessant flow of modern transportation distances these musicians from prior images of women in jazz such as the now familiar glamorous jazz portraits of post-war singers fronting big bands in ball-rooms or the unified images of all-girl groups staged in theatrical contexts of earlier decades. These newly gendered jazz scenes even depart from the sensual and attractive women instrumentalists leading their own groups in recent decades. Rather the trio here adopts the urban space to promote modern sensibilities where (young) jazz musicians pay their dues while fantasising about romantic entanglements of which they have little time to pursue in their busy lives of rehearsing, travelling, recording, and performing. There is a coolness to both the mediated representations of this trio as well as their live performances which riff on the conventions of masculine jazz culture and re-contextualise them to suit their own lived experiences as cosmopolitan Norwegian musicians.

It is the remediation and assemblage of musical texts such as these within a transnational digital and live performance landscape that contributes to the broader context of jazz participation and reception within contemporary European arts culture, a facet that enables European jazz to crystallise concretely and meaningfully through such networks. The totality of live festival performances, reception discourse, and the audiovisual ecosystem act as continual processes in the (re)negotiation of contemporary European jazz culture, one that materialises despite the inherent promotional challenges connected to such a complex cultural landscape. Through the intersections between such intimate performances within small-scale local festivals and their broader audio-mediated transnational reception, European jazz artists resist the reductive conception of 'world jazz' as a universally recognisable template persistently open to modes of flexibility, adaptability, and accommodation (Bohlman and Plastino 2016, 24). Instead, such performances speak to the local specificity and intimacy of jazz cultures, even as these contexts remain cosmopolitan and dialogically connected to global phenomena such as an enduring myth of Black popular culture and the exploitation of new contexts to acquire transnational audiences.

Concluding Thoughts on Theorising Remix in European Jazz Culture

In the previous chapters, this book examined European jazz cultures through a range of mediated platforms and cultural frames – from these more intimate performances within small-scale peripheral jazz festivals to those which engage with large-scale contemporary phenomena in a variety of contexts, especially those connected to a variety of popular music cultures and mass-mediated phenomena. By highlighting contexts which expand jazz practice into other fields of reception, I have aspired to make jazz relevant outside of the conventional spaces of instrumental jazz. The affordances of digital musical techniques, of transnational performance networks, and of the increasing interest in connecting with popular musics from throughout the world's music cultures remains critical for understanding especially jazz-influenced practices such as the remix, or of live and electronic jazz within Northern Europe.

Throughout these explorations, I have also sought to intervene in the elitism and exclusivity within both jazz practice as well as jazz scholarship. My aim was to uncover a more inclusive and representative array of artists as well as processes ranging from the experimental and alternative to the dominant and mainstream within both popular music and jazz. By embracing such a broad spectrum, I sought to recognise jazz as developing alongside and within currents in popular music. As Simon Frith (2007) asserted, in asking once again the obsessive jazz question – is jazz popular music? – the answer remains categorically yes. Jazz has regained a prominent place within popular music practices and this place has too long been disparaged or excluded from academic jazz writing.

I have also examined case studies which sought to update jazz practice in light of new technologies and forms of cultural encounters. By synthesising existing studies of European jazz in decades not frequently highlighted in jazz studies, especially the 1980s, 1990s, and 2000s, I've tried to argue against the 'jazz is dead' proclamation once levied against these decades. Paramount for this alternative view was a desire to embrace the cross-pollinations between popular musics and jazz and especially within the increasingly dominant role of electronic dance musics and the attendant artistic practices of sampling, DJing, and dancing. Further, by incorporating remix as the core framework of various cases, I've attempted to connect recent jazz practice to broader cultural, philosophical, and aesthetic debates within Europe, especially after a period of reunification and transformation of European cities.

One impact of taking remix as my point of departure, then, was to elevate the role of different kinds of jazz participants, which demanded a reconsideration of the players active in contemporary music worlds. These included the festival organisers, the event planners, the producers and DJs, the venue bookers, and dance instructors, who all played a role in promoting and cultivating contemporary jazz worlds. This broader conception allowed me to include the role of those often excluded from more traditional jazz studies, such as the pop jazz vocalist or the swing dance professional. Finally, by privileging new technological techniques such as beat-making, sampling, and the hybrid recording studio, I was able to think outside of the orthodox jazz object, mainly the analogue jazz recording. This flexibility allowed me to look closely at the influence of especially visual media within jazz or jazz-influenced cultures, such as the prominent role of music videos within vintage or electro swing or the role of vintage jazz-era films in the revival of current jazz dance movements throughout Europe.

Finally, remix has allowed me to reposition and sometimes redefine the role of the singular jazz artist labouring for a jazz record company in this transformative period from the 1990s to the 2010s to better understand the role of hybrid and highly mobile independent record companies, who have enabled and stimulated the cross-fertilisation of jazz with new techniques as well as newer modes of distribution, such as was adapted by Jazzland Recordings during the rave and techno boom of the 1990s. While some studies have recently examined the generally well-recognised European jazz labels such as ECM, during the last three decades, hundreds of local and later transnational labels and, most recently, entire media platforms have emerged to take the place of the traditional jazz major from the post-war period. The important work performed by these labels, media platforms, and networks certainly deserves more attention from both music and jazz scholars.

The cultural, gendered, abled, and class connections to European jazz culture were partially addressed in the various case studies, although I believe that a more rigorous investigation into the ways that current educational and pedagogical platforms continue to run their course could lead to fruitful debates and insights about the representation and inclusivity potential of jazz cultures today. From recent research on the incorporation of women in popular music festivals such as those performed by *Vice* and the *Guardian*, it appears that women, despite claims that they are much better represented than before the 1990s, appear to be overly optimistic. At least within popular music and electronic dance music festivals, the gender ratios appear rather 'grim', with women's participation ranging from less than 1 per cent and only very rarely spiking up to 35 per cent (Beard 2016; Smith 2019; Mitchum and Garcia-Olano 2018). Such figures reveal a consistency within the music industry, which has persistently exhibited exclusionary patterns established from the very germinal years of its internationalisation in the early twentieth century. These figures have recently motivated top–down initiatives within the EU such as the PRS Foundation's Keychange programme encouraging festivals to sign on to pledge 50 per cent gender parity by 2022.[2] Certainly, the jazz festival performance and academic world could take greater interest in integrating such socio-political initiatives now influencing the organisation and restructuring of popular music institutions. As argued in this book, popular music continues to hold a prominent place within jazz praxis and therefore it deserves more and rigorous attention from the academic field.

Together the chapters of this book have sought to invite and theorise new voices and practices within jazz culture, especially within Northern Europe. Furthermore, this project was partially motivated by a desire to seek out jazz in places where it has been ignored, shunned, or disapproved of within academic studies – especially jazz acts connected and committed to mass-mediated popular musics. The retromania or hauntology connected to reconfigurations of prior popular music cultures and related media has already been elegantly theorised by established scholars (Fisher 2014; Reynolds 2011), but few postmodern theorists have understood or accounted for the revival of the residual dialectics related to jazz as popular music as it was once hotly debated and reflected in the hot jazz swing debates of Europe before the ascendance of pop and rock as the sound of Europe's youth culture. The divorce of jazz as and from the spaces of pop culture occurred at a moment when it was no longer the driving musical culture for reconfiguring local identities and values in moments of massive transformation such as those brought on by the two world wars. Today, however, jazz is just one of many musical sources providing inspiration and cultural voice for musicians working across musical, geographical, and virtual borders and in response to a number of global phenomena, from neoliberalism more broadly, to micro-level phenomena such as diminished compensation from the exchange of jazz commodities to the changing populations of particular European metropoles.

A second area which received too little attention in this project were particular regions of Europe. Since the cases within this book cover cities and spaces largely within Northern Europe, another study could productively expand research to highlight performances and activities within Eastern and Southern Europe, two regions which deserve more attention and recognition. Further, subsequent studies might highlight alternative and particularly boundaryless and multiple spaces within these regions, such as the transnational tourist routes or the (smooth) jazz cruise ship voyages.

Finally, since the rise of feminist movements in the second and third waves, women have increasingly demanded visibility and credit for their contributions to both jazz and popular musics. In the new current of audiovisual media and individual engagements with such platforms, women have found greater visibility, especially within new media such as the music video or digital workstations (Farrugia 2012; Vernallis 2013). Given these altered promotional contexts, I have attempted to highlight a number of prominent women within these jazz-inflected musical performances and media. Women have consistently been active remixing and restaging jazz culture as instrumentalists, as composers, as vocalists, but also as dancers, choreographers, as visual artists, video-makers, and as theatrical participants and organisers within festival cultures. In this study, I have aimed to draw attention to some of them, but certainly more attention is deserved to many other women working both as jazz performers as well as those working behind the scenes.

Within all of these cases and contexts, remix here presented itself as both an ideology, practice, and overall call for a re-staging of what could be considered jazz practice in the twenty-first century. The total 'live remix concert', elevated to artistic heights within Norway's Punkt music festival, perhaps most easily coheres with existing understandings of remix as the integration of especially technological manipulations of the sonic material of jazz practice, such as the improvised jam session. However, remix as a cultural disposition allows other jams to emerge such as the jam circle of jazz dance staged in remixed settings (such as hip hop and Lindy Hop battles remediated online) to the remixes of interwar swing culture in the evocative music videos of electro swing. YouTube provides a performance-based research platform, archive, and counter-public for jazz as evidenced in the re-enactment of jazz steps of prior jazz cultures (such as the Lindy Hop) to the modern embodied dances of EDM, such as the solitary shuffle dances uploaded online by individual bedroom dancers to the electro swing tracks of DJ Parov Stelar.

Through this broad mix of styles, practices, and performance contexts, my aim has not been to dilute the meaning of jazz values but rather to understand jazz as a fluid and ever negotiated cultural field now exerting influence within popular music and within modern technological and mediated contexts for over a century. Remixing jazz culture then offers insight into how a jazz public is changing and has changed since the pervasive and far-reaching phenomena of globalisation, mass migration, and digitalisation in the last four decades. However, the changing landscape of cultural identities and of gender politics too has played out in the digital field and is here enacted within the intersections between especially jazz, popular culture, and modern electronic techniques first spawned from the DJing and production-based experiments of the 1980s to the remixes and vintage film collages accompanied by vintage remix tracks of social media.

The polygeneric music-making of all of the cases considered speaks to the "global fascinations" and sometimes "frustrated cosmopolitanisms" (Tsiouslakis 2011) of modern musicians, who seek to embody the histories of local music cultures while also participating in the broad spectrum of transnational and now a hypermobile global modernity. By continually engaging and reworking this past, such as in sampled classic blues riffs initiating Caro Emerald's 'The Ghost of You' or the combined acts of improvisation and sonic mediation through the 'live remix concert', remixed jazz cultures juxtapose such musical practices in order to make sense of the present. Remixed jazz cultures further assert long-term connections between American jazz heroes of canonised histories, the well-circulated jazz phonograph canon, and the Black Atlantic commitment and connection to early-twentieth-century jazz artists within this continent. However, these collectivities also assert connections to the fanatical European jazz clubs and youth cultures, the hot jazz clubs, the frenetic jazz dances, and the rebellious sartorial style of the jazz-loving Zazous and the "swing-heinis" (Poiger 2000, 145). In its regeneration of this European jazz past, *Remixing European Jazz Culture* then asserts this unique jazz continuum and its desire to always renew it for each new generation of European jazz publics who wish to participate in this long-standing cultural relation in ways that speak especially to the present.

Notes

1 For a recorded documentation of a similar performance of this song, see GURLS' appearance on August 18, 2017, at the Oslo Jazz Festival, published on YouTube: www.youtube.com/watch?v=pDqBG1jrR9Y (accessed December 1, 2018).
2 This initiative describes itself as

> a pioneering international initiative which transforms the future of music whilst encouraging festivals and music organisations to achieve a 50:50 gender balance by 2022.... Keychange aims to accelerate change and create a better more inclusive music industry for present and future generations.

The initiative is financed and implemented by the Creative Europe programme of the European Union, "in partnership with Musikcentrum Öst, Reeperbahn Festival, Iceland Airwaves, BIME, Tallinn Music Week, Way Out West, Liverpool Sound City and Mutek". See their website for more on obtaining support as well as lists of festivals who have signed on to this pledge: https://keychange.eu/ (accessed May 30, 2018).

BIBLIOGRAPHY

Alderman, Derek H. "Place, Naming and the Interpretation of Cultural Landscapes", in P. Howard and B. Graham (eds) *The Ashgate Companion to Heritage and Identity*. Aldershot: Ashgate, 2008, 195–213.

Adorno, Theodor and Max Horkheimer. "The Culture Industry: Enlightenment as Mass Deception", in G. Scmid Noerr (ed.) *The Dialectic of Enlightenment*. Trans. by Edmund Jephcott. Stanford: Stanford University Press, 1944/2007, 94–136.

Ake, David. *Jazz Matters: Sound, Place and Time Since Bebop*. Log Angeles: University of California Press, 2010.

All That Jazz: *Het Jazz Soul-Urban, World-Blues, Singer/Songwriter Boek*. Amsterdam: Carrera, 2009.

Andersen, Svein. "Jazz ut Mot Verden" (Jazz out to the world). *Aftenposten*, October 19, 2011.

Anderson, Chris. "The Long Tail", *Wired* 12 no. 10 (2004), www.wired.com/wired/archive/12.10/tail.html (accessed August 3, 2010).

Andrews, Marke. "Bugge Music: Keyboard Player Bugge Wesseltoft and a Few Jazz Friends in Oslo Began Playing with DJs in the Mid-90s", *The Vancouver Sun* (British Columbia), June 20, 2002, D14.

Andrews, Marke. "Pender Fire Slows but Can't Stop Maximum: Jazz Record Label Has Best of Independent, Big-Company Worlds in Promoting Artists", *The Vancouver Sun* (British Columbia), July 12, 2003, F1.

Anjou Vélo Vintage: La Rando Vélo Retro. Programme. June 22–24, 2018.

Anjou Vélo Vintage. "Le Festival Programmation", www.anjou-velo-vintage.com/fr/festival/festival-musical-retro (accessed September 10, 2018).

Appadurai, Arjun. *Modernity at Large: Cultural Dimensions of Globalization*. Minneapolis: University of Minnesota Press, 1996.

Arndt, Jurgen. "European Jazz Developments in Cross-Cultural Dialogue with the United States and Their Relationship to the Counterculture of the 1960s", in Cerchaira *et al.* (eds) *Eurojazzland: Jazz and European Sources, Dynamics, and Contexts*. Boston: Northeastern University Press, 2012, 342–365.

Arvidsson, Alf and Jörgen Adolfsson. "Minnet – Transcending Genre Boundaries, Organizing Diversity", in T. Whyton and N. Gebhardt (eds) *The Cultural Politics of Jazz Collectives: This Is Our Music*. New York and London: Routledge, 2015, 149–156.

Atkins, E. Taylor. "Toward a Global History of Jazz", in E. T. Atkins (ed.) *Jazz Planet*. Jackson, Mississippi: University of Mississippi Press, 2003, xi–xxvii.

Atkins, E. Taylor (ed.). *Jazz Planet*. Jackson: University Press of Mississippi, 2003.

Attias, Bernardo Alexander. "Subjectivity in the Groove: Phonography, Digitality, and Fidelity", in Attias *et al.* (eds) *DJ Culture in the Mix: Power, Technology, and Social Change in electronic Dance Music*. New York: Bloomsbury, 2013, 15–50.

Attias, Bernardo Alexander, Anna Gavanas and Hillegonda Rietveld (eds). *DJ Culture in the Mix: Power, Technology, and Social Change in Electronic Dance Music*. New York: Bloomsbury, 2013.

Baade, Christina. "'The Battle of the Saxes': Gender, Dance Bands, and British Nationalism in the Second World War", in N. Rustin *et al.* (eds) *Big Ears: Listening for Gender in Jazz Studies*. Durham, NC: Duke University Press, 2008, 90–128.

Baade, Christina. *Victory Through Harmony: The BBC and Popular Music in World War II*. Oxford: Oxford University Press, 2011.

Bakriges, Christopher G. "Cultural Displacement, Cultural Creation: African American Jazz Musicians in Europe from Bechet to Braxton", in N. Wynn (ed.) *Cross the Water Blues: African American Music in Europe*. Jackson: University Press of Mississippi, 2007, 250–265.

Beard, Matthey. "Is It Time We Had a Gender Quota for Music Festivals?" in *Vice*: www.vice.com/en_us/article/3devpv/is-it-time-we-had-a-gender-quota-for-music-festivals?utm_campaign=sharebutton via @vice (accessed May 30, 2018).

Beaudoin, Jedd. "Come With Us, Go Where We Go – A Chat with Caravan Palace's Hugues Payen", *Pop Matters*, June 1, 2016, www.popmatters.com/come-with-us-go-where-we-go-a-chat-with-caravan-palaces-hugues-payen-2495432192.html (accessed December 7, 2018).

Behr, Adam, Keith Negus and John Street. "The Sampling Continuum: Musical Aesthetics and Ethics in the Age of Digital Production", *Journal for Cultural Research* 21 (2017): 3.

Bellen, Joost van, Lex Breet, Felix van der EerdenAnne Hemker, Dick Koopman, Kim Tuin, Puck Verdoes, and Maz Weston. *Nachtnota: Nachtwacht, collectief voor de emancipatie van de stedelijke nacht*. Amsterdam, 2003.

Bennett, Andy and Richard Peterson (eds). *Music Scenes: Local, Trans-local and Virtual*. New York: Vanderbilt University Press, 2004.

Berliner, Paul. *Thinking in Jazz: The Infinite Art of Improvisation*. Chicago: University of Chicago Press, 1994.

"Biography: Kruder & Dorfmesiter". *Resident Advisor*. www.residentadvisor.net/dj/kruder-dorfmeister (accessed June 27, 2018).

Blair, Skippy. "Jack and Jill Competitions", in *Dance Terminology Notebook*. Altera, 1994, 37.

Bogle, Donald. *Toms, Coons, Mulattos, Mammies, and Bucks: An Interpretive History of Blacks in American Films*. New York: Bloomsbury, 2016 (1973).

Bohlman, Philip. "The Remembrance of Things Past: Music, Race, and the End of History in Modern Europe", in P. Bohlman and R. Radano (eds) *Music and the Racial Imagination* (Chicago Studies in Ethnomusicology). Chicago: University of Chicago Press, 2000, 644–676.

Bohlman, Philip and Goffredo Plastino (eds). *Jazz Worlds/World Jazz*. Chicago: University of Chicago Press, 2016.

Born, Georgina and K. Devine. "Music Technology, Gender, and Class: Digitization, Educational and Social Change in Britain", *Twentieth-Century Music*, 12 no. 2 (2015): 135–172.

Born, Georgina and David Hesmondhalgh (eds). *Western Music and Its Others*. Berkeley: University of California Press, 2000.

Braggs, Rashida K. *Jazz Diasporas: Race, Music, and Migration in Post-World War II Paris*. Oakland: University of California Press, 2016.

Brooks, Daphne. "'All That You Can't Leave Behind': Black Female Soul Singing and the Politics of Surrogation in the Age of Catastrophe", *Meridians*, 8 no. 1 (2008): 180–204.

Brown, Cecil, Anne Dvinge, Petter Frost Fadnes, Johan Fornäs, Ole Izard Høyer, Marilyn Mazur, Michael McEachrane and John Tchicai. "The Midnight Sun Never Sets: An Email Conversation about Jazz, Race and National Identity in Denmark, Norway and Sweden", in M. McEachrane (ed.) *Afro-Nordic Landscapes: Equality and Race in Northern Europe*. New York: Routledge, 2014, 57–86.

Brown, Jayna. "Dat Var Negressen Walaida Snow", *Women & Performance: A Journal of Feminist Theory*, 16 no. 1 (2006): 51–70.

Brown, Jayna. *Babylon Girls: Black Women Performers and the Shaping of the Modern*. Durham: Duke University Press, 2008.

Bruckner-Haring, Christa and Michael Kahr. "Jazz Networks in Austria – The JazzWerkstatt Initiative", in T. Whyton and N. Gebhardt (eds) *The Cultural Politics of Jazz Collectives: This Is Our Music*. London: Routledge, 2015, 177–196.

Bull, Michael. *Ipod Culture and Urban Experience*. New York: Routledge, 2008.

Butler, Mark. *Unlocking the Groove: Rhythm, Meter, and Musical Design in Electronic Dance Music*. Bloomington: Indiana University Press, 2006.

"Caravan Palace Va Faire Swinguer Art Sonic", *Le Maine Libre*, July 22, 2016.

Carrington, Ben and Brian Wilson. "Global Club Cultures: Cultural Flows and Late Modern Dance Music Culture", in M. Cieslik and G. Pollock (eds) *Young People in Risk Society: The Restructuring of Youth Identities and Transformations in Late Modernity*. Aldershot: Ashgate, 2002.

Carroll, Samantha. "Hepfidelity: Digital Technology and Music in Contemporary Australian Swing Dance Culture", *Media International Australia* 123 (May 2007): 138–149.

Carroll, Samantha. "The Practical Politics of Step-Stealing and Textual Poaching: YouTube, Audio-Visual Media and Contemporary Swing Dancers Online", *Convergence*, 14 no. 2 (2008): 183–204.

Cerchiari, Luca, Laurent Cugny, and Franz Kerschbaumer (eds). *Eurojazzland: Jazz and European Sources, Dynamics, and Contexts*. Boston: Northeastern University Press, 2012.

Cohen, Sara. *Rock Culture in Liverpool: Popular Music in the Making*. Oxford: Clarendon Press, 1991.

Cohen, Sarah. *Decline, Renewal and the City in Popular Music Culture: Beyond the Beatles*. Aldershot: Ashgate, 2007.

Cotgrove, Mark Snowboy. *From Jazz Funk & Fusion to Acid Jazz: The History of the UK Jazz Dance Scene*. Authorhouse, 2009.

Couldry, Nick and Anna McCarthy (eds). *MediaSpace: Place, Scale and Culture in a Media Age*. London: Routledge, 2004.

Crease, Robert. "The Future of the Lindy and the New York Swing Dance Society: An Epilogue", in N. Miller and E. Jensen (eds) *Swingin' at the Savoy: A Memoir of a Jazz Dancer*. Philadelphia: Temple University Press, 1996, 255–261.

Currie, Scott. "Sound Visions and Free Initiatives: The Cultural Politics of Creative Improvised Music Collectives", in T. Whyton and N. Gebhardt (eds) *The Cultural Politics of Jazz Collectives: This Is Our Music*. New York and London: Routledge, 2015, 61–85.

D'Andrea, Anthony. *Global Nomads: Techno and New Age as Transnational Countercultures in Ibiza and Goa*. London: Routledge, 2007.

Davenport, Lisa. *Jazz Diplomacy: Promoting America in the Cold War Era*. Jackson, MI: University Press of Mississippi, 2009.

Day, Morgan. "Why Swing Dancers Hate and Love Electro Swing", November 27, 2012. http://ickeroo.blogspot.com/2012/11/why-swing-dancers-love-and-hate-electro.html (accessed July 3, 2018).

Delanty, George, Liana Giogi and Monica Sassatelli (eds). *Festivals and the Cultural Public Sphere*. London and New York: Routledge, 2011.

Delaunay, Charles. "L'Histoire du Hot-Club de France (7)", *Jazz Hot*, no. 26 (October): 1948.

Delaunay, Charles. "L'Histoire du Hot-Club de France (8)", *Jazz Hot*, no. 27 (November): 1948, 16.

Delaunay, Charles. *Django Reinhardt*. Translated by Michael James. London: Cassell. Rerpint, New York: Da Capo, (1961) 1982.

Dinerstein, Joel. *Swinging the Machine: Modernity, Technology, and African American Culture Between the World Wars*. Amherst, MA: University of Massachusetts Press, 2003.

Doyle, Peter. *Echo and Reverb: Fabricating Space in Popular Music Recording, 1900–1960*. Middletown, CT: Wesleyan University Press, 2005.

Dregni, Michael. *The Life and Music of a Gypsy Legend*. New York: Oxford University Press, 2004.

Dubber, Andrew. "Collective Practice and Digital Mediation", in T. Whyton and N. Gebhardt (eds) *The Cultural Politics of Jazz Collectives: This Is Our Music*. London and New York: Routledge, 2015, 219–235.

Dulfer, Hans and Eddy Determeyer. *De Geschiedenis van de Nederlandse Jazz*. Amsterdam: de Bijenkorf, 1998.

Dvinge, Anne. "Between the Devil and the Deep Blue Sea: Afro-Danish Jazz Band Harlem Kiddies and Discourses of Race and Resistance in 1940s Denmark", *African and Black Diaspora: An International Journal*, November 18, 2013.

Electro Swing Club. *Clubs*. www.electroswingclub.com/clubs.html (accessed October 10, 2018).

Enwezor, Okwui, Markus Mueller, Diedrich Diederichsen, Kodwo Eshun and Renee Green. *ECM: A Cultural Archeology*. New York: Prestel, 2013.

Erlmann, Veit. "The Aesthetics of the Global Imagination: Reflections on World Music in the 1990s", *Public Culture*, 8 (1996): 467–487.

Farrugia, Rebekah. *Beyond the Dance Floor: Female DJs, Technology, and Electronic Dance Music*. Chicago: University of Chicago Press, 2012.

Feld, Steve. "The Poetics and Politics of Pygmy Pop", in G. Born and D. Hesmondhalgh (eds) *Western Music and Its Others: Difference, Appropriation and Representation in Music*. Berkeley: University of California Press, 2000, 254–279.

Fellezs, Kevin. *Birds of Fire: Jazz, Rock, Funk, and the Creation of Fusion*. Durham, NC: Duke University Press, 2011.

Fisher, Mark. "The Metaphysics of Crackle: Afrofuturism and Hauntology", *Dancecult*, 5 no. 2 (2013): 42–55.

Fisher, Mark. *Ghosts of My Life: Writings on Depression, Hauntology and Lost Futures*. London: Zero Books, 2014.

Florida, Richard. *Cities and the Creative Class*. New York and London: Routledge, 2005.

Fornäs, Jonas. "Swinging Differences: Reconstructed Identities in the Early Swedish Jazz Age", in E. Taylor Atkins (ed.) *Jazz Planet*. Jackson, MS: University Press of Mississippi, 2003, 207–224.

Fornäs, Jonas. *Moderna Manniskor: Folkhemmet och Jazzen*. Inbunden Svenska, 2004.

Fornäs, Jonas. "Exclusion, Polarization, Hybridization, Assimilation: Otherness and Modernity in the Swedish Jazz Age", *Popular Music and Society*, 33 no. 2 (2012): 219–236.

Friedlander, Emelie. "We Crunched the Numbers and Electronic Music Festivals Still have a Gender Equality Problem", *Thump/Vice*. July 14, 2016, https://thump.vice.com/en_us/article/qkazzq/2016-electronic-music-festivals-gender-breakdown (accessed September 17, 2018).

Frith, Simon. "Is Jazz Popular Music?" *Jazz Research Journal*, 1. no. 1 (2007): 7–23.

Fry, Andy. *Paris Blues: African American Music in France, 1920–1960*. Chicago: University of Chicago Press, 2014.

Gabbard, Krin. *Jammin at the Margins: Jazz and American Cinema*. Chicago: University of Chicago, 1996.

Garofalo, Reebee and Steve Waxman. *Rockin' Out: Popular Music in the USA*. Upper Saddle River, New Jersey: Pearson, Prentice Hall, 2005.

Gaunt, Kyra D. "YouTube, Twerking & You: Context Collapse and the Handheld Co Presence of Black Girls and Miley Cyrus", *Journal of Popular Music Studies*, 27 (2015): 244–273.

Gavanas, Anna and Rosa Reitsamer. "DJ Technologies, Social Networks and Gendered Trajectories in European DJ Cultures", in B.A. Attias *et al.* (eds) *DJ Culture in the Mix: Power, Technology and Social Change in Electronic Dance Music.* New York: Bloomsbury, 2013, 51–78.

Gebhardt, Nicholas. "When Jazz Was Foreign: Rethinking Jazz History", *Jazzforschung*, 44 (2012): 185–197.

Gendron, Bernard. "Moldy Figs and Modernists: Jazz at War (1942–1946)", in K. Gabbard (ed.) *Jazz Among the Discourses*. Durham, NC: Duke University Press, 1995, 31–56.

Gibson, William. "God's Little Toys: Confessions of a Cut and Paste Artist", *Wired*, 13 no. 7 (2005): 118–119.

Gilroy, Paul. *The Black Atlantic: Modernity and Double Consciousness*. Cambridge, MA: Harvard University Press, 1993.

Given, William. "Lindy Hop, Community, and the Isolation of Appropriation", in N. George-Graves (ed.) *The Oxford Handbook of Dance and Theater*. Oxford: Oxford University Press, 2015.

Gomes, Marcel. "Bugg the Swedish Swing Dance". https://marcelgomessweden.wordpress.com/2011/04/02/bugg-the-swedish-swing-dance/ (accessed December 5, 2018).

Gotrich, Lars. "Do Indie Jazz Labels Matter?" www.npr.org/sections/ablogsupreme/2009/07/do_jazz_record_labels_matter.html (accessed March 2, 2018).

Gottschild, Brenda Dixon. 2003. *The Black Dancing Body: A Geography from Coon to Cool*. New York: Palgrave Macmillan, 2003.

Green Guide: Netherlands. Watford: Michelin, 2001.

Grennen, Kristen. "Interview: Caravan Palace's Hugues Payen". *Sensible Reason*. April 1, 2014. http://sensiblereason.com/interview-caravan-palace/ (accessed July 12, 2018).

Gunkel, David. *Of Remixology: Ethics and Aesthics after Remix*. Cambridge, MA: MIT Press, 2015.

Hancock, Black Hawk. *American Allegory: Lindy Hop and the Racial Imagination*. Chicago: University of Chicago Press, 2013.

Harkins, Paul. "Appropriation, Additive Approaches and Accidents: The Sampler as Compositional Tool and Recording Dislocation", *Journal of the International Association for the Study of Popular Music*, 1 (2010): 1–19.

Hasse, John Edward. "'A Reason for Living': Duke Ellington in France", in L. Cerchiari, L. Cugny and F. Kerschbaumer (eds) *Eurojazzland: Jazz and European Sources, Dynamics, and Contexts*. Boston: Northeastern University Press, 2012.

HDC Weekly Magazine: Week One 2017. Ed. Annika Munter. Published by Karl Lennart Westerlund.

HDC Weekly Magazine: Week One 2018. Ed. Annika Munter. Published by Karl Lennart Westerlund.

Hebdige, Dick. *Subculture: The Meaning of Style*. London: Methuen and Co. Ltd., 1979.

Hebdige, Dick. *Cut 'n' Mix: Culture, Identity and Caribbean Music*. New York and London: Routledge, 1987.

Heffley, Mike. *Northern Sun, Southern Moon: Europe's Reinvention of Jazz*. New Haven, CT: Yale University Press, 2005.

Heile, Bjorn, Peter Elsdon and Jenny Doctor (eds). *Watching Jazz: Encounters with Jazz Performance on Screen*. Oxford: Oxford University Press, 2016.

Heinila, Harri. "Who Introduced the Lindy Hop in Europe", *Authentic Jazz Dance*. 2018. https://authenticjazzdance.wordpress.com/2018/02/05/who-introduced-the-lindy-hop-in-europe/ (accessed August 20, 2018).

Hellhund, Herbert. "Roots and Collage – Contemporary European Jazz in Postmodern Times", in L. Cerchiari, L. Cugny, and F. Kerschbaumer (eds) *Eurojazzland: Jazz and European Sources, Dynamics, and Contexts*. Boston: Northeastern University Press, 2012, 431–446.

Hesmondhalgh, David. "International Times: Fusions, Exoticism, and Antiracism in Electronic Dance Music", in G. Born and D. Hesmondhalgh (eds) *Western Music and Its Others*. Berkeley: University of California Press, 2000, 280–304.

"Historie". Melkweg, www.melkweg.nl/artikelpagina.jsp?infoid=6349&subinfoid=1370 (accessed July 28, 2008).

"History". *Swedish Dancesport Federation*: www.danssport.se/English/SwedishDancesport-Federation/DSFHistory (accessed May 6, 2018).

Hodeir, André. *Le Jazz, cet inconnu*. 1945.

Holt, Fabian. "Jazz and the Politics of Home in Scandinavia", in P. Bohlman and G. Plastino (eds) *Jazz Worlds/World Jazz*. Chicago: University of Chicago, 2016, 51–78.

Horning, Susan. *Chasing Sound: Technology, Culture and the Art of Studio Recording from Edison to the LP*. Baltimore, MD: Johns Hopkins University Press, 2015.

Hunter, Tera W. *To Joy My Freedom: Southern Black Women's Lives and Labors after the Civil War*. Cambridge, MA: Harvard University Press, 1997.

Jackson, Jeffrey H. *Making Jazz French: Music and Modern Life in Interwar Paris*. Durham, NC: Duke University Press, 2003.

James, Donald. *Some of These Days: Black Stars, Jazz Aesthetics, and Modernist Culture*. Chicago: University of Chicago, 2015.

Jankowsky, Richard. "The Medium is the Message? Jazz Diplomacy and the Democratic Imagination", in G. Plastino and P. Bohlman (eds.) *Jazz Worlds/World Jazz*. Chicago: University of Chicago Press 2016, 258–288.

Jenkins, Henry. *Fans Bloggers and Gamers: Exploring Participatory Culture*. New York: New York University, 2006.

John, Timothy. "Anjou Velo Vintage: Sun, Cycling, and All that Jazz in the Loire", *RCUK: Roadcycling UK*, https://roadcyclinguk.com/sportive/anjou-velo-vintage-sun-cycling-and-all-that-jazz-in-the-loire.html (accessed 1 February 2019).

Johnson, Martin. "Acid Jazz: Where the Past and Future Collide", *Down Beat*, 64 no. 4 (1997): 16–21.

Jones, Kevin, Phil Stafford, Sandra Bridekirk, Tom Jellett, and Deborah Jones. "In the Club with Miles of Swing", *The Weekend Australian*, July 19, 2003, B32.

Jones, Leroie and Amiri Baraka. *Blues People: Negro Music in White America*. New York: William Morrow, 1963.

Jones, Steve. "Music That Moves: Popular Music, Distribution and Network Technologies", *Cultural Studies*, 16 no. 2 (2002): 213–232.

Jordan, Matthew F. *Le Jazz and French Cultural Identity*. Chicago, IL: University of Illinois Press, 2010.

Jost, Ekkehard. *Europas Jazz 1960–1980*. Frankfurt: Fischer Taschenbuch verlag GmbH, 1987.

Jost, Ekkehard. "The European Jazz Avant-Garde of the Late 1960s and early 1970s: Where Did Emancipation Lead?", in L. Cerchiari, L. Cugny, and F. Kerschbaumer (eds) *Euro-JazzLand: Jazz and European Sources, Dynamics, and Contexts*. Boston: Northeastern University Press, 2012, 275–300.

Kan, Mischa van. *Swingin' Swedes: The Transnational Exchange of Swedish Jazz in the US*. PhD dissertation, University of Gothenburg, 2016.

Katz, Mark. *Capturing Sound: How Technology Has Changed Music*. Los Angeles: University of California Press, 2004.

Keil, Charles and Steven Feld. *Music Grooves: Essays and Dialogues*. Chicago: University of Chicago Press, 1994.

Kelman, John. "Bugge Wesseltoft: New Conceptions of Jazz Box". *All About Jazz*, March 4, 2009, www.allaboutjazz.com/bugge-wesseltoft-new-conception-of-jazz-box-by-john-kelman.php (accessed November 21, 2017).

Knauer, Wolfram. "History or Histories? Why Is It So Difficult to Draft a European Jazz History?", in T.A. Jacobsen (ed.) *National and Local Jazz History Writing in the Nordic Countries*, Conference Report, 8th Nordic Jazz Conference. Center for Dansk Jazzhistorie, Aalborg, 2009.

Knauer, Wolfram (ed.). *Jazz in Europa*. Hofheim: Wolke, 1994.

Lake, Steve and Paul Griffiths. *Horizons Touched: The Music of ECM*. London: Granata Publications, 2007.

Lee, Steve S. and Richard Peterson. "Internet-based Virtual Music Scenes: The Case of P2 in Alt Country Music", in A. Bennett and R.A. Peterson (eds) *Music Scenes: Local, Trans-Local and Virtual*. Nashville, TN: University of Vanderbilt Press, 2004, 187–204.

Lessig, Lawrence. *Remix: Making Art and Commerce Thrive in the Hybrid Economy*. New York: The Penguin Press, 2008.

Lewis, George. *A Power Stronger that Itself: The AACM and American Experimental Music*. Chicago: University of Chicago Press, 2009.

Liebman, David. "Europe: It's Role in Jazz", David Liebman website. http://upbeat.com/lieb/Feature_Articles/Europe.htm (accessed November 26, 2018).

Lipsitz, George. *Dangerous Crossroads: Popular Music, Postmodernism and the Poetics of Place*. London and New York: Verso, 1994.

Lofthus, Kai R. "Jazzland is Home for Acoustic and Electronic Jazz", *Billboard*, 114 no. 9 (2002): 64.

Lord, Tom. *The Jazz Discography*, www.lordisco.com/ (accessed October 5, 2018).

Lotz, Rainer E. *German Ragtime and Prehistory of Jazz: The Sound Documents Vol. 1*. London: LD Wright, Storyville Publications, 1985.

Lotz, Rainer E. "Cross-Cultural Links: Black Minstrels, Cakewalks, and Ragtime", in L. Cerchiari, L. Cugny and F. Kerschbaumer (eds) *Eurojazzland: Jazz and European Sources, Dynamics, and Contexts*. Boston: Northeastern University Press, 2012, 143–166.

Mäkelä, Janne (ed.). *The Jazz Chameleon: The Refereed Proceedings of the 9th Nordic Jazz Conference*. IIPC Publication Series Vol. 4. Helsinki & Turku: The Finnish Jazz & Pop Archive & International Institute for Popular Culture, 2010.

Mäkelä, Janne. "Nordic Jazz: A Historical View". *Jazz, Gender and Authenticity: Proceedings of the 10th Nordic Jazz Research Conference*, 2014.

Manning, Frankie, and Cynthia R. Millman. *Frankie Manning: Ambassador of Lindy Hop*. Philadelphia, PA: Temple University Press, 2007.

Martinelli, Francesco (ed.). *The History of European Jazz: The Music, Musicians and Audience in Context*. Sheffield: Equinox, 2018.

Mazierska, Ewa. *Popular Viennese Electronic Music, 1990–2015: A Cultural History*. New York and London: Routledge, 2018.

McGee, Kristin. *Some Liked It Hot: Jazz Women in Film and Television, 1928–1959*. Middletown, CT: Wesleyan University Press, 2009.

McGee, Kristin. "New York Comes to Groningen: Jazz Star Circuits in the Netherlands", in B. Dueck and J. Toynbee (eds) *Migrating Musics: Media, Politics and Style*. London: Routledge, 2011, 202–217.

McGee, Kristin. "Remixing Jazz Culture: Hybridity and Collectivity in the New European City", *Jazz Research Journal*, 5 no. 1/2 (2011): 67–88.

McGee, Kristin. "Collectivities, Cosmopolitanisms and Mixed-Mediations in Amsterdam's Crossover Jazz Scene", in C. Wergin and F. Holt (eds) *Musical Performance and the Changing City: Postindustrial Contexts in Europe and the United States*. New York and London: Routledge, 2013, 178–199.

McGee, Kristin. "Promoting Affect and Desire in the International World of Smooth Jazz", *Jazz Perspectives*, 7 no. 3 (2013): 251–286.

McGee, Kristin. "Assimilating and Domesticating Jazz in 1950s American Variety Television: Nat King Cole's Transformation from Guest Star to National Host", in B. Heile, P. Elsdon and J. Doctor (eds) *Watching Jazz: Encountering Jazz Performance on Screen*. Oxford: Oxford University Press, 2015, 73–102.

McGee, Kristin. "Musical Hybridity in the New European City: The Jazz Hip Hop Collectives of C-Mon and Kypski andn Kytopia", in T. Whyton and N. Gebhardt (eds) *The Cultural Politics of Jazz Collectives: This Is Our Music*. New York and London: Routledge, 2015, 86–116.

McGee, Kristin. "Staging Jazz Pasts Within Commercial European Jazz Festivals: The Case of the North Sea Jazz Festival", *European Journal of Cultural Studies*, April (2016): 1–27.

McGee, Kristin. "Straight to Baby: Scoring Female Jazz Agency and New Masculinity in Henry Mancini's Peter Gunn", in H. Pettey (ed.) *Cold War Film Genres* (Traditions in American Cinema Series). Edinburgh: Edinburgh University Press, 2018.

Miller, Norma. *SWING, BABY SWING!* 2009. www.blurb.com/b/1160083-swing-baby-swing (accessed September 17, 2018).

Miller, Norma, and Evette Jensen. *Swingin' at the Savoy: The Memoir of a Jazz Dancer*. Philadelphia, PA: Temple University Press, 2001.

Miller, Paul. *Sound Unbound: Sampling Digital Music and Culture*. Cambridge, MA: MIT Press, 2008.

Mitchell, Toni. *Global Noise: Rap and Hip Hop Outside of the USA*. Middletown, CT: Wesleyan University Press, 2001.

Mitchum, Rob and Dieogofac Garcia-Olano. "Tracking the Gender Balance of This Year's Music Festival Lineups", in *Pitchfork*. https://pitchfork.com/features/festival-report/tracking-the-gender-balance-of-this-years-music-festival-lineups/ (accessed May 30, 2018).

Monaghan, Terry. "Mama Lou Parks: Crashing Cars and Keeping the Savoy's Memory Alive", *Authentic Jazz Dance*, August 25, 2015. https://authenticjazzdance.wordpress.com/2015/04/25/mama-lou-parks-by-terry-monaghan/ (accessed July 6, 2018).

Monson, Ingrid. "The Problem with White Hipness: Race, Gender and Cultural Conceptions in Jazz Historical Discourse", *Journal of the American Musicological Society*, 48 no. 3 (1995): 396–422.

Monson, Ingrid. *Saying Something: Jazz Improvisation and Interaction*. Chicago: University of Chicago, 1996.

Morey, Justin and Phillip McIntyre. "The Creative Studio Practice of Contemporary Dance Sampling Composers", *Dancecult*, 6 no. 1 (2014): 41–60.

Mutsaers, Lutgaard. *Beat Crazy. Een Pophistorisch Onderzoek naar de Impact van de Transnationale Dansrages*. Utrecht: EML Books, 1998.

Navas, Eduardo. *Remix Theory: The Aesthetics of Sampling*. Wien: Springer, 2012.

Nettlebeck, Colin. *Dancing with DeBeauvoir: Jazz and the French*. Carlton, Victoria: Melbourne University Press, 2004.

Nicholson, Stuart. *Is Jazz Dead?: Or Has It Moved to a New Address?* New York and London: Routledge, 2005.

Niederwieser, Stefan. "Legacy: Kruder & Dorfmeister, Vienna's Gold", *Europavox*. www.europavox.com/news/legacy-kruder-dorfmeister-vienna-gold/ (accessed October 8, 2018).

Nygaard, Morten. "Beady Belles Første Sender Syllent Sollys Gjennom Sval Vårluft". *Groove.No.* April 1, 2001, www.groove.no/anmeldelse/58000818/home-beady-belle (accessed September 6, 2018).

Panassié, Hugues. *Le Jazz Hot*. Paris: Editions Correa, 1934.

Panassié, Hugues. *The Real Jazz*, trans. Anne Sorelle Williams, adapted for American publication by Charles Edward Smith. New York: Smith & Durel, 1942.

Parameshwar Gaonkar, Dilip and Elizabeth A. Povinelli. "Technologies of Public Forms: Circulation, Transfiguration, Recognition", *Public Culture*, 15 no. 3 (2003): 385–397.

Parish, P. "The Lindy-Hop – A Revival in Full Swing (The Signature Dance of the 1930s Is Back in Style)", *Dance Magazine*, 73 no. 9 (1999): 50–52.

Perchard, Tom. "Hip Hop Samples Jazz: Dynamics of Cultural Memory and Musical Tradition in the African American 1990s", *American Music*, 29 no. 3 (2011): 277–307.

Peterson, Richard and Andy Bennett. "Introducing the Scenes Perspective", in A. Bennett and R.A. Peterson (eds) *Music Scenes: Local, Trans-Local and Virtual*. Nashville, TN: University of Vanderbilt Press, 2004, 1–17.

Petters, Harold. "In Between", *Die Tageszeitung*, 2002.

PJ. "Albums: Beady Belle, Home, Jazzlands/Universal", *Independent*, June 25, 2001. www.independent.co.uk/arts-entertainment/music/reviews/albums-beady-belle-9132701.html (accessed December 8, 2018).

Poiger, Uta G. *Jazz, Rock, and Rebels: Cold War Politics and American culture in a Divided Germany*. Berkeley, CA: University of California Press, 2000.

Radano, Ronald. "Hot Fantasies: American Modernism and the Idea of Black Rhythm", in R. Radano and P. Bohlman (eds) *Music and the Racial Imagination* (Chicago Studies in Ethnomusicology). Chicago: University of Chicago Press, 1995, 459–482.

Raphael-Hernandez, Heike (ed.). *Blackening Europe: The African American Presence*. New York and London: Routledge, 2003.

Rapp, Tobias. *Lost and Sound: Berlin, Techno und der Easyjet*. Berlin: Suhrkamp Verlag, 2009.

Regev, Motti. *Pop-Rock Music: Aesthetic Cosmopolitanism in Late Modernity*. Cambridge: Polity Press, 2013.

Régnier, Gerard. *Jazz et société sous l'occupation*. Paris: Harmattan, 2009.

Reynolds, Simon. *Retromania: Pop Cultures Addiction to Its Own Past*. London: Faber & Faber, 2011.

Robertson, Roland. "Glocalization: Time-Space and Homogeneity and Heterogeneity", in M. Featherstone, S. Lash and R. Robertson (eds) *Global Modernities*. London: Sage Publications, 1995, 24–44.

Rosaldo, Renato. "Imperialist Nostalgia", *Representations*, Special Issue: Memory and Counter-Memory, no. 26 (1989): 107–122.

Rusch, Loes. "Pitched Battles: Dutch Improvised Music, Authorities and Strategies", in T. Whyton and N. Gebhardt (eds) *The Cultural Politics of Jazz Collectives: This is Our Music*. New York and London: Routledge, 2015, 42–60.

Rust, Brian. *Jazz Records 1897–1942*. Hatch End Middlesex England, 1961 (self-published).

Rutten, Paul. "Global Sounds and Local Brews: Musical Developments and Music Industry in Europe", *Soundscapes*, 2 (1999).

Salvatore, Gianfranco. "Utopian Sounds: Mimesis and Identity in European Jazz Technologies", in L. Cerchiari, L. Cugny, and F. Kerschbaumer (eds) *Eurojazzland: Jazz and European Sources, Dynamics, and Contexts*. Boston: Northeastern University Press, 2012, 407–430.

Santoro, Marco and M. Solaroli. "Ecologia Istituzionale di un Festival: il Caso Umbria Jazz", *Polis*, XXVII (2013): 81–124.

Schloss, Joseph G. *Making Beats: The Art of Sample-Based Hip-Hop*. Middletown, CT: Wesleyan University Press, 2004.

Schuiling, Floris. *The Instant Composers Pool and Improvisation Beyond Jazz*. New York and London: Routledge, 2019.

Sékiné, Anaïs Leï. "The Worlds of Lindy Hop – Cultural Appropriations and the Politics of Joy", in *NOFOD/SDHS 2013 Proceedings*. Norwegian University of Science and Technology: Society of Dance History Scholars, 2013.

Sékiné, Anaïs Leï. *Les Mondes du Lindy Hop Appropriation Culturelle et Politiques de la Joie*. PhD dissertation, Department of Sociology, University of Montreal, 2017.

Shack, William A. *Harlem in Montmartre: A Paris Jazz Story between the Great Wars*. Berkeley: University of California Press, 2001.

Shadwick, Keith. "World Music: Oslo State of Mind; Norway is a Land of Strong Contrasts and Turbulent Undercurrents; Beate Lech: My Mother Sang Old Norwegian Songs to Me for Hours. I Loved That'", *The Independent* (London), July 11, 2003, 21.

Silverman, Carol. "DJs and the Production of 'Gypsy' Music: 'Balkin Beats' as Contested Commodity", *Western Folklore*, 74 no. 1 (2015): 5–29.

Sinnreich, Aram. *Mashed Up: Music, Technology, and the Rise of Configurable Culture*. Amherst, MA: University of Massachusetts Press, 2010.

Skinner, Jonathan. "Globalization and the Dance Import-Export Business: The Jive Story", in H.N. Kringelbach and J. Skinner (eds) *Dancing Cultures: Globalization, Tourism and Identity in the Anthropology of Dance*. New York: Berghahn Books, 2012, 29–45.

Small, Christopher. *Musicking: The Meanings of Performing and Listening*. Middleton, CT: Wesleyan University Press, 1998.

Smith, Jack. "Jazzanova Mixing Review", *BBC Review*, 2003. www.bbc.co.uk/music/reviews/hhdp/.

Smith, Stacy L., Marc Choueiti and Katherine Pieper. "Inclusion in the Recording Studio? Gender and Race/Ethnicity of Artists, Songwriters & Producers across 700 Popular Songs from 2012–2018". USC Annenberg Inclusion Initiative, 2019.

Stearns, Marshall Winslow and Jean Stearns. *Jazz Dance: The Story of American Vernacular Dance*. New York: DaCapo Press, 1968/1994.

Stein, Maggie. "'In Between' May Move Ropeadope's Jazzanova Ahead", *Billboard*, 114 no. 15 (2002).

Stendahl, Bjørn. "Jazz, Hot & Swing: Jazz i Norge 1920–1940", in *Publications from the Norwegian Jazz Archives*, no. 1. Oslo: Norwegian Jazz Archives, 1987.

Stendahl, Bjørn and Johs Bergh. "Sigarett Stomp. Jazz I Norge 1940–1950", in *Publications from the Norwegian Jazz Archives*, no. 4. Oslo: Norwegian Jazz Archives, 1991.

Straw, Will. "Systems of Articulation, Logics of Change: Communities and Scenes in Popular Music", *Cultural Studies*, 5 no. 3 (1991): 368–388.

Straw, Will. "Sizing Up Record Collections: Gender and Connoisseurship in Rock Music Culture", in S. Whitely (ed.) *Sexing the Groove: Popular Music and Gender*. New York: Routledge, 1997, 3–16.

"Swinging to Electro Beats". Radio Broadcast Transcription. Host Simon Scott with Betto Arcos. *NPR Weekend Edition Saturday*. August 28, 2010.

Szeman, Ioana. "'Gypsy Music' and DJs: Orientalism, Balkanism, and Romani Musicians", *TDR*, 53 no. 3 (2009): 98–116.

Tackley Parsonage, Catherine. "Benny Carter in Britain, 1936–1937", in L. Cerchiari, L. Cugny, and F. Kerschbaumer (eds) *Eurojazzland: Jazz and European Sources, Dynamics, and Contexts*. Boston: Northeastern University Press, 2012, 167–188.

Tackley Parsonage, Catherine. *The Evolution of Jazz in Britain, 1880–1935*. New York and London: Routledge, 2005/2017.

Theakston, Rob. "Jazzanova Remixed, AllMusic Review", *AllMusic*. www.allmusic.com/album/the-remixes-1997-2000-mw0000105267 (accessed December 27, 2018).

"The Building", *Conservatorium van Amsterdam*. http://conservatoriumvanamsterdam.nl/EN/01_algemeen/02_nieuwbouw/index.jsp (accessed August 13, 2008).

Thornton, Sarah. *Club Cultures: Music, Media and Subcultural Capital*. Cambridge: Polity Press, 1996.

Toynbee, Jason, Catherine Tackley and Mark Doffman (eds). *Black British Jazz: Routes, Ownership and Performance*. Surrey: Ashgate, 2014.

Tournès, Ludovic. *New Orleans sur Seine: Histoire du Jazz en France*. Paris: Librairie Artheme Fayard, 1999.

Tsiouslakis, Ioannis. "Jazz in Athens: Frustrated Cosmopolitans in a Music Subculture", *Ethnomusicology Forum*, 20 no. 2 (2011): 175–199.

Turner, Danny. "In Pictures: Caravan Palace's Paris Studio", *Music Radar*, February 19, 2016, www.musicradar.com/news/tech/in-pictures-caravan-palaces-paris-studio-634960 (accessed December 6, 2018).

Unruh, Kendra. "From Kitchen Mechanics to 'Jubilant Spirits of Freedom': Black, Working-Class Women Dancing the Lindy Hop", *Journal of Pan African Studies*, 4 no. 6 (2011): 213–233.

Unruh, Kendra. *'Jubilant Spirits of Freedom': Representations of the Lindy Hop in Literature and Film from the Swing Era to the Swing Revival*. PhD dissertation, Purdue University, 2012.

Usner, Eric Martin. "Dancing in the Past, Living in the Present: Nostalgia and Race in Southern California Neo-Swing Dance Culture", *Dance Research Journal*, 33 no. 2 (2001): 87–101.

Vernallis, Carol. *Unruly Media: YouTube, Music Video and the new Digital Cinema*. Oxford: Oxford University Press, 2013.

Vesela, Edward. Liner Notes. *Ode to the Death of Jazz*. ECM 843 196–2.

Vintage Reboot Soiree. Facebook event page. www.facebook.com/events/1989064541407775 (accessed July 24, 2018).

Wade, Lisa. "The Emancipatory Promise of the Habitus: Lindy Hop, the Body, and Social Change", *Ethnography*, 12 no. 2 (2011): 224–246.

Wald, Gayle. "Mezz Mezzrow and the Voluntary Negro Blues", in *Crossing the Line: Racial Passing in Twentieth-Century U.S. Literature and Culture*. Durham: Duke University Press, 2000.

Wall, Tim and Simon Barber. "Collective Cultures and Live Jazz in Birmingham", in T. Whyton and N. Gebhardt (eds) *The Cultural Politics of Jazz Collectives: This Is Our Music*. New York and London: Routledge, 2015, 117–131.

Walton, Matt. "Collective: Skalpel Interview", *BBC Home*, 2004. www.bbc.co.uk/dna/collective/A2459766 (accessed July 3, 2009).

Ward, John V. "Discography, Preservation, and Cultural Crossings: The Role of the World Wide Web in the Underground Dissemination of Nordic Jazz Recordings", in J. Mäkelä (ed.) *The Jazz Chameleon. The Refereed Proceedings of the 9th Nordic Jazz Conference August 19–20, 2010, Helsinki, Finland*. Helsinki: The Finnish Jazz & Pop Archive & Turku: International Institute for Popular Culture, 2011.

Wasserberger, Igor, Antonín Matzner and Peter Motyčka. *Jazz in Europe: New Music on the Old Continent*. Bern: Peter Lang International Academic Publishers, 2018.

Webster, Emma and George McKay. "The Impact of (Jazz) Festivals: An Arts and Humanities Research Council-funded Research Report", *Jazz Research Journal*, 9 no. 2 (2016): 169–193.

Wergin, Carsten and Fabian Holt (eds). *Musical Performance and the Changing City: Postindustrial Contexts in Europe and the United States*. New York and London: Routledge, 2013.

Wells, Christopher J. "Swinging Out in Sweden: African-American Vernacular Dance's Global Revival and Its Scandinavian Roots", in *NOFOD/SDHS 2013 Proceedings*. Norwegian University of Science and Technology: Society of Dance History Scholars, 2013.

Westerlund, Lennart. "The Revival of the Revival". *HDC Weekly Magazine – Week One 2018*.

"What is Afro Swing?" *Mozambique Afroswing Exchange*: https://masx.org/what-is-afro-swing/ (accessed August 5, 2018).

Whelan, Andrew. *Breakcore: Identity and Interaction on Peer-to-Peer*. Cambridge: Cambridge Scholars Publishing, 2008.

White, Chris. "BBC Review: Parov Stelar Shine Review", *BBC*, 2008. www.bbc.co.uk/music/reviews/d5p2/ (accessed May 2, 2018).

Whitehead, Kevin. *New Dutch Swing: Jazz + Classical Music + Absurdism*. New York: Billboard Books, 1998.

Whyton, Tony. "Europe and the New Jazz Studies", in L. Cerchiari, L. Cugny, and F. Kerschbaumer (eds) *Eurojazzland: Jazz and European Sources, Dynamics, and Contexts*. Boston: Northeastern University Press, 2012, 366–380.

Whyton, Tony. *Jazz Icons: Heroes, Myths and the Jazz Tradition*. Cambridge: Cambridge University Press, 2013.

Whyton, Tony and Nicholas Gebhardt (eds). *The Cultural Politics of Jazz Collectives: This is Our Music*. New York and London: Routledge, 2015.

Wickström, Patrick. *The Music Industry: Music in the Cloud*. Cambridge: Polity Press, 2009.

Williams, Justin. "Theoretical Approaches to Quotation in Hip-Hop Recordings", *Contemporary Music Review*, 33 no. 2 (2014): 188–209.

Wipplinger, Jonathan. *The Jazz Republic: Music, Race and American Culture in Weimar Germany*. Ann Arbor, MI: University of Michigan Press, 2017.

Zwerin, Mike. *Swing under the Nazis: Jazz as a Metaphor for Freedom*. New York: Cooper Square Press, 2000.

Interviews

Bärbl Kaufer. Interview with the author, Herräng, Sweden, July 3, 2018.

Berenice van Leer. Interview with the author, Amsterdam, The Netherlands, September 29, 2009.

Beady Belle (Beate Lech). Interview with the author, Oslo, Norway, October 25, 2017.

Bianca Locatelli. Interview with the author, Herräng, Sweden, July 4, 2018.

Bugge Wesseltoft. Interview with the author, Oslo, Norway, October 26, 2017.

Caro Emerald (Caroline Esmeralda van der Leeuw). Email correspondence with the author, October 16, 2012.

Daniel Best. Interview with the author, Berlin, Germany November 27, 2017.

David Schreurs. Email correspondence with the author, October 30, 2018.

David Schreurs. Interview with the author, Groningen, Netherlands, November 3, 2011.

Ellen Andrea Wang. Telephone interview with the author, December 15, 2017.

Erland Dahlen. Interview with the author, Kristiansand, Norway, September 2, 2018.

Fe Salomon. Telephone interview with the author, September 22, 2018.

Felix Berghäll. Interview with the author, Herräng, Sweden, July 5, 2018.

Fredrik Dahlberg. Interview with the author, Herräng, Sweden, July 4, 2018.

Hasse Mattsson. Interview with the author, Herräng, Sweden, July 2, 2018.

Isabelle Montanier. Interview with the author, Saumur, Anjou, France, June 23, 2018.

Jan Ole Otnæs. Telephone interview with the author, November 3, 2017.

Jan Bang. Email correspondence with the author, November 17, 2017.

Jessica Oldin. Interview with the author, Herräng, Sweden, July 6, 2018.

Judy Prichette. "History Lecture", Herräng Dance Camp, Week One, July 6, 2018.

Lennart Westerlund. Interview with the author, Herräng, Sweden, July 5, 2018.

Lennart Westerlund. Email correspondence with the author, January 1, 2019.

Marcus Koch. Interview with the author, Herräng, Sweden, July 3, 2018.

Marie Nahnfeldt Mattsson. Interview with the author, Herräng, Sweden, July 2, 2018.

Mats Oldin. Interview with the author, Herräng, Sweden, July 6, 2018.

Mikael Bretagne. Interview with the author, Saumur, France, June 24, 2018.

Mimmi Gunnarsson. Interview with the author, Herräng, Sweden, July 6, 2018.

Nils Andrén. Interview with the author, Herräng, Sweden, July, 4, 2018.

Paul Kleber. Interview with author, Berlin, Germany, November 26, 2017.

Phil Horneman. Interview with the author, Amsterdam, The Netherlands, July 5, 2009.

Rashad Gregory. Interview with the author, Aachen, Germany, September 14, 2018.

Rashad Gregory. Email correspondence with the author, September 21, 2018.

Rikard Ekstrand. Interview with the author, Herräng, Sweden, July 4, 2018.

Rob Van de Wouw. Interview with the author, Amsterdam, The Netherlands, July 5, 2009.

Rohey Taalah. Interview with the author, Hamar, Norway, May 11, 2018.

Sonny Allen. "Library Talk", Herräng Dance Camp, Herräng, Sweden, Week 1, 2016.

Stefan Leisering. Interview with the author, Berlin, Germany, November 25, 2017.

Susanne Alt. Interview with the author, Sugar Factory, Amsterdam, the Netherlands, July 6, 2009.

Tom Hyland. Telephone interview with author, July 8, 2018.

Tom Hyland. Telephone interview with author, September 19, 2018.

Discography

Beady Belle. *Home*. Jazzland Recordings, 2001. CD.

Beady Belle. *Cewbeagappic*. Jazzland Recordings, 2003. CD.

Beady Belle. *On My Own*. Jazzland Recordings, 2016. CD.

Beady Belle. *Dedication*. Jazzland Recordings, 2018. CD.

Bruce Channel. "Hey Baby". LeCam Records, 1961. Single.

Bugge Wesseltoft. *New Conception of Jazz*. Jazzland Recordings, 1996. CD.

Bugge Wesseltoft. *Jazzland Remixed*. Jazzland 542 288–1, 2000. CD.

Bugge Wesseltoft. *Somewhere in Between*. Jazzland Recordings, 2016. CD.
Caravan Palace. *Caravan Palace*. Wagram, 2008. CD.
Caravan Palace. *Panic*. Wagram, 2012. CD.
Caravan Palace. *Panic* LP. Wagram, 2012. CD.
Caravan Palace. *Robot Face* <|°_°|>. Wagram, 2015. CD.
Caro Emerald. *Deleted Scenes from the Cutting Room Floor*. Grandmono Records, 2010. CD.
Caro Emerald. *The Shocking Miss Emerald*. Grandmono Records, 2013. CD.
Caro Emerald. *Emerald Island*. Grandmono Records, 2017. EP.
DJ Maestro. *Birds Beats*. Blue Note Trip. CD.
Electric Swing Circus. *The Electric Swing Circus*. Ragtime Records, 2013. CD.
Electric Swing Circus. *It Flew By*. Ragtime Records, 2017. CD.
Ellen Andrea Wang. *Diving*. Propeller Recordings, 2014. CD.
Ellen Andrea Wang. *Break Out*. Jazzland Recordings, 2017. CD.
Freddie Jackson. "Buck Fever". Regal Records, 1951. Single.
GURLS. *Run boy, run*. Grappa GRCD4571, 2018. CD.
Hugh Masekela. *Stimela*. Connoisseur Collection VSOP CD 200, 1994. CD.
Jazzanova. "Fedime's Flight" (12 Inch EP).
Jazzanova. *In Between*. Ropeadope Records, 2002.
Jazzanova. *Of All the Things*. Verve Records, 2008.
Jazzanova. "Stimela". *Jazzanova The Remixes 2006–2016*. Sonar Kollectiv, 2017.
Kruder & Doftmesiter. "High Noon". *G-Stone*. G-Stone Recordings, 1993. EP.
Kruder & Doftmesiter. *DJ Kicks*. 1996. Mix-Tape (compilation album).
Nina Simone. *Forever Young, Gifted and Black: Songs of Freedom and Spirit*. RCA, 1967.
Rob van de Wouw. *Neon*. Jazzland Recordings, 2013.
Skapel. *Polish Jazz*. 2000. EP.
Skapel. *Skalpel*. Ninja Tune (ZENCD87), 2004.
Sonar Kollectiv Orchester. *Guaranteed Niceness*. Sonar Kollectiv, 2007.
Susanne Alt. *Saxify*. Venus Tunes (alt008), 2016.
The Savory Collection 1935–1940. Mosaic Records. MD6–266, 2018.
Wicked Jazz Sounds. *Wicked Jazz Sounds 3*. United Records WJS003, 2007. 2 CDs.

Filmography

A Day at the Races. Directed by Sam Wood. MGM, 1937. Film.
A History of Sampling w/ Chris Read (WhoSampled) at Point Blank London. 2017. Point Blank Music School. www.youtube.com/watch?v=SZGobMX9I48&t=369s. Online course.
After Seben. Featuring Shorty Snowden. Directed by S. Kay Kaufman. 1929.
Al Minns in Sweden. Interview with Al Minns by the Swedish Swing Society, 1985. YouTube: www.youtube.com/watch?v=npONjnioOmI. Documentary.
Babylon Berlin. Directed by Henk Handloegten, Achim von Borries, and Tom Tykwer, 2017–2018. Television series.
Blast from the Past. Directed by Hugh Wilson. Forge, 1999. Film.
Caravan Palace. "Caravan Palace – Brotherswing Live", performed in Bourges for the Printemps Concert at the Phoenix, April 16, 2010. YouTube: www.youtube.com/watch?v=7YR-AvTDctk. Music Video.
Caravan Palace. "Dramophone". Directed by Frédéric de Ponchara. Le Café De La Danse, 2012. YouTube: www.youtube.com/watch?v=A7lxd7RL1To. Music Video.

Caravan Palace. "Rock it for Me". Directed by Guillaume Cassuto, Ugo Gattoni, Jeremy Pires, Wagram Music, 2012. YouTube: www.youtube.com/watch?v=fBGSJ3sbivI. Music Video.

Caro Emerald. "A Night Like This". Martini promotional video. Grandmono Records, 2009. YouTube: www.youtube.com/watch?v=74LXx0wSqMI. Music Video.

Caro Emerald. "The Ghost of You". Art Director, Donald Roos, 2017. YouTube: www. youtube.com/watch?v=bYp-opz6jHA. Music Video.

Dansa först (Dance First). Featuring the Harlem Hot Shots. Directed by Rikard Svensson, 2018. Film.

Dancing on the Edge. BBC. Television Series. 2013.

"Dawn Hampton Post Memorial Service". Herräng Dance Camp. July 4, 2017. YouTube: www.youtube.com/watch?v=vK8txh-kTSk. Video.

Electric Swing Circus. "Penniless Optimist (Demo Version)". 2011. YouTube: www.youtube. com/watch?v=u2uHgIqc5jo. Music Video.

Electric Swing Circus. "Empires". Video by Realm Pictures, 2017. YouTube: www.youtube. com/watch?v=u2uHgIqc5jo. Music Video.

"ESDC 2015 – Balboa Couples – Finals – Marcus Koch & Lana Mykhnylyuk". European Swing Dance Competition 2015. YouTube: www.youtube.com/watch?v=Rwg_ OJEDm7g. Video.

Great Gatsby. Directed by Baz Luhrmann. Warner Bros, 2013. Film.

Groovie Movie. Directed by Will Jason. MGM, 1944. Film.

Harlem Hot Shots: Shim Sham – Frankie and Chazz. Featuring Gabriella Rosati and Fatima Teffahi. 2016. YouTube: www.youtube.com/watch?v=IFH3waV26Uo.

Hellzapoppin. Directed by H.C. Potter and Edward Cline. Featuring Whitey's Lindy Hoppers. Universal, 1941.

Jammin' the Blues. Directed by Gijon Mili. Warner Bros, 1944. Short.

Jitterbug Party. Directed by Fred Waller. Featuring Cab Calloway and His Cotton Club Orchestra. Paramount Pictures. 1935. Film Short.

Like Nobody's Watching no. 1. Featuring Harlem Hot Shots' Fredrik Dahlberg. Directed by Karl-Johan Torstensson. YouTube: www.youtube.com/watch?v=YSYvy9KuVu4. Dance Video.

Moulin Rouge. Directed by Baz Luhrmann. Twentieth Century Fox, 2001. Film.

Mr Scruff. "Get A Move On". Published by Ninja Tune, 1999. YouTube: www.youtube. com/watch?v=HamLxGxeDqI. Music Video.

Rip! A Remix Manifesto. Brett Gaylor, 2008. Documentary.

Rock Around the Clock. Directed by Fred Sears. Columbia Pictures, 1956.

"RTSF 2018 – Nils & Bianca". Rock that Swing Festival, Nils & Bianca at the Deutsches Theater in Munich, Germany, February 11, 2018. YouTube: www.youtube.com/ watch?v=N-J_Mgx7eNc. Dance Competition.

Second Stops. Featuring Harlem Hot Shots' Fatima Teffahi and Rikard Ekstrand. Directed by Karl-Johan Torstensson. YouTube: www.youtube.com/watch?v=YSYvy9KuVu4. Dance Video.

Stompin' at the Savoy. Directed by Debbie Allen. Performed by Lynn Whitfield, Vanessa Williams, Jasmine Guy, and Vanessa Bell Calloway. CBS, 1992. Film.

Swing Dancers vs. Street Dancers. Dance Battle at the Montreal Swing Riot, 2015. YouTube: https://vimeo.com/142215364 (accessed August 25, 2018). Dance video.

Swing Kids. Directed by Thomas Carter. Hollywood Pictures, 1993. Film.

The Mask. Directed by Chuck Russel. New Line Cinema, 1994. Film.

The Savoy King: Chick Webb and the Music that Changed America.

The Spirit Moves: A History of Black Social Dance on Film. Directed by Mura Dehn. Dancetime Publications, 1987. Documentary.

The Talented Mr. Ripley. Directed by Anthony Minghella. Paramount Pictures, 1999. Film.

What Happened Miss Simone? Directed by Liz Garbus. Moxie Firecracker Films, 2015. Documentary film.

When Rhythm Moves Us. Directed by Karl-Johan Torstensson. Featuring the Harlem Hot Shots: Fatima Teffahi, Fredrik Dahlberg, Gabriella Rosati, Jenny Deurell, Mimmi Gunnarsson, Rikard Ekstrand, Sakarias Larsson. 2016. Dance video.

INDEX

For Product Safety Concerns and Information please contact our EU
representative GPSR@taylorandfrancis.com
Taylor & Francis Verlag GmbH, Kaufingerstraße 24, 80331 München, Germany